M

Travel Guides

Washington, DC and Baltimore

ExxonMobil
Travel Publications

Maps by
RAND MᶜNALLY

Acknowledgements

We gratefully acknowledge the help of our representatives for their efficient and perceptive inspections of the lodging and dining establishments listed; the establishments' proprietors for their cooperation in showing their facilities and providing information about them; and the many users of previous editions who have taken the time to share their experiences.

Mobil Travel Guide is also grateful to all the highly talented writers who contributed entries to this book.

Maps Copyright © 2004 Rand McNally & Company

Printing Acknowledgement: North American Corporation of Illinois

www.mobiltravelguide.com

ISBN: 0-7627-2893-0

Manufactured in the United States of America.

10 9 8 7 6 5 4 3 2 1

Contents

MAP SYMBOLS

Free limited-access highway	Interstate highway
New — under construction	U.S. highway
Toll limited-access highway	State or provincial highway
New — under construction	Other highway
Other multilane highway	Miles between arrows / One mile or less not shown
Principal highway	
Other through highway	Interchanges and interchange numbers
Other road	
Unpaved road	Time zone boundary
Ferry	

	Urbanized area in state maps; in city maps Separate cities within metro area
	National capital; state capital; cities; towns (size of type indicates relative population)
	U.S. or Canadian National Park
	State/Provincial Park or Recreation Area
	National Forest or Grassland, city park
	Point of interest
	Hospital, medical center
	Continental divide

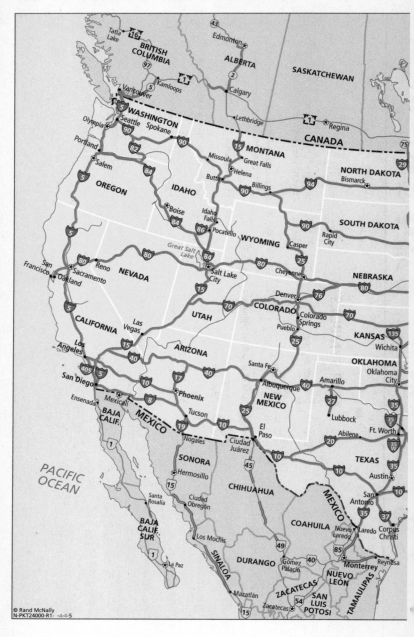

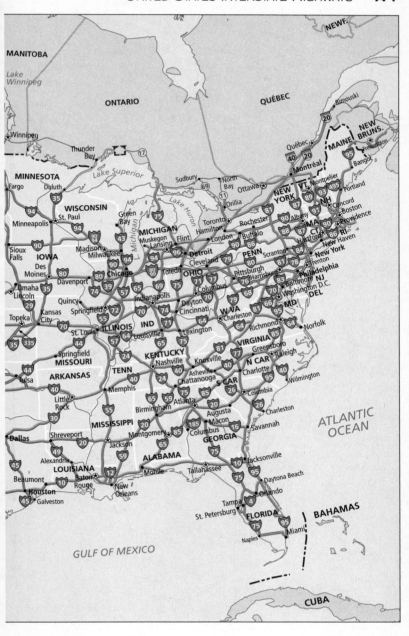

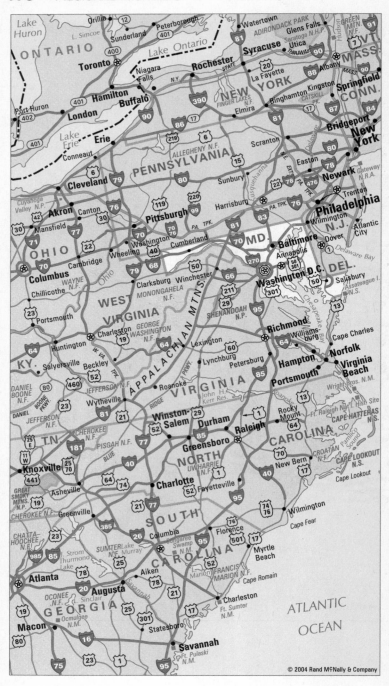

© 2004 Rand McNally & Company

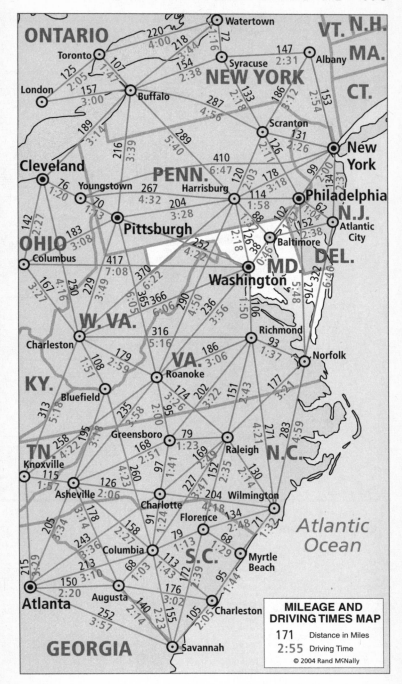

MILEAGE AND
DRIVING TIMES MAP

171   Distance in Miles
2:55   Driving Time
© 2004 Rand McNally

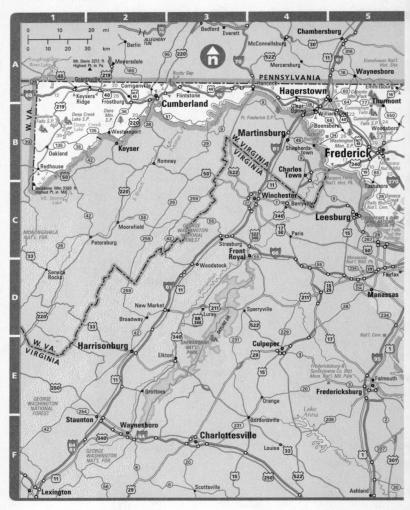

Cities and Towns

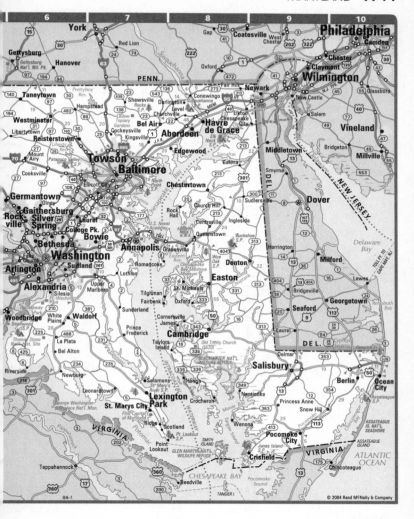

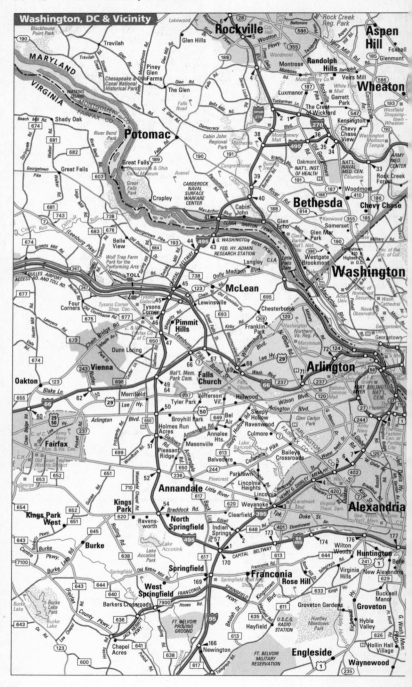

Washington, DC & Vicinity

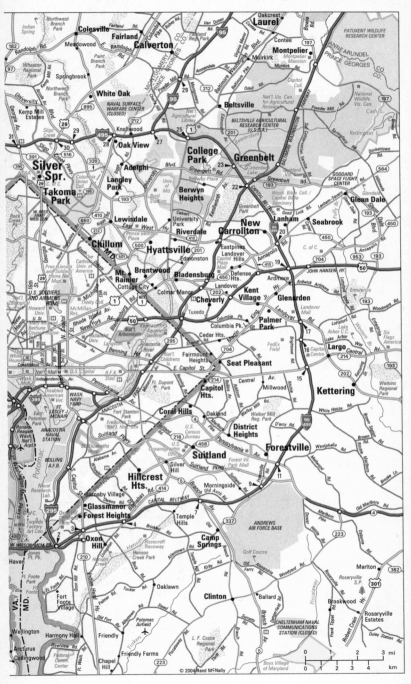

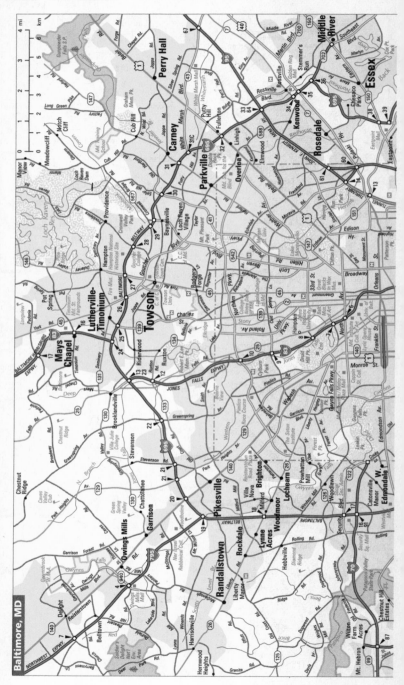

Baltimore, MD

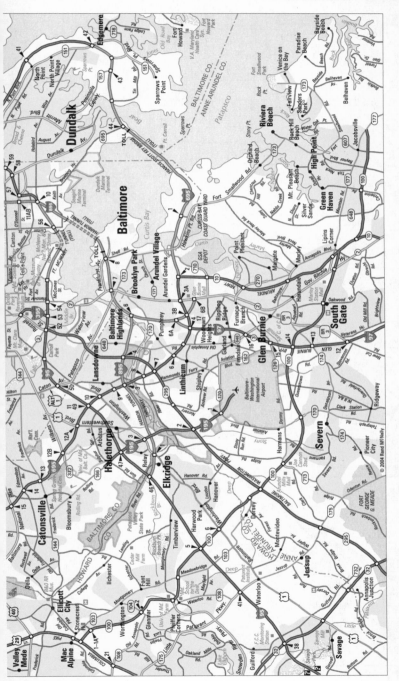

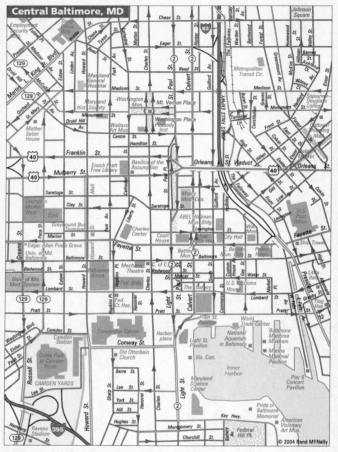

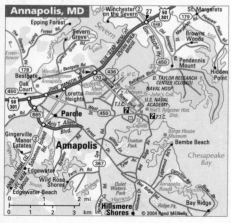

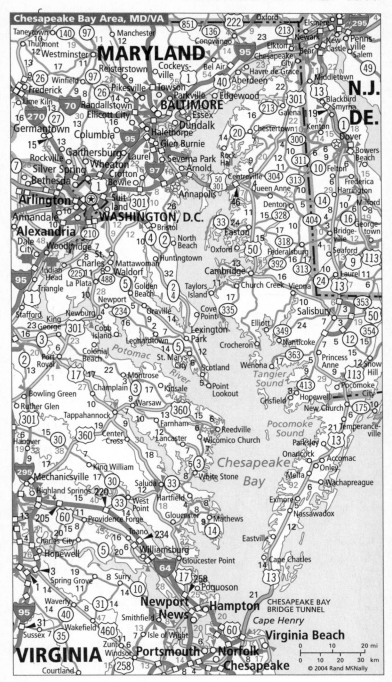

Chesapeake Bay Area, MD/VA

© 2004 Rand McNally

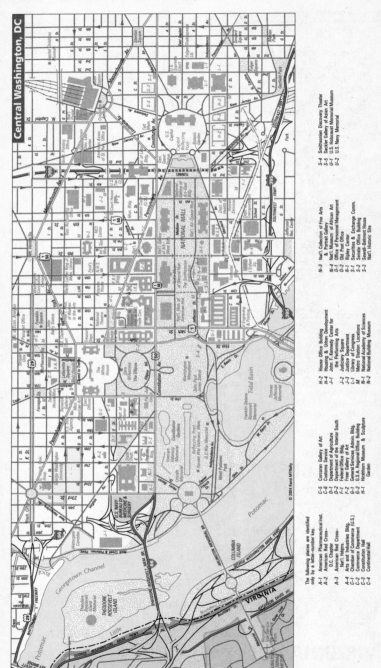

Central Washington, DC

The following places are identified only by a letter-number key.

A-1 American Pharmaceutical Inst.
A-2 American Red Cross—
     D.C. Chapter
A-3 American Red Cross—
     Nat'l. Hqtrs.
A-4 Arts and Industries Bldg.
C-1 Chamber of Commerce (U.S.)
C-2 Commerce Department
C-3 Constitution Hall
C-4 Continental Hall

C-5 Corcoran Gallery of Art
C-6 Customs Service
D-1 Department of Agriculture
D-2 Department of the Interior South
F-1 Federal Office Bldg.
F-2 Freer Gallery of Art
G-1 General Services Admin. Bldg.
G-2 G.S.A. Regional Office Building
H-1 Hirshhorn Museum & Sculpture
     Garden

H-2 House Office Building
H-4 Housing & Urban Development
J-1 John F. Kennedy Center for
     the Performing Arts
J-2 Judiciary Square
J-3 Justice Department
L-1 Library of Congress
M Metro Station Locations
N-1 National Academy of Sciences
N-2 National Building Museum

N-3 Nat'l. Collection of Fine Arts
     & Portrait Gallery
N-4 Nat'l. Museum of African Art
O-1 Office of Personnel Management
O-2 Old Post Office
R-1 Ripley Center
S-1 Securities & Exchange Comm.
S-2 Senate Office Building
S-3 Sewall-Belmont House
     Nat'l. Historic Site

S-4 Smithsonian Discovery Theater
S-5 Sackler Gallery of Asian Art
U-1 U.S. Holocaust Memorial Museum
U-2 U.S. Navy Memorial

© 2004 Rand McNally

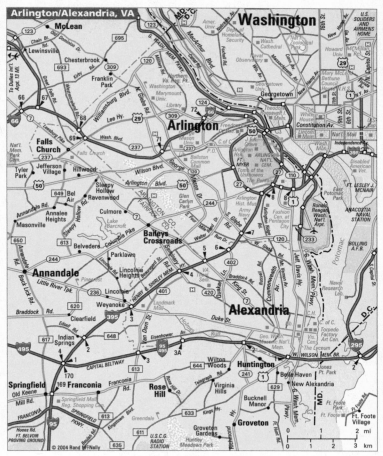

Arlington/Alexandria, VA

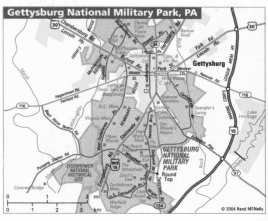

Gettysburg National Military Park, PA

© 2004 Rand McNally

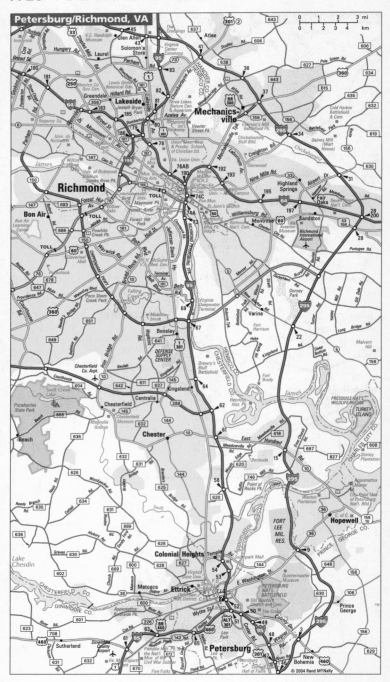

Petersburg/Richmond, VA

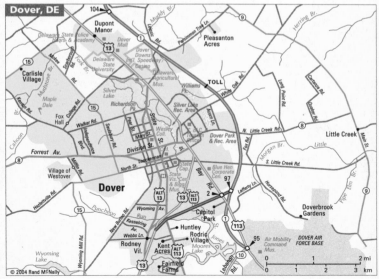

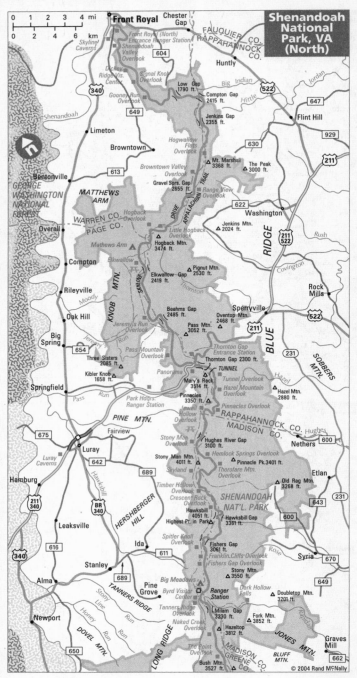

Shenandoah National Park, VA (North)

© 2004 Rand McNally

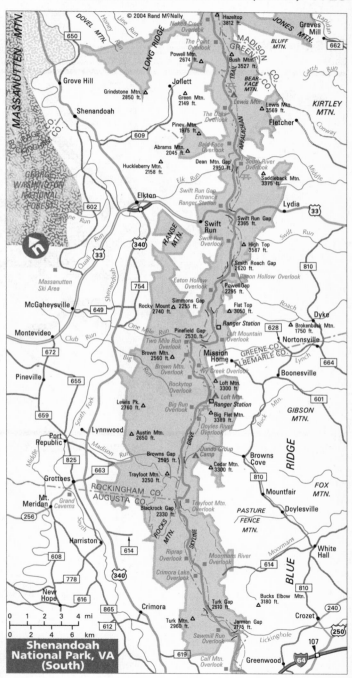

Shenandoah National Park, VA (South)

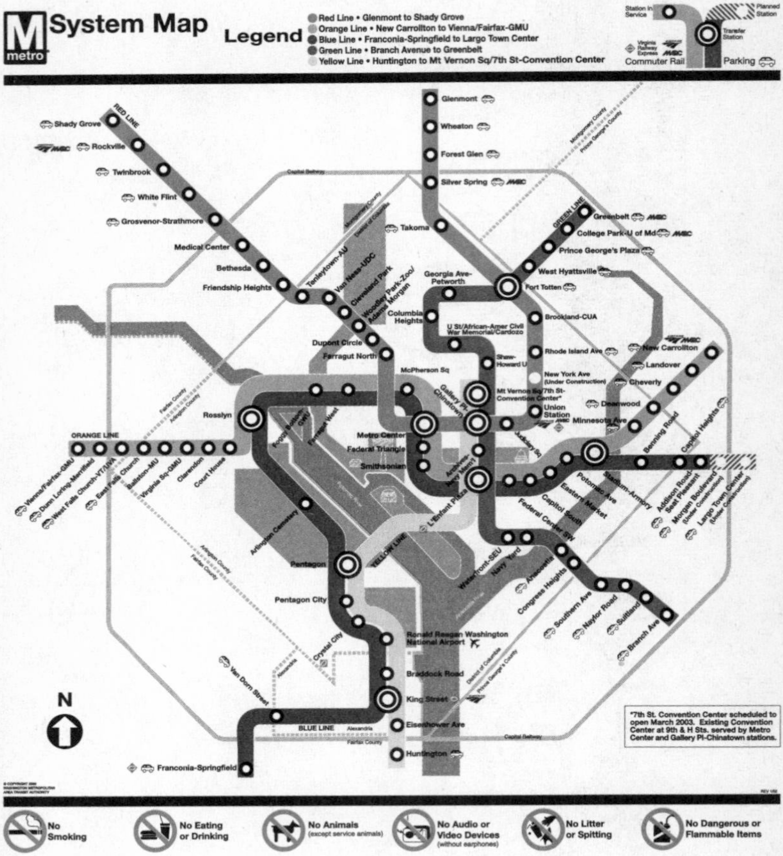

metro
System Map
Legend
Red Line • Glenmont to Shady Grove
Orange Line • New Carrollton to Vienna/Fairfax-GMU
Blue Line • Franconia-Springfield to Largo Town Center
Green Line • Branch Avenue to Greenbelt
Yellow Line • Huntington to Mt Vernon Sq/7th St-Convention Center
Station In Service
Planned Station
Transfer Station
Commuter Rail
Parking
RED LINE
Shady Grove
Rockville
Twinbrook
White Flint
Grosvenor-Strathmore
Medical Center
Bethesda
Friendship Heights
Tenleytown-AU
Van Ness-UDC
Cleveland Park
Woodley Park-Zoo/Adams Morgan
Dupont Circle
Farragut North
Glenmont
Wheaton
Forest Glen
Silver Spring
Takoma
Georgia Ave-Petworth
Columbia Heights
U St/African-Amer Civil War Memorial/Cardozo
Shaw-Howard U
GREEN LINE
Greenbelt
College Park-U of Md
Prince George's Plaza
West Hyattsville
Fort Totten
Brookland-CUA
Rhode Island Ave
New York Ave (Under Construction)
Mt Vernon Sq/7th St-Convention Center*
Union Station
New Carrollton
Landover
Cheverly
Deanwood
Minnesota Ave
McPherson Sq
Gallery Pl-Chinatown
Metro Center
Federal Triangle
Smithsonian
Judiciary Sq
Archives-Navy Mem'l
L'Enfant Plaza
Rosslyn
Foggy Bottom-GWU
Farragut West
ORANGE LINE
Vienna/Fairfax-GMU
Dunn Loring-Merrifield
West Falls Church-VT/UVA
East Falls Church
Ballston-MU
Virginia Sq-GMU
Clarendon
Court House
Benning Road
Capitol Heights
Addison Road Seat Pleasant
Morgan Boulevard (Under Construction)
Largo Town Center (Under Construction)
Stadium-Armory
Potomac Ave
Eastern Market
Capitol South
Federal Center SW
Arlington Cemetery
Pentagon
YELLOW LINE
Pentagon City
Crystal City
Ronald Reagan Washington National Airport
Braddock Road
King Street
Eisenhower Ave
Huntington
Van Dorn Street
Franconia-Springfield
BLUE LINE
Waterfront-SEU
Navy Yard
Anacostia
Congress Heights
Southern Ave
Naylor Road
Suitland
Branch Ave
Capital Beltway
Montgomery County
Prince George's County
District of Columbia
Fairfax County
Arlington County
Alexandria
N
*7th St. Convention Center scheduled to open March 2003. Existing Convention Center at 9th & H Sts. served by Metro Center and Gallery Pl-Chinatown stations.
No Smoking
No Eating or Drinking
No Animals (except service animals)
No Audio or Video Devices (without earphones)
No Litter or Spitting
No Dangerous or Flammable Items

Making road trips easy is our driving ambition.

Come and see how easy and convenient our Exxon and Mobil locations are. Before you head off for your next road trip, stop into your local Exxon or Mobil retailer and fill up on the essentials: film, batteries, cold soda for your thirst, salty snacks and candy for your hunger and, of course, automotive services and quality fuels. With over 16,000 locations nationwide, we make it effortless.

And don't forget to use your *Speedpass*™ to get back on the road even faster. After all, getting there is half the fun. How do we know? We're drivers too.

We're drivers too.

I know the long way home is shorter today.

You no longer have to listen to traffic reports telling you you're stuck in traffic. With mMode only from AT&T Wireless, you can see the real-time traffic data the radio stations use right on the screen of your phone. And if you want to take another route, getting driving directions with mMode is just as easy.

Call 1 866 reachout, go to attwireless.com/mMode, or visit any AT&T Wireless Store for more information.

reachout® with mMode™
on the wireless service America trusts℠

Meet The Stars
Mobil 2004 Five-Star Award Winners

LODGINGS

California
The Beverly Hills Hotel, *Beverly Hills*
Chateau du Sureau, *Oakhurst*
Four Seasons, San Francisco,
   San Francisco
Hotel Bel-Air, *Los Angeles*
The Peninsula Beverly Hills,
   Beverly Hills
Raffles L'Ermitage Beverly Hills,
   Beverly Hills
The Ritz-Carlton San Francisco,
   San Francisco

Colorado
The Broadmoor, *Colorado Springs*
The Little Nell, *Aspen*

Connecticut
The Mayflower Inn, *Washington*

Florida
Four Seasons Resort Palm Beach,
   Palm Beach
The Ritz-Carlton, Naples, *Naples*
The Ritz-Carlton, Palm Beach,
   Palm Beach

Georgia
Four Seasons Hotel Atlanta, *Atlanta*
The Lodge at Sea Island Golf Club,
   Sea Island

Illinois
Four Seasons Hotel Chicago, *Chicago*
Peninsula Chicago, *Chicago*
**The Ritz-Carlton, A Four Seasons
   Hotel,** *Chicago*

Massachusetts
Four Seasons Hotel Boston, *Boston*
Blantyre, *Lenox*

New York
Four Seasons Hotel New York,
   Manhattan
The Point, *Saranac Lake*

**The Ritz-Carlton New York Central
   Park,** *Manhattan*
The St. Regis, *Manhattan*

North Carolina
Fearrington House, *Pittsboro*

South Carolina
Woodlands Resort and Inn, *Summerville*

Texas
The Mansion on Turtle Creek, *Dallas*

Vermont
Twin Farms, *Woodstock*

Virginia
The Inn at Little Washington,
   Washington
The Jefferson Hotel, *Richmond*

RESTAURANTS

California
**The Dining Room at The Ritz-Carlton
   San Francisco,** *San Francisco*
The French Laundry, *Yountville*
Gary Danko, *San Francisco*

Georgia
The Dining Room, *Atlanta*
Seeger's, *Atlanta*

Illinois
Charlie Trotter's, *Chicago*
Trio, *Evanston*

New York
Alain Ducasse, *Manhattan*
Jean Georges, *Manhattan*

Ohio
Maisonette, *Cincinnati*

Pennsylvania
Le Bec-Fin, *Philadelphia*

South Carolina
The Dining Room at Woodlands,
   Summerville

Virginia
The Inn at Little Washington,
   Washington

The Mobil Travel Guide has been rating establishments since 1958. Each establishment awarded the Mobil Five-Star rating is "one of the best in the country."

Welcome

Dear Traveler,

Since its inception in 1958, Mobil Travel Guide has served as a trusted advisor to auto travelers in search of value in lodging, dining, and destinations. Now in its 46th year, the Mobil Travel Guide is the hallmark of our ExxonMobil family of travel publications, and we're proud to offer an array of products and services from our Mobil, Exxon, and Esso brands in North America to facilitate life on the road.

Whether you're looking for business or pleasure venues, our nationwide network of independent, professional evaluators offers their expertise on thousands of travel options, allowing you to plan a quick family getaway, a full-service business meeting, or an unforgettable Five-Star celebration.

Your feedback is important to us as we strive to improve our product offerings and better meet today's travel needs. Whether you travel once a week or once a year, please take the time to contact us at www.mobil travelguide.com. We hope to hear from you soon.

Best wishes for safe and enjoyable travels.

Lee R. Raymond
Chairman and CEO
Exxon Mobil Corporation

A Word to Our Readers

Travelers are on the roads in great numbers these days. They're exploring the country on day trips, weekend getaways, business trips, and extended family vacations, visiting major cities and small towns along the way. Because time is precious and the travel industry is ever-changing, having accurate, reliable travel information at your fingertips is critical. Mobil Travel Guide has been providing invaluable insight to travelers for more than 45 years, and we are committed to continuing this service well into the future.

The Mobil Corporation (known as Exxon Mobil Corporation since a 1999 merger) began producing the Mobil Travel Guide books in 1958, following the introduction of the US highway system in 1956. The first edition covered only five southwestern states. Since then, our books have become the premier travel guides in North America, covering the 48 contiguous states and Canada. Now, ExxonMobil presents the newest editions to our travel guides: city travel planners. We also recently introduced road atlases and specialty publications, a robust new Web site, as well as the first fully integrated, road-centric travel support program called MobilCompanion, the driving force in travel.

Since its founding, Mobil Travel Guide has served as an advocate for travelers seeking knowledge about hotels, restaurants, and places to visit. Based on an objective process, we make recommendations to our customers that we believe will enhance the quality and value of their travel experiences. Our trusted Mobil One- to Five-Star rating system is the oldest and most respected lodging and restaurant inspection and rating program in North America. Most hoteliers, restaurateurs, and industry observers favorably regard the rigor of our inspection program and understand the prestige and benefits that come with receiving a Mobil star rating.

The Mobil Travel Guide process of rating each establishment includes:
- Unannounced facility inspections
- Incognito service evaluations for Mobil Four- and Five-Star properties
- A review of unsolicited comments from the general public
- Senior management oversight

For each property, more than 450 attributes, including cleanliness, physical facilities, employee attitude, and courtesy, are measured and evaluated to produce a mathematically derived score, which is then blended with the other elements to form an overall score. These quantifiable scores allow comparative analysis among properties and form the basis that Mobil Travel Guide uses to assign its Mobil One- to Five-Star ratings.

This process focuses largely on guest expectations, guest experience, and consistency of service, not just physical facilities and amenities. It is fundamentally a relative rating system that rewards those properties that continually strive for and achieve excellence each year. Indeed, the very best properties are consistently raising the bar for those that wish to compete with them. These properties proactively respond to consumers' needs even in today's uncertain times.

Only facilities that meet Mobil Travel Guide's standards earn the privilege of being listed in the guide. Deteriorating, poorly managed establishments are deleted. A Mobil Travel Guide listing constitutes a positive quality recommendation; every listing is an accolade, a recognition of achievement. Our Mobil One- to Five-Star rating system highlights its level of service. Extensive in-house research is constantly underway to determine new additions to our lists.

○ The Mobil Five-Star Award indicates that a property is one of the very best in the country and consistently provides gracious and courteous service, superlative quality in its facility, and a unique ambience. The lodgings and restaurants at the Mobil Five-Star level consistently and proactively respond to consumers' needs and continue their commitment to excellence, doing so with grace and perseverance.

○ Also highly regarded is the Mobil Four-Star Award, which honors properties for outstanding achievement in overall facility and for providing very strong service levels in all areas. These award-winners provide a distinctive experience for the ever-demanding and sophisticated consumer.

○ The Mobil Three-Star Award recognizes an excellent property that provides full services and amenities. This category ranges from exceptional hotels with limited services to elegant restaurants with a less-formal atmosphere.

○ A Mobil Two-Star property is a clean and comfortable establishment that has expanded amenities or a distinctive environment. A Mobil Two-Star property is an excellent place to stay or dine.

○ A Mobil One-Star property is limited in its amenities and services but focuses on providing a value experience while meeting travelers' expectations. The property can be expected to be clean, comfortable, and convenient.

Allow us to emphasize that we do not charge establishments for inclusion in our guides. We have no relationship with any of the businesses and attractions we list and act only as a consumer advocate. In essence, we do the investigative legwork so that you won't have to.

Keep in mind, too, that the hospitality business is ever-changing. Restaurants and lodgings—particularly small chains and standalone establishments—change management or even go out of business with surprising quickness. Although we make every effort to double-check information during our annual updates, we nevertheless recommend that you call ahead to make sure the place you've selected is still open and offers all the amenities you're looking for. We've provided phone numbers; when available, we also list fax numbers and Web site addresses.

We hope that your travels are enjoyable and relaxing and that our books help you get the most out of every trip you take. If any aspect of your accommodation, dining, or sightseeing experience motivates you to comment, please drop us a line. We depend a great deal on our readers' remarks, so you can be assured that we will read your comments and assimilate them into our research. General comments about our books are also welcome. You can write to us at Mobil Travel Guide, 1460 Renaissance Dr, Suite 401, Park Ridge, IL 60068, or send an e-mail to info@mobiltravelguide.com.

Take your Mobil Travel Guide books along on every trip you take. We're confident that you'll be pleased with their convenience, ease of use, and breadth of dependable coverage.

Happy travels!

How to Use This Book

The Mobil Travel Guide City Guides are designed for ease of use. The book begins with a general introduction that provides a geographical and historical orientation to the state and gives basic statewide tourist information, from climate to highway information to seatbelt laws. The remainder is devoted to the featured cities, as well as neighboring towns and nearby tourist destinations.

The following sections explain the wealth of information you'll find in this book: information about the city and its neighborhoods, things to see and do there, and where to stay and eat.

Maps

At the front of this book in the full-color section, we have provided a US and a state map as well as detailed city maps to help you find your way around. You'll find a key to the map symbols following the Contents page at the beginning of the map section.

Driving and Walking Tours

The driving tours that we include are usually day trips that make for interesting side excursions, although they can be longer. They offer you a way to get off the beaten path and visit an area that travelers often overlook. These trips frequently cover areas of natural beauty or historical significance.

Each walking tour focuses on a particularly interesting area of the city. Again, these tours can provide a break from everyday tourist attractions, and they often include places to stop for meals or snacks.

What to See and Do

The Mobil Travel Guide offers information about nearly 20,000 museums, art galleries, amusement parks, historic sites, national and state parks, ski areas, and many other types of attractions. A white star on a black background ★ signals that the attraction is a must-see—one of the best in the area. Because municipal parks, public tennis courts, swimming pools, and small educational institutions are common to most cities, they generally are not mentioned.

In an attraction's description, you'll find the months, days, and, in some cases, hours of operation; the address/directions, telephone number, and Web site (if there is one); and the admission price category. We use the following ranges for admission fees:

⊘ **FREE**
⊘ **$** = Up to $5
⊘ **$$** = $5.01-$10
⊘ **$$$** = $10.01-$15
⊘ **$$$$** = Over $15

Special Events

Special events are either annual events that last only a short time, such as festivals and fairs, or longer, seasonal events such as horseracing, summer theater and concerts, and professional sports. The Mobil Travel Guide Special Events listings also include infrequently occurring occasions that mark certain dates or events, such as centennials and other commemorative celebrations.

Side Trips

We recognize that your travels don't always end where a city's boundaries fall, so we've included some side trips that technically fall outside the scope of this book but that travelers frequently visit when they come to this city. Nearby national parks, other major cities, and major tourist draws fall into this category. We have broken the side trips into three categories: day trips (less than a three-hour drive); overnight stays (between a three- and five-hour drive); and weekend excursions (more than a five-hour drive). You'll find the side trips at the end of the listings.

Lodging and Restaurant Listings

Lodgings and restaurants are listed under the city or town in which they are located. Lodgings and restaurants located within 5 miles of a major commercial airport are listed under a separate "Airport Area" heading that follows the city section.

LODGINGS

Travelers have different wants and needs when it comes to accommodations. To help you pinpoint properties that meet your particular needs, each lodging property is classified by type according to the following characteristics:

⊘ **Motels/Motor Lodges.** These accommodations are in low-rise structures with rooms that are easily accessible to parking, which is usually free. Properties have small, functional lobbies, and guests enter their rooms from the outdoors. Service is often limited, and dining may not be offered in lower-rated motels. Shops and businesses are generally found only in higher-rated properties, as are bellstaff, room service, and restaurants serving three meals daily.

⊘ **Hotels.** A hotel is an establishment that provides lodging in a clean, comfortable environment. Guests can expect private bathrooms as well as some measure of guest services, such as luggage assistance, room service, and daily maid service.

○ **Resorts.** A resort is an establishment that provides lodging in a facility that is typically located on a larger piece of land. Recreational activities are emphasized and often include golf, spa, and tennis. Guests can expect more than one food and beverage establishment on the property, which aims to provide a variety of food choices at a variety of price points.

○ **All Suites.** In an All Suites property, guest accommodations consist of two rooms: a bedroom and a living room. Higher-rated properties offer facilities and services comparable to regular hotels.

○ **B&Bs/Small Inns.** The hotel alternative for those who prefer the comforts of home and a personal touch. It may be a structure of historic significance and often is located in an interesting setting. Breakfast is usually included and often is treated as a special occasion. Cocktails and refreshments may be served in the late afternoon or evening. Rooms are often individually decorated, but telephones, televisions, and private bathrooms may not be available in every room.

○ **Extended Stay.** These hotels specialize in stays of three days or more and usually offer weekly room rates. Service is often limited, and dining may not be offered at lower-rated properties.

Because most lodgings offer the following features and services, information about them does not appear in the listings unless exceptions exist:

○ Year-round operation with a single rate structure

○ Major credit cards accepted (note that Exxon or Mobil Corporation credit cards cannot be used to pay for room or other charges)

○ Air-conditioning and heat, often with individual room controls

○ Bathroom with tub and/or shower in each room

○ Cable television

○ Cots and cribs available

○ Daily maid service

○ Elevators

○ In-room telephones

Each lodging listing gives the name, address/location (when no street address is available), phone number(s), fax number, and total number of guest rooms. Also included are details on business, luxury, recreational, and dining facilities on the property or nearby. A key to the symbols at the end of each listing can be found on the inside front cover of this book.

For every property, we also provide pricing information. Because lodging rates change frequently, we opt to list a pricing category rather than specific prices. The pricing categories break down as follows:

- ✪ **$** = Up to $150
- ✪ **$$** = $151-$250
- ✪ **$$$** = $251-$350
- ✪ **$$$$** = Over $350

All prices quoted by the Mobil Travel Guide are in effect at the time of publication; however, prices cannot be guaranteed. In some locations, short-term price variations may exist because of special events or holidays. Certain resorts have complicated rate structures that vary with the time of year; always confirm rates when making your plans.

RESTAURANTS

All dining establishments listed in our books have a full kitchen and offer table service and a complete menu. Parking on or near the premises, in a lot or garage, is assumed. If parking is not available, we note that fact in the listing.

Each listing also gives the cuisine type, address (or directions if no street address is available), phone and fax numbers, Web site (if available), meals served, days of operation (if not open daily year-round), reservation policy, and pricing category. We also indicate if a children's menu is offered. The price categories are defined as follows per diner and assume that you order an appetizer, an entrée, and one drink:

- ✪ **$** = $15 and under
- ✪ **$$** = $16-$35
- ✪ **$$$** = $36-$85
- ✪ **$$$$** = Over $85

QUALITY RATINGS

Mobil Travel Guide has been rating lodgings and restaurants in the United States since the first edition was published in 1958. For years, the guide was the only source of such ratings, and it remains among the few guidebooks to rate restaurants across the country and in Canada.

All listed establishments have been inspected by experienced field representatives and/or evaluated by a senior staff member. Our ratings are based on detailed inspection reports of the individual properties, on written evaluations of staff members who stay and dine anonymously, and on an extensive review of reader comments. Rating categories reflect both the features a property offers and its quality in relation to similar establishments.

Here are the definitions for the Mobil star ratings for lodgings:

⚙ ★ : A Mobil One-Star lodging is a limited-service hotel, motel, or inn that is considered a clean, comfortable, and reliable establishment.

⚙ ★ ★ : A Mobil Two-Star lodging is considered a clean, comfortable, and reliable establishment that has expanded amenities, such as a full-service restaurant on the premises.

⚙ ★ ★ ★ : A Mobil Three-Star lodging is well appointed, with a full-service restaurant and expanded amenities, such as a fitness center, golf course, tennis courts, 24-hour room service, and optional turn-down service.

⚙ ★ ★ ★ ★ : A Mobil Four-Star lodging provides a luxury experience with expanded amenities in a distinctive environment. Services may include, but are not limited to, automatic turndown service, 24-hour room service, and valet parking.

⚙ ★ ★ ★ ★ ★ : A Mobil Five-Star lodging provides consistently superlative service in an exceptionally distinctive luxury environment, with expanded services. Attention to detail is evident throughout the hotel, resort, or inn, from bed linens to staff uniforms.

The Mobil star ratings for restaurants are defined as follows:

⚙ ★ : A Mobil One-Star restaurant provides a distinctive experience through culinary specialty, local flair, or individual atmosphere.

⚙ ★ ★ : A Mobil Two-Star restaurant serves fresh food in a clean setting with efficient service. Value is considered in this category, as is family friendliness.

⚙ ★ ★ ★ : A Mobil Three-Star restaurant has good food, warm and skillful service, and enjoyable décor.

⚙ ★ ★ ★ ★ : A Mobil Four-Star restaurant provides professional service, distinctive presentations, and wonderful food.

⚙ ★ ★ ★ ★ ★ : A Mobil Five-Star restaurant offers one of few flawless dining experiences in the country. These establishments consistently provide their guests with exceptional food, superlative service, elegant décor, and exquisite presentations of each detail surrounding a meal.

TERMS AND ABBREVIATIONS IN LISTINGS

The following terms and abbreviations are used throughout the Mobil Travel Guide lodging and restaurant listings to indicate which amenities and services are available at each establishment. We've done our best to provide accurate and up-to-date information, but things do change, so if a particular feature is essential to you, please contact the establishment directly to make sure that it is available.

Complete meal Soup and/or salad, entrée, and dessert, plus a non-alcoholic beverage.

Continental breakfast Usually coffee and a roll or doughnut.

D Followed by a price, indicates the room rate for a double room—two people in one room in one or two beds (the charge may be higher for two double beds).

Each additional The extra charge for each additional person beyond the stated number of persons.

In-room modem link Every guest room has a connection for a modem that's separate from the main phone line.

Kitchen(s) A kitchen or kitchenette that contains a stove or microwave, sink, and refrigerator and is either part of the room or a separate, adjoining room. If the kitchen is not fully equipped, the listing will indicate "no equipment" or "some equipment."

Laundry service Either coin-operated laundry facilities or overnight valet service is available.

Luxury level A special section of a lodging, spanning at least an entire floor, that offers increased luxury accommodations. Management must provide no less than three of these four services: separate check-in and check-out, concierge, private lounge, and private elevator service (with key access). Complimentary breakfast and snacks are commonly offered.

Movies Prerecorded videos are available for rental or check-out.

Prix fixe A full, multicourse meal for a stated price; usually available at finer restaurants.

Valet parking An attendant is available to park and retrieve your car.

VCR VCRs are present in all guest rooms.

VCR available VCRs are available for hookup in guest rooms.

Special Information for Travelers with Disabilities

The Mobil Travel Guide **D** symbol indicates establishments that are at least partially accessible to people with mobility problems. Our criteria for accessibility are unique to our publications. Please do not confuse them with the universal symbol for wheelchair accessibility.

When the **D** symbol follows a listing, the establishment is equipped with facilities to accommodate people using wheelchairs or crutches or otherwise needing easy access to doorways and rest rooms. Travelers with severe mobility problems or with hearing or visual impairments may or may not find the facilities they need. Always phone ahead to make sure that an establishment can meet your needs.

All lodgings bearing our **D** symbol have the following facilities:

⊙ ISA-designated parking near access ramps

⊙ Level or ramped entryways to buildings

⊙ Swinging building entryway doors a minimum of 39 inches wide

⊙ Public rest rooms on the main level with space to operate a wheelchair and handrails at commode areas

⊙ Elevator(s) equipped with grab bars and lowered control buttons

⊙ Restaurant(s) with accessible doorway(s), rest rooms with space to operate a wheelchair, and handrails at commode areas

⊙ Guest room entryways that are at least 39 inches wide

⊙ Low-pile carpet in rooms

⊙ Telephones at bedside and in the bathroom

⊙ Beds placed at wheelchair height

⊙ Bathrooms with a minimum doorway width of 3 feet

⊙ Bath with an open sink (no cabinet) and room to operate a wheelchair

⊙ Handrails at commode areas and in the tub

⊙ Wheelchair-accessible peepholes in room entry door

⊙ Wheelchair-accessible closet rods and shelves

All restaurants bearing our **D** symbol offer the following facilities:

⊙ ISA-designated parking beside access ramps

⊙ Level or ramped front entryways to the building

⊙ Tables that accommodate wheelchairs

⊙ Main-floor rest rooms with an entryway that's at least 3 feet wide

⊙ Rest rooms with space to operate a wheelchair and handrails at commode areas

Making the Most of Your Trip

A few hardy souls might look back with fondness on a trip during which the car broke down, leaving them stranded for three days, or a vacation that cost twice what it was supposed to. For most travelers, though, the best trips are those that are safe, smooth, and within budget. To help you make your trip the best it can be, we've assembled a few tips and resources.

Saving Money

ON LODGING

Many hotels and motels offer discounts—for senior citizens, business travelers, families, you name it. It never hurts to ask—politely, that is. Sometimes, especially in the late afternoon, desk clerks are instructed to fill beds, and you might be offered a lower rate or a nicer room to entice you to stay. Simply ask the reservation agent for the best rate available. Also, make sure to try both the toll-free number and the local number. You may be able to get a lower rate from one than the other.

Becoming a member of MobilCompanion will entitle you to discounted rates at many well-known hotels around the country. For more information, call 877/785-6788 or visit www.mobilcompanion.com.

Timing your trip right can cut your lodging costs as well. Look for bargains on stays over multiple nights, in the off-season, and on weekdays or weekends, depending on the location. Many hotels in major metropolitan areas, for example, have special weekend packages that offer considerable savings on rooms; they may include breakfast, cocktails, and dinner discounts.

Another way to save money is to choose accommodations that give you more than just a standard room. Rooms with kitchen facilities enable you to cook some meals yourself, reducing your restaurant costs. A suite might save money for two couples traveling together. Even hotel luxury levels can provide good value, as many include breakfast or cocktails in the price of a room.

State and city taxes, as well as special room taxes, can increase your room rate by as much as 25 percent per day. We are unable to include information about taxes in our listings, but we strongly urge you to ask about taxes when making reservations so that you understand the total cost of your lodgings before you book.

Watch out for telephone-usage charges that hotels frequently impose on long-distance, credit-card, and other calls. Before phoning from your room, read the information given to you at check-in, and then be sure to review your bill carefully when checking out. You won't be expected to pay for charges that the hotel didn't spell out. Consider using your cell phone if you have one; or, if public telephones are available in the hotel lobby, your cost savings may outweigh the inconvenience of using them.

Here are some additional ways to save on lodgings:

- Stay in B&B accommodations; they're generally less expensive than standard hotel rooms, and the complimentary breakfasts cut down on food costs.
- If you're traveling with children, find lodgings at which kids stay free.
- When visiting a major city, stay just outside the city limits; these rooms are usually less expensive than those in downtown locations.
- Consider visiting national parks during the low season, when prices of lodgings near the parks drop 25 percent or more.
- When calling a hotel, ask whether it is running any special promotions or if any discounts are available; many times reservationists are told not to volunteer deals unless specifically asked about them.
- Check for hotel packages; some offer nightly rates that include a rental car or discounts on major attractions.

ON DINING

There are several ways to get a less expensive meal at a more expensive restaurant. Early-bird dinners are popular in many parts of the country and offer considerable savings. If you're interested in sampling a Mobil Four- or Five-Star establishment, consider going at lunchtime. Although the prices are probably still relatively high at midday, they may be half of those at dinner, and you'll experience the same ambience, service, and cuisine.

As a member of MobilCompanion, you can enroll in iDine. This program earns you up to 20 percent cash back at more than 1,900 restaurants on meals purchased with the credit card you register; the rebate appears on your credit card bill. For more information about MobilCompanion and iDine, call 877/785-6788 or go to www.mobilcompanion.com.

ON ENTERTAINMENT

Although some national parks, monuments, seashores, historic sites, and recreation areas may be used free of charge, others charge an entrance fee (ranging from $1 to $6 per person or $5 to $20 per carload) and/or a usage fee for special services and facilities. If you plan to make several visits to national recreation areas, consider one of the following money-saving programs offered by the National Park Service:

○ **National Parks Pass.** This annual pass is good for entrance to any national park that charges an entrance fee. If the park charges a per-vehicle fee, the pass holder and any accompanying passengers in a private noncommercial vehicle may enter. If the park charges a per-person fee, the pass applies to the holder's spouse, children, and parents as well as the holder. It is valid for entrance fees only; it does not cover parking, camping, or other fees. You can purchase a National Parks Pass in person at any national park where an entrance fee is charged; by mail from the National Park Foundation, PO Box 34108, Washington, DC 20043-4108; by calling 888/GO-PARKS; or at www.nationalparks.org. The cost is $50.

○ **Golden Eagle.** When affixed to a National Parks Pass, this sticker, available to people who are between 17 and 61 years of age, extends coverage to sites managed by the US Fish and Wildlife Service, the US Forest Service, and the Bureau of Land Management. It is good until the National Parks Pass to which it is affixed expires and does not cover usage fees. You can purchase one at National Park Service, Fish and Wildlife Service, and Bureau of Land Management fee stations. The cost is $15.

○ **Golden Age Passport.** Available to citizens and permanent US residents 62 and older, this passport is a lifetime entrance permit to fee-charging national recreation areas. The fee exemption extends to those accompanying the permit holder in a private noncommercial vehicle or, in the case of walk-in facilities, to the holder's spouse and children. The passport also entitles the holder to a 50 percent discount on federal usage fees charged in park areas, but not on concessions. Golden Age Passports must be obtained in person and are available at most National Park Service units that charge an entrance fee. The applicant must show proof of age, such as a driver's license or birth certificate (Medicare cards are not acceptable proof). The cost is $10.

○ **Golden Access Passport.** Issued to citizens and permanent US residents who are physically disabled or visually impaired, this passport is a free lifetime entrance permit to fee-charging national recreation areas. The fee exemption extends to those accompanying the permit holder in a private noncommercial vehicle or, in the case of walk-in facilities, to the holder's spouse and children. The passport also entitles the holder to a 50 percent discount on usage fees charged in park areas, but not on concessions. Golden Access Passports must be obtained in person and are available at most National Park Service units that charge an entrance fee. Proof of eligibility to receive federal benefits (under programs such as Disability Retirement, Compensation for Military Service-Connected Disability, and the Coal Mine Safety and Health Act) is required, or an affidavit must be signed attesting to eligibility.

A money-saving move in several large cities is to purchase a CityPass. If you plan to visit several museums and other major attractions, CityPass is a terrific option because it gets you into several sites for one substantially reduced price. Currently, CityPass is available in Boston, Chicago, Hollywood, New York, Philadelphia, San Francisco, Seattle, and southern California (which includes Disneyland, SeaWorld, and the San Diego Zoo). For more information or to buy one, call 888/330-5008 or visit www.citypass.net. You can also buy a CityPass from any participating CityPass attraction.

Here are some additional ways to save on entertainment and shopping:

- Check with your hotel's concierge for various coupons and special offers; they often have two-for-one tickets for area attractions and coupons for discounts at area stores and restaurants.

- Purchase same-day concert or theater tickets for half-price through the local cheap-tickets outlet, such as TKTS in New York City or Hot Tix in Chicago.

- Visit museums on their free or "by donation" days, when you can pay what you wish rather than a specific admission fee.

ON TRANSPORTATION

Transportation is a big part of any vacation budget. Here are some ways to reduce your costs:

- If you're renting a car, shop early over the Internet; you can book a car during the low season for less, even if you'll be using it in the high season.

- Rental car discounts are often available if you rent for one week or longer and reserve in advance.

- Get the best gas mileage out of your vehicle by making sure that it's properly tuned up and keeping your tires properly inflated. If your tires need to be replaced, you can save money on a new set of Michelins by becoming a member of MobilCompanion.

- Travel at moderate speeds on the open road; higher speeds require more gasoline.

- Fill the tank before you return your rental car; rental companies charge to refill the tank and do so at prices of up to 50 percent more than at local gas stations.

- Make a checklist of travel essentials and purchase them before you leave; don't get stuck buying expensive sunscreen at your hotel or overpriced film at the airport.

FOR SENIOR CITIZENS

Look for the senior-citizen discount symbol **SC** in this book's lodging and restaurant listings. Always call ahead to confirm that a discount is being offered, and be sure to carry proof of age. At places not listed in this book, it never hurts to ask if a senior-citizen discount is offered. Additional information for mature travelers is available from the American Association of Retired Persons (AARP), 601 E St NW, Washington, DC 20049; phone 202/434-2277; www.aarp.org.

Tipping

Tips are expressions of appreciation for good service. However, you are never obligated to tip if you receive poor service.

IN HOTELS

- Door attendants usually get $1 for hailing a cab.
- Bellstaff expect $2 per bag.
- Concierges are tipped according to the service they perform. Tipping is not mandatory when you've asked for suggestions on sightseeing or restaurants or for help in making dining reservations. However, a tip of $5 is appropriate when a concierge books you a table at a restaurant known to be difficult to get into. For obtaining theater or sporting event tickets, $5 to $10 is expected.
- Maids should be tipped $1 to $2 per day. Hand your tip directly to the maid, or leave it with a note saying that the money has been left expressly for the maid.

IN RESTAURANTS

Before tipping, carefully review your check for any gratuity or service charge that is already included in your bill. If you're in doubt, ask your server.

- Coffee shop and counter service waitstaff usually receive 15 percent of the bill, before sales tax.
- In full-service restaurants, tip 18 percent of the bill, before sales tax.
- In fine restaurants, where gratuities are shared among a larger staff, 18 to 20 percent is appropriate.
- In most cases, the maitre d' is tipped only if the service has been extraordinary, and only on the way out. At upscale properties in major metropolitan areas, $20 is the minimum.
- If there is a wine steward, tip $20 for exemplary service and beyond, or more if the wine was decanted or the bottle was very expensive.
- Tip $1 to $2 per coat at the coat check.

AT AIRPORTS

Curbside luggage handlers expect $1 per bag. Car-rental shuttle drivers who help with your luggage appreciate a $1 or $2 tip.

Staying Safe

The best way to deal with emergencies is to avoid them in the first place. However, unforeseen situations do happen, so you should be prepared for them.

IN YOUR CAR

Before you head out on a road trip, make sure that your car has been serviced and is in good working order. Change the oil, check the battery and belts, make sure that your windshield washer fluid is full and your tires are properly inflated (which can also improve your gas mileage). Other inspections recommended by the vehicle's manufacturer should also be made.

Next, be sure you have the tools and equipment needed to deal with a routine breakdown:

- Jack
- Spare tire
- Lug wrench
- Repair kit
- Emergency tools
- Jumper cables
- Spare fan belt
- Fuses
- Flares and/or reflectors
- Flashlight
- First-aid kit
- In winter, a windshield scraper and snow shovel

Many emergency supplies are sold in special packages that include the essentials you need to stay safe in the event of a breakdown.

Also bring all appropriate and up-to-date documentation—licenses, registration, and insurance cards—and know what your insurance covers. Bring an extra set of keys, too, just in case.

En route, always buckle up! In most states, wearing a seatbelt is required by law.

If your car does break down, do the following:

- Get out of traffic as soon as possible—pull well off the road.
- Raise the hood and turn on your emergency flashers or tie a white cloth to the roadside door handle or antenna.
- Stay in your car.
- Use flares or reflectors to keep your vehicle from being hit.

If you are a member of MobilCompanion, remember that En Route Support is always ready to help when you need it. Just give us a call and we'll locate and dispatch an emergency roadside service to assist you, as well as provide you with significant savings on the service.

IN YOUR HOTEL OR MOTEL

Chances are slim that you will encounter a hotel or motel fire, but you can protect yourself by doing the following:

- Once you've checked in, make sure that the smoke detector in your room is working properly.
- Find the property's fire safety instructions, usually posted on the inside of the room door.
- Locate the fire extinguishers and at least two fire exits.
- Never use an elevator in a fire.

For personal security, use the peephole in your room door and make sure that anyone claiming to be a hotel employee can show proper identification. Call the front desk if you feel threatened at any time.

PROTECTING AGAINST THEFT

To guard against theft wherever you go:

- Don't bring anything of more value than you need.
- If you do bring valuables, leave them at your hotel rather than in your car.
- If you bring something very expensive, lock it in a safe. Many hotels put one in each room; others will store your valuables in the hotel's safe.
- Don't carry more money than you need. Use traveler's checks and credit cards or visit cash machines to withdraw more cash when you run out.

For Travelers with Disabilities

To get the kind of service you need and have a right to expect, don't hesitate when making a reservation to question the management about the availability of accessible rooms, parking, entrances, restaurants, lounges, or any other facilities that are important to you, and confirm what is meant by "accessible."

The Mobil Travel Guide $\boxed{D}$ symbol indicates establishments that are at least partially accessible to people with special mobility needs (people using wheelchairs or crutches or otherwise needing easy access to buildings and rooms). Keep in mind that our criteria for accessibility are unique to our publication and should not be confused with the universal symbol for wheelchair accessibility. Further information about these criteria can be found in the earlier section "How to Use This Book."

A thorough listing of published material for travelers with disabilities is available from the Disability Bookshop, Twin Peaks Press, Box 129, Vancouver, WA 98666; phone 360/694-2462; disabilitybookshop.virtual ave.net. Another reliable organization is the Society for Accessible Travel & Hospitality (SATH), 347 Fifth Ave, Suite 610, New York, NY 10016; phone 212/447-7284; www.sath.org.

Important Toll-Free Numbers and Online Information

Hotels and Motels

Adams Mark 800/444-2326
www.adamsmark.com

AmericInn 800/634-3444
www.americinn.com

AmeriHost Inn Hotels 800/434-5800
www.amerihostinn.com

Amerisuites 800/833-1516
www.amerisuites.com

Baymont Inns 877/BAYMONT
www.baymontinns.com

Best Inns & Suites 800/237-8466
www.bestinn.com

Best Value Inns 888/315-BEST
www.bestvalueinn.com

Best Western International 800/WESTERN
www.bestwestern.com

Budget Host Inn 800/BUDHOST
www.budgethost.com

Candlewood Suites 888/CANDLEWOOD
www.candlewoodsuites.com

Clarion Hotels 800/252-7466
www.choicehotels.com

Comfort Inns and Suites 800/252-7466
www.choicehotels.com

Country Hearth Inns 800/848-5767
www.countryhearth.com

Country Inns & Suites 800/456-4000
www.countryinns.com

Courtyard by Marriott 888/236-2427
www.courtyard.com

Cross Country Inn 800/621-1429
www.crosscountryinns.com

Crowne Plaza Hotels and Resorts 800/227-6963
www.crowneplaza.com

Days Inn 800/544-8313
www.daysinn.com

Delta Hotels 800/268-1133
www.deltahotels.com
Destination Hotels & Resorts 800/434-7347
www.destinationhotels.com
Doubletree Hotels 800/222-8733
www.doubletree.com
Drury Inns 800/378-7946
www.druryinn.com
Econolodge 800/553-2666
www.econolodge.com
Economy Inns of America 800/826-0778
www.innsofamerica.com
Embassy Suites 800/362-2779
www.embassysuites.com
ExelInns of America 800/FOREXEL
www.exelinns.com
Extended StayAmerica 800/EXTSTAY
www.extstay.com
Fairfield Inn by Marriott 888/236-2427
www.fairfieldinn.com
Fairmont Hotels 800/441-1414
www.fairmont.com
Four Points by Sheraton 888/625-5144
www.starwood.com
Four Seasons 800/545-4000
www.fourseasons.com
Hampton Inn/Hampton Inn and Suites 800/426-7866
www.hamptoninn.com
Hard Rock Hotels, Resorts and Casinos 800/HRDROCK
www.hardrock.com
Harrah's Entertainment 800/HARRAHS
www.harrahs.com
Harvey Hotels 800/922-9222
www.bristolhotels.com
Hawthorn Suites 800/527-1133
www.hawthorn.com
Hilton Hotels and Resorts (US) 800/774-1500
www.hilton.com
Holiday Inn Express 800/HOLIDAY
www.sixcontinentshotel.com
Holiday Inn Hotels and Resorts 800/HOLIDAY
www.holiday-inn.com

Homestead Studio Suites 888/782-9473
www.stayhsd.com
Homewood Suites 800/225-5466
www.homewoodsuites.com
Howard Johnson 800/406-1411
www.hojo.com
Hyatt 800/633-7313
www.hyatt.com
Ian Schrager . . . . Contact individual hotel
www.ianschragerhotels.com
Inter-Continental 888/567-8725
www.intercontinental.com
Joie de Vivre 800/738-7477
www.jdvhospitality.com
Kimpton Hotels 888/546-7866
www.kimptongroup.com
Knights Inn 800/843-5644
www.knightsinn.com
La Quinta 800/531-5900
www.laquinta.com
Le Meridien 800/543-4300
www.lemeridien.com
Leading Hotels of the World 800/223-6800
www.lhw.com
Loews Hotels 800/235-6397
www.loewshotels.com
MainStay Suites 800/660-6246
www.choicehotels.com
Mandarin Oriental 800/526-6566
www.mandarin-oriental.com
Marriott Conference Centers 888/236-2427
www.conferencecenters.com
Marriott Hotels, Resorts, and Suites 888/236-2427
www.marriott.com
Marriott Vacation Club International 800/845-5279
www.marriott.com/vacationclub
Microtel Inns & Suites 800/771-7171
www.microtelinn.com
Millennium & Copthorne Hotels 866/866-8086
www.mill-cop.com
Motel 6 . . . . 800/4MOTEL6
www.motel6.com

Omni Hotels 800/843-6664
www.omnihotels.com
Pan Pacific Hotels and Resorts 800/327-8585
www.panpac.com
Park Inn & Park Plaza 888/201-1801
www.parkhtls.com
The Peninsula Group .... Contact individual hotel
www.peninsula.com
Preferred Hotels & Resorts Worldwide 800/323-7500
www.preferredhotels.com
Quality Inn 800/228-5151
www.qualityinn.com
Radisson Hotels 800/333-3333
www.radisson.com
Raffles International Hotels and Resorts 800/637-9477
www.raffles.com
Ramada International 888/298-2054
www.ramada.com
Ramada Plazas, Limiteds, and Inns 800/2RAMADA
www.ramadahotels.com
Red Lion Inns 800/733-5466
www.redlion.com
Red Roof Inns 800/733-7663
www.redroof.com
Regal Hotels 800/222-8888
www.regal-hotels.com
Regent International 800/545-4000
www.regenthotels.com
Relais & Chateaux 800/735-2478
www.relaischateaux.com
Renaissance Hotels 888/236-2427
www.renaissancehotels.com
Residence Inns 888/236-2427
www.residenceinn.com
Ritz-Carlton 800/241-3333
www.ritzcarlton.com
Rockresorts 888/FORROCKS
www.rockresorts.com
Rodeway Inns 800/228-2000
www.rodeway.com
Rosewood Hotels & Resorts 888/767-3966
www.rosewood-hotels.com

Scottish Inn 800/251-1962
www.bookroomsnow.com
Select Inn 800/641-1000
www.selectinn.com
Sheraton 888/625-5144
www.sheraton.com
Shilo Inns 800/222-2244
www.shiloinns.com
Shoney's Inns 800/552-4667
www.shoneysinn.com
Signature/Jameson Inns 800/822-5252
www.jamesoninns.com
Sleep Inns 800/453-3746
www.sleepinn.com
Small Luxury Hotels of the World 800/525-4800
www.slh.com
Sofitel 800/763-4835
www.sofitel.com
SpringHill Suites 888/236-2427
www.springhillsuites.com
SRS Worldhotels 800/223-5652
www.srs-worldhotels.com
St. Regis Luxury Collection 888/625-5144
www.stregis.com
Staybridge Suites by Holiday Inn 800/238-8000
www.staybridge.com
Summerfield Suites by Wyndham 800/833-4353
www.summerfieldsuites.com
Summit International 800/457-4000
www.summithotels.com
Super 8 Motels 800/800-8000
www.super8.com
The Sutton Place Hotels 866/378-8866
www.suttonplace.com
Swissotel 800/637-9477
www.swissotel.com
TownePlace Suites 888/236-2427
www.towneplace.com
Travelodge 800/578-7878
www.travelodge.com
Universal 800/23LOEWS
www.loewshotel.com

Vagabond Inns 800/522-1555
www.vagabondinns.com
W Hotels 888/625-5144
www.whotels.com
Wellesley Inn and Suites 800/444-8888
www.wellesleyinnandsuites.com
WestCoast Hotels 800/325-4000
www.westcoasthotels.com
Westin Hotels & Resorts 800/937-8461
www.westin.com
Wingate Inns 800/228-1000
www.wingateinns.com
Woodfin Suite Hotels 800/966-3346
www.woodfinsuitehotels.com
Wyndham Hotels & Resorts 800/996-3426
www.wyndham.com

Airlines

Air Canada 888/247-2262
www.aircanada.ca
Alaska 800/252-7522
www.alaskaair.com
American 800/433-7300
www.aa.com
America West 800/235-9292
www.americawest.com
ATA 800/435-9282
www.ata.com
British Airways 800/247-9297
www.british-airways.com
Continental 800/523-3273
www.flycontinental.com
Delta 800/221-1212
www.delta-air.com
Island Air 800/323-3345
www.islandair.com
Mesa 800/637-2247
www.mesa-air.com
Northwest 800/225-2525
www.nwa.com
Southwest 800/435-9792
www.southwest.com

United 800/241-6522
www.ual.com
US Airways 800/428-4322
www.usairways.com

Car Rentals

Advantage 800/777-5500
www.arac.com
Alamo 800/327-9633
www.goalamo.com
Allstate 800/634-6186
www.bnm.com/as.htm
Avis 800/831-2847
www.avis.com
Budget 800/527-0700
www.budgetrentacar.com
Dollar 800/800-4000
www.dollarcar.com
Enterprise 800/325-8007
www.pickenterprise.com
Hertz 800/654-3131
www.hertz.com
National 800/227-7368
www.nationalcar.com
Payless 800/729-5377
www.800-payless.com
Rent-A-Wreck.com 800/535-1391
www.rent-a-wreck.com
Sears 800/527-0770
www.budget.com
Thrifty 800/847-4389
www.thrifty.com

Four-Star Establishments in Washington, DC and Baltimore

Washington, DC

★★★★ Lodgings
Four Seasons Hotel
The Hay-Adams
Park Hyatt Washington
The Ritz-Carlton, Washington
The St. Regis, Washington

★★★★ Restaurants
Citronelle
Gerard's Place
Kinkead's
Willard Room

Baltimore

★★★★ Restaurant
Charleston

District of Columbia

Designed by Major Pierre Charles L'Enfant in about 1791, Washington was the first American city planned for a specific purpose. It is a beautiful city, with wide, tree-lined streets laid out according to a design that is breathtaking in its scope and imagination. For its purpose, the broad plan still works well even though

Population: 572,059
Area: 63 square miles
Elevation: 1-410 feet
Peak: Tenleytown
Entered Union: Founded in 1790
Flower: American Beauty Rose
Bird: Wood Thrush
Time Zone: Eastern
Website: www.washington.org

L'Enfant could not have foreseen the automobile or the fact that the United States would come to have a population of more than 250 million people. Nevertheless, L'Enfant's concept was ambitious, allowing for vast growth. Washington, named for the first US president, has been the nation's capital since 1800. The city's business is centered around government and tourism; there is little heavy industry.

The District of Columbia and Washington are one and the same. Originally, the District was a 10-mile-square crossing the Potomac River into Virginia, but the Virginia portion (31 square miles) was returned to the state in 1846. Residences of DC workers spill into Virginia and Maryland; so do government offices. In 1800, there were 130 federal employees; at the end of the Civil War, there were 7,000; now there are well over half a million. Although the city was a prime Confederate target in the Civil War, it was barely damaged. The assassination of Abraham Lincoln, however, struck a blow to the nation and drove home to Americans the fact that Washington was not merely a center of government. What happens here affects everyone.

This is a cosmopolitan city. Perhaps no city on earth has a populace with so many different origins. Representatives from all nations and men and women from every state work here—and vote in their home states by absentee ballot. It is a dignified, distinguished capital. Many who visit the city go first to the House of Representatives or Senate office buildings and chat with their representatives, who receive constituent visitors when they can. At these offices, visitors obtain tickets to the Senate and House galleries. From the top of the Washington Monument, there is a magnificent view of the capital. The Lincoln and Jefferson memorials cannot fail to capture the imagination.

When to Go/Climate

DC winters are relatively mild, while summers are hot and humid. The city is alive with color in spring and fall—cherry blossoms bloom in April and May, and vibrant fall foliage begins around September.

AVERAGE HIGH/LOW TEMPERATURES (°F)

Jan 47/27	**May** 76/57	**Sept** 80/63
Feb 46/29	**June** 85/67	**Oct** 69/50
Mar 57/38	**July** 89/71	**Nov** 58/41
Apr 67/46	**Aug** 87/70	**Dec** 47/32

Additional Visitor Information

Washington DC Convention and Visitors Association, 1212 New York Ave NW, Suite 600, Washington, DC 20005, has brochures and schedules of events; phone 202/789-7000 (Mon-Fri, 9 am-5 pm).

By writing to your representative or senator ahead of time, you can obtain tickets for two Congressional Tours: a guided White House tour that differs slightly from the normal tour and begins at 8:15, 8:30, or 8:45 am (Tues-Sat; specific times are assigned); or passes to the House and Senate visitors' galleries to watch congressional sessions in progress. Without this ticket, the chambers can be viewed only when Congress is not in session.

Write to your senator at the United States Senate, Washington, DC 20510. Address your representative at the United States House of Representatives, Washington, DC 20515. All tickets are free, but in peak season, which starts in spring, White House tickets may be limited. In the letter, include the dates you will be in Washington, first- and second-choice dates for the tours, and the number of people in your party. Also include your home phone number, should your representative's or senator's aide need to contact you. You can also get tickets, if available, directly from the office of your senator or representative after you arrive in Washington.

The National Park Service maintains information kiosks at several key points in the city as well as a White House Visitor Center at 1450 Pennsylvania Ave NW, which distributes free tickets to tour the White House.

Washington

Founded 1790 **Pop** 572,059 **Elev** 1-410 feet **Area code** 202
Web www.washington.org

You won't see any skyscrapers in Washington, DC—by law, no building may be taller than the 12-story-high Washington Monument—but you will find world-renowned museums, first-rate restaurants and shopping, captivating monuments and memorials, quaint neighborhoods, grassy parks and tree-lined streets, a modern and efficient mass-transit system, a thriving arts scene, and a zoological park housing not one but two giant pandas. So if you want skyscrapers, head elsewhere. For everything else, pay a visit to Washington.

Washington is best known as the capital of the United States, but the city did not even exist at the time the nation gained its independence in 1789. For a year, the nation's new government met in New York City, before relocating to Philadelphia. Dissension soon grew between the northern and southern states over the location of the permanent capital. Ultimately, it was agreed that the capital would be situated in the southern region, but only after the northern states were relieved of debts incurred during the Revolutionary War. In 1790,

City Fun Facts

1. To protect the city from possible enemy invasion during World War II, anti-aircraft guns were placed on top of several government office buildings. One of those guns accidentally went off, and the projectile hit the roof of the Lincoln Memorial.

2. The District of Columbia is named after Christopher Columbus.

3. Martha Washington is the only woman whose portrait has appeared on a US currency note. It appeared on the face of the $1 Silver Certificate of 1886 and 1891 and the back of the $1 Silver Certificate of 1896.

4. The Bureau of Engraving and Printing produces 37 million notes a day with a face value of approximately $696 million.

5. James Smithson, an Englishman who left $550,000 that founded the Smithsonian Institution, never visited the US.

6. The Gilbert Stuart oil painting of George Washington hangs in the White House today because of the efforts of Dolly Madison. The frame having been secured by screws to the wall, First Lady Dolly Madison had to have the frame broken and the canvas removed before the British invaded Washington during the War of 1812.

President George Washington selected a site for the nation's capital at the junction of the Potomac and Anacostia rivers, 14 miles north of his home in Mount Vernon. Andrew Ellicott conducted a survey of the area, which consisted mainly of swampland and dense forest. Ellicott was aided by Benjamin Banneker, a free black from Maryland. Using celestial calculations, Banneker, a self-taught astronomer and mathematician, laid out 40 boundary stones at 1-mile intervals to mark the city's borders.

President Washington chose Pierre-Charles L'Enfant to plan the new capital. L'Enfant, a French-born architect and urban designer who served in the American Revolutionary Army, created a bold and original plan, one that is widely considered the nation's greatest achievement in municipal planning. L'Enfant's plan called for a grid pattern of streets, with these streets intersected by wide, diagonal avenues. The diagonal avenues would meet at circles, and these circles would anchor the residential neighborhoods. An example can be seen today at Logan Circle, where four different thoroughfares converge, including Rhode Island and Vermont avenues. The large open circle sits at the core of a beautiful neighborhood, with many of the residences built soon after the Civil War in the Late Victorian and Richardsonian Romanesque styles.

L'Enfant envisioned the "Congress House" (now the Capitol) situated atop Jenkins Hill, which offered sweeping views of the Potomac River. To the west of Jenkins Hill, L'Enfant planned a 400-foot-wide avenue (now the National Mall) bordered by embassies and cultural institutions. Not everyone was pleased with his plan. Though he had the support of President Washington, L'Enfant faced opposition from some of the district commissioners who had been appointed to oversee the capital city's development. Secretary of State Thomas Jefferson, a noted architect in his own right, disapproved of the plan, but L'Enfant refused to compromise or modify his vision for the capital. In 1792, following a series of incidents between L'Enfant and those who challenged his plan, Washington dismissed the genius planner whom he had appointed only a year earlier. In L'Enfant's place, Washington appointed Andrew Ellicott to prepare a map of the city. With the help of his assistant, Benjamin Banneker, Ellicott produced a map of the city that adhered closely to L'Enfant's plan.

L'Enfant sought $95,500 for his services in planning the capital city, though he was ultimately paid less than $4,000. L'Enfant lived with friends during his later years. He died in 1825, financially destitute and never having received acclaim for his work in planning Washington. He was buried in Maryland, then disinterred and reburied at Arlington National Cemetery in 1909. A marble monument marks the site of his grave.

L'Enfant's visionary plan fostered the growth of the city's eclectic mix of neighborhoods, each containing its own distinct qualities: the surprising charm of Capitol Hill, with its 19th-century row houses and brick-lined streets; the massive stone monuments, museums, and government buildings in and around the National Mall; the quaint shops and restaurants of Georgetown; the cosmopolitan style and atmosphere of Dupont Circle; the bustling nightlife of Adams Morgan; and the leaf-shaded residential streets of Woodley Park. The layout of the city, with its broad avenues converging on circles and squares designated for public use, made the growth of these neighborhoods possible. As a result, the city as a whole has a small-town feel even though its population exceeds 570,000.

Most first-time visitors to Washington are surprised by the city's considerable natural beauty. L'Enfant's plan, which identified parks and open spaces as essential elements in urban design, helped to shape a city that is not merely functional but also quite lush and green, possessing the "sorts of places," as L'Enfant wrote, that "may be attractive to the learned and afford diversion to the idle." Were he alive today, L'Enfant would be pleased to see congressional staffers playing softball on the National Mall, walkers strolling alongside the Potomac River, and hikers venturing off for a trek on the trails within Rock Creek Park. Pulitzer Prize-winning historian David McCullough has expressed his appreciation of the capital's natural beauty. "In many ways it is our most civilized city," McCullough wrote of Washington. "It accommodates its river, accommodates trees and grass, makes room for nature as other cities don't."

The C&O Canal Towpath is a popular destination for bikers and hikers. The towpath begins in Georgetown and parallels the Potomac River, meandering 184 miles west to Cumberland, Maryland. Just outside of Washington, the towpath cuts through Great Falls Park. The park's ferocious rapids and giant boulders may cause visitors to forget that they're only a few miles from the city. The George Washington Parkway leads from the park back to the capital. McCullough penned of this route, "There is no more beautiful entrance to any of our cities than the George Washington Parkway, which sweeps down the Virginia side of the Potomac. The views of the river gorge are hardly changed from Jefferson's time."

Beyond the gorge, the capital unfolds in a rich blend of people, neighborhoods, parks, embassies, offices, memorials, monuments, and museums. Rising above it all, the white marble of the Washington Monument stretches for the sky, a constant reminder of the capital's namesake and the remarkable history and growth of not just this great city but also the nation it serves and represents.

Additional Visitor Information

For additional attractions and accommodations, see ARLINGTON COUNTY (RONALD REAGAN WASHINGTON-NATIONAL AIRPORT AREA) and DULLES INTERNATIONAL AIRPORT AREA in Virginia. Also see BALTIMORE/WASHINGTON INTERNATIONAL AIRPORT AREA in Maryland.

The following suburbs and towns in the Washington, DC metropolitan area are included in this book. For information about any of them, see the individual alphabetical listing. In Virginia: Alexandria, Arlington County (Ronald Reagan Washington-National Airport Area), Fairfax. In Maryland: Bethesda.

Transportation

CAR RENTAL AGENCIES
See IMPORTANT TOLL-FREE NUMBERS.

PUBLIC TRANSPORTATION

The Metrorail system is the least expensive means of getting around the capital. Metro (as it is called) provides a coordinated transportation system between buses and rail. The rapid rail system links major commercial districts and neighborhoods from the Capitol to the Pentagon and from the National Zoo to the National Airport and beyond. Trains operate every 6-12 minutes on the average: Monday-Friday, 5:30 am-midnight; Saturday and Sunday from 8 am. Phone 202/637-7000.

RAIL PASSENGER SERVICE

Amtrak 800/872-7245.

Adams-Morgan/ U Street Corridor

The historic U Street Corridor sits to the immediate west of Adams-Morgan and north of downtown. Until being surpassed by Harlem in the 1920s, this neighborhood was the largest African-American community in the nation. Jazz great Duke Ellington once called this neighborhood home, and a mural at 1214 U Street honors his talent. Across the street, the Lincoln Theatre, first opened in 1922, has been restored to its past splendor and continues to offer live entertainment. The likes of Ella Fitzgerald, Louis Armstrong, and Billie Holliday performed at the Lincoln Theatre during its heyday. The U Street Corridor maintains its musical heritage through a number of popular nightclubs, as well as the Center for the Preservation of Jazz and Blues. To the northeast, Howard University has attracted top African-American students since its founding in 1868.

Two miles north of the White House, the Adams-Morgan neighborhood offers the city's most vibrant nightlife. Here, amid turn-of-the-century row houses and apartment buildings, people from throughout the metro region gather each night to enjoy the neighborhood's ethnic restaurants and trendy clubs. The neighborhood's diversity is reflected in the wide range of cuisines offered by its restaurants, ranging from Caribbean to Ethiopian to Vietnamese. The second half of the 20th century saw an influx of Cubans and Central Americans to Adams-Morgan, and the neighborhood now serves as the center of the Latino community in Washington. Art lovers visit Adams-Morgan to view its many large, colorful street murals, which were first painted by Latinos in the 1970s.

What to See and Do

2:K:9. *2009 8th St NW (20001). Phone 202/667-7750.* Flash helps you get in the door here (no jeans or athletic wear, please); pulsating hip-hop, house, and techno beats will keep you dancing until all hours. Dazzling lighting effects and a powerful sound system make the enormous dance floor rock. Exhausted? Take a breather at the swank 42-foot bar or just hang back and watch the dancers in cages—always inspiring. The place draws a glam, multi-ethnic crowd of under-30s. **$$$**

African American Civil War Memorial. *1200 U St NW (20001). Phone 202/667-2667.* Sculpture pays tribute to the more than 200,000 African American soldiers who fought in the Civil War.

Basilica of the National Shrine of the Immaculate Conception. *400 Michigan Ave NE (20017). Phone 202/526-8300.* Largest Roman Catholic church in the US and one of the largest in the world. Byzantine and Romanesque architecture; extensive and elaborate collection of mosaics and artwork. (Daily) Carillon concerts (Sun afternoons); organ recitals (June-Aug, Sun evenings). Guided tours (daily). **FREE**

Catholic University of America. *620 Michigan Ave NE (20064). Phone 202/319-5000.* (1887) 5,510 students. Open to all faiths. Performances at Hartke Theatre (year-round).

Franciscan Monastery. *1400 Quincy St NE (20017). Phone 202/526-6800.* Within the church and grounds is the "Holy Land of America"; replicas of sacred Holy Land shrines including the Manger at Bethlehem, the Garden of Gethsemane, and the Holy Sepulchre. Also the Grotto at Lourdes and the Roman catacombs. Guided tours by the friars (daily). **DONATION**

Howard University. *Main campus: 2400 6th St NW between W and Harvard sts NW (20059). West campus: 2900 Van Ness St NW (20008). Three other campuses in the area. Phone 202/806-6100.* (1867) 12,000 students. Main campus has a Gallery of Fine Art with a permanent Alain Locke African Collection; changing exhibits (Sept-July, Mon-Fri).

US National Arboretum. *3501 New York Ave NE (20002). Phone 202/245-2726. www.usna.usda.gov.* Floral displays in spring, summer, fall, and winter on 446 acres; Japanese garden, National Bonsai and Penjing Museum (daily); National Herb Garden, major collections of azaleas (15,000), wildflowers, ferns, magnolias, crabapples, cherries, and dogwoods; aquatic plantings; dwarf conifers (the world's largest evergreen collection). (Daily; closed Dec 25) Under 16 years admitted only with adult. **FREE**

Motel/Motor Lodge

★ **WINDSOR PARK HOTEL.** *2116 Kalorama Rd NW (20008). Phone 202/483-7700; toll-free 800/247-3064; fax 202/332-4547. www.windsorpark hotel.com.* 43 rooms, 5 story. Complimentary continental breakfast. Check-out noon. TV; cable (premium). **$**

⊠ SC

Hotels

★ ★ **CENTER CITY HOTEL.** *1201 13th St NW (20005). Phone 202/682-5300; toll-free 800/458-2817; fax 202/371-9624. www.centercityhotel.com.* 100 rooms, 8 story. Complimentary continental breakfast. Check-out 11 am. TV; cable (premium). Laundry services. Restaurant. **$**

D ⊠ SC

★ ★ ★ **THE CHURCHILL HOTEL.** *1914 Connecticut Ave NW (20009). Phone 202/797-2000; fax 202/462-0944. www.thechurchillhotel.com.* Near Embassy Row and Dupont Circle, this hotel has a pleasant French style. 144 rooms, 9 story. TV; cable (premium). In-room modem link. Restaurant, bar. Room service. Health club privileges. In-house fitness room. Valet parking. Concierge. Refurbished apartment building; built 1904. **$$**

🕅 📡 **SC**

★ ★ **COURTYARD BY MARRIOTT.** *1900 Connecticut Ave NW (20009). Phone 202/332-9300; fax 202/328-7039. www.courtyard.com.* 147 rooms, 9 story. Check-out noon. TV; cable (premium), VCR available. In-room modem link. Laundry services. Restaurant, bar. In-house fitness room. Health club privileges. Outdoor pool. Valet parking. **$**

D 🏊 🕅 📡

★ ★ **JURYS NORMANDY INN.** *2118 Wyoming Ave NW (20008). Phone 202/483-1350; fax 202/387-8241. www.jurysdoyle.com.* 75 rooms, 6 story. Check-out noon. TV; cable (premium). In-room modem link. Laundry services. Health club privileges. **$**

D 📡

B&B/Small Inns

★ **KALORAMA GUEST HOUSE.** *1854 Mintwood Pl NW (20009). Phone 202/667-6369; fax 202/319-1262. www.washingtonpost.com/yp/kgh.* 30 rooms, some share bath, 3 story. Complimentary continental breakfast. Check-out 11 am, check-in noon. TV in common room. Limited parking. Created from four Victorian townhouses (1890s); rooms individually decorated. Totally nonsmoking. **$**

📡 **SC**

★ **KALORAMA GUEST HOUSE.** *2700 Cathedral Ave NW (20008). Phone 202/328-0860; fax 202/328-8730.* 19 rooms, 7 share baths, 4 story. No room phones. Children over 5 years only. Complimentary continental breakfast. Check-out 11 am, check-in noon. TV in sitting room. Laundry services. Limited off-street parking. Two early 20th-century townhouses (1910). **$**

📡

★ **TAFT BRIDGE INN.** *2007 Wyoming Ave NW (20009). Phone 202/387-2007; fax 202/387-5019. www.taftbridgeinn.com.* 12 rooms, 7 share bath, 3 story. Complimentary full breakfast. Check-out 11 am, check-in 2 pm. TV in some rooms; VCR available. In-room modem link. Laundry services. Georgian-style house built in 1905; eclectic antique, art collection. Totally nonsmoking. **$**

📡

★ **WINDSOR INN.** *1842 16th St NW (20009). Phone 202/667-0300; toll-free 800/423-9111; fax 202/667-4503.* 45 rooms, 3 story. No elevator.

Complimentary continental breakfast. Check-out noon, check-in 2 pm. TV; cable (premium). Health club privileges. Originally a boarding house (1922). **$**

⊠ **SC**

Restaurants

★ **AFTERWORDS.** *1517 Connecticut Ave NW (20036). Phone 202/387-1462; fax 202/232-6777. www.kramers.com.* Closed Thanksgiving, Dec 25. Breakfast, lunch, dinner, brunch. Bar; entertainment Wed-Sat. Outdoor seating. In two-story greenhouse and terrace behind Kramer Books bookshop. **$**

D

★ ★ **ANNA MARIA'S.** *1737 Connecticut Ave NW (20009). Phone 202/667-1444; fax 202/667-2699.* Italian menu. Closed holidays. Lunch, dinner. Bar. **$$**

★ ★ **CAFE ATLANTICO.** *405 8th St NW (20004). Phone 202/393-0812; fax 202/393-0555. www.cafeatlanticodc.com.* Nuevo Latino menu. Menu changes biweekly. Closed holidays. Lunch, dinner. Bar. Valet parking. Outdoor seating. **$$$**

D

★ ★ **CASHION'S EAT PLACE.** *1819 Columbia Rd NW (20009). Phone 202/797-1819; fax 202/797-0048. www.cashionseatplace.com.* American menu. Closed Mon, holidays. Dinner, Sun brunch. Bar. Valet parking. Outdoor seating. **$$$**

D

★ ★ **FASIKA'S.** *2447 18th St (20009). Phone 202/797-7673. www.fasikas.com.* Ethiopian menu. Closed Dec 25. Dinner. Bar. Casual attire. Outdoor seating. **$$**

★ ★ **FELIX RESTAURANT & SPY LOUNGE.** *2406 18th St NW (20009). Phone 202/483-3549.* American menu. Closed major holidays. Lunch, dinner. Bar. Casual attire. **$$**

D

★ **GRILL FROM IPANEMA.** *1858 Columbia Rd NW (20009). Phone 202/986-0757; fax 202/265-4229.* Brazilian menu. Closed major holidays. Dinner, brunch. Bar. **$$**

D

★ ★ **LA FOURCHETTE.** *2429 18th St NW (20009). Phone 202/332-3077.* French menu. Closed holidays. Lunch, dinner, brunch. Outdoor seating. **$$**

★ ★ **LAURIOL PLAZA.** *1835 18th St NW (20009). Phone 202/387-0035; fax 202/362-5649. www.lauriolplazarestaurant.com.* Latin American menu. Lunch, dinner, brunch. Bar. Outdoor seating. **$$**

D

★ ★ **MESKEREM.** *2434 18th St NW (20009). Phone 202/462-4100; fax 202/362-5812. www.meskeremonline.com.* Ethiopian menu. Closed Thanksgiving, Dec 25. Lunch, dinner. Bar. **$$**

D

★ **SAIGONNAIS.** *2307 18th St NW (20009). Phone 202/232-5300. www.dcnet.com/saigonnais.* Vietnamese menu. Closed Jan 1, Thanksgiving, Dec 25. Lunch, dinner. Outdoor seating. **$$**

Capitol Hill

Capitol Hill is home, of course, to the United States Capitol. But the heart of the neighborhood lies to the east of the Capitol building, amid the narrow, tree-lined streets of the Capitol Hill Historic District. Quaint 19th-century row houses fill the blocks within the Historic District. The neighborhood is a popular place to live for congressional staffers, given its close proximity to the offices of the elected officials in the Senate and House of Representatives. The Eastern Market, a public market and favored gathering place at 7th and C streets, keeps the Historic District well supplied in fresh produce, meats, fish, and flowers.

The US Capitol and its majestic dome, made of cast iron and weighing nearly 9 million pounds, sit atop Capitol Hill, formerly known as Jenkins Hill. The east side of the Capitol faces the Supreme Court and the Library of Congress, while the west side offers a clear view of the National Mall.

Thousands of commuters, business travelers, and tourists access the city every day via the train and Metro lines at Union Station. Situated in the northwest reaches of Capitol Hill, Union Station is more than just a train station; the Beaux Arts-inspired building includes more than 130 shops and restaurants, as well as a nine-screen cineplex. Union Station's bold, white granite exterior, coupled with its ornate and spacious interior, makes for an appropriately inspiring gateway to the nation's capital.

What to See and Do

Capital Children's Museum. *800 3rd St NE (20002). Phone 202/675-4120. www.ccm.org.* Make delicious tortillas and hot chocolate in "Mexico," slide down a fire pole in "Cityscapes," or design a cartoon character in "Chuck Jones: An Animated Life"—learning and playing feel pretty much the same at this lively, hands-on museum. Young problem-solvers will enjoy the challenge of the 20 puzzling tasks of "Brain Teasers," while their younger siblings can take on "Teasers for Tots." The charming old building that houses the museum is a former convent. (Daily 10 am-5 pm; closed Mon during school year except holidays) **$$**

⭐ **The Capitol.** *Capitol Hill (20002). Between Constitution and Independence aves, at Pennsylvania Ave, E end of the Mall. Phone 202/225-6827. www.aoc.gov.* With its graceful dome making it one of the most famous American landmarks, the Capitol has been the seat of the legislative branch of the US government for more than 200 years. Visitors can take guided tours of several sections, including the beautifully restored Old Supreme Court Chamber and Old Senate Chamber. The breathtaking Rotunda, a ceremonial space beneath the soaring dome, is a gallery for paintings and sculptures of historic significance. Below it is the Crypt, built for the remains of George Washington (who asked to be buried at Mount Vernon instead), now used for exhibits. Don't miss the National Statuary Hall, where statues of prominent citizens have been donated by all 50 states, and the ornate Brumidi Corridors, named for the Italian artist who designed their murals and many other decorative elements in the Capitol. A state-of-the-art visitor center, currently under construction, is scheduled to open in 2005. (Mon-Sat; closed Jan 1, Thanksgiving, Dec 25) Tickets for tours are available at the Capitol Guide Service kiosk near the intersection of First St SW and Independence Ave. **FREE**

Congress. *Capitol Hill (20002).* Tickets to the House and Senate visitors' galleries can be obtained from the office of your representative or senator. Foreign visitors can obtain passes to the Senate Gallery from the appointment desk, first floor, Senate Wing; and to the House of Representatives Gallery from the check stand, third floor, House wing (identification required).

Old Senate Chamber. *First and Constitution aves NE (20001). N of rotunda. Phone 202/225-6827.* Original Senate chamber has been restored to its 1850s appearance.

West Front. *Phone 202/225-6827.* Along the Capitol's west front are terraces, gardens, and lawns designed by Frederick Law Olmstead, who also planned New York City's Central Park. Halfway down the hill are the Peace Monument (on the north) and the Garfield Monument (on the south). At the foot of Capitol Hill is Union Square with a reflecting pool and Grant Monument.

Capitol City Brewing Company. *2 Massachusetts Ave NE (20002). Phone 202/842-2337. www.capcitybrew.com.* Shiny copper vats and a large oval copper bar are the centerpieces of this huge—and hugely popular—brew pub situated in the beautifully restored 1911 Postal Square Building. Hill staffers and tourists crowd in for made-on-the-premises ales, lagers, and pilsners that go down well with warm pretzels and mustard or with whole meals. This is one of four Capitol City pubs in the area, and the only one swathed in neoclassical marble. (Daily)

DC United (MLS). *RFK Memorial Stadium. 2400 E Capitol St (20003). Phone 202/547-9077. www.dcunited.com.* Professional soccer team.

Eastern Market. *225 7th St SE. Phone 202/546-2698.* Meat, fish, and produce are sold. Also crafts and farmers market on weekends. (Tues-Sun)

Emancipation Statue. *Lincoln Park, E Capitol St NE between 11th and 13th sts NE (20003).* Bronze work of Thomas Ball paid for by voluntary subscriptions from emancipated slaves, depicting Lincoln presenting the Emancipation Proclamation to a black man, was dedicated on April 14, 1876, the 11th anniversary of Lincoln's assassination, with Fredrick Douglass in attendance. Also here is

Mary McLeod Bethune Memorial. *E Capitol St, SE (20003).* Honors the noted educator and advisor to President Lincoln and founder of the National Council of Negro Women.

Fort Dupont Park. *Randle Cir and Minnesota Ave SE (20019). Phone 202/426-7723; 202/426-7745. www.nps.gov/fodu/.* Picnicking, hiking, and bicycling in hilly terrain; cultural arts performances in summer (see SPECIAL EVENTS). Also films, slides, and activities involving natural science; environmental education programs; nature discovery room; Junior Ranger program; programs for senior citizens and disabled persons; and garden workshops and programmed activities by reservation. **FREE** Nearby is

Fort Dupont Sports Complex. *3779 Ely Pl SE (20019). E on Pennsylvania Ave SE; N on Minnesota Ave; E on Ely Pl. Phone 202/584-5007 (ice rink).* Skating, ice hockey (fee); tennis courts, basketball courts, ball fields (daily; free), jogging.

Frederick Douglass National Historic Site. *1411 W St SE (20020). Phone 202/426-5961; 800/967-2283 (tour reservations). www.nps.gov/frdo/freddoug.html.* This 21-room house on 9 acres is where Douglass, a former slave who became minister to Haiti and a leading black spokesman, lived from 1877 until his death in 1895; visitor center with film, memorabilia. (Daily; closed Jan 1, Thanksgiving, Dec 25) **FREE**

Government Printing Office. *710 N Capitol St NW (20403). On N Capitol St, between G and H sts. Phone 202/512-0132.* Four buildings with 35 acres of floor space where most of the material issued by US government, including production and distribution of the Congressional Record, Federal Register, and US passports, is printed. (No public tours; for information on the agency, call 202/512-1991.) Office includes the **Main Government Bookstore.** Nearly 20,000 publications available (Mon-Fri; closed holidays).

House Office Buildings. *Along Independence Ave, south side of Capitol grounds at Independence and New Jersey aves (20500). Phone 202/224-3121.* Pedestrian tunnel connects two of the oldest House office buildings with the Capitol.

Kenilworth Aquatic Gardens. *Anacostia Ave and Douglas St NE (20019). Phone 202/426-6905.* Water lilies, lotuses, and other water plants bloom from mid-May until frost. Gardens (daily). Guided walks (Memorial Day-Labor Day, Sat, Sun, and holidays, also by appointment; closed Jan 1, Thanksgiving, Dec 25). **FREE**

Labor Department. *Francis H. Perkins Building, 200 Constitution Ave NW (20210). Phone 202/219-6992 (library); toll-free 866/4-USA-DOL. www.dol.gov.* Lobby contains the Labor Hall of Fame, an exhibit depicting labor in the US; the library on the second floor is open to the public. (Mon-Fri; closed holidays) **FREE**

Library of Congress. *10 1st St SE (20540). Phone 202/707-8000 (reading room schedule, calendar of events); 202/707-8000 (information on exhibitions and free guided tours). www.loc.gov.* (1800) Treasures include a Gutenberg Bible, the first great book printed with movable metal type; the Giant Bible of

Mainz, a 500-year-old illuminated manuscript. Collection includes books, manuscripts, newspapers, maps, recordings, prints, photographs, posters, and more than 30 million books and pamphlets in 60 languages. In the elaborate Jefferson Building is the Great Hall, decorated with murals, mosaics, and marble carvings; exhibition halls. In the Madison Building, a 22-minute audiovisual presentation, *America's Library,* provides a good introduction to the library and its facilities. (Mon-Sat; closed federal holidays) **FREE** The library complex includes

Folger Shakespeare Library. *201 E Capitol St SE (20540). Phone 202/544-4600. www.folger.edu.* (1932) Houses the finest collection of Shakespeare materials in the world, including the 1623 First Folio edition and large holdings of rare books and manuscripts of the English and continental Renaissance. The Great Hall offers year-round exhibits from the Folger's extensive collection. The Elizabethan Theatre, which was designed to resemble an innyard theater of Shakespeare's day, is the site of the Folger Shakespeare Library's series of museum and performing arts programs, which include literary readings, drama, lectures, and education and family programs. Self-guided tours. Guided tours (11 am). (Mon-Sat; closed federal holidays) **FREE**

Lincoln Museum. *511 10th St NW (20004). Phone 202/347-4833.* Exhibits and displays focus on Lincoln's life and assassination. (Daily; closed Dec 25) **FREE**

Navy Yard. *901 M St SE (20374). Between 1st and 11th sts SE. Phone 202/433-4882.* Along the Anacostia River at a location chosen by George Washington, the yard was founded in 1799 and was nearly destroyed during the War of 1812. Outside the yard at 636 G St SE is the John Philip Sousa house, where the "March King" wrote many of his famous compositions; the house is private.

Marine Barracks. *Entrance to Navy Yard is at end of 9th St at M St SE. Inside is G St between 8th and 9th sts SE. Phone 202/433-6060.* The parade ground, more than two centuries old, is surrounded by handsome and historic structures, including the Commandant's House facing G St, which is said to be the oldest continuously occupied public building in the city. The spectacular parade is open to the public Tues and Fri evenings in summer (see SPECIAL EVENTS).

Marine Corps Museum. *Building 58 in Navy Yard. 901 M St SE (20374). Phone 202/433-3840.* Weapons, uniforms, maps, flags, and other artifacts describe the history of the US Marine Corps. Housed in a restored 19th-century structure; also used as marine barracks from 1941 to 1975. (Mon, Wed-Fri; Sat, Sun by appointment only; closed Jan 1, Dec 25) **FREE**

Navy Museum. *Building 76, Washington Navy Yard, 805 Kidder Breese SE. Phone 202/433-6897 or 202/433-4882.* History of the US Navy from the Revolutionary War to the space age. Dioramas depict achievements of early naval heroes; displays development of naval weapons; fully rigged foremast fighting top and gun deck from frigate *Constitution* on display; World War II guns that can be trained and elevated; submarine room has operating periscopes. Approximately 5,000 objects on display including paintings, ship models, flags, uniforms, naval decorations, and the bathy-scaphe *Trieste*. Two-acre outdoor park displays 19th- and 20th-century guns, cannon, other naval artifacts; US Navy destroyer *Barry* located on the waterfront. (Daily; closed holidays) Tours (Mon-Fri). **FREE**

Senate Office Buildings. *114 Constitution Ave NE (20002). Constitution Ave on both sides of 1st St NE.* Linked by private subway to the Capitol.

Sewall-Belmont House. *144 Constitution Ave NE (20002). Phone 202/546-1210. www.sewallbelmont.org.* (1680, 1800) The Sewall-Belmont House is a monument to Alice Paul, the author of the Equal Rights Amendment. From this house, she spearheaded the fight for the passage of the amendment. Now a national landmark, the house contains portraits and sculptures of women from the beginning of the suffrage movement; extensive collection of artifacts of the suffrage and equal rights movements; historic headquarters of the National Woman's Party. (Tues-Fri 11 am-3 pm, Sat noon-4 pm; closed Jan 1, Thanksgiving, Dec 25) **FREE**

Supreme Court of the United States. *1st St NE at Maryland Ave (20543), E of the Capitol. Phone 202/479-3211.* Designed by Cass Gilbert in Neoclassical style. Court is in session Oct-Apr (Mon-Wed, at two-week intervals from the first Mon in Oct) and on the first workday of each week in May and June; court sessions are open to the public (10 am and 1 pm), on a first-come, first-served basis; lectures are offered in the courtroom (Mon-Fri except when court is in session; 20-minute lectures hourly on half-hour); on the ground floor are exhibits and film (23 minutes), cafeteria, snack bar, gift shop (Mon-Fri; closed holidays). **FREE**

Union Station. *50 Massachusetts Ave NE (20002). On Massachusetts Ave between 1st and 2nd sts. Phone 703/371-9441. www.unionstationdc.com.* Restored Beaux Arts train station designed by Daniel Burnham and completed in 1907 features lavish interior spaces under a 96-foot-high, coffered, gold-leafed ceiling. Located within the original station and train shed are 130 shops, restaurants, and a movie theater complex. Original spaces, such as the presidential suite, have been turned into restaurants without extensive alteration. Also located within the station are the Amtrak depot and Gray Line and Tourmobile Sightseeing operators (see SIGHTSEEING TOURS). (Daily) **FREE**

US Botanic Garden. *100 Maryland Ave SW (20002), at base of Capitol Hill. Phone 202/225-8333. www.usbg.gov.* The Botanic Garden, one of the oldest in the country, was established by Congress in 1820 for public education and exhibition. It features plants collected by the famous Wilkes Expedition of the South Seas. Conservatory has tropical, subtropical, and desert plants; seasonal displays. Exterior gardens are planted for seasonal blooming; also here is **Bartholdi Fountain,** designed by the sculptor of the Statue of Liberty. (Daily) **FREE**

Special Events

Evening Parade. *US Marine Barracks, I St between 8th and 9th sts SE (20390). Phone 202/433-6060.* Spectacular parade with Marine Band, US Marine

Drum and Bugle Corps, Color Guard, Silent Drill Team, and marching companies. Submitting a written request for reservations at least three weeks in advance is recommended. Tues and Fri evenings, early May-late Aug.

Fort Dupont Summer Theatre. *Fort Dupont Park. Minnesota Ave and Randle Cir (20019). Phone 202/426-7723 or 202/426-5961.* Musicals, concerts, plays, and dancing. Fri evenings, late June-late Aug. **FREE**

Hotels

★ ★ **HOLIDAY INN.** *415 New Jersey Ave NW (20001). Phone 202/638-1616; toll-free 800/638-1116; fax 202/638-0707. www.holiday-inn.com.* 343 rooms, 10 story. Check-out noon. TV; cable (premium). In-room modem link. Restaurant, bar. In-house fitness room. Outdoor pool, poolside service. **$**

[D] [≈] [⫯] [⊴] [SC]

★ ★ ★ **HOTEL GEORGE.** *15 E St NW (20001). Phone 202/347-4200; toll-free 800/576-8331; fax 202/347-4213. www.hotelgeorge.com.* If you need to be downtown but are tired of the traditional options, the Neoclassical atmosphere of this business- and leisure-friendly hotel is just what you need. The guest rooms are individually designed, with a comfortable, but elegant, residential feel. 139 rooms, 8 story. Check-out noon, check-in 3 pm. TV; cable (premium), VCR, CD available. Restaurant, bar. Sauna, steam room. Health club privileges. Valet parking. Concierge. **$$$**

[D] [⊴]

★ ★ ★ **LOEWS L'ENFANT PLAZA HOTEL.** *480 L'Enfant Plz SW (20024). Phone 202/484-1000; fax 202/646-4456. www.loewshotels.com.* Sitting just blocks from the Mall, this hotel cannot be beat for its central location. 370 rooms. Pets accepted. Check-out 1 pm. TV; cable (premium), VCR available. In-room modem link. Restaurant, bar. In-house fitness room. Outdoor pool, poolside service. Valet parking. Business center. Concierge. **$$**

[D] [🐾] [≈] [⫯] [⊴] [⫯]

★ ★ **PHOENIX PARK HOTEL.** *520 N Capitol St NW (20001). Phone 202/638-6900; toll-free 800/824-5419; fax 202/393-3236. www.phoenix parkhotel.com.* 148 rooms, 9 story. Check-out 1 pm. TV; cable (premium). In-room modem link. Restaurant, bar; entertainment. In-house fitness room. Valet parking. Business center. Near the Capitol; traditional European décor. **$$**

[D] [⫯] [⊴] [SC] [⫯]

★ ★ ★ **WASHINGTON COURT HOTEL.** *525 New Jersey Ave NW (20001). Phone 202/628-2100; toll-free 800/321-3010; fax 202/879-7918. www.washingtoncourthotel.com.* The elegant four-story lobby sets the stage at this luxury business hotel, two blocks from the Capitol Building. 264 rooms, 15 story. Check-out noon. TV; cable (premium), VCR available. In-room modem link. Restaurant, bar; entertainment. In-house fitness room. Valet parking. Concierge. **$$**

D 𝄂 ⊠ SC

Restaurants

★ ★ ★ **BISTRO BIS.** *15 E St NW (20001). Phone 202/661-2700; fax 202/661-2747. www.bistrobis.com.* The long zinc bar is the only concession to the bistro theme at this sleek downtown spot. The food is classic French bistro, with well-executed items. As unstuffy as DC gets; a fun night out. Closed Dec 25. Lunch, dinner, brunch. Entertainment. Children's menu. **$$**

D

★ ★ **LA COLLINE.** *400 N Capitol St NW (20001). Phone 202/737-0400; fax 202/737-3026.* French menu. Closed Sun; holidays. Breakfast, lunch, dinner. Bar. Outdoor seating. Across from Union Station. **$$**

D

★ **MARKET INN.** *200 E St SW (20024). Phone 202/554-2100; fax 202/863-1052. www.marketinndc.com.* American menu. Closed Thanksgiving, Dec 25. Lunch, dinner, Sun brunch. Bar; entertainment. Children's menu. Outdoor seating. English pub ambience. **$$**

D

★ ★ **MONOCLE.** *107 D St NE (20002). Phone 202/546-4488; fax 202/546-7235.* American menu. Closed Sat, Sun; holidays. Lunch, dinner. Bar. Children's menu. Located in 1865 Jenkens Hill building. Valet parking. Close to the Capitol; frequented by members of Congress and other politicians. **$$**

★ ★ **TWO QUAIL.** *320 Massachusetts Ave NE (20002). Phone 202/543-8030; fax 202/543-8035.* American menu. Closed Dec 25. Lunch, dinner. **$$**

Downtown

In recent years, Washington's downtown has experienced more development than any other neighborhood in the city. The newly constructed Washington Convention Center and MCI Center (home to the National Basketball Association's Wizards and National Hockey League's Capitals), along with the opening of many new hotels, restaurants, and office buildings, have revitalized the downtown area, giving it an energy and verve that had been missing for decades.

Situated north of the National Mall and bordered to the west by the White House and to the east by Union Station, downtown Washington features a number of different museums, including the National Museum of American Art, the National Building Museum, National Archives, the National Museum of Women in the Arts, and the Jewish Historical Society. The downtown area's south side (Penn Quarter) is known for its thriving theater scene, with venues such as the National Theatre, Shakespeare Theatre, Warner Theatre, and historic Ford's Theatre, where President Lincoln was assassinated in 1865. Visitors to downtown may want to schedule time to visit the US Navy Memorial & Naval Heritage Center, as well as the National Law Enforcement Officers Memorial.

Washington's Chinatown can be found downtown, a block north of the MCI Center. At 7th and H streets, the Gateway Arch welcomes visitors to Chinatown. This landmark is the world's largest single-span Chinese arch. The colorful wooden arch features 7,000 tiles and nearly 300 painted dragons. Not surprisingly, Chinatown is home to some of the city's finest authentic Chinese restaurants.

What to See and Do

Chinatown. *G and H sts, between 6th and 8th sts NW (20431).* Recognizable by the Chinatown Friendship Archway at 7th and H sts. The archway is decorated in Chinese architectural styles of Qing and Ming dynasties and is topped with nearly 300 painted dragons.

✪ **Ford's Theatre.** *511 10th St NW (20004). Phone 202/426-6924 (visitor information); 202/347-4833 (box office). www.fordstheatre.org.* Seeing a play in this historic old theater, famous as the site of Abraham Lincoln's assassination, is deeply moving. A museum in the basement exhibits the clothes the president was wearing that night, as well as John Wilkes Booth's derringer; upstairs, the presidential box has been restored to its 1865 condition. Ford's became a working theater again in 1968; recent productions have included the play *Inherit the Wind* and a one-man show about George Gershwin. Self-guided tours (daily; closed Dec 25).

General Services Administration Building. *18th and F sts NW (20405).* (1917) Was originally the Department of Interior.

Glow. *714 6th St NW (20001). Phone 202/271-1171. www.clubglow.com.* Mix eye-popping special effects—heavy, high-tech lighting with a state-of-the-art sound system, add some of the city's hippest DJs and hundreds of gotta-dance clubgoers, and you've got—on Saturday nights, anyway—the party to end all parties. A once-a-week club within a club, Glow fills gigantic Club Insomnia with the hottest trance, techno, British, and Latin sounds, working the young, sexily dressed crowd (no boots or athletic wear) into a froth of sensory overload. (Sat) **$$$$**

Gray Line bus tours. *50 Massachusetts Ave NE (20002). Phone 301/386-8300; toll-free 800/862-1400.* Tours of city and area attractions depart from Union Station. Contact 5500 Tuxedo Rd, Tuxedo, MD 20781.

HR-57. *1610 14th St NW (20009). Phone 202/667-3700. www.hr57.org.* This ultra-friendly, bare-bones spot is the performance arm of the Center for the Preservation of Jazz and Blues, a not-for-profit cultural center that named its club after a 1987 House Resolution designating jazz as "a rare and valuable national American treasure." Musical integrity—and the ability to appreciate a great jam—are everything here; expect to hear well-known and lesser-known artists at the top of their game, and a crowd that eats it up. (Wed-Sat) **$$**

International Spy Museum. *800 F St NW (20004). Phone 202/393-7798; toll-free 866/779-6873. www.spymuseum.org.* Learn more about people who keep secrets for a living at this private museum that opened in 2002. It sheds light on the world of international espionage with artifacts that run the gamut from invisible ink and high-tech eavesdropping devices to a through-the-wall camera and a KGB lipstick pistol. Find out how codes were made and broken throughout history, how successful disguises are created, and what real-life James Bonds think of the high-stakes "game" of spying. (Daily from 10 am; closed Jan 1, Thanksgiving, Dec 25). **$$$$**

Judiciary Square. *D and 4th sts NW (20001).* Two square blocks of judiciary buildings, including five federal and district courts, the US District Court (1820), and the US Court of Appeals (1910). At D St halfway between 4th and 5th sts is the first completed statue of Abraham Lincoln (1868).

MCI Center. *601 F St NW (20004). Phone 202/628-3200. www.mcicenter.com.* This 20,000-seat, state-of-the-art arena, home to the NBA's Washington Wizards, the WNBA's Washington Mystics, the NHL's Washington Capitals, and the Georgetown Hoyas, is also a popular venue for concerts and other events, from Liza Minnelli to the Harlem Globetrotters. Even when nothing is scheduled, you can check out Nick and Stef's Steakhouse (open for dinner every day, lunch Mon-Fri), the F Street Sports Bar, or Modell's Sporting Goods for team-themed athletic wear. (Mon-Sat; closed major holidays; days and fees for events vary)

MCI National Sports Gallery. *601 F St NW (20004). Phone 202/661-5133.* This 25,000-square-foot museum commemorates and showcases the best of American sports history. Includes sports memorabilia collections; participatory and technology-driven exhibits with basketball, football, hockey, and baseball themes. Rotating exhibits feature special-interest sports. Home of the American Sportscasters Association Hall of Fame and Museum, honoring the memorable voices that brought great sports moments. **$$$**

National Archives. *700 Pennsylvania Ave NW (20408). Between 7th and 9th sts NW; exhibition entrance is on Constitution Ave. Phone 202/501-5205; 202/501-5000 (recording). www.archives.gov.* (1934) Original copies of the Declaration of Independence, the Bill of Rights, and the Constitution; a 1297 version of the Magna Carta and other historic documents, maps, and photographs. Guided tours by appointment only. Archives are also available to the public for genealogical and historical research (Mon-Sat; closed federal holidays). (Daily; closed Dec 25) **FREE**

National Building Museum. *Housed in the Old Pension Building, 401 F St NW (20001). Phone 202/272-2448. www.nbm.org.* Deals with architecture, design, engineering, and construction. Permanent exhibits include drawings, blueprints, models, photographs, artifacts; architectural evolution of Washington's buildings and monuments. The museum's enormous Great

Hall is supported by eight of the world's largest Corinthian columns. Guided tours (afternoons: weekdays, one tour; weekends, two tours). Museum (Mon-Sat 10 am-5 pm, Sun 11 am-5 pm; closed Jan 1, Thanksgiving, Dec 25). **FREE**

National Museum of Women in the Arts. *1250 New York Ave NW (20005). Phone 202/783-5000; toll-free 800/222-7270. www.nmwa.org.* Focus on women's contributions to the arts. More than 1,200 works by women artists from the Renaissance to the present. Paintings, drawings, sculpture, pottery, prints. Library, research center by appointment. Performances. Guided tours (by appointment). (Mon-Sat 10 am-5 pm, Sun noon-5 pm; closed Jan 1, Thanksgiving, Dec 25) **$**

National Portrait Gallery. *8th and F sts NW (20560). Phone 202/275-1738. www.npg.si.edu.* Portraits and statues of people who have made significant contributions to the history, development, and culture of the United States. (Daily; closed Dec 25)

National Theatre. *1321 Pennsylvania Ave NW (20004). Phone 202/628-6161 (information); toll-free 800/447-7400 (tickets). www.nationaltheatre.org.* Sarah Bernhardt, Laurence Olivier, and the Barrymores are just some of the theatrical luminaries who have performed at this historic playhouse, which is said to be haunted by the ghost of a murdered actor. These days, you'll see touring productions of such shows as *The Tale of the Allergist's Wife* and *42nd Street.* On Mondays, there are films in summer and performances drawing on local talent the rest of the year. Saturday mornings feature children's shows. Tours (Mon-Fri) by reservation, phone 202/783-6854. Fees vary by performance.

New York Avenue Presbyterian Church. *1313 New York Ave NW (20005). Phone 202/393-3700. www.nyapc.org.* The church where Lincoln worshipped. It was rebuilt 1950-1951, with Lincoln's pew. Dr. Peter Marshall was pastor from 1937 to 1949. Mementos on display include the first draft of the Emancipation Proclamation. (Daily, services Sun morning; closed holidays)

Pavilion at the Old Post Office. *1100 Pennsylvania Ave NW (20004). Phone 202/289-4224. www.oldpostofficedc.com.* (1899) Romanesque structure, which for years was headquarters of the US Postal Service, has been remodeled into a marketplace with 100 shops and restaurants and daily entertainment. In the 315-foot tower are replicas of the bells of Westminster Abbey, a Bicentennial gift from Great Britain; the tower, which is the second-highest point in DC, offers spectacular views from an open-air observation deck (free). Above the Pavilion shops are headquarters for the National Endowment for the Arts. (Daily; closed Jan 1, Thanksgiving, Dec 25) **FREE**

Petersen House. *516 10th St NW (20004).* The house where President Lincoln was taken after the shooting at Ford's Theatre; he died here the following morning. The house has been restored to its appearance at that time. (Daily; closed Dec 25) **FREE**

Polly Esther's. *605 12th St NW (20005). Phone 202/737-1970. www.pollyesthers.com.* Sometimes familiarity breeds fun! If your idea of the good old days is the 1970s, '80s, or '90s, you'll love it here, where dancing to a retro beat is all the rage and the Hustle is more than a memory. Period kitsch adds to the ambience; the moderately priced drink list includes potions made with Tang. Part of a New York-based chain, this Polly Esther's is especially popular for bachelorette parties. (Thurs-Sat) **$$**

Shakespeare Theatre at the Lansburgh. *450 7th St NW (20004). Phone 202/547-1122. www.shakespearedc.org.*

Shops at National Place. *1331 Pennsylvania Ave NW (20004); enter at 13th and F sts. Phone 202/662-1200.* Trilevel marketplace—at, above, and below street grade—featuring more than 100 specialty shops and restaurants. (Daily)

Shops at Union Station. *50 Massachusetts Ave NE (20002). Phone 202/289-1908. www.unionstationdc.com.* This is shopping in some of the most elegant surroundings imaginable—architect Daniel Burnham's extraordinary 1907 Union Station, restored to its former glory and reopened in 1988. The white granite Beaux Arts masterpiece is still a functioning train station and is now home to more than 130 upscale restaurants and shops, many of them catering to the special needs of travelers. But many locals patronize the shops too (including President Bill Clinton, who regularly bought holiday presents here). (Daily)

US Navy Memorial. *701 Pennsylvania Ave NW (20001). Phone 202/737-2300. www.lonesailor.org.* Dedicated to those who have served in the Navy in war and in peacetime. A 100-foot-diameter granite world map dominates the Plaza, where the *Lone Sailor,* a 7-foot bronze sculpture, stands and the US Navy Band stages performances (Memorial Day-Labor Day, Tues evenings). Visitor Center features electronic kiosks with interactive video displays on naval history; also Navy Memorial Log Room and US Presidents Room. (Tues-Sat) **FREE** Also here is

   At Sea. *Arleigh and Roberta Burke Theater. 701 Pennsylvania Ave NW (20001). Phone toll-free 800/777-2238.* Underwritten by ExxonMobil, this award-winning high-resolution 70mm film conveys the experience of being at sea aboard a US Navy aircraft carrier. The 241-seat theater employs a two-story, 52-foot-wide screen and six-track digital audio to surround the audience with the sights and sounds of carrier operations. Showings (Mon-Sat, four times daily; Sun, two times).

Warner Theatre. *13th and E sts NW (20004). Phone 202/783-4000. www.warnertheatre.com.*

Washington Capitals (NHL). *MCI Center. 601 F St NW (20004). Phone 202/661-5050. www.washingtoncapitals.com.* The Capitals advanced to the NHL finals once in the 1990s, but success has been sporadic, at best. The team plays its home games in the MCI Center, one of the newer facilities in the league, which the team shares with the Washington Wizards (see) of the NBA. Going to games provides a good chance to see Washington movers and shakers like politicians and celebrities—and it could be argued that more people go for this reason than for the hockey.

Washington Mystics (WNBA). *MCI Center. 601 F St NW (20004). Phone 202/661-5050. www.wnba.com/mystics/.* Professional women's basketball team.

Washington Wizards (NBA). *MCI Center. 601 F St NW (20004). Phone 202/661-5050. www.nba.com/wizards.* The Wizards got a publicity boost in the early 2000s, as Michael Jordan came out of retirement for a second time to play for the team. Still, the team never made the playoffs under Jordan, and he retired again after the 2003 season finale. The team plays its home games in the MCI Center, and tickets are easy to come by on most nights, depending on who the Wizards' competition is.

Special Event

Taste of DC. *Pennsylvania Ave NW (20004). Between 7th and 14th sts. Phone 202/789-7002. www.washington.org/taste/.* Enjoy sample-size portions of scrumptious fare from local restaurants at the biggest, liveliest food and music festival on the East Coast. In an area as culturally diverse as DC, the vendors represent many of the world's great cuisines, including Indian, Jamaican, Italian, and Thai. Enjoy music and other live entertainment as you munch on your jerk chicken and vegetable samosas, and make sure to save room for key lime pie or an old-fashioned funnel cake. Columbus Day weekend.

Hotels

★ ★ ★ **CAPITAL HILTON.** *1001 16th St NW (20036). Phone 202/393-1000; toll-free 800/774-1500; fax 202/639-5784.* 544 rooms, 15 story. Check-out noon, check-in 3 pm. TV; cable (premium). Restaurant, bar. Room service. In-house fitness room, massage, steam room. Business center. **$**

D 🛪 🖳 🏃

★ **THE GOVERNORS HOUSE HOTEL.** *1615 Rhode Island Ave NW (20036). Phone 202/296-2100; toll-free 800/821-4367; fax 202/463-6614. www.governorshousewdc.com.* 149 rooms, 9 story. Check-out noon. TV; cable (premium). In-room modem link. Restaurant, bar. In-house fitness room. Health club privileges. Outdoor pool. Valet parking. On the original site of the governor of Pennsylvania's house. **$**

D 🏊 🛪 🖳

★ ★ ★ **GRAND HYATT WASHINGTON.** *1000 H St NW (20001). Phone 202/582-1234; toll-free 800/633-7313; fax 202/634-4781. www.grand washington.hyatt.com.* A convenient downtown location, situated close to the MCI Center, the US Capitol, and other federal agencies, makes this hotel a popular choice for travelers. 888 rooms, 12 story. Check-out noon, check-in 3 pm. TV; cable (premium). In-room modem link. Laundry services. Restaurant, bar; entertainment. Room service 24 hours. Babysitting services available. In-house fitness room, massage, sauna, steam room. Health club privileges. Indoor pool, whirlpool. Valet parking. Business center. Three-story cascading waterfall. **$$**

D 🏊 🛪 🖳 🏃

★ ★ **THE HAMILTON CROWNE PLAZA.** *1001 14th St NW (20005). Phone 202/682-0111; fax 202/682-9525. www.crowneplazawashington.com.*

318 rooms, 14 story. Check-out noon, check-in 3 pm. TV; cable. Restaurant, bar. Valet parking. Business center. Concierge. **$$**

[icons]

★ ★ ★ ★ **HAY-ADAMS HOTEL.** *16th and H sts NW (20006). Phone 202/638-6600; toll-free 800/424-5054; fax 202/638-2716. www.hayadams.com.* The Hay-Adams seems to radiate the power of the nation's capital. Set on Lafayette Square across from the White House, the hotel has been welcoming notables since the 1920s. Reading like a Who's Who of American history, the Hay-Adams' guest list is truly fascinating. If only these walls could talk! Originally designed as the private residences of two influential men, the hotel retains the majestic style of its former incarnation. The guest rooms are a happy marriage of historic preservation and 21st-century conveniences; intricately carved plaster ceilings and ornamental fireplaces reside alongside high-speed Internet access and multiline telephones. Windows frame views of the White House, St. John's Church, and Lafayette Square, further convincing visitors that they are in the center of Washington's universe. All-day dining is available at Lafayette, while the Off the Record bar is a popular watering hole for politicians and hotel guests. 145 rooms, 8 story. Pets accepted, some restrictions. Check-out noon, check-in 3 pm. TV; cable (premium). In-room modem link. Fireplaces. Restaurant, bar. Room service 24 hours. Babysitting services available. Concierge. **$$$$**

[icons]

★ ★ ★ **HENLEY PARK HOTEL.** *926 Massachusetts NW (20001). Phone 202/638-5200; toll-free 800/222-8474; fax 202/414-0513. www.henleypark.com.* This intimate, historic hotel is within walking distance of the Washington Convention Center and convenient to various DC attractions. All rooms have a charming European style. 96 rooms, 8 story. Check-out noon. TV; cable (premium). In-room modem link. Restaurant, bar; entertainment. Room service 24 hours. Health club privileges. Valet parking. Tudor detailing; 1918 structure. **$$**

[icons]

★ ★ **HOTEL HARRINGTON.** *436 11th St NW (20004). Phone 202/628-8140; toll-free 800/424-8532; fax 202/347-3924. www.hotel-harrington.com.* 260 rooms, 11 story. Pets accepted, some restrictions. Check-out noon. TV; cable (premium). Laundry services. Restaurant, bar. **$**

[icons]

★ ★ **HOTEL WASHINGTON.** *Pennsylvania Ave at 15th St NW (20004). Phone 202/638-5900; toll-free 800/424-9540; fax 202/638-1595. www.hotelwashington.com.* 344 rooms, 11 story. Pets accepted. Check-out 1 pm, check-in 3 pm. TV; cable (premium). In-room modem link. Restaurant, bar. In-house fitness room, sauna. Business center. One of the oldest continuously operated hotels in the city. Original Jardin d'Armide tapestry (1854). **$$**

[icons]

★ ★ ★ **JW MARRIOTT HOTEL ON PENNSYLVANIA AVENUE.** *1331 Pennsylvania Ave NW (20004). Phone 202/393-2000; toll-free 800/228-9290; fax 202/626-6991. www.marriotthotels.com/wasjw.* Located in the heart of Washington, this elegant hotel offers guests superb service and a relaxing stay. Centrally located to theaters, shops, and some wonderful sightseeing, this hotel has something for everyone. 772 rooms, 12 story. Check-out noon. TV; cable (premium). In-room modem link. Restaurant. Room service 24 hours. In-house fitness room, sauna. Massage. Indoor pool, whirlpool. Valet parking. Business center. Concierge. Luxury level. **$$**

D ⇌ ✗ ⇟ SC ✗

★ ★ **MARRIOTT WASHINGTON METRO CENTER.** *775 12th St NW (20005). Phone 202/737-2200; fax 202/347-5886. www.marriotthotels.com.* Located in the heart of downtown. Business travelers will appreciate the location and amenities of this hotel. 345 rooms, 15 story. Check-out noon, check-in 4 pm. TV; cable (premium). In-room modem link. Restaurant, bar. Room service to midnight. Babysitting services available. In-house fitness room, sauna. Indoor pool, whirlpool. Valet parking. Business center. Concierge. Luxury level. **$$**

D ⇌ ✗ ⇟ ✗

★ ★ ★ **RENAISSANCE MAYFLOWER HOTEL.** *1127 Connecticut Ave NW (20036). Phone 202/347-3000; toll-free 800/HOTELS-1; fax 202/466-9082. www.renaissancehotels.com.* If you like to get comfortable in stately old hotels, you'll want to book a room at this high-rise property in the heart of the city's business district. Built in 1925 for Calvin Coolidge's inauguration, this hotel played host to the likes of Franklin Delano Roosevelt and J. Edgar Hoover. You'll find popular shops and restaurants just outside its front doors; the White House is only four blocks away. Be ready for the eye-pleasing view when you check in: all the gilded trim, crystal chandeliers, and Oriental rugs in the block-long lobby will awe you. The guest rooms themselves are quite homey, so you'll likely feel right at home in yours. For business travelers, each room has a desk with work lamp, a two-line phone with a dataport, and a speakerphone. For groups, the Mayflower offers state-of-the-art meeting facilities. 660 rooms, 10 story. Pets accepted, some restrictions; fee. Check-out noon, check-in 3 pm. TV; cable (premium). In-room modem link. Restaurant, bar; entertainment. Room service 24 hours. Babysitting services available. In-house fitness room. Health club privileges. Valet parking. Business center. Concierge. Foreign currency exchange. **$$$**

D ✎ ✗ ⇟ ✗

★ ★ ★ ★ **THE ST. REGIS, WASHINGTON, DC.** *923 16th and K sts NW (20006). Phone 202/638-2626; toll-free 800/562-5661; fax 202/638-4231. www.starwood.com/stregis/.* The St. Regis is a treasure in the nation's capital. Since 1926, the St. Regis has been a preferred residence of discerning travelers visiting Washington. Just a stone's throw from the White House, the hotel enjoys a prime city location with nearly all of Washington's attractions nearby. Stepping into this esteemed hotel offers an enchanting glimpse of a grander time. Its gilded lobby of coffered ceilings and sparkling chandeliers is a work of art. Reflecting its Italian Renaissance roots, the rooms and suites recall the splendor of European palaces with silk-covered walls and antique furnishings. English-style butlers attend to the individual needs of each guest. Formal afternoon tea is served to the gentle strains of a harp, and dining at the

Library Restaurant completes this sublimely elegant experience. 193 rooms, 8 story. Pets accepted, some restrictions; fee. Check-out 1 pm, check-in 3 pm. TV; cable (premium), VCR available. In-room modem link. Restaurant, bar. Room service 24 hours. Babysitting services available. In-house fitness room. Health club privileges. Valet parking. Concierge. **$$$**

[D] 🍴 🏋 ⛵

★ ★ **TOPAZ HOTEL.** *1733 North St NW (20036). Phone 202/393-3000; toll-free 800/424-2950; fax 202/785-9581. www.topazhotel.com.* 99 rooms, 10 story. Complimentary continental breakfast. Check-out noon. TV; cable (premium), VCR available. In-room modem link. Restaurant, bar. Health club privileges. On the site of the "Little White House" where Theodore Roosevelt lived during his vice-presidency and the first weeks of his presidency. **$$**

⛵ **SC**

★ ★ ★ **WILLARD INTERCONTINENTAL WASHINGTON.** *1401 Pennsylvania Ave NW (20004). Phone 202/628-9100; toll-free 800/327-0200; fax 202/637-7326. www.washington.interconti.com.* The Willard InterContinental is steeped in history. Only two blocks from the White House, this legendary Beaux Arts hotel has been at the center of Washington's political scene since 1850. The Willard's lobby has always served as a drawing room to the world; it is here that Lincoln held fireside staff meetings, Grant escaped the rigors of the White House to enjoy brandy and cigars, and the term "lobbyist" was coined. Henry Clay shared the secret of the mint julep in the Round Robin Bar, while the Willard Room's continental cuisine (see) makes history today. This landmark's guest rooms and suites are a traditional blend of Edwardian and Victorian styles furnished in deep jewel tones. The Jenny Lind suite is perfect for honeymooners with its mansard roof and canopy bed, while the Oval suite, inspired by the office of the same name, makes guests feel like masters of the universe. 341 rooms, 12 story. Pets accepted. Check-out noon, check-in 3 pm. TV; cable (premium), VCR available. In-room modem link. Restaurant, bar. Room service 24 hours. Babysitting services available. In-house fitness room. Valet parking, covered parking. Business center. Concierge. **$$$$**

[D] 🍴 🏋 ⛵ **SC** 🏃

All Suite

★ **EMBASSY SQUARE SUMMERFIELD SUITES.** *2000 North St NW (20036). Phone 202/659-9000; toll-free 800/424-2999; fax 202/429-9546. www.summerfieldsuites.com.* This hotel is just a mile from the White House and near more than 40 restaurants and shops. 278 rooms, 10 story. Complimentary continental breakfast. Check-out noon. TV; cable (premium). In-room modem link. Laundry services. In-house fitness room. Outdoor pool. **$**

[D] 🏊 🏋 ⛵ **SC**

B&B/Small Inn

★ ★ ★ **MORRISON CLARK HOTEL.** *1015 L St NW (20001). Phone 202/898-1200; toll-free 800/332-7898; fax 202/289-8576. www.morrisonclark.com.*

This small, elegant hotel has historic charm, architecture, furnishings, and paintings. The guest rooms are all renovated with up-to-date amenities. 54 rooms, 4 story. Complimentary continental breakfast. Check-out noon, check-in 3 pm. TV; cable (premium), VCR available. In-room modem link. Dining room. Room service. In-house fitness room, health club privileges. Restored Victorian mansion (1864); period furnishings. **$$**

🏋 ➷ **SC**

Restaurants

★ ★ ★ **701 RESTAURANT.** *701 Pennsylvania Ave NW (20004). Phone 202/393-0701; fax 202/393-0242.* Overlooking the Navy Memorial fountains, this restaurant features a varied menu as well as a caviar bar. The roomy tables, comfortable chairs, and live piano music provide a nice atmosphere. Continental menu. Closed holidays. Lunch, dinner. Bar. Outdoor seating. **$$$**

D

★ ★ ★ **BOMBAY CLUB.** *815 Connecticut Ave NW (20006). Phone 202/ 659-3727; fax 202/659-5012.* This restaurant maintains its position as one of the most respected Indian restaurants in the area. The menu is divided into sections including house, vegetarian, Goan, Moghlai, and Northwest Frontier specialties. Indian menu. Closed Jan 1, Dec 25. Lunch, dinner, Sun brunch. Bar. Outdoor seating. **$$**

D

★ ★ **BOMBAY PALACE.** *2020 K St NW (20006). Phone 202/331-4200; fax 202/331-1505. www.bombay-palace.com.* Northern Indian menu. Indian décor and original art; 350-gallon fish tank. Lunch, dinner. Bar. Reservations accepted. Totally nonsmoking. **$$**

D

★ **BURMA.** *740 6th St NW (20001). Phone 202/638-1280.* Burmese menu. Closed holidays. Lunch, dinner. **$**

★ ★ ★ **CAFE 15.** *806 15th St NW (20005). Phone 202/737-8800; fax 202/ 730-8500.* Located in the sophisticated Sofitel, Cafe 15 does a strong job of competing in the culinary politics of high-end DC dining. You'll find an airy, bright dining room with a gracious staff and an ambitious team of chefs turning out contemporary French-Alsatian fare of the lofty, super-foodie variety. The wine list is deep and rare and well suited to heavy-hitter expense accounts. French menu. Breakfast, lunch, dinner. Bar. Casual attire. Outdoor seating. **$$$**

D

★ **CAFE MOZART.** *1331 H St NW (20005). Phone 202/347-5732; fax 202/ 347-4958. www.cafemozartgermandeli.com.* Austrian, German menu. Closed Jan 1, Thanksgiving, Dec 25. Breakfast, lunch, dinner. Bar; entertainment Thurs-Sat. Children's menu. German deli on premises. **$$**

D

★ ★ ★ **THE CAPITAL GRILLE.** *601 Pennsylvania Ave NW (20004). Phone 202/737-6200; fax 202/637-8821. www.thecapitalgrille.com.* Steak menu. Closed Thanksgiving, Dec 25. Lunch, dinner. Bar. Free valet parking (dinner). Totally nonsmoking. **$$$**

D

★ ★ ★ **CHRISTOPHER MARKS.** *1301 Pennsylvania Ave NW (20004). Phone 202/628-5939; fax 202/737-0072.* You'll feel like a power player upon stepping into this clubby restaurant. The menu is a bit predictable, but all of the choices are well executed and served by a professional staff. Seafood menu. Closed Sun. Lunch, dinner. Entertainment. Children's menu. **$$$**

D

★ ★ ★ **DC COAST.** *1401 K St NW (20005). Phone 202/216-5988; fax 202/371-2221. www.dccoast.com.* Seafood menu. Closed Sun; holidays. Lunch, dinner. **$$$**

D

★ ★ **DISTRICT CHOPHOUSE.** *509 7th St NW (20004). Phone 202/347-3434; fax 202/347-3388. www.districtchophouse.com.* American menu. Closed Thanksgiving, Dec 25. Lunch, dinner. Bar. Brewery. Children's menu. **$$**

D

★ ★ ★ **GEORGIA BROWN'S.** *950 15th St NW (20005). Phone 202/393-4499; fax 202/393-7134. www.gbrowns.com.* At this McPherson Square spot, one of Washington's favorite restaurants for several years running, diners have trouble choosing from among the many creative, modern dishes. The dining room is the definition of "casual elegance." Southern menu. Closed Dec 25. Lunch, dinner, Sun brunch. Bar; entertainment. **$$**

D

★ ★ ★ ★ **GERARD'S PLACE.** *915 15th St NW (20005). Phone 202/737-4445; fax 202/737-5555.* Gerard's Place is an intimate little hideaway for people who love the art of dining. Elegant and civilized, it is perfect for romance, special occasions, or dinner with close friends. The menu is a product of meticulous attention to detail. Fresh ingredients are at work here, as are classic French technique and a healthy dose of creativity. Aromatic herbs like sage, mint, basil, lavender, sorrel, and lemon thyme often play supporting roles. Meals are served on mismatched china plates—a nice touch that adds a sweet sense of home to this prized establishment. The kitchen offers a five-course tasting menu as well as a tempting à la carte menu. The wine list is lengthy and features mostly French bottles, with a more modest American selection. Desserts are all made to order and must be selected at the beginning of the meal, or at least 25 minutes before you'd like to dig in. These desserts are worth the wait, so don't miss out. French menu. Closed Sun; holidays. Lunch, dinner. Outdoor seating. **$$$**

D

★ **HAAD THAI.** *1100 New York Ave NW (20005). Phone 202/682-1111; fax 202/682-0824. www.haadthai.com.* Thai menu. Closed holidays. Lunch, dinner. Bar. **$**

[D]

★ ★ **HUNAN CHINATOWN.** *624 H St NW (20001). Phone 202/783-5858; fax 202/393-1375. www.marriottworldcenter.com.* Hunan, Szechwan menu. Lunch, dinner. **$$**

★ ★ **JALEO.** *480 7th St NW (20004). Phone 202/628-7949; fax 202/628-7952.* Spanish menu. Closed Thanksgiving, Dec 24, 25. Lunch, dinner. Bar. Sevillanas dancers Wed nights. Valet parking. Murals of flamenco dancers. **$$**

[D]

★ **LES HALLES.** *1201 Pennsylvania Ave NW (20004). Phone 202/347-6848; fax 202/347-6911. www.leshalles.net.* American, French menu. Lunch, dinner, brunch. Bar. Children's menu. Outdoor seating. Three-level dining area. **$$$**

[D] [SC]

★ ★ **LUIGINO.** *1100 New York Ave NW (20005). Phone 202/371-0595; fax 202/371-6482. www.luigino.com.* Nothern Italian menu. Closed holidays. Lunch, dinner. Bar. Children's menu. Outdoor seating. **$$**

[D]

★ ★ **MORRISON-CLARK.** *1015 L St NW (20001). Phone 202/289-8580; fax 202/289-8576. www.morrisonclark.com.* American, Caribbean menu. Closed holidays. Lunch, dinner, Sun brunch. Bar. Outdoor seating. **$$$**

[D]

★ **MR. YUNG'S.** *740 6th St NW (20001). Phone 202/628-1098; fax 202/628-1128.* Chinese menu. Lunch, dinner. Outdoor seating. **$$$**

[D]

★ ★ **OCCIDENTAL GRILL.** *1475 Pennsylvania Ave NW (20004). Phone 202/783-1475; fax 202/783-1478. www.occidentaldc.com.* American menu. Closed Thanksgiving, Dec 25. Lunch, dinner. Bar. **$$$**

[D]

★ ★ **OLD EBBITT GRILL.** *675 15th St NW (20005). Phone 202/347-4800; fax 202/347-6136. www.ebbitt.com.* Proximity to the White House, monuments, and museums makes this famous watering hole a draw for the power-hungry as well as the merely hungry. Known for big breakfasts in the early hours and oysters and burgers later, Old Ebbitt also serves seasonal specialties such as corn on the cob and berry cobbler. Its Beaux Arts façade and glamorous marble, brass, and mahogany interior allow tourists to feel like high-placed political insiders. Seafood menu. Breakfast, lunch, dinner, Sun brunch. Bar. In a vaudeville theater built in the early 1900s. **$$**

[D]

★ ★ **OVAL ROOM.** *800 Connecticut Ave NW (20006). Phone 202/463-8700; fax 202/785-9863. www.ovalroom.com.* American menu. Menu changes seasonally. Closed Sun; July 4, Dec 25. Lunch, dinner. Bar. Outdoor seating. **$$$**

D

★ ★ ★ **PRIME RIB.** *2020 K St NW (20006). Phone 202/466-8811; fax 202/466-2010. www.theprimerib.com.* This K Street spot remains one of the best steakhouses inside the Beltway. Seafood, steak menu. Closed Sun; holidays. Lunch, dinner. Bar. Jacket required. **$$$**

D

★ ★ ★ **RED SAGE.** *605 14th St NW (20005). Phone 202/638-4444; fax 202/628-8430. www.redsage.com.* The flavors of colors of the vibrant Southwest come to the Northeast at Red Sage, one of DC's trendiest and liveliest venues. Political movers and shakers, media magnates, and the like crowd into Red Sage nightly to relax and wind down with chilly, potent margaritas, and fiery new-wave fare that incorporates the robust chile-centric ingredients of the American Southwest. This is a perfect spot for dinner with friends who crave heat, and the scene, with dinner. American, continental menu. Closed major holidays. Lunch, dinner. Bar. Children's menu. Casual attire. Outdoor seating. **$$$**

D

★ ★ ★ **TABERNA DEL ALABARDERO.** *1776 I St NW (20006). Phone 202/429-2200; fax 202/775-3713. www.americascuisine.com/dc/taberna.html.* The joyousness of this restaurant (a favorite of DC celebrities for birthdays) is only matched by the highly skilled staff. Spanish menu. Closed Sun; holidays. Lunch, dinner. Bar. Guitarists. Jacket required. Outdoor seating. **$$$**

D

★ **THAI KINGDOM.** *2021 K St NW (20006). Phone 202/835-1700; fax 202/466-4147.* Thai menu. Closed holidays. Lunch, dinner. Bar. **$$**

D

★ ★ **TONY CHENG'S MONGOLIAN BARBECUE.** *619 H St NW (20001). Phone 202/842-8669; fax 202/842-3669.* Mongolian barbecue menu. Lunch, dinner. Food bar encircles a Mongolian grill. **$$**

D

★ ★ ★ ★ **WILLARD ROOM.** *1401 Pennsylvania Ave NW (20004). Phone 202/637-7440; fax 202/637-7326. www.washington.interconti.com.* Located in the Willard InterContinental Washington hotel (see), The Willard Room may look familiar to you if you've seen the Steven Spielberg film *Minority Report*—a scene was filmed in the restaurant. But you needn't be Tom Cruise on a mission to enjoy a meal at this sophisticated Victorian-style dining room. An eclectic American menu that changes with the seasons is offered at lunch and dinner. Spa selections are popular choices for those on a waistline-preservation plan; these dishes are marked with an asterisk to indicate that they are lower in fat, cholesterol, and sodium.

Those who have no interest in anything labeled "Spa," unless it means a massage, will be fine with the menu's other choices—innovative takes on fish, shellfish, game, lamb, beef, and poultry prepared with a French flair. In addition to dessert, the restaurant offers an after-dinner cheese course for those who are extremely anti-spa. The Willard Room also houses a wonderful selection of wines from France and Italy, as well as new-world bottles from Australia and North America. Another perk is the classic cocktail list that adds to the old-world charm of dining here. *Secret Inspector's Notes:* This restaurant has been (and continues to be) a hotbed of politicos. You'll feel as if coalitions are being formed around you as you glance from table to table. American menu. Closed Sun. Breakfast, lunch, dinner. Bar. Piano. Jacket required. Reservations required. Valet parking. **$$$**

D

Dupont Circle

Dupont Circle is widely regarded as Washington's most cosmopolitan neighborhood, a deserved reputation given the area's diverse collection of art galleries, ethnic restaurants, unique shops, and palatial mansions. The neighborhood derives its name from the landscaped circle at the confluence of Connecticut, Massachusetts, and New Hampshire avenues. A magnificent white marble fountain stands in the center of the circle. Designed by Lincoln Memorial sculptor Daniel Chester French, the Dupont Memorial Fountain serves as a popular gathering place for locals and tourists alike.

Following the Civil War, developers descended upon Dupont Circle, transforming the area from open fields and marshland to a mansion-filled haven for the city's powerful and wealthy. Most of these mansions still stand and have been well preserved, offering passersby the opportunity to view the finest architectural styles of the late 19th century, including Queen Anne, Richardsonian Romanesque, and Italian Renaissance.

While some of Dupont Circle's mansions remain privately owned residences, others have been converted into embassies and museums. The nation's first museum of modern art, the Phillips Collection, is located in a Georgian Revival mansion on 21st Street. At 17th and M streets in Dupont Circle, the National Geographic Society presents Explorers Hall, which offers exhibits and presentations on cultural and natural history.

What to See and Do

Dupont-Kalorama Museum Walk. *www.dkmuseums.com.* A joining of forces of seven museums to create an awareness of the area. Information and brochures are available at any of the museums in the group. Participating museums are

> **Anderson House Museum.** *2118 Massachusetts Ave NW (20008). Phone 202/785-2040.* Museum of the Revolutionary War and national headquarters of the Society of the Cincinnati has portraits by early American artists; 18th-century paintings; 17th-century tapestries; decorative arts of

Europe and Asia; and displays of books, medals, swords, silver, glass, and china. (Tues-Sat afternoons; closed holidays) **FREE**

Fondo del Sol. *2112 R St NW (20008). Phone 202/483-2777.* Dedicated to presenting, promoting, and preserving cultures of the Americas, the museum presents exhibitions of contemporary artists and crafters, holds special events, and hosts traveling exhibits for museums and other institutions. (Tues-Sat afternoons; closed holidays) **$$**

Meridian International Center. *1624 Crescent Pl NW (20009). Phone 202/939-5568. www.meridian.org.* Housed in two historic mansions designed by John Russell Pope, the center hosts international exhibits, concerts, lectures, and symposia promoting international understanding. Period furnishings, Mortlake tapestry; gardens with linden grove. (Wed-Sun afternoons; closed holidays) **FREE**

Phillips Collection. *1600 21st St NW (20009). Phone 202/387-2151 or 202/387-0961. www.phillipscollection.org.* First museum of modern art in the nation. Founded in 1918, the museum continues to emphasize the work of emerging as well as established international artists. Permanent collection of 19th- and 20th-century Impressionist, Post-Impressionist, and modern painting and sculpture. (Tues-Sun; closed holidays) Introductory tours (Wed and Sat). Concerts (Sept-May, Sun). Weekday admission by donation. **$$**

Textile Museum. *2320 S St NW (20008). Phone 202/667-0441. www.textilemuseum.org.* Founded in 1925 with the collection of George Hewitt Myers, the museum features changing exhibits of non-Western textiles, Oriental rugs, and other handmade textile art. Guided tours (Sept-May, Wed, Sat, Sun; by appointment). (Daily) **DONATION**

Woodrow Wilson House. *2340 S St NW (20008). Phone 202/387-4062. www.woodrowwilsonhouse.org.* (1915) Red brick Georgian Revival town house to which President Wilson retired after leaving office; family furnishings and gifts-of-state. A National Trust for Historic Preservation property. (Tues-Sun; closed Jan 1, Thanksgiving, Dec 25) **$$**

Eighteenth Street Lounge. *1212 18th St NW (20036). Phone 202/466-3922. www.eslmusic.com.* Lovers of modern dance music and techno all over the world know about ESL, the music label; DC residents and visitors flock to the lounge itself, a cooler-than-cool, atmospheric three-story space where the music, often spun by the DJ duo Thievery Corporation (one member is an owner), never stops. Relax by a fireplace or hang out on the patio, depending on the weather. A strict door policy weeds out wearers of athletic garb and the attitudinally impaired. (Tues-Sat) **$$$$**

Fresh Farm Market. *20th St NW (20036) between Massachusetts Ave and Q St NW. Phone 202/331-7300. www.farmland.org/market/market.htm.* Looking for the slenderest stalks of asparagus? Herbs that really taste like herbs? How about a bright bouquet of tulips? You'll find those delights and many others, including in-season fruits, mushrooms, artisanal cheeses, and organic offerings, at this weekly market, which brings together more than 25 local farmers with customers who prefer to skip the middleman. Vendors here sell only goods grown or produced on their land; every dollar spent goes directly to them. (Apr-Dec, Sun)

Hotels

★ ★ ★ **THE JEFFERSON.** *1200 16th St NW (20036). Phone 202/347-2200; toll-free 800/235-6397; fax 202/331-7982. www.thejeffersondc.com.* Just four blocks from the White House, this Beaux Arts hotel, dating to 1923, is a masterpiece of quiet luxury. The antique-filled public rooms recall the elegance of the past, and the museum-quality collection of artwork and original documents signed by Thomas Jefferson is astounding. The guest rooms are a stylish blend of old and new. The seamless, attentive service is outstanding and satisfies every need. A fitness center is available, as are privileges at the University Club, with its Olympic-size pool. The restaurant feels like old Washington with its faux tortoiseshell walls and leather chairs, yet its New American cuisine is all the rage. 100 rooms, 8 story. Pets accepted, some restrictions. Check-out 1 pm. TV; cable (premium), VCR (movies). In-room modem link. Restaurant, bar. Room service 24 hours. Health club privileges. Garage, valet parking. Concierge. Opened in 1923; individually decorated rooms have four-poster beds. **$$**

🅳 🔧 🏊 📶

★ ★ ★ ★ **PARK HYATT WASHINGTON.** *24th at M St NW (20037). Phone 202/789-1234; toll-free 800/633-7313; fax 202/457-8823. www.hyatt.com.* The awe-inspiring monuments and world-class museums of Washington, DC are within easy reach of the Park Hyatt. Located in the city's West End, the hotel is several blocks from Georgetown and downtown. The Park Hyatt maintains a handsome style throughout the hotel, from the gleaming lobby with its palette of gold and cream to the guest rooms and suites, which include the latest technology while maintaining a cozy ambience. Rivaling a small museum, the hotel boasts an impressive art collection: Picasso, Leger, Matisse, and Miro adorn the walls of the public and private spaces. Melrose (see) is recognized for its distinguished cuisine, served in the formal dining room or outside on the terrace during warmer months. The health club is comprehensive, including the latest exercise equipment, indoor pool, whirlpool, and sauna. 223 rooms, 10 story. Pets accepted. Check-out noon, check-in 3 pm. TV; cable (premium), VCR available. Restaurant, bar. Room service 24 hours. In-house fitness room, spa, steam room, sauna, massage. Indoor pool, whirlpool, poolside service. Valet parking. **$$$**

🅳 🔧 🏊 🧍 📶

Restaurants

★ ★ **BACCHUS.** *1827 Jefferson Pl NW (20036). Phone 202/785-0734. www.bacchusdc.net.* Lebanese menu. Closed Sun; holidays. Lunch, dinner. **$$**

★ ★ **BEDUCI.** *2100 P St NW (20037). Phone 202/223-3824; fax 202/296-1143. www.beduci.com.* Mediterranean menu. Closed holidays; late Aug. Lunch, dinner. Bar. Three dining areas. **$$$**

★ **BUA.** *1635 P St NW (20036). Phone 202/265-0828. www.buathai.com.* Thai menu. Closed Thanksgiving, Dec 25. Lunch, dinner. Bar. Outdoor seating. **$$**

D

★ **C. F. FOLKS.** *1225 19th St NW (20036). Phone 202/293-0162; fax 202/ 457-9078. www.cffolks.com.* Old-fashioned lunch counter. Closed Sat, Sun; holidays. Outdoor seating. **$**

D

★ **FRAN O'BRIEN'S STADIUM STEAK HOUSE.** *1001 16th St NW (20036). Phone 202/783-2599; fax 202/783-3444. www.fobss.com.* Seafood, steak menu. Closed holidays. Lunch, dinner. Bar. Children's menu. **$$$**

D

★ ★ **GABRIEL.** *2121 P St NW (20037). Phone 202/956-6690; fax 202/956-6641. www.washingtonpost.com/yp/gabriel.* American menu. Closed Mon; Dec 25. Breakfast, dinner, Sun brunch. Bar. Business casual attire. **$$**

D

★ **GRILLE 88.** *1910 18th St NW (20009). Phone 202/588-5288; fax 202/ 588-8829.* American menu. Closed Mon; major holidays. Dinner. Bar. Casual attire. Outdoor seating. **$$**

★ ★ ★ **THE JEFFERSON.** *1200 16th St NW (20036). Phone 202/833-6206; fax 202/331-7982. www.thejeffersondc.com.* Here, diners seeking an intimate, secluded restaurant find professional and discreet service, perfect for those seeking anonymity in this high-profile town. The chef demonstrates a high degree of culinary talent and sensibility with the freshest seasonal ingredients. American menu. Breakfast, lunch, dinner, Sun brunch. Bar. Valet parking. **$$**

D

★ ★ ★ **MELROSE.** *24th at M St (20037). Phone 202/955-3899; fax 202/ 408-6118.* Finding a hotel restaurant that feels like a dining experience and not just an obligatory feeding ground for the hotel's guests can be a tough task. The Melrose Restaurant, located in the Park Hyatt (see), is far from a standard hotel feeder. It is fairly formal in its décor, with cushioned neutral-toned seating, cream-colored walls, high ceilings, lots of windows, and lots of sunlight. The room is lovely, but in a battle between décor and food, the food wins hands down. The kitchen sees food as an inspiration for energy and creativity, and this contemporary menu is filled with dishes that are alive with flavor and ingenuity. It is clear that the chefs behind closed doors are not afraid to play with products from around the world. The menu shows a special fondness for Asian ingredients, but nods are also made to Spanish, Italian, and regional American styles of cooking. Contemporary American menu. Breakfast, lunch, dinner, Sun brunch. Piano. Children's menu. Valet parking. Outdoor seating. **$$$**

D

★ ★ ★ **OBELISK.** *2029 P St NW (20036). Phone 202/872-1180.* Italian menu. Menu changes daily. Closed Sun, Mon; holidays. Dinner. Totally non-smoking. Intimate dining room on the second floor of a townhouse. **$$$**

★ ★ ★ **PALM.** *1225 19th St NW (20036). Phone 202/293-9091; fax 202/775-1468. www.thepalm.com.* Seafood, steak menu. Closed holidays. Lunch, dinner. Bar. Valet parking (dinner). **$$$**

D

★ ★ **PESCE.** *2016 P St NW (20036). Phone 202/466-3474; fax 202/466-8302. www.pescebistro.com.* Seafood menu. Closed holidays. Lunch, dinner. Valet parking. **$$**

D

★ **PIZZERIA PARADISO.** *2029 P St NW (20036). Phone 202/223-1245; fax 202/223-5699.* Italian menu. Closed holidays. Lunch, dinner. Totally nonsmoking. **$$**

★ **RAKU.** *1900 Q St NW (20009). Phone 202/265-7258; fax 202/265-5488. www.raku/dc.com.* Pan-Asian menu. Closed Thanksgiving, Dec 25. Lunch, dinner. Bar. Outdoor seating. **$$**

D

★ ★ ★ **RESTAURANT NORA.** *2132 Florida Ave NW (20008). Phone 202/462-5143; fax 202/234-6232. www.noras.com.* Organic seasonal ingredients, many purchased from local family farms, are the stars of this intimate, former 19th-century grocery store turned organic American eatery. Chef-owner Nora Pouillon is a pioneer in the organic movement; Restaurant Nora was the first certified organic restaurant in the country (95 percent of the products used are organic). And it's not only the purity of the edible ingredients that is attended to—all the water used at Nora is filtered three times on premises, including the water that washes your dishes and is used for cooking. While Nora's focuses on healthful cooking, this is not flavorless spa cuisine. Pouillon coaxes intense flavors from nature's superstar ingredients, creating stylish, delicious meals that integrate accents from places far and near—from the American South to Spain, and from Latin America to Asia and India. (If you're looking for a soy burger on spelt bread, this is not the place.) The mouthwatering and imaginative menu changes daily and includes a selection of starters, main-course salads, and entrées, as well as two tasting menus. The rustic dining room is decorated with dried flowers and museum-quality antique Mennonite and Amish quilts. Soothing amber lighting warms the room, and Nora's wonderful food warms the tummy. Continental menu. Closed Sun; holidays; late Aug-early Sept. Dinner. Bar. Atrium dining. Totally nonsmoking. **$$$**

★ ★ ★ **SAM AND HARRY'S.** *1200 19th St NW (20036). Phone 202/296-4333; fax 202/785-1070. www.samandharrys.com.* Seafood, steak menu. Closed Sun; holidays. Lunch, dinner. Bar. Valet parking. **$$$**

D

★ ★ ★ **VIDALIA.** *1990 M St NW (20036). Phone 202/659-1990; fax 202/223-8572. www.vidaliadc.com.* Chef-owner Jeffrey Buben, taking his lead from the South as well as from the Chesapeake Bay area, transforms regional cuisine into a delectable art. American, Southern menu. Closed Sun; Jan 1, Dec 25. Lunch, dinner. Bar. Wine bar. **$$$**

D

Embassy Row/ Woodley Park

The majority of Washington, DC's 150 international embassies can be found in the city's northwest quadrant along Massachusetts Avenue. The neighborhood is fittingly known as Embassy Row. The embassies originally existed as mansions for the city's elite. Many are fashioned in the Beaux Arts style of the late 19th and early 20th centuries. Each embassy flies the national flag of its occupant, creating a colorful display up and down Massachusetts Avenue.

The US Naval Observatory sits behind guarded gates in Embassy Row. The grounds of the observatory include the official residence for the vice president, a Queen Anne-style mansion built in 1893. In the 1970s, Walter Mondale became the first vice president to live here. Before Mondale, the mansion was the residence of the observatory's superintendent. The observatory serves as the nation's leading authority in astronomical and time data. The official time of the United States is kept by an atomic clock at the observatory. The clock gains or loses about one second every 6 million years.

The serene, mostly residential neighborhood of Woodley Park rests to the immediate north of Embassy Row. Connecticut Avenue cuts through the middle. Independent shops and restaurants line the avenue, along with an eclectic mix of architectural styles, ranging from Classic Revival to Mission to Queen Anne.

The National Zoological Park can be accessed via Connecticut Avenue. Hundreds of animals call the zoo home, including two giant pandas, Mei Xiang and Tian Tian, who were loaned to the zoo for ten years by the China Wildlife Conservation Association. Rock Creek Park is adjacent to the National Zoo. Established as a park in 1890, the woods and trails surrounding Rock Creek offer a tranquil respite from the hustle and bustle of life in the capital.

At the south end of Woodley Park, where Massachusetts and Wisconsin avenues converge, the Washington National Cathedral welcomes 700,000 annual visitors and worshippers. Stunning in size and beauty, the cathedral features 215 stained-glass windows, 110 gargoyles, an organ with 10,000 pipes, and a 24,000-pound carillon. Martin Luther King, Jr., delivered his final Sunday sermon at the cathedral in 1968. Five days after his sermon, the cathedral was the site of a memorial service for Dr. King.

What to See and Do

Embassy Row. *Massachusetts Ave and 23rd St NW (20036).* This neighborhood, within the city's northwest quadrant, is centered around Sheridan Circle. Dozens of foreign legations can be found in the area and north along Massachusetts Ave.

Fort Stevens Park. *13th and Quackenbos St NW (20019). Phone 202/895-6000.* General Jubal Early and his Confederate troops tried to invade Washington at this point on July 11-12, 1864. President Lincoln risked his life at the fort during the fighting. (Daily) **FREE**

Islamic Center. *2551 Massachusetts Ave NW (20008). Phone 202/332-8343.* Leading mosque in the US has landscaped courtyard, intricate interior mosaics. (Daily; no tours during Fri prayer service)

National Museum of Health and Medicine. *Walter Reed Army Medical Center, Building #54. 6900 Georgia Ave and Elder St NW (20307). Phone 202/782-2200.* One of the most important medical collections in America. Interprets the link between history and technology; AIDS education exhibit; an interactive exhibit on human anatomy and lifestyle choices; and a collection of microscopes, medical teaching aids, tools, and instruments (1862-1965) and famous historical icons exhibits. (Daily; closed Dec 25) **FREE**

National Presbyterian Church and Center. *4101 Nebraska Ave NW (20016). Phone 202/537-0800. www.natpresch.org.* Chapel of the President contains memorabilia of past US presidents; faceted glass windows depict the history of man and church. Self-guided tours (daily; no tours holidays). Guided tours (Sun following service).

Washington Dolls' House & Toy Museum. *5236 44th St NW (20015). Phone 202/244-0024. www.dollshousemuseum.com.* Splendid collection of antique doll houses, dolls, toys, and games; museum shop. (Tues-Sun; closed Jan 1, Thanksgiving, Dec 25) **$$**

⭐ **Washington National Cathedral.** *3000 Wisconsin Ave NW (20016). Phone 202/537-6207 (tours); 202/537-6200 (recording). www.cathedral.org/cathedral.* This inspiring edifice, 83 years in the making, was completed in 1990, its $65 million cost covered by private donations. It was built largely of Indiana limestone using traditional methods, with flying buttresses rather than steel providing support. Graced with intricate carvings inside and out, it has a 30-story central tower and 215 stained-glass windows, including one that contains a piece of lunar rock presented by the astronauts of *Apollo XI*. Bring binoculars if you want to see, close up, the more than 100 gargoyles, which depict not just dragons but also a child with his hand in a cookie jar and *Star Wars* villain Darth Vader. Worshippers of all faiths are welcome at services held daily. There are also frequent musical events, including recitals given on the magnificent pipe organ most Sundays at 5 pm. Famous Americans interred at the cathedral include Woodrow Wilson and Helen Keller. **DONATION**

Special Events

Goodwill Industries Embassy Tour. *220 S Dakota Ave NE (20018). Phone 202/636-4225.* This is a walking tour with shuttle bus transportation between embassies. Tickets are limited. No children under age 10 permitted. Second Sat in May.

Musical programs. *In Carter Barron Amphitheater, Rock Creek Park. 5000 Glover Rd NW (20015). Phone 202/619-7222.* Mid-June-Aug.

Washington National Cathedral Open House. *3000 Wisconsin Ave NW (20016). Phone 202/537-6200.* It's the only day of the year when the central tower is open to the public. Sat nearest Sept 29.

Hotels

★ ★ ★ **HILTON WASHINGTON EMBASSY ROW.** *2015 Massachusetts Ave NW (20036). Phone 202/265-1600; toll-free 800/774-1500; fax 202/328-7526. www.hilton.com.* This European-style boutique hotel is located on the "Avenue of the Embassies," just half a block from Dupont Circle and the metro system. 193 rooms, 9 story. Check-out noon. TV; cable (premium). In-room modem link. Laundry services. Restaurant, bar; entertainment. Room service 24 hours. In-house fitness room. Outdoor pool, poolside service. Valet parking. Business center. Concierge. **$$**

⬚ ⬚ ⬚ ⬚ ⬚

★ ★ ★ **MARRIOTT WARDMAN PARK HOTEL.** *2660 Woodley Rd NW (20008). Phone 202/328-2000; fax 202/234-0015. www.marriott.com.* Located in a prestigious area of the capital, this hotel is just minutes from the National Zoo. 1,350 rooms, 10 story. Pets accepted, some restrictions. Check-out noon. TV; cable (premium), VCR available. Restaurant, bar. In-house fitness room, sauna. Outdoor pool. Valet parking. Business center. Concierge. **$$**

⬚ ⬚ ⬚ ⬚ ⬚ ⬚

★ ★ ★ **OMNI SHOREHAM HOTEL.** *2500 Calvert St NW (20008). Phone 202/234-0700; toll-free 800/843-6664; fax 202/265-7972. www.omnihotels.com.* A retreat in the middle of the city, this hotel is located on 11 acres in Rock Creek Park. 836 rooms, 8 story. Pets accepted, some restrictions; fee. Check-out noon. TV; cable (premium), VCR available. Restaurant, bar; entertainment. In-house fitness room, sauna. Outdoor pool, children's pool, poolside service. Valet parking. Business center. **$$$**

⬚ ⬚ ⬚ ⬚ ⬚ SC ⬚

★ ★ ★ **THE WESTIN EMBASSY ROW.** *2100 Massachusetts Ave NW (20008). Phone 202/293-2100; toll-free 800/434-9990; fax 202/293-0641. www.westin.com.* Since 1927, this Embassy Row property has welcomed guests with turn-of-the-century style. All rooms and suites are decorated with Federal and Empire furnishings, and boast beautiful views of Washington National Cathedral and historic 206 rooms, 8 story. Check-out noon. TV; cable (premium), VCR available. In-room modem link. Restaurant, bar; entertainment. In-house fitness room. Health club privileges. Massage. Sauna. Valet parking. Business center. Concierge. **$$$**

⬚ ⬚ ⬚ ⬚ ⬚

Restaurants

★ **GUAPO'S.** *4515 Wisconsin Ave NW (20016). Phone 202/686-3588; fax 202/686-5490. www.guaposrestaurant.com.* Latin American, Mexican menu. Lunch, dinner. Bar. Outdoor seating. **$$**

D

★ ★ **KRUPIN'S.** *4620 Wisconsin Ave NW (20016). Phone 202/686-1989; fax 202/686-3566.* American menu. Closed Dec 25. Breakfast, lunch, dinner. Children's menu. Totally nonsmoking. **$$**

D

★ ★ **LAVANDOU.** *3321 Connecticut Ave NW (20008). Phone 202/966-3002; fax 202/966-0982. www.lavandourestaurant.net.* Southern French menu. Closed holidays. Lunch, dinner. Reservations required. **$$**

D

★ ★ **LEBANESE TAVERNA.** *2641 Connecticut Ave NW (20008). Phone 202/265-8681; fax 202/483-3007. www.lebanesetaverna.com.* Lebanese menu. Closed major holidays. Lunch, dinner. Bar. **$$$**

D

★ **MURPHY'S OF DC.** *2609 24th St NW (20008). Phone 202/462-7171; fax 202/462-7901. www.murphysofdc.com.* American, Irish menu. Lunch, dinner. Children's menu. Outdoor seating. **$$**

★ ★ **NEW HEIGHTS.** *2317 Calvert St NW (20008). Phone 202/234-4110; fax 202/234-0789. www.newheightsrestaurant.com.* New American cuisine. Menu changes seasonally. Closed holidays. Dinner, brunch. Bar. Outdoor seating. **$$$**

★ ★ **SAIGON GOURMET.** *2635 Connecticut Ave NW (20008). Phone 202/265-1360; fax 202/265-2092.* Vietnamese menu. Closed Thanksgiving. Lunch, dinner. Valet parking. Outdoor seating. **$$**

D

Foggy Bottom

Nestled alongside the Potomac River, overlooking the heavily forested Theodore Roosevelt Island, Foggy Bottom is home to prestigious institutions in the arts, education, and government. At the west end of this neighborhood, the John F. Kennedy Center for the Performing Arts offers live music, dance, theatre, and comedy from internationally acclaimed performers. The Kennedy Center also sponsors education programs in the arts; over 6 million people participate in these programs annually. George Washington University's main campus occupies 43 acres on Foggy Bottom's north side. The headquarters for the State Department, Department of Interior, and Peace Corps are all located in Foggy Bottom.

Foggy Bottom, so named for the mists that tend to rise above its marshy topography, features a varied assortment of public sculptures, ranging from one of Albert Einstein standing outside the National Academy of Sciences to a trio of sculptures along Virginia Avenue honoring Latino heroes Benito Juarez, Simon Bolivar, and José de San Martin.

Pennsylvania Avenue slices through Foggy Bottom, leading to Lafayette Square, a 7-acre park situated directly across from the White House. Construction on the White House began in 1792, though it was not suitable for occupancy until 1800, when the nation's second president, John Adams, and his wife, Abigail, moved into the home. During the war of 1812, the White House was torched by the British, leaving it almost completely destroyed. President James Madison brought in the White House's original designer, James Hoban, to oversee the rebuilding of the home. Since the time of its reconstruction, the White House has undergone numerous restorations and additions, though the home still possesses its original exterior stone walls.

Not far from the White House, you can visit the Eisenhower Executive Office Building, an architectural marvel constructed more than a century ago in the Second Empire style. The Department of the Treasury is also nearby. Completed in 1869, the Treasury building's Greek Revival style influenced the design of many other government buildings in Washington.

What to See and Do

B'nai B'rith Klutznick Museum. *B'nai B'rith International Center, 1640 Rhode Island Ave NW (20036).* Phone 202/857-6583. Permanent exhibition of Jewish ceremonial and folk art. Changing exhibits. (Mon-Fri, Sun; closed holidays, Jewish holidays) **FREE**

Explorers Hall. *1145 17th St NW (20036).* Phone 202/857-7588 *(recording).* National Geographic Society headquarters. Several traveling exhibits, call for information. (Daily; closed Dec 25) **FREE**

George Washington University. *19th to 24th sts NW, F St to Pennsylvania Ave.* Phone 202/994-1000. www.gwu.edu. (1821) 20,000 students. Theater; art exhibits in Dimock Gallery (Mon-Fri; closed holidays) and University Library.

The Improv. *1140 Connecticut Ave NW (20036).* Phone 202/296-7008. www. dcimprov.com. The crowd is youngish and the comedy free-flowing here, where almost anything is good for a laugh, especially the local industry: politics. Onstage talent includes established stars as well as hilariously original newcomers you may have caught on Comedy Central or elsewhere on TV. Open mic nights enable wannabe comics to step into the limelight and compete for prizes. Appetizers, sandwiches, beer, and wine are available. (Daily) **$$$$**

John F. Kennedy Center for the Performing Arts. *2700 F St NW (20566).* Phone 202/467-4600; 202/416-8340 *(tours);* toll-free 800/444-1324. www.kennedy-center.org. The glittering home of the National Symphony Orchestra and Washington Opera hosts an impressive array of internationally known artists in dance, theater, and music. It opened in 1971 as a memorial to John F. Kennedy; a large bronze bust of the former president graces the Grand Foyer. The sleekly designed complex houses a number of dazzling performance spaces and reception areas, as well as paintings, sculptures, and other artwork presented by foreign governments. (Daily) **FREE**

Lulu's Club Mardi Gras. *1217 22nd St, NW (20013). Phone 202/861-5858. www.lulusclub.com.* This freewheeling spot is all about raucous music, dancing, and checking out members of the opposite sex. Beer is the beverage of choice; food is served until 10 pm. Salsa lessons draw regular crowds, but Lulu's is also known for special events such as "Shred Your Ex, Meet Your Next," where patrons are invited—in a spirit of communal catharsis—to run photos of formerly significant others through a shredder. (Daily) **$$**

National Aquarium. *Dept of Commerce Bldg, 14th and Constitution Ave (20230). Phone 202/482-2825. www.nationalaquarium.com.* The nation's oldest public aquarium was established in 1873. It now exhibits more than 1,700 specimens representing approximately 260 species, both freshwater and saltwater. Touch tank; theater. Shark feedings (Mon, Wed, Sat); piranha feedings (Tues, Thurs, Sun). (Daily 9 am-5 pm; closed Dec 25) **$**

Rock Creek Park. *3545 Williamsburg Ln NW (20008). From downtown DC, take the Rock Creek and Potomac Pkwy north to Beach Dr. Exit onto Beach Dr north, take it to Broad Branch Rd, make a left and then a right onto Glover Rd, and follow the signs to the Nature Center. Phone 202/895-6070 or 202/426-6829. www.nps.gov/rocr.* Leave urban commotion behind by going for a brisk hike in Rock Creek Park. Just 5 miles from the White House are dozens of miles of clearly marked, well-maintained, easy and moderately hard hiking trails through the park's 1,754 acres of meadows and woodlands. There's also a gentle walk along Beach Drive that takes you through dramatic Rock Creek Gorge; on weekends and holidays, cars are prohibited, making it even more peaceful. (Daily) **FREE** Also here are

Art Barn. *2401 Tilden St NW (20008). Phone 202/244-2482.* Historic carriage house (1831). Art exhibitions. (Thurs-Sun afternoons) **FREE**

Carter Barron Amphitheatre. *16th St and Colorado Ave NW (20011). Phone 202/426-0486. www.nps.gov/rocr/cbarron/cbarron.htm.* This 4,200-seat outdoor theater in a wooded area is the setting for summer performances of symphonic, folk, pop, and jazz music and Shakespearean theater.

National Zoo. *3001 Connecticut Ave NW (20008). Main entrance at 3000 block of Connecticut Ave NW; other entrances at Beach Dr (Rock Creek Pkwy) and the junction of Adams Mill Rd and Harvard St. Phone 202/673-4800. natzoo.si.edu.* A branch of the Smithsonian Institution, the National Zoo features 5,000 animals of 500 species. Come when the zoo first opens or after 2 pm if you want to see giant pandas Tian Tian and Mei Xiang without waiting in long lines. The pair, on ten-year loan from China, are this lovely and interesting zoological park's most famous residents, but the other animals, from butterflies to American bison, have charms of their own and shouldn't be missed. The zoo is set amid the urban greenery of Rock Creek Park. (Daily from 10 am; closed Dec 25) **FREE**

Nature Center. *5200 Glover Rd NW (20015). Phone 202/865-6070.* Planetarium, films, exhibits, nature demonstrations. (Wed-Sun 9 am-5 pm; closed holidays) **FREE**

Theodore Roosevelt Memorial. *18050 W Basin Dr SW (20024). N end of Theodore Roosevelt Island, accessible only by footbridge from George Washington Memorial Pkwy, northbound lane, in Arlington, VA.* The island is an 88-acre wilderness preserve; the 17-foot statue of Roosevelt was designed by Paul Manship. (Daily; closed Dec 25) **FREE**

Hotels

★ ★ ★ **MARRIOTT WASHINGTON.** *1221 22nd St NW (20037). Phone 202/872-1500; toll-free 800/228-9290; fax 202/872-1424. www.marriott.com/ waswe.* Located in the West End, just on the edge of Georgetown, this hotel offers the facilities, amenities, and services that business travelers have come to expect, as well as comfort and convenience for leisure travelers, minutes from DC attractions. 416 rooms, 9 story. Check-out noon, check-in 4 pm. TV; cable (premium). In-room modem link. Restaurant, bar. In-house fitness room, sauna. Indoor pool, poolside service. Business center. Concierge. Luxury level. **$$**

D ⊨ 术 ⊭ 木

★ ★ **THE MELROSE HOTEL WASHINGTON.** *2430 Pennsylvania Ave NW (20037). Phone 202/955-6400; toll-free 800/MELROSE; fax 202/ 775-8489. www.melrosehotel.com.* 240 rooms, 8 story. Check-out noon. TV, cable; VCR available. In-room modem link. Restaurant, bar. Room service 24 hours. In-house fitness room. Valet, garage parking. Concierge. Classic English furnishings, art. **$$**

D 术 ⊭ SC

★ ★ **ONE WASHINGTON CIRCLE HOTEL.** *1 Washington Cir NW (20037). Phone 202/872-1680; toll-free 800/424-9671; fax 202/887-4989. www.onewashcirclehotel.com.* 151 rooms, 9 story. Check-out noon. TV; cable (premium), VCR available. In-room modem link. Restaurant, bar; entertainment. In-house fitness room. Outdoor pool. Concierge. Elegant furnishings; landscaped grounds. **$$**

⊨ 术 ⊭ SC

★ ★ ★ ★ **THE RITZ-CARLTON, WASHINGTON, DC.** *1150 22nd St NW (20037). Phone 202/835-0500; toll-free 800/241-3333; fax 202/974- 5519. www.ritzcarlton.com.* A convenient West End location, stylish accommodations, and superior service make The Ritz-Carlton, Washington, DC a favorite of sophisticated travelers. The supremely knowledgeable staff truly pampers its guests. The Ritz-Carlton's attention to detail is marvelous, and it continues to exceed expectations with innovative amenities. On-call technology butlers assist with computer woes, while the Luggage-less Travel program is offered to frequent guests, inviting them to leave behind items for their next visit. Traditional European décor defines the rooms and suites, and Club Level accommodations are treated to five food and beverage presentations daily. Perhaps most impressive is the Sports Club/LA access granted to all guests of The Ritz-Carlton. Adjacent to the hotel, this massive 100,000-square-foot complex is a veritable nirvana for fitness buffs with cutting-edge fitness programming, multiple athletic courts, and a pool.

The complex also includes Splash, one of Washington's leading day spas. 300 rooms, 15 story. Pets accepted, some restrictions. Check-out noon, check-in 3 pm. TV; cable (premium). In-room modem link. Restaurant, bar. Room service 24 hours. Babysitting services available. In-house fitness room, spa. Indoor pool, whirlpool. Valet parking. Business center. Concierge. **$$$**

★ ★ ★ **SWISSOTEL WASHINGTON–THE WATERGATE.** *2650 Virginia Ave NW (20037). Phone 202/965-2300; toll-free 800/424-2736; fax 202/337-7915. www.swissotel.com.* Neighboring the Kennedy Center along the Potomac River, this luxury hotel is walking distance to the mall and historic Georgetown. Views from the expansive guest rooms make any extended stay a pleasure. 232 rooms, 13 story. Pets accepted, some restrictions; fee. Check-out noon. TV; cable (premium), VCR available. In-room modem link. Restaurant, bar. Room service 24 hours. In-house fitness room. Massage. Sauna, steam room. Indoor pool, whirlpool. Valet parking. Business center. Concierge. **$$**

★ ★ ★ **THE WESTIN GRAND.** *2350 M St NW (20037). Phone 202/429-0100; toll-free 888/627-8406; fax 202/429-9759. www.westin.com.* Not as glitzy as many of the other top DC hotels, the Westin offers attentive service and a more private, low-key environment. The rooms are comfortable and stylish, with ultra-comfortable beds and sizeable bathrooms. 263 rooms, 4 story. Check-out noon. TV; cable (premium), VCR available. In-room modem link. Restaurant, bar. Room service 24 hours. In-house fitness room. Outdoor pool, poolside service. Covered valet parking. Business center. Concierge. Luxury level. **$$**

★ ★ **WYNDHAM CITY CENTER HOTEL.** *1143 New Hampshire Ave NW (20037). Phone 202/775-0800; toll-free 800/544-5064; fax 202/331-9491. www.wyndham.com.* 352 rooms, 9 story. Check-out noon. TV; cable (premium). In-room modem link. Restaurant, bar; entertainment. In-house fitness room. Health club privileges. Business center. Concierge. Luxury level. **$$**

All Suites

★ ★ **EMBASSY SUITES.** *1250 22nd St NW (20037). Phone 202/857-3388; toll-free 800/362-2779; fax 202/293-3173. www.embassysuites.com.* 318 rooms, 9. story. Complimentary full breakfast. Check-out noon. TV; cable (premium). In-room modem link. Restaurant, bar. In-house fitness room, sauna. Game room. Indoor pool, whirlpool. Business center. Concierge. **$$**

★ ★ **RIVER INN.** *924 25th St NW (20037). Phone 202/337-7600; toll-free 800/424-2741; fax 202/337-6520. www.theriverinn.com.* 126 rooms. Pets accepted; fee. Check-out noon. TV; cable (premium). In-room modem link. Restaurant, bar. Health club privileges. **$$**

D 🐾 ⊠ SC

Restaurants

★ ★ ★ **AQUARELLE.** *2650 Virginia Ave NW (20037). Phone 202/298-4455; fax 202/298-4483.* Continental menu. Breakfast, lunch, dinner, Sun brunch. Bar. Valet parking. **$$**

D

★ **ART GALLERY GRILLE.** *1712 I St NW (20006). Phone 202/298-6658.* American menu. Closed Sat-Sun; holidays. Breakfast, lunch, dinner. Bar. Casual attire. Outdoor seating. **$$**

D

★ **THE BREAD LINE.** *1751 Pennsylvania Ave NW (20006). Phone 202/ 822-8900; fax 202/822-8256.* Closed Sat-Sun. Breakfast, lunch. Outdoor seating. The menu is inspired by international street foods. **$**

D

★ ★ ★ **GALILEO.** *1110 21st St NW (20036). Phone 202/293-7191; fax 202/331-9364. www.robertodonna.com.* This is the flagship enterprise of Roberto Donna, the celebrity chef whose reputation in the area is legendary (he is also behind Il Radicchio, I Matti, and many others). In keeping with the cutting-edge trends, there's even a much-sought-after kitchen table. Northern Italian menu. Closed holidays. Lunch, dinner. Bar. Outdoor seating. **$$$**

D

★ ★ ★ **THE GRILL AT RITZ-CARLTON.** *1150 22nd St NW (20037). Phone 202/835-0500; fax 202/835-1588. www.ritzcarlton.com.* American menu. Breakfast, lunch, dinner. **$$$**

★ ★ ★ ★ **KINKEAD'S.** *2000 Pennsylvania Ave NW (20006). Phone 202/296-7700; fax 202/296-7688. www.kinkead.com.* Senators, journalists, models, financiers, and media moguls rub elbows at chef-owner Bob Kinkead's stunning spot for jazzy, distinctive, and fun-to-eat global fare. The deep cherry wood-paneled dining room has an intimate, clubby feel to it, with warm, low lighting, vintage wrought-iron staircases, tufted chocolate leather seating, and elegant table settings. As for what to eat, diners here have a tough choice to make. The palatial raw bar is a great place to start. But then again, the menu, which changes daily and draws influences from Spain, France, Italy, Morocco, and Asia, offers a terrific selection of appetizers, soups, salads, chops, and seafood, not to mention incredibly creative side dishes. It is not possible to order a disappointment. To complement the menu, you'll find one of the most user-friendly wine lists in the capital. The list is color coded from light to dark according to nose, weight, body, and flavor. Kinkead's hosts live jazz in the evenings and is a perfect choice for a lively meal with family, friends, or colleagues. American, seafood menu. Closed major holidays. Lunch, dinner. Bar. Jazz pianist. **$$$**

D

★ ★ ★ **TEATRO GOLDONI.** *1909 K St (20036). Phone 202/955-9494; fax 202/955-9584. www.teatrogoldoni.com.* This restaurant serves innovative, complex Venetian dishes. Italian menu. Closed Sun; holidays. Lunch, dinner. Bar. Valet parking. **$$$**

D

Georgetown

Georgetown holds worldwide acclaim for its rich history, eclectic architecture, and glamorous social scene. Founded as a Maryland tobacco port in 1751, Georgetown was annexed by the District of Columbia when Washington became the nation's capital in 1791. Wealthy merchants and land speculators settled here during the 1800s, building beautiful residences, many of which still stand today. The neighborhood's vast array of architectural styles include Federal and Classical Revival houses, Georgian mansions, and Queen Anne and Richardsonian Romanesque row houses.

After a period of economic decline following World War I, Georgetown once again became a trendy place to live when government workers flocked here during Franklin Delano Roosevelt's years in office. Georgetown's reputation for glamour heightened during the Kennedy years; JFK and his wife, Jacqueline, moved here in 1954, shortly after they were married. Today, the neighborhood continues to maintain its image as an enclave for the rich and powerful, although it draws visitors of all backgrounds to its historic cobblestone streets and many charming shops and restaurants.

The Gothic architecture of Georgetown University towers above the banks of the Potomac River. Founded in 1789 as the nation's first Jesuit university, Georgetown has many accomplished alumni, most notably the nation's 42nd president, Bill Clinton. Patrick Healy became the first African American to head a white university when he became Georgetown's president in 1873.

What to See and Do

Blues Alley. *1073 Wisconsin Ave NW (20007). Phone 202/337-4141. www.bluesalley.com.* For nearly 40 years, serious jazz lovers have flocked to this intimate club to hear such noted artists as Dizzy Gillespie, Sarah Vaughan, and Maynard Ferguson, along with a host of outstanding but lesser-known musicians. Nightly shows run the gamut from vocal and instrumental sounds to solo performers to larger ensembles. Housed in an 18th-century brick carriage house in Georgetown, the club has a sophisticated ambience and a Creole-themed dinner menu to match.

Chesapeake & Ohio Canal Boat Rides. *Thomas Jefferson and 30th sts (20007). Departs from 1057 Thomas Jefferson St NW, between 30th and 31st sts. Phone*

202/653-5190. Narrated one-hour round-trip canal tours by park rangers in period clothing aboard mule-drawn boats. The ticket office is adjacent. (Apr-Nov, Wed-Sun) **$$**

Chesapeake & Ohio Canal Towpath. *1057 Thomas Jefferson St NW (Georgetown Visitor Center) (20007). Phone 202/653-5190 or 301/739-4200. www.nps.gov/choh/co_visit.htm.* Biking (or simply strolling) along the fascinating Chesapeake & Ohio Canal towpath is a great way to immerse yourself in both history and nature. The canal, which runs 184.5 miles between Georgetown and Cumberland, Maryland, was completed in 1850. The mostly level path takes you past locks, lockhouses, aqueducts, and other intriguing original structures from the route's commercial heyday. Expect spectacular scenery and all manner of wildlife along the way, including deer, fox, and woodpeckers. Fee (**$**) per cyclist at Great Falls. Georgetown Visitor Center (Sat, Sun).

Dumbarton Oaks. *1703 32nd St NW (20007). Garden entrance at 31st and R sts. Phone 202/339-6401. www.doaks.org.* (1800) Famous gardens spanning 16 acres are both formal and Romantic in design. Mansion has antiques and European art, including El Greco's *The Visitation,* galleries of Byzantine art, and a library of rare books on gardening and horticulture. Museum of pre-Columbian artifacts housed in structure by Philip Johnson. Gardens (daily afternoons; closed holidays); house and museum (Tues-Sun afternoons; closed holidays). **$$**

Georgetown Flea Market. *Wisconsin Ave NW (20007). Just north of S St. Phone 202/296-4989. www.georgetownfleamarket.com.* This friendly neighborhood flea market has been giving local collectors of antique furniture, jewelry, books, rugs, toys, linens, and other vintage treasures a reason to get out of the house on Sundays since 1973. It's also known as a place to spot celebrities (actress Diane Keaton has been a frequent patron). About 70 dealers set up booths year-round; come early for the biggest selection or late for the best bargains, but feel free to dicker anytime. (Sun)

Georgetown University. *Main entrance at 37th and O sts NW (20007). Phone 202/687-0100. www.georgetown.edu.* (1789) 12,000 students. Oldest Catholic college in the US, a Jesuit school. Campus tours (Mon-Sat, by reservation).

Old Stone House. *3051 M St NW (20007). Phone 202/426-6851 (also TTY service). www.nps.gov/rocr/oldstonehouse/.* (1765) Believed to be the oldest pre-Revolutionary building in Washington. Constructed on parcel No. 3 of the original tract of land that was then Georgetown, the house was used as both a residence and a place of business; five rooms are furnished with household items that reflect a middle-class residence of the late 18th century. The grounds are lush with fruit trees and seasonal blooms. (Wed-Sun; closed holidays) **FREE**

Shops at Georgetown Park. *3222 M St NW (20007). Phone 202/298-5577. www.shopsatgeorgetownpark.com.* This stylish urban mall has four levels of upscale shops and restaurants to explore, and is especially strong in apparel. Look for Ann Taylor, Abercrombie & Fitch, J. Crew, Talbots, and other nationally popular brands. If your energy flags, you'll find fresh-baked pretzels and cookies to munch on, as well as Godiva chocolates.

An accommodating Concierge Center on Level One offers gift wrapping, stroller and wheelchair loan, postal services, parking validation, photocopying, faxing, and other amenities. (Daily)

St. John's Church Georgetown Parish. *3240 O St NW (20007). Phone 202/ 338-1796.* Oldest Episcopal congregation in Georgetown, established 1796; original design of church by William Thornton, architect of the Capitol. Many presidents since Madison have worshiped here. Francis Scott Key was a founding member. Tours (by appointment).

Tudor Place. *1644 31st St NW (20007). Phone 202/965-0400. www.tudor place.org.* (1805) This 12-room Federal-style mansion was designed by Dr. William Thornton, architect of the Capitol, for Martha Custis Peter, granddaughter of Martha Washington. The Peter family lived in the house for 180 years. All furnishings and objets d'art are original. More than 5 acres of gardens (Mon-Sat). Guided tours (Tues-Sat, by reservation; closed holidays). **$$**

Washington Harbour. *3000 K St NW (20007).* Dining and shopping complex that features lavish fountains, life-size statuary, and a boardwalk with a view of the Potomac River.

Yellow House. *1430 33rd St NW (20007).* (1733) One of Georgetown's oldest homes (a private residence), typical of the area's mansions.

Special Events

Georgetown Garden Tour. *3224 N St NW (20007). Phone 202/333-6896.* Fourteen or more different gardens open to the public. Proceeds go to Georgetown Children's House; includes "Evermay" garden, which features grand expanses, fountains, and sculptures. Self-guided tours. Second Sat in May.

Georgetown House Tour. *3240 O St NW (20007). Phone 202/338-1796. www.georgetownhousetour.com.* Held since 1927, participants view 12 well-known and less well-known houses in Georgetown. St. John's Episcopal Church members serve as hosts and guides, and serve tea in the Parish Hall in the afternoon. Late Apr.

Hotels

★ ★ ★ ★ **FOUR SEASONS HOTEL.** *2800 Pennsylvania Ave NW (20007). Phone 202/342-0444; fax 202/944-2076. www.fourseasons.com.* This Four Seasons Hotel is nestled within Washington's lovely and historic Georgetown neighborhood. Just outside the hotel's doors are enticing shops, energetic nightlife, and delectable dining. The warm and inviting atmosphere of the Four Seasons is instantly recognizable in the gracious lobby, where bountiful floral displays and Oriental rugs set a refined, residential tone. The guest accommodations are some of the most spacious in the city and are magnificently appointed with polished formal furnishings, beautiful fabrics, and exquisite attention to detail. The views of Rock Creek Park (see) and the C & O Canal further enhance the relaxing mood. Popular fitness classes are offered in the extremely well-equipped fitness center, complete with a lap pool, while the seven spa treatment rooms provide a restful alternative for personal well-being. Consistently delicious meals are available at Seasons (see), or you can retreat to the cozy Garden Lounge for afternoon tea or cocktails. Not only is the food memorable, but the politically charged crowd is unparalleled! *Secret Inspector's Notes:* No time to finish your e-mails before lunch? No problem! When dining at Seasons for lunch, guests are greeted not only with gracious charm but also with the offer of wireless connectivity from an available laptop. 260 rooms, 6 story. Pets accepted, some restrictions. Check-out noon. TV; cable (premium), VCR available (movies). In-room modem link. Restaurant, bar. Room service 24 hours. In-house fitness room, steam room. Spa. Indoor pool. Valet parking. Business center. Concierge. **$$$$**

★ ★ **GEORGETOWN INN.** *1310 Wisconsin Ave NW (20007). Phone 202/333-8900; toll-free 800/368-5922; fax 202/333-8308. www.georgetowninn.com.* 98 rooms, 6 story. Check-out noon, check-in 3 pm. TV; cable (premium), VCR available. In-room modem link. Restaurant, bar. Babysitting services available. In-house fitness room. Valet parking. **$$**

★ ★ **HOLIDAY INN.** *2101 Wisconsin Ave NW (20007). Phone 202/338-4600; toll-free 800/465-4329; fax 202/338-4458. www.holiday-inn.com.* 296 rooms, 7 story. Check-out noon. TV; cable (premium). In-room modem link. Laundry services. Restaurant, bar. In-house fitness room. Outdoor pool. **$**

★ ★ ★ **THE LATHAM HOTEL GEORGETOWN.** *3000 M St NW (20007). Phone 202/726-5000; toll-free 800/368-5922; fax 202/337-4250. www.thelatham.com.* The quaintness of Georgetown sits just steps away from this European-style boutique hotel, given its prime location on the city's main street. Simply walk outside its front doors and you'll find good shopping and tasty food. For the latter, however, you may not even want to leave The Latham. Michel Richard, a high-profile local chef with an international reputation, owns and operates the onsite Citronelle (see) restaurant, where diners savor award-winning French and American cuisine. The well-appointed guest rooms come with marble showers, high-speed Internet access, and more. In summer, cool off in the rooftop swimming pool. 143 rooms, 10 story. Check-out 11 am, check-in 3 pm. TV. In-room modem link. Restaurant. Outdoor pool. Valet parking. Concierge. Overlooks the historic Chesapeake and Ohio Canal. **$$**

★ ★ ★ **MONARCH HOTEL.** *2401 M St NW (20037). Phone 202/429-2400; toll-free 877/222-2266; fax 202/457-5010. www.monarchdc.com.* This recently renovated hotel is within walking distance of Georgetown and minutes from many national attractions. 415 rooms, 10 story. Pets accepted, some restrictions; fee. Check-out 1 pm. TV; cable (premium), CD player available. In-room modem link. Restaurant, bar; entertainment.

Room service 24 hours. In-house fitness room, sauna, steam room. Indoor pool, whirlpool. Squash, racquetball courts. Valet parking. Business center. Concierge. **$$**

D 🏊 🛌 🏋 🔄 SC 🚶

THE RITZ-CARLTON GEORGETOWN. *Too new to be rated. 3100 South St NW (20007). Phone 202/835-0500; toll-free 800/241-3333; fax 202/974-5519. www.ritzcarlton.com.* Embassy delegations often stay at this elegant, intimate hotel that blends contemporary décor with a historical setting. It's located on the banks of the Potomac River in Washington Harbour, an entertainment/residential/office complex located on land that was once the site of the original village of George Towne. Many of its executive suites and deluxe rooms offer gorgeous river views, and each comes with all the extra creature comforts you'd expect from a Ritz-Carlton, including feather duvets, goose-down pillows, and oversized marble baths. But don't spend all your time in your cushy room. Sip one of the fire-red martinis served in the Degrees Bar and Lounge, and then dine in Fahrenheit, which dishes out American/Italian cuisine. Soothe yourself with a facial or a full-body massage at the Boutique Spa, or tone those muscles at the fully equipped fitness center. 86 rooms. Pets accepted, some restrictions. Check-out noon, check-in 3 pm. TV; cable (premium). Restaurant, bar. Babysitting services available. In-house fitness room, spa. **$$$$**

D 🏋 🔄

All Suite

★ **WASHINGTON SUITES GEORGETOWN.** *2500 Pennsylvania Ave NW (20037). Phone 202/333-8060; toll-free 877/736-2500; fax 202/338-3818. www.washingtonsuiteshotel.com.* 123 rooms, 10 story. Pets accepted, some restrictions; fee. Check-out noon. TV; cable (premium). In-room modem link. Health club privileges. **$**

🔄 SC

Restaurants

★ ★ ★ **1789.** *1226 36th St NW (20007). Phone 202/965-1789; fax 202/337-1541. www.1789restaurant.com.* This quietly elegant establishment, located just on the edge of Georgetown University's campus, is a top destination for students with visiting relatives. The service is extraordinary. American menu. Closed Dec 25. Dinner. Bar. In a restored mansion; five dining rooms on three levels. Jacket required. **$$$**

★ ★ **ADITI.** *3299 M St NW (20007). Phone 202/625-6825.* Indian menu. Closed Thanksgiving. Lunch, dinner. Bar. **$**

★ **AUSTIN GRILL.** *2404 Wisconsin Ave NW (20007). Phone 202/337-8080. www.austingrill.com.* Tex-Mex menu. Closed Thanksgiving, Dec 25. Lunch, dinner, Sun brunch. Bar. **$$**

★ **BILLY MARTIN'S TAVERN.** *1264 Wisconsin Ave NW (20007). Phone 202/333-7370; fax 202/333-6089. www.billymartinstavern.com.* Seafood, steak menu. Closed Dec 25. Breakfast, lunch, dinner, Sat-Sun brunch. Bar. Established 1933. Reservations accepted. Outdoor seating. **$**

★ ★ **BISTRO FRANCAIS.** *3128 M St NW (20007). Phone 202/338-3830; fax 202/338-1421.* Country French menu. Closed Dec 24-25. Lunch, Sat-Sun brunch. **$$**

D

★ ★ **BISTROT LEPIC.** *1736 Wisconsin Ave NW (20007). Phone 202/333-0111; fax 202/333-2209. www.bistrotlepic.net.* French menu. Closed Mon; holidays. Lunch, dinner. Storefront restaurant. **$$$**

★ ★ **BUSARA.** *2340 Wisconsin Ave NW (20007). Phone 202/337-2340; fax 202/333-1364. www.busara.us.* Thai menu. Closed holidays. Lunch, dinner. Bar. Reservations required. Outdoor seating. **$$**

D

★ ★ **CAFE MILANO.** *3251 Prospect St NW (20007). Phone 202/333-6183; fax 202/333-6594. www.cafemilano.net.* Italian menu. Closed Thanksgiving, Dec 25. Lunch, dinner. Bar. Outdoor seating. **$$$**

D

★ ★ ★ ★ **CITRONELLE.** *3000 M St NW (20007). Phone 202/625-2150; fax 202/339-6326. www.citronelledc.com.* Citronelle's chef-owner Michel Richard is one talented guy. Not only has he created a restaurant that has stood the test of time (he's had it for more than ten years), but he has also managed to keep the menu vibrant, exciting, and just on the safe side of daring. Like his food, the restaurant is stylish and elegant. Filled with fresh flowers and lit with a creamy, golden glow, the room has a chic vibe and an open kitchen for a bird's-eye view of the chefs, dressed in white and hard at work. This is a terrific spot for most any occasion so long as fine dining is the order of business. Ingredients are the stars here; the chef manages to wow diners by highlighting the simple flavors of each dish's main component. Global accents—herbs, spices, fruits, nuts, and vegetables—come into play to draw out flavors, to spotlight sweetness or acidity, and to maintain balance on the palate. Richard is a poetic culinarian. Nabbing a seat at one of his coveted tables is like winning the lottery. French menu. Closed major holidays. Breakfast, lunch, dinner. Bar. Children's menu. Jacket required. Outdoor seating. **$$$**

D

★ ★ **CLYDE'S OF GEORGETOWN.** *3236 M St NW (20007). Phone 202/333-9180. www.clydes.com/restaurants/cl-georgetown.html.* One of the oldest saloons in Washington, this is the original Clyde's (now one of a dozen establishments owned by the Clyde's Group). Its cozily crowded main bar draws a loyal following with its nice selection of draft beers. The brass-and-wood dining room features ambitious menu choices well beyond the burgers and chili for which the place is famous. Its afternoon appetizer offerings were the inspiration for the 1976 pop hit "Afternoon Delight." American, seafood menu. Closed Dec 25. Lunch, dinner, Sun brunch. Bar. Children's menu. Atrium dining. **$$**

D

★ ★ **FILOMENA.** *1063 Wisconsin Ave NW (20007). Phone 202/338-8800; fax 202/338-8806. www.filomena.com.* Italian menu. Closed Jan 1, Thanksgiving, Dec 25. Lunch, dinner, brunch. Bar. **$$$**

★ **GARRETT'S.** *3003 M St NW (20007). Phone 202/333-1033; fax 202/333-8055. www.garrettsdc.com.* American menu. Lunch, dinner. Bar. 1794 landmark building; originally the house of Maryland governor T. S. Lee. **$$**

★ **GUARDS.** *2915 M St NW (20007). Phone 202/965-2350; fax 202/342-6112.* Continental, seafood menu. Lunch, dinner, Sun brunch. Bar. **$$**

★ **J. PAUL'S.** *3218 M St NW (20007). Phone 202/333-3450; fax 202/342-6721. www.j-pauls.com.* American menu. Lunch, dinner, Sun brunch. Bar. Children's menu. **$$**

D

★ ★ **LA CHAUMIERE.** *2813 M St NW (20007). Phone 202/338-1784; fax 202/965-4597. www.washingtonpost/yp/lachaumiere.* Country French menu. Closed Sun, holidays. Lunch, dinner. **$$**

D

★ ★ ★ **MAKOTO RESTAURANT.** *4822 MacArthur Blvd NW (20007). Phone 202/298-6866; fax 202/625-6602.* Looking for the best Japanese food in town? Come here, but be forewarned that reservations at this 25-seat restaurant are limited. For the uninitiated, we recommend the eight- to ten-course prix fixe meal. No matter what you select, you are guaranteed impeccable service of the freshest ingredients presented in artful creations. Closed Mon. Lunch, dinner. Reservations recommended. **$$$**

★ ★ ★ **MENDOCINO GRILL AND WINE BAR.** *2917 M St NW (20007). Phone 202/333-2912; fax 202/625-7888.* The excellent, all-American wine list is the most impressive feature of this wine bar-cum-restaurant. The food is designed to complement the wine, and the menu comprises creative choices that all sound tempting. The décor is upscale 1960s modern (think Brady Bunch wine bar), but it somehow manages to work. American menu. Lunch, dinner. Entertainment. **$$$**

D

★ ★ ★ **MORTON'S OF CHICAGO.** *3251 Prospect St NW (20007). Phone 202/342-6258; fax 202/338-8033. www.mortons.com.* This Georgetown location of the national steakhouse chain is one of three in the DC area. Seafood, steak menu. Closed holidays. Dinner. Bar. Valet parking. **$$$**

D

★ **MR. SMITH'S.** *3104 M St NW (20007). Phone 202/333-3104. www.mrsmiths.com.* American menu. Lunch, dinner, Sat-Sun brunch. Bar. Outdoor seating. **$$**

★ ★ **NATHAN'S.** *3150 M St NW (20007). Phone 202/338-2000; fax 202/333-2509.* American, northern Italian menu. Dinner, Sat-Sun brunch. Bar. **$$**

★ ★ **OLD EUROPE.** *2434 Wisconsin Ave NW (20007). Phone 202/333-7600; fax 202/625-0553. www.old-europe.com.* German menu. Closed July 4, Dec 24. Lunch, dinner. Bar. Children's menu. Casual attire. **$$**

[D] [SC]

★ ★ **PAOLO'S.** *1303 Wisconsin Ave NW (20007). Phone 202/333-7353; fax 202/342-2846. www.capitalrestaurants.com.* California, Italian menu. Lunch, dinner, Sat-Sun brunch. Bar. Outdoor seating. Wood-burning pizza oven. **$$**

[D]

★ ★ **SEA CATCH.** *1054 31st St NW (20007). Phone 202/337-8855; fax 202/337-7159. www.seacatchrestaurant.com.* Seafood menu. Closed Sun. Lunch, dinner. Bar. Valet parking. Outdoor seating on a deck overlooking the historic Chesapeake and Ohio Canal. **$$$**

[D]

★ ★ ★ **SEASONS.** *2800 Pennsylvania Ave NW (20007). Phone 202/342-0444; fax 202/944-2076. www.fourseasons.com.* Enclosed in glass and tastefully decorated with deep armchairs, dark wood, fresh flowers, and a good dose of style, Seasons is the elegant flagship restaurant of the Four Seasons Hotel (see). The sophisticated American menu offers simple, elegant fare that makes this an ideal locale for a business meal. The kitchen is not trying to win awards for wild, far-out food. The dishes here will all be familiar, but even the most familiar foods can surprise you when they're prepared with the best ingredients, passion, and skill. To complement the classic menu, you can choose from old-world or North American wines, or an extensive selection of wines by the glass. For an afternoon delight, stop by the Garden Terrace for tea service with all the trimmings—scones with clotted cream, cucumber and watercress sandwiches with the crusts cut off, petit fours, chocolate-dipped strawberries, and assorted butter cookies. American menu. Breakfast, lunch, dinner, Sun brunch. Bar. Piano. Children's menu. Valet parking. **$$$**

[D]

★ ★ **SEQUOIA.** *3000 K St NW (20007). Phone 202/944-4200; fax 202/944-4210. www.arkrestaurants.com.* American menu. Lunch, dinner, Sun brunch. Bar. Outdoor seating. **$$$**

[D]

★ **SUSHI-KO.** *2309 Wisconsin Ave NW (20007). Phone 202/333-4187; fax 202/333-7594. www.sushiko.us.* Japanese menu. Closed July 4, Thanksgiving, Dec 25. Lunch, dinner. Casual attire. **$$$**

[D]

★ **THE TOMBS.** *1226 36th St NW (20007). Phone 202/337-6668; fax 202/337-1541. www.clydes.com.* Did someone say "Rah"? Since 1962, this classic sports-themed bar and grill has been dear to the hearts of Georgetown University students, faculty, and alums—raucously dear to them when GU teams have a home game or are playing on TV. Vintage sporting prints and rowing paraphernalia contribute to the ambience. You'll find burgers, pizza, and other bar standards on the menu, as well as desserts (and a good wine list) from the restaurant upstairs, 1789 (see). American menu. Closed Thanksgiving, Dec 24-25. Lunch, dinner, Sun brunch. Bar. **$$**

★ ★ **TONY AND JOE'S SEAFOOD PLACE.** 3000 K St NW (20007). Phone 202/944-4545; fax 202/944-4587. www.tonyandjoes.com. Seafood menu. Closed Dec 25. Lunch, dinner, Sun brunch. Bar; entertainment. Outdoor seating. **$$**

D

★ **ZED'S ETHIOPIAN CUISINE.** 1201 28th St NW (20007). Phone 202/333-4710; fax 202/333-1085. www.zeds.net. Ethiopian menu. Closed Thanksgiving, Dec 25. Lunch, dinner. Silverware provided at customer's request; communal dining from trays. **$$**

The Mall and the Waterfront

Envisioned by Pierre L'Enfant as a 400-foot-wide promenade, the grounds of the National Mall nonetheless existed for more than 100 years as a mix of forest, nondescript open space, and railroad tracks. During the Civil War, the Mall grounds were used to house and train troops, produce arms, and slaughter cattle. In 1902, the McMillan Commission submitted plans to Congress that called for dramatic modifications to the Mall, creating a space that revived—and expanded on—L'Enfant's vision. Over the course of the 20th century, considerable changes were made to the Mall, most of which adhered to the principles of the McMillan Commission's plan. Today, the National Mall serves as a national stage for remembrance, recreation, and protest.

Three different parks occupy the long stretch of land that—begins at—the west steps of the Capitol building and continues to the Washington Monument, where it widens and extends to the Lincoln Memorial and the banks of the Potomac River. Technically, the three parks—the National Mall, Washington Monument Grounds, and West Potomac Park—comprise National Capital Parks-Central, though the whole expanse of space is more commonly regarded as being part of the National Mall.

Thousands of tourists flock to the Mall daily to visit the area's many memorials, monuments, and museums. At the west end of the Mall, the Reflecting Pool leads to the base of the Lincoln Memorial. Martin Luther King, Jr., delivered his "I Have a Dream" speech here in 1963. Nearby, you'll find the Korean War Veterans Memorial and the Vietnam Veterans Memorial. At the center of the Mall stands the Washington Monument, a 555-foot-high obelisk honoring the nation's first president. The Thomas Jefferson and Franklin Delano Roosevelt memorials border the Mall to the south, alongside the Tidal Basin. Several world-renowned museums are located near the Mall, including the Smithsonian National Air and Space Museum, the National Gallery of Art, and the Holocaust Memorial Museum.

The National Mall's well-maintained grounds make it a wonderful place to sit and relax or go for a stroll. The Mall features more than 170 flower beds, 35 ornamental pools and fountains, 2,000 American elms, and 3,000 Japanese cherry trees. Bordering the Tidal Basin, the cherry trees, a gift from the people of Tokyo in 1912, draw visitors from around the world each spring to enjoy the their bright blooms.

What to See and Do

American Red Cross. *1730 E St NW (20006). Phone 202/737-8300. www.redcross.org. National headquarters includes three buildings bounded by 17th, 18th, D, and E sts NW.* The 17th St building includes marble busts *Faith, Hope,* and *Charity* by sculptor Hiram Powers and three original Tiffany stained-glass windows. (Daily 8:30 am-4 pm, closed most federal holidays) **FREE**

Arena Stage. *1101 6th St at Maine Ave SW (20024). Phone 202/488-3300. www.arena-stage.org.*

Art Museum of the Americas, OAS. *201 18th St NW (20006). Phone 202/458-6016. www.museum.oas.org.* Dedicated to Latin American and Caribbean contemporary art; paintings, graphics, sculpture. (Tues-Sun; closed holidays) **FREE**

Black History Recreation Trail. *1100 Ohio Dr SW (20001). Phone 202/619-7222.* Trail through Washington neighborhoods highlights important sites in African American history.

Blair-Lee House. *1651 Pennsylvania Ave NW (20503).* (1824) Guest house for heads of government and state who are visiting the US as guests of the president. Not open to the public.

Bureau of Engraving and Printing. *14th and C sts SW (20228). S of the Mall; enter on 14th St. Phone 202/874-3019. www.bep.treas.gov.* Watch millions of dollars being made—printed, that is—on the tour of this site, which takes visitors through many of the steps involved in producing currency. You'll see large, blank sheets of paper transformed, as if by magic, into wallet-size bills and learn about the latest high-tech steps the Bureau has taken to thwart counterfeiting. You can buy uncut sheets of bills in different denominations, as well as shredded cash, at the BEP store. Guided tours 9 am-2 pm. (Closed weekends, federal holidays, and Dec 24-Jan 3) **FREE**

Constitution Gardens. *Constitution Ave and 18th St (20011). Phone 202/426-6841.* This 50-acre park, with a man-made lake, is also the site of the Signers of the Declaration of Independence Memorial. **FREE**

Corcoran Gallery of Art. *500 17th St NW (20006). 17th St between New York Ave and E St NW. Phone 202/639-1700. www.corcoran.org.* The city's oldest art museum—and its largest non-federal one—is also one of its liveliest. Known for its strong collection of 19th-century American art (don't miss John Singer Sargent's luminous *Oyster Gatherers of Cancale*) and its support for local artists, the museum also shows important European pieces and eye-opening contemporary works, including photography, performance art, and new media. A glamorous, Frank Gehry-designed addition to the landmark

Beaux Arts building is in the works. (Wed-Mon; closed Jan 1, Thanksgiving, Dec 25) Free admission Mon, Thurs after 5 pm. **$**

DAR Headquarters. *1776 D St NW (20006). Phone 202/628-1776. www.dar.org.* Includes Memorial Continental Hall (1904) and Constitution Hall (1920); DAR Museum Gallery, located in the administration building, has 33 state period rooms; outstanding genealogical research library (fee for nonmembers). Guided tours (Mon-Sat). **FREE**

Department of Commerce Building. *1401 Constitution Ave NW (20230). Phone 202/482-4883. www.commerce.gov.* (1932)

Department of Energy. *1000 Independence Ave SW (20585). Phone 202/586-5575. www.energy.gov.* Includes the **Interstate Commerce Commission** (1934), Constitution Ave between 12th and 13th sts NW; **Customs Department,** Constitution Ave between 13th and 14th sts NW; and the **District Building,** Pennsylvania Ave between 13th and 14th sts NW, Washington's ornate 1908 city hall.

Department of Justice Building. *950 Pennsylvania Ave (20530).* (1934) Pennsylvania Ave between 9th and 10th sts NW. (Not open to the public) Across Pennsylvania Ave is

FBI Headquarters. *J. Edgar Hoover Bldg, 935 Pennsylvania Ave NW (20530), between 9th and 10th sts NW; tour entrance on 9th St NW. Phone 202/324-3000. www.fbi.gov.* Tours of historical exhibits, includes FBI laboratory; very large firearm collection; demonstration of firearms. (At press time, FBI Tour was closed for renovations, and no re-opening date had been posted. Call above phone number for further information.) (Previous hours: Mon-Fri; closed holidays) **FREE**

Department of State Building. *2201 C St NW (20520). Phone 202/647-3241.* The State Department's diplomatic reception rooms, furnished with 18th-century American furniture and decorative art, are used by the Secretary of State and cabinet members for formal entertaining. Tours (Mon-Fri; closed federal holidays and special events; three to four weeks advance reservations; children over 12 years only preferred). **FREE**

Department of the Interior. *1849 C St NW (20240). Between 18th and 19th sts NW. Phone 202/208-3100. www.doi.gov.* (1938) Within is a museum including exhibits and dioramas depicting the history and activities of the department and its various bureaus. A photo ID is required for admission. (Mon-Fri; closed holidays) Reference library is open to the public. **FREE**

Department of the Treasury. *1500 Pennsylvania Ave NW (20501). E of the White House. Phone 202/622-0896. www.treasury.gov.* According to legend, this Greek Revival building, one of the oldest (1836-1869) in the city, was built in the middle of Pennsylvania Ave because Andrew Jackson, tired of endless wrangling over the location, walked out of the White House, planted his cane in the mud, and said, "Here." The building has been extensively restored. **FREE**

Federal Reserve Building. *C and 21st sts NW (20002). Phone 202/452-3149.* (1937) Primarily an office building but noteworthy for its architecture; rotating art exhibits; film (20 minutes). **FREE**

Federal Trade Commission Building. *6th St and Pennsylvania Ave NW (20001). Phone 202/326-2222. www.ftc.gov.* (1938) (Mon-Fri; closed holidays) **FREE**

Federal Triangle. *Pennsylvania Ave and 13th St NW (20004).* The Triangle consists of a group of government buildings, nine of which were built for $78 million in the 1930s in modern classic design. The "crown jewel" of the triangle is the Ronald Reagan International Trade Center, located on Pennsylvania Ave at 13th St NW.

⭐ **Franklin Delano Roosevelt Memorial.** *West Basin Dr (20003). West Potomac Park near the Lincoln Memorial. Phone 202/426-6841. www.nps.gov/fdrm.* This newer memorial, dedicated in 1997, features a series of sculptures depicting the 32nd US President Franklin Roosevelt and his wife, Eleanor. Four outdoor rooms represent each of FDR's four presidential terms, which began in the Great Depression and ended at the close of World War II. Visitors can feel his presence in broadcasts of his "fireside chats" throughout the exhibits. (Daily 24 hours; interpretive ranger staff on site 8 am-11:45 pm; closed Dec 25) **FREE**

Korean War Memorial. *French Dr SW and Independence Ave (20242). Adjacent to the Lincoln Memorial. Phone 202/426-6841. www.nps.gov/kwvm.* This massive sculpture honors the Americans who served in the Korean conflict, showing 19 soldiers dressed and armed for battle heading toward the American flag, their symbolic goal. The adjacent wall features etched photographs that pay tribute to military support personnel. (Daily 8 am-midnight; closed Dec 25) **FREE**

Lafayette Square. *Pennsylvania Ave NW (20004). Phone 202/673-7647.* Statue of Andrew Jackson on horseback in the center was the first equestrian figure in Washington (1853). One of the park benches was known as Bernard Baruch's office in 1930s and is dedicated to him.

   Decatur House Museum. *748 Jackson Pl NW (20006). Phone 202/842-0920. www.decaturhouse.org.* (1818) Federal townhouse built for naval hero Commodore Stephen Decatur by Benjamin H. Latrobe, second architect of the Capitol. After Decatur's death in 1820, the house was occupied by a succession of American and foreign statespeople and was a center of political and social life in the city. The ground floor family rooms reflect Decatur's Federal-period lifestyle. Operated by the National Trust for Historic Preservation. (Tues-Sun; closed Jan 1, Thanksgiving, Dec 25) **FREE**

⭐ **Lincoln Memorial.** *23rd St NW at Daniel French and Henry Beacon Dr (20242). Phone 202/426-6841. www.nps.gov/linc.* Dedicated in 1922, Daniel Chester French's Abraham Lincoln looks across a reflecting pool to the Washington Monument and the Capitol. Lincoln's Gettysburg Address and Second Inaugural Address are inscribed on the walls of the templelike structure, which is particularly impressive at night. The 36 columns represent the 36 states in the Union in existence at the time of Lincoln's death. (Daily 8 am-11:45 pm; closed Dec 25) **FREE**

Martin Luther King, Jr. Memorial Library. *901 G St NW (20001).* *www.dclibrary.org/mlk.* (1972) Main branch of the DC public library was designed by architect Mies van der Rohe. Martin Luther King mural. Books, periodicals, photographs, films, videocassettes, recordings, microfilms, Washingtoniana, and the *Washington Star* collection. Library for the visually impaired; librarian for the hearing impaired; black studies division; AP wire service machine; community information service. Underground parking. (Mon-Sat, also Sun afternoons; closed holidays) **FREE**

National Academy of Sciences. *2100 C St NW (20418). Between 21st and 22nd sts NW. Phone 202/334-2000. www.nationalacademies.org.* (1924) Established in 1863 to stimulate research and communication among scientists and to advise the federal government in science and technology. A famous 21-foot bronze statue of Albert Einstein by Robert Berks is on the front lawn. Art exhibits, concerts. (Schedule varies) **FREE**

National Gallery of Art. *600 Constitution Ave NW (20002). Between 3rd and 7th sts. Phone 202/737-4215. www.nga.gov.* The West Building (1941), designed by John Russell Pope, contains Western European and American art spanning periods between the 13th and 20th centuries: highlights include the only Leonardo da Vinci painting in the western hemisphere, *Ginevra de' Benci;* a comprehensive collection of Italian paintings and sculpture; major French Impressionists; numerous Rembrandts and examples of the Dutch school; masterpieces from the Mellon, Widener, Kress, Dale, and Rosenwald collections; special exhibitions. The East Building (1978), designed by architect I. M. Pei, houses the gallery's growing collection of 20th-century art, including Picasso's *Family of Saltimbanques* and Jackson Pollock's *Lavender Mist.* (Daily; closed Jan 1, Dec 25) **FREE**

The Octagon Museum. *1799 New York Ave NW (20006). At 18th and E sts NW. Phone 202/638-3221. www.archfoundation.org/octagon/.* (1799-1801) Federal townhouse built for Colonel John Tayloe III, based on designs by Dr. William Thornton. It served as temporary quarters for President and Mrs. James Madison after the White House burned in War of 1812; it also was the site of the ratification of the Treaty of Ghent. Restored with period furnishings (1800-1828). Changing exhibits on architecture and allied arts. (Tues-Sun 10 am-4 pm; closed Jan 1, Thanksgiving, Dec 25) **$**

Old Executive Office Building. *17th St and Pennsylvania Ave NW (20501). Phone 202/395-5895.* (1875) Second Empire/Victorian architecture. Built as War Office; was also home to State Department; now offices for president's staff. Guided tours by appointment (Sat morning only). **FREE**

Organization of American States (OAS). *17th St NW and Constitution Ave (20006). Phone 202/458-3000. www.oas.org.* Headquarters of OAS, set up to maintain international peace and security and to promote integral development in the Americas. Tropical patio, Hall of Heroes and Flags, Hall of the Americas, Aztec Garden, Council Chamber. (Mon-Fri; closed holidays) **FREE**

Potomac Park (East and West). *1100 Ohio St SW (22213). NW and SE of the Jefferson Memorial. Phone 202/619-7222 (park information). www.nps.gov/nacc/.* A more beautiful urban playground would be hard to find. Seven hundred twenty riverfront acres are divided by Washington's famous Tidal Basin into East and West Potomac Parks. East Potomac Park has three golf courses, a large swimming pool, picnic grounds, tennis courts, and biking and hiking paths. Pedal boats can be rented at the Tidal Basin. At West Potomac Park, you'll find the Vietnam, Korean, Lincoln, Jefferson, and FDR memorials; Constitution Gardens; a small island where ducks live; and the Reflecting Pool. Beyond these family-friendly activities, you'll find one of the most glorious—albeit one of the briefest—sights of the city: the famous two-week burst of pink and white cherry blossoms from more than 3,000 trees, a 1912 gift of friendship from Japan, in late Mar/early Apr. The Cherry Blossom Festival (see SPECIAL EVENTS) begins each year with the lighting of the 300-year-old Japanese Stone Lantern, presented by the governor of Tokyo back in 1954.

⭐ **Smithsonian Institution.** *1000 Jefferson Dr SW (20560). Phone 202/357-2700 (general information and schedule). www.si.edu.* The majority of Smithsonian museums are located on the National Mall. Smithsonian headquarters are in the Smithsonian Institution Building, the "Castle" (1855), located at 1000 Jefferson Dr SW, on the Mall. The headquarters contain administrative offices, Smithson's crypt, and the Smithsonian Information Center, which has information on all Smithsonian museums. Many visitors begin their day here. (All buildings open daily 10 am-5:30 pm; closed Dec 25; Anacostia Museum and National Zoo hours vary) **FREE** Smithsonian museums on the mall include

Anacostia Museum. *1901 Fort Place SE (20020). Phone 202/357-2700. www.si.edu.* An exhibition and research center for black heritage in the historic Anacostia section of southeast Washington. Changing exhibits. (Daily; closed Dec 25) **FREE**

Arthur M. Sackler Gallery. *1200 Jefferson Dr SW (20560). Phone 202/357-2700.* Changing exhibitions of Asian art, both Near- and Far-Eastern, from major national and international collections. Permanent collection includes Chinese and South and Southeast Asian art objects presented by Arthur Sackler. Between the Freer Gallery and the Arts and Industries Building is the **Enid A. Haupt Garden,** 4 acres that compose the "roof" of the Sackler Gallery, the International Gallery, an underground Smithsonian research and education complex, and 1050 Independence Ave SW. **FREE**

Arts and Industries Building. *900 Jefferson Dr SW (20560). Phone 202/357-2700. www.si.edu/ai/.* The south hall contains the Experimental Gallery, an exhibit space dedicated to innovative and creative exhibits from museums in the Smithsonian and from around the world. Discovery Theater (fee) hosts performances for children. **FREE**

Freer Gallery. *1200 Jefferson Dr SW (20560). Phone 202/357-2700. www.asia.si.edu.* Asian art with objects dating from Neolithic period to the early 20th century. Also works by late 19th- and early 20th-century American artists, including a major collection of James McNeill Whistler's work, highlighted by the famous Peacock Room. Next to the Freer is the Smithsonian Institution Building, or "the Castle." **FREE**

Hirshhorn Museum and Sculpture Garden. *Independence Ave and 7th St SW (20560). Phone 202/357-2700 or 202/633-6474. www.hirshhorn.si.edu.* The cool modernity of the paintings and sculptures here—and of the curvy building itself—are a delicious respite for history-sated visitors. Inside is some of the most interesting art produced in the last 100 years: everything from Constantin Brancusi's egglike "Sleeping Muse I" to Nam June Paik's "Video Flag" made with 70 video monitors. Outdoors, the greenery of the plaza (7:30 am-5:30 pm) and sculpture garden (7:30 am-dusk) make this an inviting spot for a National Mall rendezvous. (Daily 10 am-5:30 pm; closed Dec 25) **DONATION**

⭐ **National Air and Space Museum.** *600 Independence Ave SW (20560). Between 7th and 4th sts SW. Phone 202/357-1387. www.nasm.si.edu.* This popular museum thrills those who have lived through the age of space exploration, as well as those whose memories go back further. View the Wright brothers' *1903 Kitty Hawk Flyer,* Charles Lindbergh's *Spirit of St. Louis,* and the command module *Columbia,* which carried the first men to walk on the moon. World War II buffs will want to see not only American fighter planes but also the British *Supermarine Spitfire,* the Japanese *Mitsubishi Zero,* and the German *Messerschmitt.* In the Apollo to the Moon exhibit, you'll see lunar rocks, spacesuits, and John Glenn's squeeze-tube beef stew, among other artifacts. An IMAX theater enables you to view on a huge, five-story-high screen Earth as seen from the space shuttle. And don't miss the high-tech shows at the Albert Einstein Planetarium, which combine ideas about the size and origins of the universe with eye-popping images taken from the Hubble Space Telescope and Mars Global Surveyor. (Daily 10 am-5:30 pm; closed Dec 25) **FREE**

National Museum of African Art. *950 Independence Ave SW (20560). Phone 202/357-4600 or 202/357-4814. www.nmafa.si.edu.* With everything from masks to musical instruments, sacred objects to simple wooden headrests, the diverse cultures of Africa past and present are on view at this small but fascinating museum. Permanent exhibits display ceramics, textiles, household tools, and the visual arts of the sub-Sahara. Traveling shows cover even more ground; recent ones have featured colonial-era photography and Ethiopian religious icons. A full schedule of films, musical presentations, lectures, and children's events keeps things lively. (Daily 10 am-5:30 pm; closed Dec 25) **FREE**

⭐ **National Museum of American History.** *14th St and Constitution Ave NW (20560). Phone 202/357-2700 or 202/357-1729 (TTY). www.american history.si.edu/.* More than 17 million artifacts cover aspects of American cultural heritage large and small, public and private. Want to see Julia Child's gleaming black six-burner stove? Check out the cheerfully comfortable kitchen from the famous chef's longtime home in Cambridge, Massachusetts, reassembled here in 2001. Or watch textile conservators take painstaking steps to restore the fragile Star-Spangled Banner, the actual flag that inspired Francis Scott Key in 1814 to write the poem that became America's national anthem. The museum's endlessly fascinating collections include everything from the lap desk at which Thomas

Jefferson drafted the Declaration of Independence to Henry Ford's 1913 Model-T, from first ladies' inaugural gowns to Dorothy's ruby slippers from The Wizard of Oz. Children will especially enjoy the Hands On History Room, where they can harness a life-size model of a mule or tap out a telegraph message in Morse code. (Daily 10 am-5:30 pm; closed Dec 25) **FREE**

National Museum of Natural History. *Constitution Ave and 10th St NW (20560). Phone 202/357-2700. www.mnh.si.edu.* Before you enter this museum, stop on the Ninth St side of the building to see the mesmerizing Butterfly Garden. You'll see the different relationships between plants and butterflies in four separate habitats: wetland, meadow, wood's edge, and urban garden. But the fascination only begins here. The National Museum of Natural History holds more than 124 million artifacts and specimens dating back to the Ice Age. For a fun first stop, try the first-floor Discovery Room. Here the whole family can learn about different cultures and other aspects of natural history through a wealth of interactive activities. Other museum exhibits include an insect zoo with thousands of live specimens, a section on gems (including the 45.52-carat, billion-year-old Hope Diamond), dinosaur skeletons, a live coral reef, and botanical, zoological, and geological materials. This is where Western civilization can be traced, literally, to its roots. (Daily 10 am-5:30 pm; closed Dec 25) **FREE**

Renwick Gallery at the American Art Museum. *Pennsylvania Ave at 17th St NW (20006). Phone 202/275-1500 or 202/357-2700. www.americanart.si.edu.* The Patent Office Building, home of the American Art Museum, is closed for renovations until 2006, but the museum's Renwick Gallery, housed in an elegant Second Empire-style building, remains open, and its exhibitions of American crafts and decorative arts are knockouts. The permanent collection features superb, one-of-a-kind pieces in clay, fiber, glass, metal, and wood. Make sure to see the sculptural furniture by Sam Maloof and the playful "Game Fish" by Larry Fuente. (Daily 10 am-5:30 pm; closed Dec 25) **FREE**

★ **Thomas Jefferson Memorial.** *East Basin Dr SW (20003). S edge of Tidal Basin. Phone 202/426-6841. www.nps.gov/thje.* This memorial, dedicated in 1943, honors the third President of the United States and the author of both the Declaration of Independence and the Bill of Rights. The white marble dome surrounded by columns, representing the classic style that Jefferson introduced to the US, is a memorable Washington landmark and is quite beautiful especially when lit up at night. In the basement, you'll find a museum and the plaster statue from which the 19-foot bronze one in the center of the monument was created. (Daily 8 am-midnight; closed Dec 25) **FREE**

Tourmobile Sightseeing. *1000 Ohio Dr SW (20024). Phone 202/554-5100. www.tourmobile.com.* Narrated shuttle tours to 18 historic sites on the National Mall and in Arlington National Cemetery. Unlimited reboarding throughout day (daily; no tours Dec 25). Additional tours separately or in combinations: Arlington National Cemetery; Mount Vernon (seasonal) and Frederick Douglass Home (seasonal). **$$$$**

⭐ **US Holocaust Memorial Museum.** *100 Raoul Wallenberg Pl SW (20024). Entrances at Raoul Wallenberg Pl (15th St SW) and at 14th St SW. Phone 202/488-0400 or 202/488-0406 (TTY). www.ushmm.org.* Opened in 1993, this privately funded museum is noteworthy for its effective presentation of information, images, and artifacts in an architectural setting that enhances visitors' understanding of the Holocaust. Temporary exhibits cover everything from the diary of Anne Frank to the role of Oskar Schindler in saving the lives of hundreds of Jews. At the heart of the museum is its self-guided Permanent Exhibition, which includes powerful photos; film footage; eyewitness testimonies; clothing, suitcases, children's drawings, and other victims' belongings; and reconstructions of concentration camp buildings. Especially stirring is the Hall of Faces, a narrow, three-story-high space crammed with framed photographs of the Jewish residents of a single Lithuanian town, more than 3,000 of whom were murdered in September 1941. Visitors are welcome to reflect privately on their experience in the quiet, skylighted Hall of Remembrance and to light memorial candles in the niches of its walls. (Daily 10 am-5:30 pm; closed Yom Kippur, Dec 25). Timed daily-use passes are necessary for visiting the museum's permanent exhibition and can be obtained each day at the museum starting at 10 am or in advance by calling 800/400-9373. **FREE**

⭐ **Vietnam Veterans Memorial.** *900 Ohio Dr SW (20242). Constitution Ave between Henry Bacon Dr and 21st St NW. Phone 202/426-6841. www.nps.gov/vive.* Designed by Maya Ying Lin and funded by private citizens' contributions, this memorial's polished black granite walls are inscribed with the names of the 58,175 US servicemen who died in or remain missing from the Vietnam War (a large directory helps visitors locate specific names). Deliberately apolitical, the memorial aims to foster reconciliation and healing given the divisiveness the war caused in American society. Also on site are the Three Servicemen Statue and Flagpole and the Vietnam Women's Memorial. (Daily 8 am-11:45 pm; closed Dec 25) **FREE**

Voice of America. *330 Independence Ave SW (20237). Between 3rd and 4th sts SW; enter on C St. Phone 202/619-3919.* Live radio broadcasts to foreign countries; 45-minute guided tours (Mon-Fri, reservations required; closed holidays). **FREE**

⭐ **Washington Monument.** *15th St SW (20242). Parking lot on N side, off Constitution Ave. Phone 202/426-6841 or 202/426-6839. www.nps.gov/wamo.* This obelisk, the tallest masonry structure in the world at 555 feet, was dedicated in 1885 to the memory of the first US president, George Washington. Before its dedication, it had been under construction for almost 40 years, a lack of funds and the Civil War both getting in the way of its completion. You can see where construction resumed after a 28-year delay about a quarter of the way up the monument, where two different shades of marble meet. Views of the majestic structure can be enjoyed anytime, but to enter, you must have a ticket. You can try your luck at getting one of the free tickets distributed at the kiosk at 15th and Madison starting at 8 am for same-day tours, or you can reserve tickets ahead of time by calling 800/967-2283. There is an elevator to the observation room at the 500-foot level. To take the 898 steps up or down, arrangements must be made in advance. (Daily 9 am-4:45 pm; closed Dec 25) **FREE**

Washington Walks. *Phone 202/484-1565. www.washingtonwalks.com.* Guided tours sponsored by Washington Walks are a great way to see the city up close. The group (along with Children's Concierge) runs two tours that kids will especially like: for Goodnight Mr. Lincoln, children can show up in pajamas at the Lincoln Memorial for stories, games, and music about Honest Abe. The White House Un-Tour offers role-playing (you might be asked to impersonate the president who loved bowling) and fun facts about the executive mansion. (Apr-Oct, days vary; rest of year by appointment) **$$**

⭐ **The White House.** *1600 Pennsylvania Ave NW (20502). Phone 202/456-7041 (recording). www.whitehouse.gov.* Constructed in 1800 under the supervision of George Washington, the house has been lived in by every US president since John Adams. It was burned by the British during the War of 1812 and reconstructed under the guidance of James Monroe (1817-1825). The West Wing, which includes the Oval Office, was built during Theodore Roosevelt's administration (1901-1909); before its construction, executive offices shared the second floor with the president's private quarters. The interior of the White House was gutted and rebuilt, using modern construction techniques, during the Truman administration; President Truman and family resided at Blair House for four years during the reconstruction. The Library and the Vermeil Room (on the Ground Floor); the East, Green, Blue, and Red Rooms; and the State Dining Room (on the State Floor) are accessible to groups often for tours. In this era of heightened security, you'll find Secret Service agents in every room, doubling as tour guides. Obtain tickets through your congressperson or senator. (Tues-Sat 7:30-11:30 am; closed Jan 1, Dec 25, and presidential functions) **FREE**

Special Events

Cherry Blossom Festival. *Tidal Basin and Ohio Dr NW (20003). Tidal Basin, West Potomac Park, East Potomac Park, Washington Monument grounds. Phone 202/547-1500. www.nationalcherryblossomfestival.org.* Nothing says spring more spectacularly than the sight of thousands of cherry trees in full bloom around the Jefferson Memorial. About 150 trees remain from the original 1912 gift of 3,000 from the city of Tokyo, but thousands of others have been planted in parks along the Tidal Basin, and for two weeks each year their lush pink and white blooms transform the cityscape. The festival celebrates this annual event with activities that appeal to visitors of all ages. Don't miss the Smithsonian's Kite Festival on the National Mall, the rousing parade, or Sakura Matsuri, a day-long Japanese street festival. Visitors can enjoy drummers, traditional dancers, and musical performances; demonstrations of flower arranging, calligraphy, and martial arts; a Taste of Japan food fair (who says that sushi isn't street food?); and the bustling Ginza Arcade, with shops selling everything from origami paper to antique kimonos. Late Mar-early Apr.

Concerts. *Independence and 15th St NW (20008). Phone 202/619-7222.* **Sylvan Theater,** Washington Monument grounds, June-Aug, days vary, phone 202/619-7222. **US Capitol,** west terrace, June-late Aug, Mon-Wed, Fri, Sun, phone 202/619-7222. **National Gallery of Art,** west garden court, Oct-June, Sun evenings; first-come basis, phone 202/842-6941. **Phillips Collection,** at Dupont-Kalorama Museum, Sept-May, Sun, phone 202/387-2151.

Easter Egg Roll. *White House Lawn. 1600 Pennsylvania Ave NW (20502). Phone 202/456-2200.* First introduced to Washington by Dolley Madison. Mon after Easter.

Festival of American Folklife. *National Mall. Constitution Ave (20004). Phone 202/357-2700.* Festival of folklife traditions from America and abroad. Sponsored by the Smithsonian Institution and National Park Service. Late June-early July.

July 4th Fireworks on the Mall. *National Mall (20001). Phone 202/426-6841. www.nps.gov/nama/events/july4/july4.htm.* You have to like a city that holds its fireworks show on the Fourth of July and not on the 3rd or whenever it's convenient. This display is extra-spectacular because the bombs burst in air over the monuments on the National Mall—a truly stirring sight. One of the best viewing spots is the Capitol, where the National Symphony Orchestra gives a rousing concert before the fireworks begin. Arrive early (the crowds get quite large) and picnic while you wait. July 4. **FREE**

Pageant of Peace. *Ellipse, south of White House. 15th and E sts NW (20319). Phone 202/619-7222.* Seasonal music, caroling; giant Christmas tree near the White House is lit by the president. Dec.

Motel/Motor Lodge

★ ★ **CHANNEL INN HOTEL.** *650 Water St SW (20024). Phone 202/554-2400; toll-free 800/368-5668; fax 202/863-1164. www.channelinn.com.* 100 rooms, 3 story. Check-out noon. TV; cable (premium). In-room modem link. Restaurant, bar; entertainment. Health club privileges. Outdoor pool. Near piers. **$**

D ⌖ SC

Hotel

★ ★ **HOLIDAY INN.** *550 C St SW (20024). Phone 202/479-4000; toll-free 800/465-4329; fax 202/479-4353. www.holiday-inn.com.* 516 rooms, 9 story. Check-out noon. TV; cable (premium). In-room modem link. Restaurant, bar. Health club privileges. In-house fitness room. Outdoor pool. **$$**

D ⌖ ⋀ ⌖ SC

Restaurant

★ **CANTINA MARINA.** *600 Water St SW (20024). Phone 202/554-8396.* Cajun menu. Closed holidays. Lunch, dinner. Bar. Outdoor seating. **$$**

D

★ ★ **HOGATE'S.** *800 Water St SW (20024). Phone 202/484-6300; fax 202/484-3840.* American menu. Closed Dec 25. Lunch, dinner, Sun brunch. Bar. Brunch entertainment. Children's menu. Outdoor seating. **$$$**

D

Maryland

Maryland prides itself on its varied terrain and diverse economy. Metropolitan life around the great cities of Baltimore and Washington, DC (the land was ceded from Maryland in 1791), is balanced by the rural atmosphere in central and southern Maryland and on the Eastern Shore, across the Chesapeake Bay. Green mountains in the western counties contrast with white Atlantic beaches. A flourishing travel industry, agricultural and dairy wealth in central Maryland, the seafood industry of the Bay and its tidal rivers, manufacturing and commerce in the cities, plus federal government and defense contracts combine to make the state prosperous.

Population: 5,296,486
Area: 9,838 square miles
Elevation: 0-3,360 feet
Peak: Backbone Mountain (Garrett County)
Entered Union: Seventh of original 13 states (April 28, 1788)
Capital: Annapolis
Motto: Manly deeds, womanly words
Nickname: Old Line State, Free State
Flower: Black-Eyed Susan
Bird: Baltimore Oriole
Tree: White Oak
Fair: Late August-early September in Timonium
Time Zone: Eastern
Website: www.mdisfun.org

Maryland's three-and-one-half centuries of history began in March 1634 when Lord Baltimore's brother, Leonard Calvert, solemnly knelt on tiny St. Clements Island, near the wide mouth of the Potomac, and named his new province in honor of Henrietta Maria, wife of Charles I, King of England. Calvert's awkward little ships, the *Ark* and the *Dove,* then carried the 222 passengers, including religious refugees, to a Native American village a few miles away. They purchased the village and named it Saint Maries Citty (now St. Mary's City). Religious tolerance was practiced from the colony's founding and was assured by law in 1649. The land was cleared, tobacco was planted, and over the years, profits built elegant mansions, many of which still stand.

Maryland was one of the 13 original colonies. Its first capital was St. Mary's City. In 1694, the capital was transferred to Annapolis, where it remains today.

Every war waged on US soil has seen major action by Marylanders. In 1755, British General Edward Braddock, assisted by Lieutenant Colonel George Washington, trained his army at Cumberland for the fight against the French and Indians. In the Revolution, General William Howe invaded Maryland at the head of Chesapeake Bay, and a battle was joined at Brandywine Creek in Pennsylvania before the British moved on to capture Philadelphia. Maryland troops in the Battle of Long Island made a heroic bayonet coverage of the retreat. The courageous action of the "Old Line" gave the state one of its nicknames. The War of 1812 saw Fort McHenry at Baltimore withstand attack by land and sea, with the action immortalized in the national anthem by Francis Scott Key, a Frederick lawyer. In the Civil War, Maryland was a major battleground at Antietam; troops moved back and forth through the state for the four bloody years of destruction.

A border state with commercial characteristics of both North and South, Maryland found its original dependence on tobacco relieved by the emerging Industrial Revolution. Modern factories, mills, and ironworks around Baltimore became important to the state's economy. Educational institutions were established and the port of Baltimore, at the mouth of the Patapsco River, flourished. In the mid-19th century, with the Baltimore & Ohio Railroad and the Chesapeake & Ohio Canal carrying freight to the fast-developing western states, Maryland thrived.

Sports enthusiasts have always thought well of Maryland. The state's thousands of miles of tidal shoreline allow plenty of elbow room for aquatic diversion. Maryland's race tracks include Pimlico (see BALTIMORE), featuring the nationally known Preakness Stakes, and Laurel. The "Maryland Million" is held alternately at Laurel and Pimlico. Deer hunting is allowed in most counties and goose hunting on the Eastern Shore. Historical sites cover the landscape, and more are constantly being opened up to the public by the state and National Park Service. Highways are good; reaching places in the Baltimore-Washington, DC, area is simplified by direct, high-speed, four-lane highways constructed around, between, and radiating from these cities.

When to Go/Climate

Spring and autumn are popular times to visit Maryland. Winter weather is unpredictable and summers can be hot and humid.

AVERAGE HIGH/LOW TEMPERATURES (°F)

Baltimore

Jan 40/23	**May** 74/53	**Sept** 79/58
Feb 44/26	**June** 83/62	**Oct** 67/46
Mar 54/34	**July** 87/67	**Nov** 57/37
Apr 64/43	**Aug** 85/66	**Dec** 42/28

Parks and Recreation

Water-related activities, hiking, riding, various other sports, picnicking and visitor centers, as well as camping, are available in many of Maryland's parks. Most state-maintained areas have small charges for parking and special services. Camping: $2-$22/site/night; stays limited to two weeks; most areas are open late March-early December, but the season varies from one park to the next; check-out is 3 pm; reservations for a stay of one week are available at Assateague—they may be obtained by writing directly to the park. Pets are allowed at the following parks (some special restrictions may apply; phone ahead): Green Ridge Forest, Elk Neck, Patapsco (Hollofield), Point Lookout, Rocky Gap, Savage River Forest, Susquehanna, Swallow Falls, Garrett Forest, Potomac Forest, and Pocomoke River (Milburn Landing). Day use: 8 am-sunset; closed Dec 25; fee Mar-Oct. For complete information, including information on cabins, contact the Maryland Department of Natural Resources, State Forest and Park Service, Tawes State Office Building E-3, 580 Taylor Ave, Annapolis 21401; phone toll-free 888/432-2267 or 800/830-3974. It is advisable to call parks before visiting, as some may be closed during the off-season.

FISHING AND HUNTING

Nontidal, nonresident fishing license, $20; five-day, $7; trout stamp, $5. Chesapeake Bay nonresident fishing license, $12; five-day, $4.

Nonresident hunting licenses: consolidated, $86-$135, depending on state of residence; three-day, $35; waterfowl stamp $6; regular deer stamp, $9.50; bow hunting deer stamp, $3.50; black powder deer stamp, $3.50; second deer stamp, $10. For the latest information, including *Maryland Sportfishing Guide* or the *Guide to Hunting, Trapping in Maryland,* contact Maryland Department of Natural Resources, Licensing & Registration Service, 580 Taylor Ave B-1, Annapolis 21404-1869; phone 410/260-8200.

Driving Information

Safety belts are mandatory for the driver and passengers in the front seat of a vehicle. Any child 10 years and under must be in an approved passenger restraint anywhere in a vehicle. Any child under 4 years or weighing 40 pounds or less must be in an approved safety seat. For more information, phone 410/486-3101.

INTERSTATE HIGHWAY SYSTEM

The following alphabetical listing of Maryland towns shows that these cities are within 10 miles of the indicated interstate highways. Check a highway map for the nearest exit.

Highway Number	Cities/Towns within 10 Miles
Interstate 68	Cumberland.
Interstate 70	Baltimore, Columbia, Ellicott City, Frederick, Hagerstown.

Interstate 81	Hagerstown.
Interstate 83	Baltimore, Cockeysville, Towson.
Interstate 95	Aberdeen, Baltimore, College Park, Elkton, Havre de Grace, Laurel, Silver Spring, Towson.

Additional Visitor Information

The Maryland guide to travel, *Destination Maryland,* and a calendar of events can be obtained from the Maryland Office of Tourism Development, 217 E Redwood St, Baltimore 21202; phone 800/543-1036.

There are several visitor information centers in Maryland; visitors who stop by will find information and brochures helpful in planning stops at points of interest. Their locations are as follows: on I-95 (N & S) near Laurel; on I-70 (E & W) between Hagerstown and Frederick; on US 15 S at Emmitsburg; on I-95 S near North East; on US 48 E near Friendsville; on US 13 N near Maryland-Virginia line; in the State House, Annapolis; Crain memorial, on US 301 N, Newburg; and in Bay Country, on US 301 N/S, Centreville. (Daily; closed holidays)

Calendar Highlights

FEBRUARY

National Outdoor Show *(Cambridge). Phone 800/522-TOUR.* Goose and duck calling, log sawing, crab picking, and trap setting contests; entertainment.

APRIL

Point-to-Point Steeplechase *(Cockeysville). Phone 410/557-9466.* Three well-known meets on consecutive weekends—My Lady's Manor, Grand National, and Maryland Hunt Cup.

MAY

Maryland Preakness Celebration *(Baltimore). Phone 410/837-3030.* Statewide festival; events include a hot-air balloon festival, parade, steeplechase, celebrity golf tournament, block parties, and schooner race.

Mid-Atlantic Maritime Festival *(St. Michaels). Chesapeake Bay Maritime Museum. Phone 410/745-2916.* Nautical celebration with fly-fishing demonstration, skipjack races, boat building contest, boat parade, seafood festival, and cooking contest.

AUGUST

Montgomery County Agricultural Fair *(Gaithersburg). Phone 301/926-3100.* One of the East Coast's leading county fairs; emphasis on agriculture, 4-H activities; animal exhibits, home arts; antique farm equipment; tractor pull, horse pull, demolition derby; rodeo; entertainment.

State Fair *(Towson). Timonium Fairgrounds. Phone 410/252-0200.* Ten-day festival of home arts; entertainment, midway; agricultural demonstrations, thoroughbred horse racing, livestock presentations.

SEPTEMBER

New Market Days *(Frederick). In New Market. Phone 301/831-6755.* Nostalgic revival of the atmosphere of a 19th-century village; costumed guides, period crafts, and events held in the "Antiques Capital of Maryland."

OCTOBER

St. Mary's County Oyster Festival *(Leonardtown). County Fairgrounds. Phone 301/863-5015.* National oyster shucking contests; oyster cook-off, seafood and crafts.

Autumn Glory Festival *(Oakland). Phone 301/387-4386.* Celebrates fall foliage. Features arts and crafts, five-string banjo contest, state fiddle contest, western Maryland tournament of bands, parades, and antique show.

NOVEMBER

Annapolis by Candlelight *(Annapolis). For information, contact Historic Annapolis Foundation, phone 800/603-4020.*

DEEP CREEK LAKE, MARYLAND'S WESTERN PLAYGROUND

Out in western Maryland's Garrett County, the local folks like to call massive Deep Creek Lake the state's "hidden secret." But the secret is getting out, and the massive lake has become the centerpiece for a wealth of vigorous outdoor adventures: water skiing, whitewater rafting, hiking, back-road bicycling, kayaking, fly-fishing, canoeing, sailing, and swimming. On a drive around the lake, you can partake in as many activities as you choose—outfitters are on hand to rent all the necessary equipment—or simply enjoy the sublime mountain views. Maryland's largest freshwater lake, Deep Creek, is 12 miles long, but so etched with fingerlike coves that the shoreline stretches for 65 miles. Surrounded by the forested ridges and splashing streams of mountain wilderness, the lake, at an altitude of 2,300 feet, treats summer visitors to a cooling respite from the city. Begin this two-day, 400-mile drive in Baltimore and head west on I-70 and I-68 to exit 14 at Keysers Ridge. Take US 219 south to the Visitor Center, which is on the right just outside the village of McHenry. Plan to spend the night in one of McHenry's inns, hotels, or motels. The trip from Baltimore to McHenry is about 180 miles, a scenic ride that carries you across a series of green mountain ridges. To break up the trip, pull off I-68 at Cumberland, immediately recognizable by the castle-like spires and turrets of its courthouse and churches. George Washington is said to have assumed his first military command at Fort Cumberland, and his one-room log cabin and remnants of the fort can still be seen here. Cumberland is the terminus of the Chesapeake and Ohio Canal, which originates in Washington, DC, and you can rent a bicycle and ride along the tow path for miles. At Deep Creek Lake, follow the signs to Deep Creek Lake State Park, which maintains a nice 700-foot-long sandy swimming beach, a lovely place to relax after the trip from the city. The Discovery Center, an attractive structure of stone, wood, and soaring windows, features displays about the region's natural history and mining heritage. Ranger talks, walks, and canoe trips are offered. On the second day of your trip, take US 219 south from McHenry to the turn-off to Swallow Falls State Park. For an easy hike, follow the 1 1/2-mile path that scrambles in a loop past four waterfalls. At the trail head, the park has preserved a 37-acre stand of virgin hemlock and white pine estimated to be 300 years old. After 1/4 mile, Muddy Creek Falls—the state's highest at 52 feet—cascades down a staircase of rocks into a large pool. You are welcome to splash in the many pools along this trail. Next, follow signs south to the town of Oakland and then begin your scenic return to Baltimore via Route 135 northeast to US 220 north to I-68 east. Just beyond Bloomington on Route 135, make a detour left on Savage River Road. For about 5 1/2 miles along this road, the Savage River splashes. So narrow, mean, and harrowing is the course, say local tourism officials, that it was picked as the site of the 1989 Whitewater World Championships and the 1992 US Canoe & Kayak Team Olympic Trials. A couple of suspension bridges built for the events still leap the river. While here, imagine yourself trying to negotiate a kayak through the frenzied chaos of water and rocks. Retrace your path to Route 135 northeast. About 10 miles east of Cumberland, take a break at Rocky Gap State Park, two minutes off the interstate, which tempts with a couple of fine sandy beaches in a forested mountain setting. **(Approximately 400 miles)**

EASTERN SHORE OF THE CHESAPEAKE BAY

North America's largest estuary, the Chesapeake Bay commands more than 4,500 miles of shoreline, much of it in Maryland. A vast sea known for its rich history and savory shellfish, it is one of the Mid-Atlantic's most popular destinations. Inviting inns, other lodgings, and fine seafood restaurants are plentiful on Maryland's Eastern Shore. A two-day driving tour covering about 250 miles makes a fine introduction to the bay and to the watermen and their families who harvest the seafood that appears on every menu. Begin your drive in Annapolis, Maryland's beautiful old capital, which doubles as the bay's sailing headquarters. In summer, catch the regular Wednesday evening races, when as many as 100 boats may compete. The finish is easily visible from City Dock at the foot of the city's colonial-era streets. From Annapolis, take US 50 east across the soaring Chesapeake Bay Bridge. Just before you reach the bridge, a five-minute detour leads to Sandy Point State Park, the only stop on this drive where you can take a dip in the bay. At the eastern end of the bridge, turn north onto US 301 to State Route 213 north to Chestertown. Founded in 1706, Chestertown is a pretty village with a collection of 18th- and 19th-century homes, several of them situated along the scenic Chester River. After browsing in the shops of High and Cross streets, take Route 20 west to Rock Hall, a sailing and charter fishing port. Retrace your path to Chestertown, and take Route 213 south to US 50 south. In Easton, take Route 33 west to the historic sailing port of St. Michaels, an inviting place to spend the night. One of the Mid-Atlantic's prettiest little towns, its lovely inns, fine restaurants, offbeat shops on Talbot Street, and expansive bay views are irresistible. So, too, are the charming little back streets, lined with lovely homes dating back to the 18th and 19th centuries. Your first stop should be the Chesapeake Bay Maritime Museum, which focuses on the Chesapeake. The museum's 18-acre harbor site features more than a dozen historic structures, including a fully restored 1879 lighthouse complete with flashing light. Stop by Waterman's Wharf, where you can try your skill at crab fishing. The Waterfowling Building displays beautifully carved duck decoys. Boat builders are often at work restoring historic bay work boats for the museum's large collection. The *Patriot,* a cruise ship departing from the museum's dock, takes visitors on a 60-minute tour up the Miles River, a bay tributary. From St. Michaels, follow Route 33 to its end at Tilghman Island, a charter fishing port. Plan on having lunch at one of its waterside seafood houses. On the return trip to St. Michaels, stop about 3 miles east of the city and take the road south (right) to Bellevue. There you can catch the little Bellevue-Oxford Ferry for a ten-minute ride across the Tred Avon River to Oxford, a sleepy pleasure boat port dating back to 1694. To stretch your legs, take a walk along the Strand, a lovely river promenade, or rent a bicycle and pedal among the quiet streets. From Oxford, return to Annapolis via Route 333 and US 50, stopping briefly in Easton to admire its attractive, colonial-looking town center and to investigate its engaging shops and galleries. **(Approximately 250 miles)**

Baltimore

Settled 1661 **Pop** 654,154 **Elev** 32 ft **Area code** 410 and 443

Information Baltimore Area Convention & Visitors Association, 100 Light St, 12th floor, 21202; 410/659-7300 or 800/343-3468

Web www.baltimore.org

Suburbs Aberdeen, Cockeysville, Columbia, Ellicott City, Pikesville, Towson.

Metropolis of Maryland and one of America's great cities, Baltimore is a city of neighborhoods built on strong ethnic foundations, a city of historic events that helped shape the nation, and a city that has achieved an incredible downtown renaissance in the past 20 years. It is a major East Coast manufacturing center and, almost from its beginning, a world seaport. Several colleges and universities, foremost of which is Johns Hopkins, make their home here.

Lying midway between North and South and enjoying a rich cultural mixture of both, Baltimore is one of the nation's oldest cities. When British troops threatened Philadelphia during the Revolutionary War, the Continental Congress fled to Baltimore, which served as the nation's capital for a little more than two months.

In October 1814, a British fleet attacked the city by land and sea. The defenders of Fort McHenry withstood the naval bombardment for 25 hours until the British gave up. Francis Scott Key saw the huge American flag still flying above the fort and was inspired to pen "The Star-Spangled Banner."

Rapid growth in the early 19th century resulted from the opening of the National Road and then the nation's first railroad, the Baltimore & Ohio.

Politics was a preoccupation in those days, and the city hosted many national party conventions. At least seven presidents and three losing candidates were nominated here. Edgar Allan Poe's mysterious death in the city may have been at the hands of shady electioneers.

Untouched physically by the Civil War, effects came later when Southerners flooded in to rebuild their fortunes and commerce was disrupted by the loss of Southern markets. A disastrous fire in 1904 destroyed 140 acres of the business district but the city recovered rapidly and, during the two World Wars, was a major shipbuilding and naval repair center.

In the 1950s and early 1960s, Baltimore was the victim of the apathy and general decay that struck the industrial Northeast. But the city fought back, replacing hundreds of acres of slums, rotting wharves, and warehouses with gleaming new office plazas, parks, and public buildings. The Inner Harbor was transformed into a huge public area with shops, museums, restaurants, and frequent concerts and festivals. Millions of tourists and proud Baltimoreans flock downtown to enjoy the sights and activities.

Famous residents and native sons and daughters include Babe Ruth; Edgar Allan Poe; H. L. Mencken; Mother Elizabeth Ann Seton; Eubie Blake; Ogden Nash; Thurgood Marshall; Wallis Warfield Simpson, who became the Duchess of Windsor; and more recent sports legends Brooks Robinson, Johnny Unitas, Jim Palmer, and Cal Ripken.

Additional Visitor Information

For additional accommodations, see BALTIMORE/WASHINGTON INTERNATIONAL AIRPORT AREA, which follows BALTIMORE.

Maps, brochures, and calendars of events are available at the Baltimore Area Visitors Center, 301 E Pratt St, Constellation Pier, 21202; phone 410/837-INFO or 800/282-6632.

Transportation

AIRPORTS
See BALTIMORE/WASHINGTON INTERNATIONAL AIRPORT AREA.

CAR RENTAL AGENCIES
See IMPORTANT TOLL-FREE NUMBERS.

PUBLIC TRANSPORTATION
Bus and subway (Mass Transit Administration), phone 410/539-5000.

RAIL PASSENGER SERVICE
Amtrak 800/872-7245; MARC (commuter train serving Baltimore and Washington, DC) 800/325-RAIL or 410/291-4267.

What to See and Do

American Visionary Art Museum. *800 Key Hwy (21230). Phone 410/244-1900. www.avam.org.* Visitors with a penchant for the offbeat or the just plain bizarre should not miss this singular museum. The Whirligig—a 55-foot-tall, wind-powered, pinwheel-like sculpture made from bicycle wheels, car parts, and cables—stands in Sculpture Plaza as a towering symbol of the museum's mission. The museum defines visionary art as works produced by individuals without formal training whose art stems from an inner vision. Opened in 1995, the museum has more than 4,000 pieces in its collection. The main building holds seven indoor galleries. Separate from this building are the wildflower garden, a wedding chapel and altar built out of tree limbs and flowers, and the tall sculpture barn, which once showcased psychic Uri Geller's art, including a car he covered with 5,000 psychically bent forks and spoons. The museum also plans to add a "Thou Art Creative Center," an interactive area for visitors. (Tues-Sun 10 am-6 pm; closed Mon, Thanksgiving, Dec 25) **$$**

Antique Row. *N Howard and W Read sts (21201).* Antique Row, which has existed in Baltimore for over 100 years, is an antique lover's paradise. With more than 20 dealers and shops that also include restoration services, the area offers enough displayed and hidden treasures to satisfy diehard shoppers and casual browsers alike. The different shops specialize in items such as European furniture, Tiffany lamps, china, and rare books.

The Avenue in Hampden. *36th St (21211). www.hampdenmainstreet.org* Although the four blocks that make up the Avenue total only a half mile, visitors will be amazed at all there is to see in this eclectic North Baltimore neighborhood. Novelty shops, vintage clothing stores, casual restaurants, and art galleries line Hampden's main drag, and the treasures that guests can find in these shops range from kitschy to sublime. If you're looking for a down-home meal, drop in at Mamie's Café or Café Hon.

B & O Railroad Museum. *901 W Pratt St (21223). Phone 410/752-2490. www.borail.org.* This museum, affiliated with the Smithsonian, celebrates the birthplace of railroading in America and depicts the industry's economic and cultural influences. Encompassing 40 acres, the museum's collection of loco-motives is the oldest and most comprehensive in the country. Its exhibits are divided among three main buildings. In the Roundhouse, visitors can board and explore more than a dozen of the "iron horses," which include a rail post office car and the Tom Thumb train. The second floor of the Annex building has an impressive display of working miniature-scale trains. The Mount Clair Station, exhibiting the story of the B & O railroad, was built in 1851 to replace the 1829 original, which was the first rail depot in the country. Outside, the museum features more trains, such as the Chessie, the largest steam locomo-tive. On certain weekends, visitors can take a train ride. In 2003, the museum marked its 175th anniversary. (Daily; closed major holidays) **$$**

Babe Ruth Birthplace and Museum. *216 Emory St (21230). Phone 410/727-1539. www.baberuthmuseum.com.* Although Babe Ruth played for the New York Yankees, Baltimore calls him one of its native sons. The house where this legend was born has been transformed into a museum that showcases his life and career. Visitors can see rare family photographs as well as a com-plete record of his home runs. The museum also features exhibits about the Baltimore Colts and Orioles. Every February 6, the museum commemorates Babe Ruth's birthday by offering free admission to all visitors.(Daily 10 am-5 pm, until 4 pm Nov-Mar; closed Jan 1, Thanksgiving, Dec 25) **$$**

Baltimore crab. *Throughout the city.* A visit to Charm City wouldn't be com-plete without a sampling of the local delicacy. Crab is a staple of Maryland's economy and diet. It comes prepared in a variety of forms: deep-fried, soft-shelled, or flaked and served as crab cakes. However, the classic version is steamed hard crabs. Restaurants serve steamed crab without adornment. Don't be put off when your waiter covers the table with plain brown paper and then hands you a wooden mallet, paper napkins, and a plastic bib. When the crabs come to the table, they will be hot, red from the steam, and covered in Old Bay Seasoning. Once you crack open the shell and taste the sweet, white meat, you'll be hooked. Crab is in season from March to October, but peak season is July through September.

Baltimore Maritime Museum. *802 S Caroline St (21231). Inner Harbor area. Phone 410/396-3453. www.baltomaritimemuseum.org.* This museum's featured ships include the USS *Torsk*, a World War II submarine; the Coast Guard cutter *Taney*; and the lightship *Chesapeake*. All the ships have been designated National Historic Landmarks. (Spring, summer, and fall, Sun-Thurs 10 am-5:30 pm, Fri-Sat until 6:30 pm; winter, Fri-Sun 10:30 am-5 pm) **$$**

Baltimore Museum of Art. *10 Art Museum Dr (21218). Near N Charles and 31st sts. Phone 410/396-7100. www.artbma.org.* Located near Johns Hopkins University, this museum opened in 1923 and was designed by John Russell Pope, the architect of the National Gallery in Washington, DC. The museum has eight permanent exhibits featuring works from the periods of Impressionism to modern art. It boasts the second largest collection of works by Andy Warhol. However, its jewel is the Cone collection, which includes more than 3,000 pieces by artists such as Picasso, Van Gogh, Renoir, Cezanne, and Matisse. The Matisse collection is the largest in the Western Hemisphere. Visitors will also want to see the 3-acre sculpture garden, which contains art by Alexander Calder and Henry Moore. (Wed-Fri 11 am-5 pm, Sat-Sun 11 am-6 pm; free admission first Thurs of each month; closed Mon, Tues, major holidays) **$$**

Baltimore Museum of Industry. *1415 Key Hwy, Inner Harbor South (21230). Phone 410/727-4808. www.thebmi.com.* This museum educates visitors about the vital role that industry and manufacturing played in Baltimore's economic and cultural development. Located in a renovated oyster cannery on the west side of the Inner Harbor, the museum opened in 1977. Its exhibits showcase such trades as printing, garment making, canning, and metalworking. Guests will learn about the invention of Noxema, the disposable bottle cap, and even the first umbrella. Or they can explore the SS *Baltimore*, the only operating coal-fired tugboat on the East Coast that is now a National Historic Landmark. Visitors can also see the Mini-Mariner, a restored 1937 working prototype of the World War II boat bomber. The museum also has "Theatre on the Harbor," which presents touring and in-house productions. Past shows have included "Gizmo's Invention Show" and "Right Place, Right Time, Wright Brothers." (Mon-Sat; closed Thanksgiving, Dec 24 and 25) **$$$**

Baltimore Patriot. *Pier 1, 301 E Pratt St (21202). Phone 410/685-4288.* Ninety-minute tours around Baltimore's Inner Harbor. (Apr-Oct, daily)

Baltimore Streetcar Museum. *1901 Falls Rd, under North Ave Bridge (21201). Phone 410/547-0264. www.baltimoremd.com/streetcar/.* Eleven electric streetcars and two horsecars used in the city between 1859 and 1963; 1 1/4-mile rides (fee). (June-Oct, Sat noon-5 pm; rest of year, Mon-Fri, Sun noon-5 pm; also open Memorial Day, July 4, Labor Day) **$$**

Baltimore Zoo. *1 Druid Hill Park Lake Dr (21217). Phone 410/366-5466. www.baltimorezoo.org.* Located in Druid Hill Park, this third oldest zoo in the United States covers 180 acres and features more than 2,250 animals. Children will be intrigued by the scaly inhabitants of the reptile house. They can also travel to another continent by visiting the giraffes and elephants in the African Safari exhibit, as well as ride the carousel or try out the climbing wall. The zoo also hosts special events during Halloween and Christmas. (Daily; closed Thanksgiving, Dec 25) **$$$$**

Basilica of the National Shrine of the Assumption. *408 N Charles St (21201). Phone 410/727-3565. www.baltimorebasilica.org.* Now a co-cathedral, this was the first Roman Catholic cathedral in the US. Bishop John Carroll, head of the diocese of Baltimore from its establishment in 1789, blessed the cornerstone in 1806. The church was dedicated in 1821. Architectural design by B. H. Latrobe. Tours Sun after 10:45 am mass or by appointment. (Daily)

Battle Monument. *Calvert St at Fayette St (21222).* (1815) Memorial to those who fell defending the city in the War of 1812.

Boordy Vineyards. *12820 Long Green Pike, Fork (21051). Phone 410/592-5015. www.boordy.com.* Guests who live by the maxim *In Vino Veritas* should visit Maryland's oldest family-run winery. Only a 15-minute drive from Baltimore, Boordy sits in the serene countryside. With its rows and rows of delicate plants and 19th-century farm buildings, this winery will surely charm visitors. Daily tours are available, and Boordy hosts special events, such as wine tastings and live musical performances. **FREE**

Charles Center. *36 S Charles St (21201).* Business area with European-style plazas, part of an overhead walkway system, shops, restaurants, and outdoor activities. Prize-winning office building by Mies van der Rohe borders center plaza. Also here is

Morris A. Mechanic Theatre. *25 Hopkins Plz (21201). Phone 410/481-SEAT. www.themechanic.org.* Hosts Broadway productions.

Church Home and Hospital. *Broadway and Fairmount aves (21231), in East Balitimore.* Edgar Allan Poe died here in 1849.

City Court House. *100 N Calvert St (21202).* (1900) On the steps is a statue of Cecil Calvert, brother of Leonard and founder of Maryland as the second Lord Baltimore.

City Hall. *100 N Holiday St (21202), downtown. Tours by appointment, Phone 410/396-3100.* Post-Civil War architecture, restored to original detail. **FREE**

City of Baltimore Conservatory. *Druid Hill Park. 2600 Madison Ave (21217). Phone 410/396-0180.* This graceful building (circa 1885) houses a large variety of tropical plants. Special shows during Easter, Nov, and the Christmas season. (Thurs-Sun) **FREE**

Cylburn Arboretum. *4915 Greenspring Ave (21209). Phone 410/396-0180.* Marked nature trails. Nature museum, ornithological room, horticultural library in restored mansion; shade and formal gardens, All-American Selection Garden, Garden of the Senses. (Daily 6 am-4 pm) **FREE**

Duckpin Bowling. *Throughout the city. Phone 410/377-8115.* Despite its name, no ducks play a part in this game, which originated in Baltimore in 1900. The object of the game is similar to that of bowling except that the pins and balls are smaller. However, first-time players should not be fooled by the diminutive pieces. They'll soon discover that the smaller pins are, in fact, even harder to knock down! Alleys are open throughout Baltimore, including at **Taylor's Stoneleigh Duckpin Bowling Center,** 6703 York Rd. **$**

Edgar Allan Poe Grave. *At Westminster Hall and Burial Grounds, Fayette and Green sts, downtown.* Baltimore's oldest cemeteries also contain the graves of many prominent early Marylanders. Westminster Burying Ground and Catacomb tours by appointment (Apr-Nov, first and third Fri and Sat). **$$**

Edgar Allan Poe House and Museum. *203 N Amity St (21223). Phone 410/396-7932. www.ci.baltimore.md.us/government/historic/poehouse.html.* The famed author and father of the macabre lived in this house from 1832 to 1835. The faint of heart should beware, as several psychics have reported ghostly presences here. Haunted or not, the house and museum scare up many Poe artifacts, such as period furniture, a desk and telescope owned by Poe, and Gustave Dore's illustrations of *The Raven.* Around January 19, the museum hosts a birthday celebration that includes readings and theatrical performances of Poe's work. (Apr-Dec) **$**

Enoch Pratt Free Library. *400 Cathedral St, at Franklin St, downtown (21201). Phone 410/396-5430. www.pratt.lib.md.us.* City's public library. H. L. Mencken and Edgar Allan Poe collections. (Sept-May, daily; rest of year, Mon-Sat; closed holidays)

Federal Hill. *Bordered by Hughes St, Key Hwy, Hanover St, and Cross St (21227). Inner Harbor area.* View of the city harbor and skyline. Named after a celebration that occurred here in 1788 to mark Maryland's ratification of the Constitution.

Fell's Point. *812 S Ann St (21231). Broadway, S of Fleet St to the harbor. ww.fellspoint.us.* Shipbuilding and maritime center, this neighborhood dates back to 1730; approximately 350 original residential structures. Working tugboats and tankers can be observed from the docks.

First Unitarian Church. *Charles and Franklin sts (21201). Phone 410/685-2330. www.toad.net/~firstubalt/.* (1817) William Ellery Channing preached a sermon here that hastened the establishment of the Unitarian denomination. Example of Classic Revival architecture.

Fort McHenry National Monument and Historic Shrine. *End of E Fort Ave (21230). Phone 410/962-4299.* Fort McHenry boasts a stunning view of the harbor, authentic re-created structures, and a wealth of living history that will fascinate both history buffs and casual visitors. In addition to being the site of the battle that inspired Francis Scott Key to pen "The Star-Spangled Banner" in 1814, the fort was a defensive position during the Revolutionary War, a POW camp for Confederate prisoners during the Civil War, and an army hospital during World War I. The fort's exhibits showcase these exciting events. Park rangers are knowledgeable and helpful, and they encourage visitors to participate in the twice-daily flag changes. Summer weekends feature precision drill and music performed by volunteers in Revolutionary War uniforms. (Daily; closed Jan 1, Dec 25) **$$**

Narrated cruises. *Phone 410/962-4299.* The *Baltimore Patriot* departs from Inner Harbor Finger Pier to Fort McHenry and Fell's Point (Memorial Day-Labor Day). Also departures from Fort McHenry and Fell's Point. For other tours, contact Maryland Tours, Inc. **$$$**

Gunpowder Falls State Park. *2813 Jerusalem Rd, Kingsville (21087). Phone 410/592-2897.* Approximately 16,000 acres, located in the Gunpowder River Valley. **Hammerman Area,** E on US 40, right onto Ebenezer Rd, 5 miles to the park entrance in Chase, is a developed day-use area. Offers swimming beach, windsurfing beach, boating, marina (Dundee Creek); picnicking, playground. Other areas offer hiking/biking trails, canoeing, and trout fishing. Standard fees.

Harborplace. *200 E Pratt St (21202). Phone 410/332-4191. www.harbor place.com.* This shopping center is the most recognizable symbol of Baltimore's downtown and harbor renaissance. With its architecture of glass and exposed pipes and beams, Harborplace serves as a model for other cities' revitalization plans. Developed by James W. Rouse, the shopping mecca opened in 1980 and boasts more than 130 stores and restaurants. Visitors who want to take a break can go outside and walk on the brick-paved promenade that runs along the water's edge. Harborplace also has a small outdoor amphitheater, where, in good weather, guests are treated to free performances by jugglers, musicians, singers, and military and concert bands. (Daily)

Holocaust Memorial. *Corner of Water, Gay, and Lombard sts (21202), downtown. Phone 410/752-2630.* Simple stone memorial to the victims of the Holocaust.

Jewish Historical Society of Maryland. *15 Lloyd St (21202), downtown. Phone 410/732-6400. www.jhsm.org.* Buildings include Lloyd St Synagogue (1845), the oldest in Maryland; B'nai Israel Synagogue (1876); and the Jewish Museum of Maryland. (Tues-Thurs and Sun noon-4 pm; or by appointment; closed Jewish holidays) Research archives (Mon-Fri, by appointment). **$**

Johns Hopkins Medical Institutions. *550 N Broadway (21205). Phone 410/955-7894. www.hopkinsmedicine.org.* (1889) Widely known as a leading medical school, research center, and teaching hospital. Victorian buildings.

Johns Hopkins University. *3400 N Charles St (21218). Phone 410/516-8000. www.jhu.edu.* Founded in 1876 and located in northern Baltimore, Johns Hopkins is an impressive institution of scholarship and research. It enrolls 18,000 students and is renowned for the Bloomberg School of Public Health, the Peabody Institute (a music conservatory) and its Applied Physics Laboratory, located 30 minutes outside of Baltimore. *US News & World Report* continuously ranks its affiliated hospital, which has its own separate campus in eastern Baltimore, as one of the top medical facilities in the country. Guests to the campus should visit the Homewood mansion. This elegant, Federal red-bricked building was once owned by Charles Carroll, one of the signers of the Declaration of Independence. It was deeded to the university in 1902 and now serves as a historic home. Guided tours are available. Located on the campus grounds are

Bufano Sculpture Garden. *Dunning Park, behind Mudd Hall.* A wooded retreat with animals sculpted by artist Beniamino Bufano. **FREE**

Evergreen House. *4545 N Charles St (21210), approximately 2 miles N of Homewood campus. Phone 410/516-0341. www.jhu.edu/~evrgreen/evergreen.html.* On 26 wooded acres; features Classical Revival architecture and a formal garden. Library (35,000 volumes).

Post-impressionist paintings, Japanese and Chinese collections, and Tiffany glass. Tours (daily). **$$**

Homewood House Museum. *Near 34th St. Phone 410/516-5589. www.jhu.edu/~hwdhouse/.* (1801) Former country home of Charles Carroll, Jr., whose father was a signer of the Declaration of Independence; period furnishings. (Tues-Sat, also Sun afternoons) Guided tours (hourly). **$$$**

Joseph Meyerhoff Symphony Hall. *1212 Cathedral St (21201). Phone 410/783-8000 or 410/783-8100. www.baltimoresymphony.org.* Permanent residence of the Baltimore Symphony Orchestra.

Lacrosse Hall of Fame Museum. *113 W University Pkwy (21210). Phone 410/235-6882. www.lacross.org/museum/.* Team trophies, display of lacrosse artifacts and memorabilia, including rare photographs and art, vintage equipment and uniforms. Also historical video documentary. (Feb-May, Tues-Sat; June-Jan, Mon-Fri; closed holidays) **$**

Lexington Market. *400 W Lexington St (21201). Between Eutaw and Paca sts, downtown. Phone 410/685-6169. www.lexingtonmarket.com.* This under-roof market is more than two centuries old. Covering two blocks, it has more than 130 stalls offering fresh vegetables, seafood, meats, baked goods, and prepared foods that will whet any appetite. Vendors outside the market sell clothing, jewelry, T-shirts, and other miscellaneous items. Throughout the year, the market hosts several events, such as the Chocolate Festival in October, which boasts free samples and a chocolate-eating contest. But the most anticipated event at the market is Lunch with the Elephants. Every March, Ringling Brothers and Barnum & Bailey Circus elephants parade up Eutaw Street accompanied by fanfare, live music, and clowns. When they finally reach the market, they are served "lunch," which consists of 1,100 oranges, 1,000 apples, 500 heads of lettuce, 700 bananas, 400 pears, and 500 carrots. (Mon-Sat; closed holidays) **FREE**

Lovely Lane Museum. *2200 St. Paul St (21218). Phone 410/889-4458.* Permanent and changing exhibits of items of Methodist church history since 1760. Guided tours (Mon-Fri; also Sun after services and by appointment; closed holidays). **FREE**

Maryland Historical Society. *201 W Monument St (21201). Phone 410/685-3750. www.mdhs.org.* The state's oldest cultural institution includes a library, a museum, and even a small press that promotes scholarship about Maryland's history and material culture. The library has more than 5.4 million works and is a valuable resource for genealogists. The society's collection of historical artifacts includes the original draft of "The Star Spangled Banner" and the world's largest collection of 19th-century American silver. It also sponsors educational programs, such as lectures and living history presentations. (Daily) **$**

Maryland Institute, College of Art. *1300 Mount Royal Ave (21217). Phone 410/669-9200. www.mica.edu.* (1826) 880 students. Institute hosts frequent contemporary art exhibitions. Campus distinguished by recycled buildings and white marble Italianate main building. (Daily)

Maryland Science Center & Davis Planetarium. *601 Light St (21230). Phone 410/685-5225 (recording). www.mdsci.org.* This interactive center proves that science is anything but boring. Located in the Inner Harbor, the three-story building contains hundreds of exhibits guaranteed to spark young (and older) minds. In the Chesapeake Bay exhibit, you can learn about the delicate ecosystem that exists beneath the water. Or you can explore the mysteries of the human body in BodyLink. The Kids Room, for guests 8 and younger, gives children the chance to operate a fish camera or dress up like turtles. Don't miss the Hubble Space Telescope National Visitor Center, a 4,000-square-foot interactive space gallery, which has more than 20 hands-on activities and 120 high-resolution images that allow guests to see space through the Hubble's eye. Those who can't get enough of outer space should also visit the Davis Planetarium and the Crosby-Ramsey Memorial Observatory, both on site. The center's IMAX theater will thrill guests with its five-stories-tall movie screen and 3-D capability. (Daily) **$$$**

Minnie V Harbor Tours. *Docks near Pier 1, Pratt St, Inner Harbor area. Phone 410/685-9062.* A 45-foot Chesapeake Bay skipjack sloop built in 1906. Ninety-minute harbor tours give 24 passengers the opportunity to help crew the boat (open weekends).

Morgan State University. *1700 E Cold Spring Ln (21251). Phone 443/885-3333. www.morgan.edu.* (1867) 5,100 students. The James E. Lewis Museum of Art has changing exhibits (Mon-Fri; weekends by appointment; closed holidays).

Mother Seton House. *600 N Paca St (21201), downtown. Phone 410/523-3443.* Home of St. Elizabeth Ann Bayley Seton from 1808 to 1809. Here she established the forerunner of the parochial school system, as well as an order of nuns that eventually became the Daughters & Sisters of Charity in the US and Canada. (Sat and Sun afternoons, also by appointment; closed Jan 1, Easter, Dec 25) **FREE**

Mount Clare Museum House. *In Carroll Park at 1500 Washington Blvd (21230). Phone 410/837-3262.* (1760) Oldest mansion in Baltimore, former home of Charles Carroll, barrister. Eighteenth- and 19th-century furnishings. Guided tours on the hour. (Tues-Sun; closed Jan, holidays) **$$**

Mount Vernon Place United Methodist Church. *10 E Mount Vernon Pl (21202). Phone 410/685-5290.* (circa 1850) Brownstone with balcony and grillwork extending the entire width of the house; spiral staircase suspended from three floors; library with century-old painting on the ceiling; drawing room. (Mon-Fri; closed holidays and Mon after Easter) **FREE**

MPT (Maryland Public Television). *11767 Owings Mills Blvd # 2 (21117). Phone 410/356-5600 or 800/223-3MPT (surrounding states). ww.mpt.org.* Tours of the state's television network studios. (By appointment) **FREE**

MV Lady Baltimore. *West Bulkhead, 301 Light St (21202). Phone 410/727-3113 or 800/695-LADY.* Round-trip cruises to Annapolis (June-Aug, Wed); also cruises to the Chesapeake & Delaware Canal (three selected Sun in Oct). *Bay Lady* has lunch and dinner cruises (Apr-Oct, daily; limited schedule rest of year).

⭐ **National Aquarium.** *501 E Pratt St (21202). Inner Harbor area. Phone 410/576-3800. www.aqua.org.* This aquarium's glass-and-steel pyramid shape is as unusual and stunning as the more than 15,000 sea creatures it houses. Located in the Inner Harbor, the National Aquarium introduces guests to stingrays, sharks, puffins, seals, and even a giant Pacific octopus. Visitors can explore the danger and mystery of a living South American tropical rain forest complete with poisonous frogs, exotic birds, piranha, and swinging tamirin monkeys, or delight in the underwater beauty of the replicated Atlantic coral reef. The Children's Cove, a touch pool, provides an interactive experience for kids. In the Marine Mammal Pavilion, a high-tech dolphin show entertains and teaches guests about these intelligent creatures. Visitors particularly enjoy watching trainers feed the animals. Daily feeding schedules are posted in the lobby. (Daily 9 am-7 pm, Fri until 10 pm; closed Thanksgiving, Dec 25) **$$$$** Visitors cross an enclosed skywalk to reach the adjacent wing, which houses

Marine Mammal Pavilion. *501 E Pratt St (21202). Phone 410/576-3800. www.aqua.org.* This unique structure features a 1,300-seat amphitheater surrounding a 1.2-million-gallon pool, which houses Atlantic bottlenose dolphins; underwater viewing areas enable visitors to observe the mammals from below the surface. (Daily) Special video programs about dolphins and whales; educational arcade with computerized video screens and other participatory exhibits around the pavilion's upper deck. Visitor service area located in the atrium. Gift shop. Café. A life-size replica of a humpback whale spans two levels of the atrium. Discovery Room houses a collection of marine artifacts. Resource Center is an aquatic learning center for school visitors; library boasts extensive collection of marine science material.

Old Otterbein United Methodist Church. *112 W Conway St (21201). Inner Harbor area. Phone 410/685-4703. www.oldotterbein.com.* (1785-1786) Fine Georgian architecture; mother church of United Brethren. Tours of historic building (Apr-Oct, Sat).

Old Town Mall. *400 N Gay St.* This 150-year-old, brick-lined commercial area has been beautifully refurbished; it's closed to vehicular traffic. Nearby is

Stirling Street. *1000 block of Monument St, 1 block W of mall.* First community urban "homesteading" venture in the US. Renovated homes date to the 1830s. Original façades have been maintained; interior rehabilitation ranges in style from the antique to the avant garde.

Oriole Park at Camden Yards. *333 W Camden St (21201). Phone 410/685-9800. baltimore.orioles.mlb.com.* The crack of the bat and the roar of the crowd signal that the Orioles are home. Opened in 1992 and located just blocks from the Inner Harbor, Camden Yards is considered by many to be the best baseball stadium in the US. With its steel trusses, arched brick façade, and natural turf, the stadium's design is reminiscent of the great ballparks built in the early 1900s. It holds 48,876 fans and memorializes local legends Brooks Robinson, Earl Weaver, and Cal Ripken, Jr. The old B & O Warehouse sits behind right field and has long been a target for batters aiming for a home run. Guests can sit anywhere in the stadium and enjoy an unobstructed view of the game. Tours of the stadium are also available and allow visitors to sit in the dugout, see the press box, and explore the clubhouse. (Season Mar-Sept; tours held mid-Feb-late Dec, daily except on days of afternoon home games)

Otterbein "Homesteading." *Area around S Sharp St, Inner Harbor area.* The original neighborhood dates back to 1785. Houses have been restored.

Patterson Park. *200 S Linwood Ave (21231). Baltimore St, Eastern and Patterson Park aves. Phone 410/396-7931.* Defenses here helped stop the British attack in 1814. Breastworks and artillery pieces are displayed.

Peabody Institute of the Johns Hopkins University. *609 N Charles St (21202). In Mount Vernon Place area. Phone 410/659-8124 (box office). www.peabody.jhu.edu.* (1857) 550 students. Music conservatory founded by philanthropist George Peabody; now affiliated with Johns Hopkins. Research and reference collection in library accessible to the public (Mon-Fri; closed holidays). The Miriam A. Friedberg Concert Hall seats 800. Orchestral, recital, and opera performances.

Port Discovery. *35 Market Pl (21202). Phone 410/727-8120. www.port discovery.org.* Port Discovery is three floors and 80,000 square feet of pure imagination. Ranked the fourth best children's museum in the country by *Child* magazine, the museum opened in 1998 in collaboration with Walt Disney Imagineering. Its exhibits are interactive, innovative, and educational. Kids will have a blast exploring the three-story urban tree house. In MPT Studioworks, they can become producers of their own television broadcasts. Sensation Station will overload their senses of sight, sound, and touch. Kids can even travel back to ancient Egypt and uncover the mystery of the pyramids and Pharaoh's tomb. The museum also operates the HiFlyer, a giant helium balloon that's anchored 450 feet above the Inner Harbor. The enclosed gondola holds 20 to 25 passengers and offers a spectacular view of the city. (Memorial Day-Labor Day, daily; rest of year, Tues-Sun; closed Thanksgiving, Dec 25) **$$$**

The Power Plant. *601 E Pratt St (21202). Phone 410/752-5444.* As its name implies, this commercial complex was once a power plant owned by Baltimore Gas & Electric. Located in the Inner Harbor next to the National Aquarium (see), the renovated plant now houses a two-story Barnes & Noble bookstore; a Hard Rock Café; and the original ESPN Zone, a 35,000-square-foot sports-themed restaurant and arcade.

Pride of Baltimore II. *Inner Harbor (21202). Phone 410/752-2490; toll-free 888/55-PRIDE. www.intandem.com/newpridesite.* This replicated 1812-style Baltimore Clipper is Maryland's goodwill ambassador. The ship has sailed to more than 40 countries in North and South America, Europe, and Asia to promote the state's tourism and economical interests. In 1986, the original *Pride of Baltimore* sank in a storm near Puerto Rico, killing the entire crew. When the *Pride of Baltimore II* is docked in the Inner Harbor, visitors can board for a tour. Day sails and overnight passages between ports are also available (**$$$$**). (Daily; closed holidays) **FREE**

Public Works Museum & Streetscape. *751 Eastern Ave (21202), at Inner Harbor East. Phone 410/396-5565.* Museum exhibits the history and artifacts of public works. Located in a historic sewage pumping station. Streetscape sculpture outside depicts the various utility lines and ducts under a typical city street, in a walk-through model. (Tues-Sun 10 am-5 pm; closed Mon) **$$**

Sail Baltimore. *1809 Thames St (21231). Phone 410/522-7300. www.sail baltimore.org.* Because boats are to Baltimore as cows are to farms, Sail Baltimore, a nonprofit organization, informs the public about a variety of citywide boating events that take place throughout the year. Its Web site provides an updated schedule of the different boats and ships that will be visiting the Inner Harbor. It also hosts the Great Chesapeake Bay Schooner Race in October, among other seasonal events.

Senator Theatre. *5904 York Rd (21212). Phone 410/435-8338. www.senator .com.* Movie buffs will appreciate the charm and history of the Senator, which *USA Today* rated one of the top theaters in the country. Showing first-run, independent, and classic films, the theater seats 900 and has a 40-foot-wide screen. Listed on the National Register of Historic Places, its architecture is elegant Art Deco. The theater has also premiered several films by directors John Waters and Barry Levinson, who are Baltimore natives. The theater recently added its own mini "Walk of Fame" outside its entrance. **$$$**

Sherwood Gardens. *Stratford Rd and Greenway, in the residential community of Guilford in northern Baltimore.* More than 6 acres in size, the gardens reach their peak of splendor in late April and early May, when thousands of tulips, azaleas, and flowering shrubs bloom.

Six Flags America. *13710 Central Ave, Mitchellville, MD (20721). From Baltimore, take I-695 to I-97 S, Rte 3/301 S to Rte 214 W, and go 3 miles (follow signs). From Washington, take I-495/I-95 to exit 15 A and go 5 miles (follow signs). Phone 301/249-1500. www.sixflags.com/parks/america/home.asp.* This colorful theme park offers thrills both gentle and extreme, with everything from an old-fashioned carousel to classic 50-mph wooden roller coasters and the high-tech Batwing, which gives riders the feeling of free-flight. Smaller kids will love Looney Tunes MovieTown, where Bugs Bunny and his cartoon pals roam free. Too hot to ride? Cool down with Paradise Island Water Park's splash-happy water slides, wave pool, inner-tube ride, and interactive water tree house. (Daily June-Aug; limited schedule in Apr, May, Sept, and Oct) **$$$$**

⭐ **Star-Spangled Banner Flag House and War of 1812 Museum.** *844 E Pratt St (21202). Phone 410/837-1793. www.flaghouse.org.* Open to the public for over 75 years, this museum was the home of Mary Pickersgill, sewer of the flag that Francis Scott Key eternalized in America's national anthem. Although the flag now hangs in the Smithsonian's National Museum of American History, visitors can tour the house to learn about its origins and Pickersgill's life. The house has an adjoining War of 1812 museum, which exhibits military and domestic artifacts and presents an award-winning video. (Tues-Sat) **$**

Top of the World. *World Trade Center, 401 E Pratt St (21202). Inner Harbor area. Phone 410/837-8439.* Observation deck and museum on the 27th floor of the World Trade Center, which was designed by I. M. Pei. Exhibits describe the city's history, famous residents, and the activities of the port. (Daily) **$$**

University of Maryland at Baltimore. *520 W Lombard St (21201). Lombard, Greene, and Redwood sts, downtown. Phone 410/706-7820. www.umaryland.edu.* 5,476 students. The 32-acre downtown campus includes six professional schools; the University of Maryland Medical System, and the Graduate School. Davidge Hall (1812) is the oldest medical teaching building in continuous use in the western hemisphere.

USS *Constellation.* *Pier 1, 301 E Pratt St (21202). Phone 410/539-1797. www.constellation.org.* This retired sloop has a proud naval history that spans from the Civil War to World War II. Anchored at Pier 1 in the Inner Harbor, visitors can board the ship for a self-guided audio tour. Kids can participate in the Powder Monkey program, in which they learn what it was like to serve in President Lincoln's navy. In 1999, a restoration project returned the ship to its original Civil War appearance. (Daily; closed Jan 1, Thanksgiving, Dec 25) **$$$**

Vagabond Players. *806 S Broadway (21231). Phone 410/563-9135 (box office).* Oldest continuously operating "little theater" in the US. Recent Broadway shows, revivals, and original scripts are performed. (Fri-Sun) **$$**

Walters Art Museum. *600 N Charles St (21201). Phone 410/547-9000. www.the walters.org.* This museum's collection is so comprehensive that it spans 55 centuries and traces the history of the world from ancient times to the present day. Father and son William and Henry Walters gifted the museum and its numerous holdings to Baltimore, although the New York Metropolitan Museum of Art also coveted it. Located in the historic neighborhood of Mount Vernon and containing more than 30,000 pieces of art, the collection, which is housed in three buildings, is renowned for its French paintings and Renaissance and Asian art. The museum also exhibits Faberge eggs; paintings by the Old Masters, such as Raphael and El Greco; and an impressive assortment of ivories and Art Deco jewelry. Visitors will also want to check out the unique Roman sarcophagus. (Tues-Sun; closed Mon, major holidays) **$$**

Washington Monument. *Charles and Monument sts, in Mount Vernon Pl area (21202). Phone 410/396-1049.* (1815-1842) The first major monument to honor George Washington. There's a museum in the base; view the city from the top. Other monuments nearby honor Lafayette, Chief Justice Roger Brooke Taney, philanthropist George Peabody, lawyer Severn Teackle Wallis, and Revolutionary War hero John Eager Howard.

Special Events

American Craft Council Baltimore-Winter Show. *Convention Center. 1 W Pratt St (21201). Phone 410/649-7000.* Craft festival features the works of nearly 800 artisans, with crafts ranging from clay and glass to furniture and toys. Three-day weekend in late Feb. **$$$**

Artscape. *1200 block of Mount Royal Ave (21217). Phone 877/BALTIMORE. www.artscape.org.* This festival celebrates the area's abundance of visual, literary, and performing arts. The three-day event, which occurs in late July, takes place in the "cultural corridor" of the city's Bolton Hill neighborhood. It features live music performances, poetry and fiction readings by regional writers, and even a one-act opera. Past festival performers and guests have included John Waters, Buckwheat Zydeco, Kool & the Gang, and India.Arie. The Artists' Market exhibits and sells the work of more than 140 artists. The festival includes a wide variety of activities for children, which in the past have included a youth Shakespearean performance and an interactive art tent. The event also presents a charity wine-tasting hosted by a regional vineyard. Late July.

Cockpit in Court Summer Theatre. *Essex Community College. 7201 Rossville Blvd (21237). Phone 410/780-6369.* Theater in residence at Essex Community College. Four separate theaters offer a diverse collection of plays, including Broadway productions, contemporary drama, revues, and Shakespeare. Mid-June-mid-Aug.

Harbor Expo. *3001 Boston St (21224). Phone 410/396-7931. Middle Branch and Canton waterfront.* Boat parades, seafood festival; entertainment; events. Mid-June.

Maryland Film Festival. *107 E Read St (21202). Phone 410/752-8083. www.mdfilmfest.com.* Initiated in 1999, this four-day festival has become a premiere cinema event for Baltimore, presenting more than 120 foreign, domestic, and short films throughout the city's movie houses, including the famous Senator Theatre (see). Most screenings are followed by a discussion with the film's director or producer; past directors in attendance have included Barry Levinson and John Waters. In addition to featuring cutting-edge contemporary movies, its Guest Host Program invites members from the film community to screen and discuss films that have influenced their own work. The festival has also hosted films for children, such as a silent movie version of *Peter Pan* accompanied by an orchestra. The festival's committee holds film-related events in Baltimore throughout the year. Late Apr or early May. **$$$$**

Maryland House and Garden Pilgrimage. *1105-A Providence Rd (21286). Phone 410/821-6933. www.mhgp.org.* More than 100 homes and gardens throughout the state are open. To purchase tour book contact address or phone number above. Late Apr-early May.

New Year's Eve Extravaganza. *Convention Center and Inner Harbor. 1 W Pratt St (21201). Phone 410/649-7144.* Parties, entertainment, big bands, and fireworks.

Pier 6 Concert Pavilion. *Pier 6, 731 Eastern Ave (21202). Inner Harbor area. Phone 410/625-3100 for schedule.* Summertime outdoor concerts and plays at the water's edge. Some covered seating. (June-Sept, evenings) **$$$$**

Pimlico Race Course. *5201 Park Heights Ave (21215). Phone 410/542-9400. www.marylandracing.com.* Home to the world-famous Preakness Stakes (see), this track is well steeped in thoroughbred horseracing tradition. Pimlico features a 70-foot-wide and 1-mile-long track. It can easily meet the needs of horseracing fans with more than 750 betting windows and a clubhouse and two grandstands that can accommodate more than 13,000 people. In the lounge, visitors can view broadcasts of races at other tracks. (Wed-Sun, Apr-June) **$**

Preakness Stakes and Celebration Week. *Pimlico Race Course, 5201 Park Heights Ave (21215). Also Statewide festival. Phone 410/837-3030.* The Preakness Stakes, the second jewel in horse racing's Triple Crown, is a time-honored tradition in Baltimore. Every year, on the third Saturday in May, nearly 100,000 people from Maryland and around the world gather at the Pimilico Race Course. Celebration festivities begin one week before the race. The week is packed with activities that include a parade, a hot-air balloon festival, outdoor concerts, boat races, and 5K and 10K runs. On race day, the track's gates open at 8:30 am, with the first races beginning at 11 am. The Preakness itself is the second-to-last race of the day and begins at around 5:30 pm. Visitors looking for a good value and an eye-level view of the horses should reserve seats in the infield. Those willing to spend more money—and dress more formally—should choose seats in the clubhouse or grandstand.

Showcase of Nations Ethnic Festivals. *200 W Lombard St (21201). Various downtown locations. Phone 410/752-8632.* Presenting the food, music, and crafts of a different culture each weekend. June-Sept.

Motels/Motor Lodges

★ ★ **BEST WESTERN HOTEL & CONFERENCE CENTER.** *5625 O'Donnell St (21224). Phone 410/633-9500; toll-free 800/633-9511; fax 410/633-4314. www.bestwestern.com.* 175 rooms, 12 story. Check-out noon. TV; cable (premium). In-room modem link. Laundry services. Restaurant, bar. Room service. In-house fitness room, sauna. Game room. Indoor pool, whirlpool. **$**

D ⇌ 🏋 ⇲ SC

★ ★ **DAYS INN.** *100 Hopkins Pl (21201). Phone 410/576-1000; toll-free 800/329-7466; fax 410/576-9437. www.daysinn.com.* 250 rooms, 9 story. Check-out 11 am. TV; cable (premium). In-room modem link. Laundry services. Restaurant, bar. Room service. Health club privileges. Pool, pool-side service. Business center. Concierge. **$**

D ⇌ ⇲ SC 🏋

★ **HAMPTON INN.** *8225 Town Ctr Dr (21236). Phone 410/931-2200; toll-free 800/426-7866; fax 410/931-2215. www.hamptoninn.com.* 127 rooms, 4 story. Complimentary continental breakfast. Check-out noon, check-in 3 pm. TV; cable (premium). In-room modem link. Laundry services. In-house fitness room. Health club privileges. Outdoor pool. **$**

D ⇌ 🏋 ⇲

★ ★ **HOLIDAY INN.** *1800 Belmont Ave (21244). Phone 410/265-1400; toll-free 800/465-4329; fax 410/281-9569. www.holiday-inn.com.* 133 rooms, 2 story. Check-out noon. TV; cable (premium). In-room modem link. Laundry services. Restaurant, bar. Room service. Health club privileges. Pool. **$**

D ⇌ ⇲ SC

★ ★ **HOLIDAY INN SELECT.** *2004 Greenspring Dr (21093). Phone 410/252-7373; toll-free 800/289-4499; fax 410/561-0182. www.holiday-inn.com.* 245 rooms, 5 story. Check-out noon. TV; cable (premium). In-room modem link. Laundry services. Restaurant, bar; entertainment. Room service. In-house fitness room. Indoor, outdoor pool; whirlpool. Concierge. **$**

D ⌖ ⼍ ⼓ SC

Hotels

★ ★ ★ **BROOKSHIRE INNER HARBOR SUITE HOTEL.** *120 E Lombard St (21202). Phone 410/625-1300; toll-free 800/647-0013; fax 410/649-2635. www.harbormagic.com.* This hotel welcomes guests with the quiet elegance and sophisticated grace of a luxury retreat. 97 rooms, 11 story. Pets accepted, some restrictions. Complimentary full breakfast. Check-out noon, check-in noon. TV; cable (premium), VCR available. In-room modem link. Laundry services. Restaurant, bar. Room service. In-house fitness room. Health club privileges. Valet parking. **$$**

D ⌖ ⼍ ⼓ SC

★ ★ **CLARION HOTEL.** *612 Cathedral St (21201). Phone 410/727-7101; fax 410/789-3312. www.clarioninn.com.* 104 rooms, 14 story. Complimentary breakfast buffet. Check-out 11 am. TV; cable (premium), VCR available (movies). In-room modem link. Laundry services. Restaurant, bar. Health club privileges. Concierge. Restored hotel built in 1927. Marble floors, stairs in lobby. Period furnishings, artwork, crystal chandeliers. **$$**

D ⼓ SC

★ ★ ★ **HARBOR COURT HOTEL.** *550 Light St (21202). Phone 410/234-0550; res 800/824-0076; fax 410/659-5925. www.harborcourt.com.* Gracious style defines this hotel. With beautiful guest suites, 24-hour room service, and massage, visitors will have a great experience here. Relax at Hampton's (see), well known for great service, to experience the ultimate in dining. 200 rooms, 8 story. Check-out noon. TV; cable (premium), VCR available, CD player in suites. In-room modem link. Restaurant, bar; entertainment. Room service 24 hours. In-house fitness room, massage, sauna. Indoor pool, whirlpool, poolside service. Outdoor tennis. Lawn games. Racquetball. Self-park, valet parking. Airport transportation. Business center. Concierge. Elegant retreat located on the Inner Harbor; panoramic view of the city. **$$$**

D ⼝ ⌖ ⼍ ⼓ ⼈

★ ★ **HOLIDAY INN.** *301 W Lombard St (21201). Phone 410/685-3500; toll-free 800/465-4329; fax 410/727-6169. www.holiday-inn.com.* 373 rooms, 13 story. Check-out noon. TV; cable (premium). In-room modem link. Laundry services. Restaurant, bar. Room service. In-house fitness room, sauna. Indoor pool. Concierge. **$$**

D ⌖ ⼍ ⼓ SC

★ ★ ★ **HYATT REGENCY BALTIMORE.** *300 Light St (21202). Phone 410/528-1234; toll-free 800/233-1234; fax 410/685-3362. www.hyatt.com.* For business or pleasure, this grand hotel is conveniently located in Baltimore's Inner Harbor. It's linked by a skywalk to the convention center and mall. Amenities also include a basketball court, two restaurants, an outdoor pool, and 29,000 square feet of meeting space. 511 rooms, 15 story. Check-out noon, check-in 3 pm. TV; cable (premium). In-room modem link. Laundry services. Restaurant, bar; entertainment Fri, Sat. Room service. Supervised children's activities. In-house fitness room, sauna. Indoor, outdoor pools; whirlpool, poolside services available. Outdoor tennis. Valet parking. Business center. Concierge. Luxury level. **$$**

D 🎣 🏊 🏋 🚲 SC 🏃

★ ★ **INN AT THE COLONNADE.** *4 W University Pkwy (21218). Phone 410/235-5400; toll-free 800/222-8733; fax 410/235-5572. www.doubletree.com.* With its rich European elegance, this hotel has spacious guest suites, an indoor pool, exercise facilities, and much more. Enjoy fine dining at the award-winning Four West, or visit the local aquariums and museums. 125 rooms, 3 story. Check-out noon. TV; cable (premium). In-room modem link. Laundry services. Restaurant. Room service. In-house fitness room. Indoor pool, whirlpool, poolside service. Business center. Biedermeier-inspired furnishings; extensive collection of 18th-century European masters. Adjacent to Johns Hopkins University. **$$**

D 🏊 🏋 🚲 SC 🏃

★ ★ ★ **MARRIOTT BALTIMORE INNER HARBOR.** *110 S Eutaw St (21201). Phone 410/962-0202; toll-free 800/228-9290; fax 410/625-7892. www.marriott.com.* With a great location, this hotel is within walking distance to local aquariums, shopping, and sightseeing. It also has 14,000 square feet of meeting space, an indoor pool, and a health club. 534 rooms, 10 story. Check-out noon, check-in 4 pm. TV; cable (premium), VCR available. In-room modem link. Laundry services. Restaurant, bar; entertainment. Room service. In-house fitness room, sauna. Indoor pool, whirlpool. Business center. Concierge. Luxury level. Opposite the baseball stadium at Camden Yards. **$$**

D 🏊 🏋 🚲 🏃

★ ★ ★ **MARRIOTT BALTIMORE WATERFRONT.** *700 Aliceanna St (21202). Phone 410/385-3000; toll-free 800/228-9290; fax 410/895-1900. www.marriott.com.* 777 rooms, 32 story. Check-out noon, check-in 4 pm. TV; cable (premium). In-room modem link. Laundry services. Restaurant, bar. Room service. In-house fitness room, sauna. Indoor pool, whirlpool. Business center. Concierge. Luxury level. **$$**

D 🏊 🏋 🚲 SC 🏃

★ ★ **RADISSON HOTEL AT CROSS KEYS.** *100 Village Sq (21210). Phone 410/532-6900; res 800/333-3333; fax 410/532-2403. www.radisson.com.* With stylish French country-decorated rooms, this hotel offers tennis, swimming, and much more. Minutes from Baltimore's Inner Harbor and Camden Yards, the hotel provides complimentary shuttles to both. 148 rooms, 4 story. Check-out noon. TV; cable (premium). In-room modem link. Restaurant, bar. Room service. In-house fitness room. Health club privileges. Pool, poolside service. **$$**

★ ★ **RADISSON PLAZA LORD BALTIMORE.** *20 W Baltimore St (21201). Phone 410/539-8400; toll-free 800/333-3333; fax 410/625-1060. www.radisson.com.* Built in 1928, this elegant hotel is a registered historical landmark that continues to welcome guests with attentive service; handsomely appointed guest rooms, some offering spectacular views of scenic downtown Baltimore; and a refined elegance that continues to delight guests. 458 rooms, 23 story. Check-out noon, check-in 3 pm. TV; cable. In-room modem link. Restaurant, bar. In-house fitness room, sauna. Health club privileges. Valet parking. Historic landmark; near harbor. **$$**

★ ★ ★ **RENAISSANCE HARBORPLACE HOTEL.** *202 E Pratt St (21202). Phone 410/547-1200; toll-free 800/535-1200; fax 410/539-5780. www.renaissancehotels.com.* Located on the waterfront at Baltimore's scenic Inner Harbor and amidst all of downtown's delights, this hotel offers scenic views, friendly service, and elegantly appointed guest rooms. Nearby attractions include the Gallery, Convention Center, and World Trade Center. 657 rooms, 12 story. Check-out noon. TV; cable (premium), VCR available. In-room modem link. Laundry services. Restaurant, bar; entertainment. Room service 24 hours. In-house fitness room, sauna. Health club privileges. Indoor pool, whirlpool, poolside service. Garage, valet parking. Business center. Concierge. Luxury level. **$$**

★ ★ ★ **SHERATON INNER HARBOR HOTEL.** *300 S Charles St (21201). Phone 410/962-8300; toll-free 800/325-3535; fax 410/962-8211. www.sheraton.com/Innerharbor.* This hotel is connected to the Baltimore Convention Center as well as to Inner Harbor attractions. 357 rooms, 15 story. Check-out noon, check-in 3 pm. TV; cable (premium), VCR available (movies). In-room modem link. Laundry services. Restaurant, bar. Room service. In-house fitness room, sauna. Health club privileges. Pool. Valet parking. Business center. Concierge. **$$$**

★ ★ **TREMONT PARK HOTEL.** *8 E Pleasant St (21202). Phone 410/576-1200; toll-free 800/873-6668; fax 410/244-1154. www.tremontsuitehotels.com.* 58 rooms, 13 story. Complimentary continental breakfast. Check-out noon. TV; VCR available. Laundry services. Restaurant, bar. Health club privileges. Valet parking. Concierge. **$$**

★ ★ ★ **WYNDHAM BALTIMORE INNER HARBOR HOTEL.** *101 W Fayette St (21201). Phone 410/752-1100; toll-free 800/996-3426; fax 410/752-0832. www.wyndham.com.* Just fifteen minutes from BWI Airport, this modern high-rise hotel offers everything one would expect from a luxury hotel. Its grand style leaves guests feeling pampered. Oversized rooms and a great sports bar add to the experience. 732 rooms, 27 story. Check-out noon, check-in 4 pm. TV; cable (premium). In-room modem link. Laundry services. Restaurant, bar. In-house fitness room. Pool, poolside service. Valet parking. Business center. Concierge. **$$**

[D] [≈] [♁] [↕] [SC] [♁]

B&B/Small Inns

★ ★ ★ **ABACROMBIE BADGER BED AND BREAKFAST.** *58 W Biddle St (21201). Phone 410/244-7227; toll-free 888/9-BADGER; fax 410/244-8415. www.badger-inn.com.* Originally an 1880s townhouse, this delightful inn welcomes both business and leisure travelers, enveloping guests with gracious tranquility and a serene atmosphere. Nearby attractions include the Meyerhoff Symphony Hall, Lyric Opera House, and the start to the fashionable Antique Row. 12 rooms, 4 story. Children over 10 years only. Complimentary continental breakfast. Check-out 11 am, check-in 4-6 pm. TV. Restaurant, bar. Turn-of-the-century building; many antique furnishings. Totally nonsmoking. **$**

[↕]

★ ★ ★ **ADMIRAL FELL INN.** *888 S Broadway, Historic Fell's Point (21231). Phone 410/522-7377; toll-free 800/292-4667; fax 410/522-0707. www.admiralfell.com.* This renovated urban inn is conveniently located downtown in the scenic historic waterfront area. From the custom-designed Federal-style furnishings and meeting rooms, which offers guests an empowering view of the skyline and harbor, to the warm and attentive service, this hotel is a delight. Enjoy a stroll along the quaint brick sidewalks to the numerous antique shops, gourmet restaurants, galleries, and friendly pubs. 83 rooms, 5 story. Pets accepted. Complimentary continental breakfast. Check-out noon, check-in 4 pm. TV; cable (premium). Dining room, bar. Health club privileges. **$$**

[D] [🐾] [↕] [SC]

★ ★ ★ **CELIE'S WATERFRONT INN.** *1714 Thames St (21231). Phone 410/522-2323; toll-free 800/432-0184; fax 410/522-2324. www.celieswaterfront. com.* Located in the heart of the Fell's Point waterfront district, this inn beckons to travelers with its atmospheric seafaring past and its welcome of utter relaxation and timeless tranquility. Rooms are airy and graced with skylights, offering scenic views of the harbor and well-maintained gardens. 9 rooms, 3 story. Children over 10 years only. Complimentary continental breakfast. Check-out 11 am, check-in 3 pm. TV; VCR. In-room modem link. Fireplaces. Health club privileges. Roof deck. Totally nonsmoking. **$**

[D] [↕]

★ ★ ★ **HOPKINS INN.** *3404 St. Paul St (21218). Phone 410/235-8600; fax 410/235-7051. www.bichotels.com/hopkinsinn.* This charming bed-and-breakfast is just blocks from the Baltimore International College. Guests will enjoy the handsomely appointed rooms and friendly service. 25 rooms, 4 story. Complimentary continental breakfast. Check-out 11 am, check-in

3 pm. TV. Covered parking $6. 1920s Spanish Revival building. Rooms individually furnished in a variety of styles. Totally nonsmoking. **$**

⊠ SC

★ ★ ★ **INN AT GOVERNMENT HOUSE.** *1125 N Calvert St (21202). Phone 410/539-0566; fax 410/539-0567. www.baltimorecity.gov/visitor.* Located in the scenic Mount Vernon historic district, this elegant inn is known to welcome Baltimore's visiting dignitaries. Comprised of three townhouses and charmingly appointed with an elegant Victorian décor, this inn guarantees a welcoming respite as well as warm and friendly service. 18 rooms, 4 story. Complimentary continental breakfast. Check-out noon, check-in 3-8 pm. TV. Part of a complex of several Federal and Victorian mansions and town houses (1888). Totally nonsmoking. **$**

D ⊠ SC

★ ★ **INN AT HENDERSON'S WHARF.** *1000 Fell St (21231). Phone 410/522-7777; toll-free 800/522-2088; fax 410/522-7087. www. hendersonswharf.com.* 38 rooms. Pets accepted; fee. Complimentary continental breakfast. Check-out noon, check-in 3 pm. TV; cable (premium). In-room modem link. Laundry services. In-house fitness room. 19th-century tobacco warehouse. On the waterfront; dockage available. **$$**

D ⊁ 🕇 ⊠ SC

★ ★ ★ **MR. MOLE BED AND BREAKFAST.** *1601 Bolton St (21217). Phone 410/728-1179; fax 410/728-3379. www.mrmolebb.com.* Built in the 1860s and carefully restored, this charming inn is charmingly appointed with beautiful 18th- and 19th-century antiques, as well as elegant marble fireplaces and handsomely furnished guest rooms. 5 rooms, 5 story. Children over 10 years only. Complimentary breakfast. Check-out 11 am, check-in 4-6 pm. In-room modem link. Garage parking. Totally nonsmoking. **$**

⊠

Restaurants

★ ★ **ANGELINA'S.** *7135 Harford Rd (21234). Phone 410/444-5545; toll-free 800/272-2225. www.crabcake.com.* Italian, American menu. Closed Mon; Thanksgiving, Dec 25. Lunch, dinner. Bar. Entertainment Fri. Children's menu. Casual attire. **$$$**

D

★ ★ **BAYOU BLUES CAFE.** *8133-A Honeygo Blvd (21236). Phone 410/ 931-2583. www.thebayoucafe.com.* American, Cajun menu. Lunch, dinner. Bar. Children's menu. Casual attire. Outdoor seating. **$$$**

D

★ **BERTHA'S.** *734 S Broadway (21231). Phone 410/327-5795; fax 410/ 732-1548. www.berthas.com.* Seafood menu. Closed major holidays. Lunch, dinner, Sun brunch. Bar. Entertainment. Historic 19th-century building. Reservations required for Scottish afternoon tea (Mon-Sat). **$$$**

D

★ ★ ★ **BLACK OLIVE.** *814 S Bond St (21231). Phone 410/276-7141; fax 410/276-7143. www.theblackolive.com.* Greek, Middle Eastern menu. Closed major holidays. Dinner. Entertainment. Casual attire. **$$$**

D

★ ★ ★ **BOCCACCIO.** *925 Eastern Ave (21231). Phone 410/234-1322; fax 410/727-6318.* Northern Italian menu. Closed most major holidays. Lunch, dinner. Bar. Casual attire. **$$$**

D

★ **CAFE HON.** *1002 W 36th St (21211). Phone 410/243-1230; fax 410/243-6461. www.cafehon.com.* Closed most major holidays. Breakfast, lunch, dinner, Sun brunch. Bar. Children's menu. Totally nonsmoking. **$$**

D

★ ★ ★ ★ **CHARLESTON.** *1000 Lancaster St (21202). Phone 410/332-7373; fax 410/332-8425. www.charlestonrestaurant.com.* Chef-owner Cindy Wolf's stunning, regional American restaurant is one of the most exciting and luxurious dining experiences to be had in Baltimore. This upscale bistro-style room is warmed by an amber glow that makes you feel ten years younger. And the food is even better. Sautéed heads-on gulf shrimp with andouille sausage and Tasso ham with creamy stone-milled grits, a signature dish, is a perfect example of the robust, home-style low-country cooking served here nightly. The restaurant also has an impressive wine program that includes several dozen sparkling wines and a hefty selection of about 400 well-chosen whites and reds from the new world (Australia, South Africa, New Zealand, and Chile) and the old (France, Italy, and Spain). If wine doesn't call you, Charleston offers more than a dozen microbrews and imported beers and a splashy cocktail list that contains some inventive sippers as well as a great variety of classics. American menu. Menu changes daily. Closed Sun; holidays. Dinner. Bar. Entertainment. Outdoor seating. **$$$**

D

★ ★ **CHIAPPARELLI'S OF LITTLE ITALY.** *237 S High St (21202). Phone 410/837-0309; fax 410/783-7985. www.chiapparellis.com.* Southern Italian menu. Closed Thanksgiving, Dec 25. Lunch, dinner. Bar. Children's menu. Casual attire. Valet parking. Built in 1870; original brick walls, oak paneling. Seven dining rooms on two levels. **$$$**

★ ★ **CITY LIGHTS.** *301 Light St (21202). Phone 410/244-8811; fax 410/244-8815. www.citylightsseafood.com.* Closed Thanksgiving, Dec 24-25. Lunch, dinner. Bar. Children's menu. Outdoor seating. **$$**

D

★ ★ ★ **DALESIO'S OF LITTLE ITALY.** *829 Eastern Ave (21202). Phone 410/539-1965; fax 410/576-8749. www.dalesios.com.* Located in Little Italy, this newly renovated restaurant serves northern Italian and spa cuisine selections and special featured wine dinners. Northern Italian menu. Closed Thanksgiving. Lunch, dinner. Bar. Casual attire. Valet parking. Outdoor seating. **$$**

D

★ ★ ★ **DELLA NOTTE.** *801 Eastern Ave (21202). Phone 410/837-5500; fax 410/837-2600.* Italian menu. Closed Dec 25. Lunch, dinner. Bar. Children's menu. Casual attire. **$$**

D

★ ★ **GERMANO'S TRATTORIA.** *300 S High St (21202). Phone 410/752-4515; fax 410/625-6472. www.germanostrattoria.com.* Tuscan, regional Italian menu. Closed Thanksgiving, Dec 25. Lunch, dinner. Bar. Children's menu. Casual attire. **$$**

D

★ ★ ★ **HAMPTON'S.** *550 Light St (21202). Phone 410/234-0550; fax 410/659-5925. www.harborcourt.com.* Located in the Harbor Court Hotel (see), Hampton's is a luxurious restaurant that serves marvelous seasonal American fare matched by serene and romantic views of Baltimore's Inner Harbor. The kitchen stays true to classic technique, using pristine regional ingredients and clever modern tweaks to add a savvy edge to the plate. Specialties include lobster bisque flecked with chives and mushrooms, seared dry-aged beef tenderloin, and a kickin' horseradish Caesar salad. The wine list is exceptional as well, focusing on small, independent producers and rare vintages that pair up seamlessly with the inspired menu. Nightly live piano and a jazz quartet on the weekends fill the room with an old-world elegance and charm. American menu. Closed Mon. Dinner, Sun brunch. Jacket required. Reservations required. Valet parking. Totally nonsmoking. **$$$**

D

★ **HENNINGER'S TAVERN.** *1812 Bank St (21231). Phone 410/342-2172. www.henningerstavern.com.* American menu. Closed Sun, Mon; Jan 1, Dec 25. Dinner. Bar. Casual attire. **$$**

★ ★ **IKAROS.** *4805 Eastern Ave (21224). Phone 410/633-3750.* Greek, American menu. Closed Tues; Thanksgiving, Dec 25. Lunch, dinner. **$$**

D

★ ★ **JEANNIER'S.** *105 W 39th St (21211). Phone 410/889-3303; fax 410/889-6813.* French, continental menu. Closed Sun; most major holidays. Lunch, dinner. Bar. **$$**

D

★ ★ **JOHN STEVEN, LTD.** *1800 Thames St (21231). Phone 410/327-5561; toll-free 877/732-3460; fax 410/327-0513. www.johnstevensltd.com.* American, eclectic, seafood menu. Lunch, dinner. Bar. Building built in 1838. Casual attire. Outdoor seating. **$$**

D

★ ★ ★ **JOY AMERICA CAFE.** *800 Key Hwy (21230). Phone 410/244-6500; fax 410/244-6363. www.avam.org/joyamerica/.* "Nothing Without Joy" is the fitting motto at this whimsical restaurant housed on the top floor of Baltimore's unique Visionary Arts Museum. The food is as creative as the décor, and many dishes have a Latin flair. Contemporary American menu. Closed Mon; Labor Day, Thanksgiving, Dec 25. Lunch, dinner, Sun brunch. Bar. Children's menu. Outdoor seating. **$$$**

D

★ ★ **KAWASAKI.** *413 N Charles St (21201). Phone 410/659-7600; fax 410/625-0607. www.kawasaki-restaurant.com.* Japanese menu. Closed Sun; major holidays. Lunch, dinner. Bar. Casual attire. **$$**

D

★ **KISS CAFE.** *2400 Boston St (24224). Phone 410/327-9889; fax 410/327-8318.* American menu. Closed major holidays. Breakfast, lunch, dinner. Bar. Casual attire. Outdoor seating. **$**

D

★ ★ ★ **LA SCALA.** *1012 Eastern Ave (21202). Phone 410/783-9209; fax 410/783-5949. www.lascaladining.com.* Italian menu. Closed Jan 1, Thanksgiving, Dec 25. Dinner. Bar. Casual attire. **$$$**

★ ★ **MT. WASHINGTON TAVERN.** *5700 Newbury St (21209). Phone 410/367-6903; fax 410/542-9023. www.mtwashingtontavern.com.* Closed Dec 25. Lunch, dinner, Sun brunch. Bar. Entertainment Wed, Sat. Children's menu. Outdoor seating. **$$**

★ ★ **OBRYCKI'S CRAB HOUSE.** *1727 E Pratt St (21231). Phone 410/732-6399; fax 410/522-4637. www.obryckis.com.* Closed mid-Dec-Mar. Lunch, dinner. Bar. Children's menu. **$$$**

D

★ ★ **PIERPOINT.** *1822 Aliceanna St (21231). Phone 410/675-2080; fax 410/563-2855. www.pierpointrestaurant.com.* American menu. Closed Mon; Jan 1, Dec 25. Lunch, dinner. Bar. Casual attire. **$$**

★ ★ ★ **THE PRIME RIB.** *1101 N Calvert St (21202). Phone 410/539-1804; fax 410/837-0244. www.theprimerib.com.* Voted the best steakhouse in town, The Prime Rib has been consistently good for three decades. Upscale atmosphere. Closed Thanksgiving. Dinner. Bar. Pianist. Jacket required. Black lacquered walls. **$$$**

D

★ ★ **ROCCO'S CAPRICCIO.** *846 Fawn St (21202). Phone 410/685-2710; toll-free 888/685-2710; fax 410/539-4261.* Northern Italian, Mediterranean menu. Closed Thanksgiving, Dec 25. Lunch, dinner. Bar. Children's menu. Casual attire. **$$$**

★ ★ ★ **RUBY LOUNGE.** *802 N Charles St (21201). Phone 410/539-8051.* This is a sophisticated spot to spend an evening. The elegantly apportioned restaurant and bar are upscale. The menu presents appetizers and entrées that are a cut above, and the skilled and efficient bar staff whip up fanciful concoctions that are sure to please. American menu. Closed Sun, Mon; also most major holidays. Dinner. Bar. Casual attire. Valet parking. **$$**

★ ★ ★ **RUTH'S CHRIS STEAK HOUSE.** *600 Water St (21202). Phone 410/783-0033; toll-free 800/544-0808; fax 410/783-0049. www.ruthschris.com.* Sizzling hot, custom-aged steaks are the specialty at this branch of Ruth Fertel's famed national chain. Portions are big enough to share, and there's a courtesy shuttle to all major Inner Harbor hotels. Closed Jan 1, Thanksgiving, Dec 25; also Super Bowl Sun. Dinner. Bar. **$$$**

D

★ ★ **SOTTO SOPRA.** *405 N Charles St (21201). Phone 410/625-0534; fax 410/625-2642. www.sottosoprainc.com.* Northern Italian menu. Lunch, dinner. Entertainment. Casual attire. **$$$**

D

★ ★ ★ **SPIKE AND CHARLIE'S.** *1225 Cathedral St (21201). Phone 410/752-8144. www.spikeandcharlies.com.* Here, food is art. Eclectic culinary creations are served in an ultrachic dinner salon. American menu. Closed Mon; most major holidays. Dinner. Bar. Reservations required. **$$**

D

★ ★ ★ ★ **THE OREGON GRILLE.** *1201 Shawan Rd (21030). Phone 410/771-0505; fax 410/771-9837. www.theoregongrille.com.* American menu. Closed Dec 25. Lunch, dinner, Sun brunch. Bar. Jacket required after 5 pm. Outdoor seating. **$$$**

D

★ ★ **TIO PEPE.** *10 E Franklin St (21202). Phone 410/539-4675; fax 410/837-7288.* Spanish menu. Closed most major holidays. Lunch, dinner. Bar. Jacket required. Reservations required. **$$$**

D

★ ★ **VELLEGGIA'S.** *829 E Pratt St (21202). Phone 410/685-2620; fax 410/837-5176.* Italian menu. Closed Dec 24-25. Lunch, dinner. Bar. Children's menu. Casual attire. **$$**

D

Baltimore/Washington International Airport Area

See also Baltimore; also see Washington, DC

Services and Information

Information. 410/859-7100.

Lost and Found. 410/859-7387.

Weather. 410/936-1212.

Cash Machines. Main Terminal, Pier C.

Airlines. Aer Lingus, Air Canada Jazz, Air Jamaica, Air Tran, America West, American, British Airways, Continental, Delta, Frontier Airlines, Ghana Airways, Hooters Air, Icelandair, Midwest, Northwest, Pan Am, Southwest, United, USAir, USA 3000.

Motel/Motor Lodge

★ **HAMPTON INN.** *829 Elkridge Landing Rd, Linthicum (21090). Phone 410/850-0600; toll-free 800/426-7866; fax 410/691-2119. www.hampton inn.com.* 139 rooms, 5 story. Pets accepted. Complimentary continental breakfast. Check-out noon. TV; cable (premium). In-room modem link. Laundry services. Free airport transportation. **$**

[D] [🛎] [✈] [⬡] [SC]

Hotels

★ ★ ★ **MARRIOTT BALTIMORE WASHINGTON INTER-NATIONAL AIRPORT.** *1743 W Nursery Rd, Linthicum (21240). Phone 410/859-8300; toll-free 800/228-9290; fax 410/691-4555. www.marriott.com.* 310 rooms, 10 story. Check-out noon. TV; cable (premium). In-room modem link. Laundry services. Restaurant, bar. Room service. In-house fitness room. Health club privileges. Massage. Indoor pool, whirlpool. Free airport transportation. Business center. Luxury level. **$$**

[D] [≈] [🖈] [⬡] [SC] [🏃]

★ ★ ★ **SHERATON INTERNATIONAL HOTEL ON BWI AIRPORT.** *7032 Elm Rd (21240). Phone 410/859-3300; fax 410/859-0565. www.sheraton.com.* 201 rooms, 2 story. Check-out noon. TV; cable (premium). In-room modem link. Restaurant, bar; entertainment. Room service 24 hours. In-house fitness room. Pool, poolside service. Airport transportation. Luxury level. **$$**

[D] [≈] [🖈] [⬡]

All Suite

★ ★ **EMBASSY SUITES.** *1300 Concourse Dr, Linthicum (21090). Phone 410/850-0747; toll-free 800/EMBASSY; fax 410/850-0895. www.embassy suites.com.* 251 rooms, 8 story. Complimentary breakfast. Check-out noon. TV; cable (premium). In-room modem link. Laundry services. Restaurant, bar. Room service. In-house fitness room, sauna. Health club privileges. Indoor pool, whirlpool. Airport transportation. Business center. **$**

[D] [≈] [🖈] [⬡] [SC] [🏃]

Side Trips — **Day Trips**

Not only is there a cornucopia of activities in Washington, DC, but there is plenty to keep you busy just outside the city limits. In less than two hours, you could picnic in beautiful Shenandoah National Park, tour the naval academy at Annapolis, or soak up more US history in Gettysburg.

Alexandria, VA

10 minutes; 7 miles from Washington, DC
See also Arlington County (Ronald Reagan Washington-National Airport Area), Fairfax

Settled 1670 **Pop** 128,283 **Elev** 52 ft **Area code** 703

Information Convention/Visitors Association, 421 King St, 22314-3209; 703/838-4200

Web www.funside.com

A group of English and Scottish merchants established a tobacco warehouse at the junction of Hunting Creek and the "Potowmack" River in the 1740s. The little settlement prospered and 17 years later surveyor John West, Jr., and his young assistant, George Washington, arrived and "laid off in streets and 84 half-acre lots" the town of Alexandria. Among the first buyers on the July morning in 1749 when the lots were offered for public sale were Lawrence Washington and his brother Augustus, William Ramsay, the Honorable William Fairfax, and John Carlyle. Erecting handsome town houses, these gentlemen soon brought a lively and cosmopolitan air to Alexandria with parties, balls, and horse racing. It was also the hometown of George Mason and Robert E. Lee and home to George Washington.

In 1789, Virginia ceded Alexandria to the District of Columbia, but in 1846, the still Southern-oriented citizens asked to return to the Old Dominion, which Congress allowed.

During the Civil War, Alexandria was cut off from the Confederacy when Union troops occupied the town to protect Potomac River navigation. Safe behind Union lines, the city escaped the dreadful destruction experienced by many other Southern towns. After the war, even with seven railroads centering here for transfer of freight, Alexandria declined as a center of commerce and was in trade doldrums until about 1914, when the Alexandria shipyards were reopened and the

Naval Torpedo Station was built. Today, it has developed into a trade, commerce, transportation, and science center. More than 250 national associations are based here.

What to See and Do

Alexandria Black History Resource Center. *638 N Alfred St (22314). Phone 703/838-4356.* Photographs, letters, documents, and artifacts relate the history of African Americans in Alexandria. (Tues-Sat; closed holidays) **DONATION**

The Athenaeum. *201 Prince St (22314). Phone 703/548-0035.* Greek Revival structure (1851) built as a bank now houses the Fine Arts Association. Art shows, dance performances. (Wed-Fri and Sat-Sun afternoons; closed holidays)

Atlantic Kayak. *1201 N Royal St (22314). Phone 703/838-9072; toll-free 800/297-0066. www.atlantickayak.com.* See the capital's sights from a new perspective: as a kayaker on the Potomac. Atlantic Kayak runs short trips that include a brief lesson; all equipment is included, and no experience is required. Sunset and moonlight tours are an especially beautiful way to view DC's monuments. Another outing takes you to the Dyke Marsh Wildlife Area, where you'll see ospreys, great blue herons, and other birds. There's even a tour with fireworks viewing on July 4. (Apr-Oct, daily)

Doorways to Old Virginia. *Departs from Ramsay House, 221 King St (22314). Phone 703/548-0100. www.chesapeakejubilee.org.* Offers guided walking tours of the historic district. (Mar-Oct, Fri-Sun, evenings) **$$$**

Fort Ward Museum and Historic Site. *4301 W Braddock Rd (22304). Phone 703/838-4848.* Restored Union Fort from the Civil War; museum contains a Civil War collection. Museum (Tues-Sun; closed Jan 1, Thanksgiving, Dec 25). Park, picnicking (daily to sunset). **FREE**

George Washington Masonic National Memorial. *101 Callahan Dr, W end of King St (22301). Phone 703/683-2007.* American Freemasons' memorial to their most prominent member, this 333-foot-high structure houses a large collection of objects that belonged to George Washington, which were collected by his family or the masonic lodge where he served as the first master. Guided tours explore a replica of Alexandria-Washington Lodge's first hall, a library, museum, and an observation deck on the top floor. (Daily 9 am-4 pm; closed Jan 1, Thanksgiving, Dec 25) **FREE**

Gunston Hall. *10709 Gunston Rd, Mason Neck (22079). 18 miles S on US 1, then 4 miles E on VA 242. Phone 703/550-9220. www.gunstonhall.org.* (1755-1759) The 550-acre estate of George Mason, framer of the Constitution and father of the Bill of Rights. Restored 18th-century mansion with period furnishings; reconstructed outbuildings; display of historic livestock on a working farm; museum; boxwood gardens on grounds; nature trail; picnic area; gift shop. (Daily 9:30 am-5 pm; closed Jan 1, Thanksgiving, Dec 25) **$$**

King Street. *In Old Town.* Street is lined with trendy restaurants, shops, and fine antique stores.

Oxon Hill Farm. *6411 Oxon Hill Rd, Oxon Hill, MD (20745). Entrance from Oxon Hill Rd, 300 yds W of jct MD 210 and I-95. Phone 301/839-1177.* Living history farm (circa 1898-1914) located on a working farm with livestock; participatory activities. Represents life from early 1800s to present. (Daily; closed Jan 1, Thanksgiving, Dec 25) **FREE**

Pohick Bay Regional Park. *6501 Pohick Bay Dr, Lorton (22079). Phone 703/ 339-6104. www.nvrpa.org/pohickbay.html/.* Near Gunston Hall. Activities in this 1,000-acre park include swimming (Memorial Day-Labor Day), boating (ramp, rentals, fee); 18-hole golf, miniature and Frisbee golf, camping (7-day limit; electric hookups available; fee), picnicking. Park (all year). Fee charged for activities.

Pohick Episcopal Church. *9301 Richmond Hwy, Lorton (22079), 16 miles S on US 1. Phone 703/550-9449.* (1774) The colonial parish church of Mount Vernon and Gunston Hall. Built under the supervision of George Mason and George Washington; original walls; interior fully restored. (Daily) **FREE**

Sightseeing boat tours. *Phone 703/684-0580.* Tours of the Alexandria waterfront. Contact the Potomac Riverboat Company. **$$$**

Torpedo Factory Arts Center. *105 N Union St (22314). Phone 703/838-4565. www.torpedofactory.org.* Renovated munitions plant houses an artists' center with more than 160 professional artists of various media. Studios, cooperative galleries, school. Also the home of Alexandria Archaeology offices, lab, and museum; phone 703/838-4399. (Daily 10 am-5 pm; closed holidays) **FREE**

⭐ **Walking tour of historic sites.** *Tours depart from the Ramsay House, 221 King St (22314). Phone 703/838-4200.* Start at Visitors Center in **Ramsay House** (circa 1725). Oldest house in Alexandria and later used as a tavern, grocery store, and cigar factory. Here, vistors can obtain special events information and a free visitors guide, as well as purchase "block tickets" good for reduced admission to three of the city's historic properties. Guided walking tours depart from here (spring-fall, weather permitting). The bureau also issues free parking permits, tour and highway maps, and hotel, dining, and shopping information. (Daily; closed Jan 1, Thanksgiving, Dec 25) Sites included in the tour are

> **Boyhood Home of Robert E. Lee.** *607 Oronoco St (22314). Phone 703/548-8454.* Federalist architecture. Famous guests include Washington and Lafayette.

> **Carlyle House.** *121 N Fairfax St (22314). Phone 703/549-2997.* (1753) This stately stone mansion built in Palladian style was the site of a 1755 meeting between General Edward Braddock and five British colonial governors to plan the early campaigns of the French and Indian War. (Tues-Sun; closed holidays) **$$**

> **Christ Church.** *118 N Washington St (22314). Phone 703/549-1450. www.historicchristchurch.org.* (1773) Washington and Robert E. Lee were pewholders. Fine Palladian window; interior balcony; wrought-brass and crystal chandelier brought from England. Structure is extensively restored but has changed little since it was built. Exhibit, gift shop at

Columbus St entrance. (Mon-Sat, also Sun afternoons; closed holidays; also for weddings, funerals)

Gadsby's Tavern Museum. *134 N Royal St (22314). Phone 703/838-4242.* (1770, 1792) Famous hostelry frequented by Washington and other patriots. Combines two 18th-century buildings; interesting architecture. (Tues-Sun; closed holidays) **$$**

Home of General Henry "Light Horse Harry" Lee. *611 Cameron St (22314).* (Private)

Lafayette House. *301 S St. Asaph St (22314).* Fine example of Federal architecture. House was loaned to Lafayette for his last visit to America (1825). (Private)

Lee-Fendall House. *614 Oronoco St (22314). Phone 703/548-1789. www. leefendallhouse.org.* (1785) Built by Phillip Richard Fendall and lived in by Lee family for 118 years. Both George Washington and Revolutionary War hero "Light Horse Harry" Lee were frequent visitors to the house. Remodeled in 1850, the house is furnished with Lee family belongings. (Tues-Sat 10 am-4pm, Sun 1-4 pm, weekend hours may vary; closed holidays) **$**

The Lyceum. *201 S Washington St (22314). Phone 703/838-4994.* Museum, exhibitions; Virginia travel information (limited). (Daily; closed Jan 1, Thanksgiving, Dec 25) **FREE**

Old Presbyterian Meeting House. *321 S Fairfax St (22314). Phone 703/ 549-6670. www.opmh.org.* (1774) Tomb of the unknown soldier of the Revolution is in the churchyard. (Mon-Fri) **FREE**

Stabler-Leadbeater Apothecary Museum. *105 S Fairfax St (22314). Phone 703/836-3713.* (1792) Largest collection of apothecary glass in its original setting in the country; more than 1,000 apothecary bottles. Original building is now a museum of early pharmacy; collection of old prescriptions, patent medicines, scales, and other 18th-century pharmacy items. George Washington, Robert E. Lee, and John Calhoun were regular customers. (Daily; closed Jan 1, Thanksgiving, Dec 25)

Special Events

George Washington Birthday Celebrations. Events include a race and a Revolutionary War reenactment; climaxed by a birthday parade on the federal holiday. Feb.

House tours. *Tours depart from the Ramsay House, 221 King St (22314). Phone 703/838-4200.* Fine colonial and Federalist houses are open to the public: Historic Garden Week (Apr); Hospital Auxiliary Tour of Historic Houses (Sept); Scottish Christmas Walk (Dec). Tickets, additional information at Alexandria Convention/Visitors Association.

Red Cross Waterfront Festival. *123 N Alfred St (22314). Phone 703/549-8300.* Commemorates Alexandria's maritime heritage. Features "tall ships," blessing of the fleet, river cruises, races, arts and crafts, exhibits, food, a variety of music, and fireworks. June.

Scottish Christmas Walk. *Ramsay House, 221 King St (22314). Phone 800/388-9119.* Parade, house tour, concerts, greens and heather sales, and a dinner/dance to emphasize city's Scottish origins. First Sat in Dec.

Virginia Scottish Games. *Ramsay House, 221 King St (22314). Phone 703/838-4200.* Athletic competition, Highland dance and music, antique cars, displays, and food. Fourth weekend in July.

Motels/Motor Lodges

★ **BEST WESTERN MOUNT VERNON.** *8751 Richmond Hwy (22309). Phone 703/360-1300; toll-free 800/780-7234; fax 703/799-7713. www.bestwestern.com.* 132 rooms, 4 story. Complimentary continental breakfast. Check-out 11 am. TV; cable (premium). Laundry services. Sauna. In-house fitness room. **$**

[D] [大] [≦] [SC]

★ **BEST WESTERN OLD COLONY INN.** *1101 N Washington St (22314). Phone 703/739-2222; toll-free 800/780-7234; fax 703/549-2568. www.bestwestern.com.* 49 rooms, 2 story. Complimentary full breakfast. Check-out noon. TV; cable (premium). In-room modem link. Laundry services. Pool. Free airport transportation. **$**

[D] [≃] [✕] [≦] [SC]

★ ★ **COURTYARD BY MARRIOTT.** *2700 Eisenhower Ave (22314). Phone 703/329-2323; toll-free 800/321-2211; fax 703/329-6853. www.courtyard.com.* 176 rooms, 8 story. Check-out noon. TV; cable (premium). Laundry services. Restaurant, bar. Room service. In-house fitness room. **$**

[D] [大] [✦] [≦]

★ **HAMPTON INN.** *4800 Leesburg Pike (22302). Phone 703/671-4800; toll-free 800/426-7866; fax 703/671-2442. www.hamptoninn.com.* 130 rooms, 4 story. Complimentary continental breakfast. Check-out noon. TV; cable (premium). In-room modem link. Laundry services. In-house fitness room. Health club privileges. Pool. **$**

[D] [≃] [大] [≦] [SC]

★ ★ **HOLIDAY INN SELECT.** *480 King St (22314). Phone 703/549-6080; toll-free 800/465-4329; fax 703/684-6508. www.holiday-inn.com.* 227 rooms, 6 story. Pets accepted, some restrictions. Check-out noon. TV; cable (premium). In-room modem link. Laundry services. Restaurant, bar. In-house fitness room, sauna. Indoor pool. Free airport transportation. Business center. Concierge. **$$**

[D] [✈] [≃] [大] [≦] [SC] [大]

★ ★ **RADISSON HOTEL OLD TOWN ALEXANDRIA.** *901 N Fairfax St (22314). Phone 703/683-6000; toll-free 800/333-3333; fax 703/683-5750. www.radisson.com.* 258 rooms, 12 story. Check-out noon. TV; cable (premium). In-room modem link. Restaurant, bar. Pool. Free airport transportation. **$**

[D] [≃] [≦] [SC]

Hotels

★★**HILTON ALEXANDRIA MARK CENTER.** *5000 Seminary Rd (22311). Phone 703/845-1010; toll-free 800/774-1500; fax 703/845-7662. www.hilton.com.* 495 rooms, 30 story. Check-out noon. TV; cable (premium), VCR available (free movies). In-room modem link. Restaurant, bar. In-house fitness room, sauna. Game room. Indoor, outdoor pools; whirlpool. Outdoor tennis. Covered parking, valet parking. Free airport transportation. Business center. Luxury level. Located on 50 wooded acres with nature preserve. **$**

D ⤢ ⊷ 🏋 🚶 ⊵ SC 🏃

★★★**MORRISON HOUSE.** *116 S Alfred St (22314). Phone 703/838-8000; toll-free 800/367-0800; fax 703/684-6283. www.morrisonhouse.com.* The quaint, brick-lined streets of charming Old Town Alexandria are a perfect match for the historical flavor of the Morrison House. Just down the river from the Capitol, this Federal-style mansion presents visitors with a peaceful alternative to the bustling city. Decorative fireplaces, four-poster mahogany beds, and silk sofas define the guest rooms, all furnished in early American décor. The amenities are decidedly 21st century, however, with oversized marble bathrooms and luxurious Frette linens. The Grille attracts a smart casual set with its clubby ambience and live piano music, but it is the exceptional Elysium (see) that is not to be missed. Menus are banished here, the dishes determined by the chef's conversations with each patron. Diners sip Champagne and fine wines as he concocts creative, personalized meals. Rather like having a private chef for the evening, this is truly a singular experience. 45 rooms, 5 story. Check-out noon, check-in 3 pm. TV; cable (premium), VCR available. In-room modem link. Restaurant, dining room, bar; entertainment Thurs-Sat. Room service 24 hours. Babysitting services available. Covered parking. **$$**

D ⊵

All Suites

★★★**SHERATON SUITES.** *801 N St. Asaph St (22314). Phone 703/836-4700; toll-free 800/325-3535; fax 703/548-4514. www.sheraton.com.* Located just 2 miles from National Airport and the Pentagon, this hotel offers amenities for both business and leisure travelers. 247 rooms, 10 story. Check-out 1 pm. TV; cable (premium). In-room modem link. Laundry services. Restaurant, bar. In-house fitness room. Indoor pool, whirlpool. Garage parking. Free airport transportation. Luxury level. **$**

D ⊷ 🏋 🛫 ⊵ SC

★★**WASHINGTON SUITES.** *100 S Reynolds St (22304). Phone 703/370-9600; fax 703/370-0467. www.washingtonsuiteshotel.com.* 225 rooms, 9 story. Pets accepted, some restrictions; fee. Complimentary continental breakfast. Check-out noon. TV; cable (premium). Laundry services. Restaurant, bar. In-house fitness room. Health club privileges. Pool. Business center. **$$**

D 🐾 ⊷ 🏋 🚶 ⊵ 🏃

Restaurants

★ **THE ALAMO.** *100 King St (22314). Phone 703/739-0555; fax 703/549-8441.* Nouvelle Southwestern menu. Closed Thanksgiving, Dec 25. Lunch, dinner. Bar. Entertainment. In 1871 Corn Exchange Building. **$$**

★ ★ **BILBO BAGGINS.** *208 Queen St (22314). Phone 703/683-0300; fax 703/683-1857. www.bilbobaggins.net.* Continental menu. Closed Dec 25. Lunch, dinner, Sun brunch. Bar. Upstairs in an 1898 structure; stained glass, skylights. **$$**

D

★ ★ **BISTRO EUROPA.** *715 King St (22314). Phone 703/549-0533. www.bistro-europa.com.* Continental menu. Lunch, dinner. Bar. Casual attire. **$$**

D

★ ★ **BLUE POINT GRILL.** *600 Franklin St (22314). Phone 703/739-0404; fax 703/684-1853. www.suttongourmet.com.* Seafood menu. Closed Dec 25. Lunch, dinner, Sun brunch. Outdoor seating. **$$**

D

★ ★ **BULLFEATHERS RESTAURANT-OLD TOWN.** *112 King St (22314). Phone 703/836-8088; fax 703/836-3246.* American menu. Lunch, dinner. Bar. Children's menu. Casual attire. **$**

★ ★ **CALVERT GRILLE.** *3106 Mt. Vernon Ave (22305). Phone 703/836-8425; fax 703/836-0539.* Breakfast, lunch, dinner, Sat-Sun brunch. Bar. Children's menu. **$$**

D

★ **CHADWICK'S.** *203 Strand St (22314). Phone 703/836-4442.* American menu. Closed Dec 25. Lunch, dinner, late night. Bar. Children's menu. Casual attire. Outdoor seating. **$$**

D

★ ★ **CHART HOUSE.** *1 Cameron St (22314). Phone 703/684-5080; fax 703/684-7364. www.chart-house.com.* Contemporary American menu. Lunch, dinner, Sun brunch. Bar. Children's menu. Reservations required Fri-Sun. **$$**

D

★ ★ ★ **CHEZ ANDRE.** *10 E Glebe Rd (22305). Phone 703/836-1404; fax 703/836-2530.* Choose from three different dining rooms at this restaurant that has been family owned for nearly 40 years. French menu. Closed Sun; major holidays. Lunch, dinner. Bar. Reservations required. **$$**

★ ★ **COPELAND'S OF NEW ORLEANS.** *4300 King St (22302). Phone 703/671-7997; fax 703/578-1082. www.alcopeland.com.* Cajun/Creole menu. Closed Thanksgiving, Dec 25. Lunch, dinner, Sun brunch. Bar. Children's menu. Outdoor seating. **$**

D

★ ★ **EAST WIND.** *809 King St (22314). Phone 703/836-1515; fax 703/836-2380.* Vietnamese menu. Closed major holidays. Lunch, dinner. Bar. **$$**

★ ★ **ECCO CAFE.** *220 N Lee St (22314). Phone 703/684-0321; fax 703/684-1785. www.eccocafe.com.* American, Italian menu. Closed Thanksgiving, Dec 25. Lunch, dinner, Sun brunch. Bar. Jazz Sun. In a restored 1890s warehouse building; eclectic décor. **$$**
[D]

★ ★ ★ **ELYSIUM.** *116 S Alfred St (22314). Phone 703/838-8000; toll-free 800/367-0800; fax 703/684-6283. www.morrisonhouse.com.* Have you ever dreamed of having a chef of your very own—someone who would come to your table and say something like, "Good evening. So nice to see you. What would you like me to make for you this evening?" Open your eyes. This is not a dream. You are at Elysium, a magical restaurant in the Morrison House hotel in historic Alexandria, where you create your very own "Flight of Food" based on what the chef has purchased from local markets and farmers that very day. Instead of a dinner menu, you'll be presented with a wine list (a nice big one with lots of terrific international choices) and then a personal visit from the chef to discuss what you're in the mood to eat. He'll give you the list of ingredients, and you work together to develop the menu. It's very interactive and very exciting. This is living. After dinner, a butler will escort you to the parlor for an after-dinner drink or a wonderful, aromatic pot of special-blend lose tea made for the Morrison House. Eclectic, continental menu. Closed Jan 1. Breakfast, dinner. Bar. Children's menu. Casual attire. **$$$**
[D]

★ **FACCIA LUNA.** *823 S Washington St (22314). Phone 703/838-5998. www.faccialuna.com.* American, Italian menu. Closed some major holidays. Lunch, dinner. Bar. Children's menu. Outdoor seating. **$$**
[D]

★ ★ **FISH MARKET.** *105 King St (22314). Phone 703/836-5676; fax 703/836-4659. www.fishmarketoldtown.com.* Closed Thanksgiving, Dec 25. Lunch, dinner. Bar. Ragtime pianist. In a restored 18th-century warehouse built of bricks carried to the New World as a ballast in the ship's hold; nautical décor. Outdoor seating. **$$**

★ ★ **GADSBY'S TAVERN.** *138 N Royal St (22314). Phone 703/548-1288; fax 703/548-5324. www.gadsbys.org.* Closed Jan 1, Dec 25. Lunch, dinner, Sun brunch. Children's menu. Built in 1792; Georgian architecture; colonial décor and costumes. Reservations required. Outdoor seating. Strolling minstrels. Gadsby's Tavern Museum adjacent. Totally nonsmoking. **$$**
[D]

★ ★ ★ **GERANIO.** *722 King St (22314). Phone 703/548-0088; fax 703/548-0091. www.geranio.net.* A roaring fireplace and stylish décor create a comfortable blend of old and new at this innovative restaurant. Regional favorites make up the diverse and gratifying menu. Italian, Mediterranean menu. Closed some major holidays. Lunch, dinner. Bar. Reservations required. **$$**
[D]

★ **HARD TIMES CAFE.** *1404 King St (22314). Phone 703/683-5340; fax 703/683-8801. www.hardtimes.com.* Specializes in chili. Closed some major holidays. Lunch, dinner. Housed in a former church; rustic décor; collection of state flags. **$**

D

★ ★ **IL PORTO.** *121 King St (22314). Phone 703/836-8833; fax 703/836-8835. www.ilportoristorante.com.* A very skilled kitchen staff turns out classic dishes at this cozy restaurant, a local favorite for years. Set in a renovated warehouse, the atmosphere is just as rustic as the food. Northern Italian menu. Closed Thanksgiving. Lunch, dinner. Bar. Children's menu. Casual attire. Reservations required. **$$**

D

★ ★ ★ **LA BERGERIE.** *218 N Lee St (22314). Phone 703/683-1007; fax 703/519-6114. www.labergerie.com.* A historic brick warehouse is the setting for this restaurant that is a local favorite. Pleasant, tuxedoed waiters serve classic, often-forgotten dishes from the Basque region. French menu. Closed Sun except Mother's Day; major holidays. Lunch, dinner. Restored 1890s warehouse. Reservations required. **$$**

D

★ ★ **LANDINI BROTHERS.** *115 King St (22314). Phone 703/836-8404; fax 703/549-2211. www.landinibrothers.com.* Italian menu. Closed major holidays. Lunch, dinner. Bar. Reservations required. 1790s building. **$$**

D

★ ★ **LE GAULOIS.** *1106 King St (22314). Phone 703/739-9494; fax 703/739-9496.* French menu. Closed major holidays. Lunch, dinner. Casual attire. Reservations required. Outdoor seating. **$$**

D

★ ★ **LE REFUGE.** *127 N Washington St (22314). Phone 703/548-4661.* French menu. Closed Sun; some major holidays. Lunch, dinner. Bar. Reservations required. **$$$**

★ **MANGO MIKE'S.** *4580 Duke St (22304). Phone 703/823-1166; fax 703/370-4424. www.mangomikes.com.* Caribbean menu. Closed Thanksgiving, Dec 25. Lunch, dinner, Sun brunch. Bar. Children's menu. Outdoor seating. **$**

D

★ ★ **MONROE'S.** *1603 Commonwealth Ave (22301). Phone 703/548-5792; fax 703/548-5914.* Italian menu. Closed most major holidays. Dinner, Sun brunch. Bar. Children's menu. Reservations required. Outdoor seating. Contemporary trattoria with large murals. Totally nonsmoking. **$$**

D

★ ★ **R. T.'S.** *3804 Mt. Vernon Ave (22305). Phone 703/684-6010; fax 703/548-0417. www.rts.com.* Cajun/Creole menu. Closed some major holidays. Lunch, dinner. Bar. Children's menu. **$$**

D

★ ★ **SANTA FE EAST.** *110 S Pitt St (22314). Phone 703/548-6900; fax 703/519-0798. www.santafeeast.com.* Southwestern menu. Closed July 4, Thanksgiving, Dec 25. Lunch, dinner, Sun brunch. Bar. In historic (1790) building. Outdoor seating. Fountain in courtyard. **$$**

D

★ ★ **SCOTLAND YARD.** *728 King St (22314). Phone 703/683-1742; fax 703/683-6989. www.scotlandyardrestaurant.com.* Scottish menu. Closed Mon; Thanksgiving. Dinner. Reservations required. Totally nonsmoking. **$$$**

D

★ ★ **STELLA'S.** *1725 Duke St (22314). Phone 703/519-1946; fax 703/519-7610. www.stellas.com.* American menu. Closed Jan 1, July 4, Thanksgiving, Dec 25. Lunch, dinner. Bar. Children's menu. Casual attire. Outdoor seating. **$$**

D

★ ★ **TAVERNA CRETEKOU.** *818 King St (22314). Phone 703/548-8688. www.tavernacretekou.com.* Greek, seafood menu. Closed Mon; some major holidays. Lunch, dinner, Sun brunch. Bar; entertainment. Reservations required. Outdoor seating. **$$**

★ ★ **TEMPO.** *4231 Duke St (22304). Phone 703/370-7900; fax 703/370-7902. www.temporestaurant.com.* Italian, French menu. Closed most major holidays. Lunch, dinner, Sun brunch. Bar. Reservations required. Outdoor seating. **$$**

D SC

★ ★ **THAI HUT.** *408 S Van Dorn St (22304). Phone 703/823-5357; fax 703/823-2931.* Thai menu. Closed Thanksgiving, Dec 25. Lunch, dinner. **$$**

D

★ ★ **THAI LEMONGRASS.** *506 S Van Dorn St (22304). Phone 703/751-4627; fax 703/751-4627.* Thai menu. Closed Dec 25. Lunch, dinner. Bar. Casual attire. **$$**

D

★ ★ **UNION STREET PUBLIC HOUSE.** *121 S Union St (22314). Phone 703/548-1785; fax 703/548-0705. www.usphalexandria.com.* Closed Thanksgiving, Dec 25. Lunch, dinner, Sun brunch. Bar. Children's menu. In a sea captain's house and warehouse (circa 1870). **$$**

★ ★ **VILLA D'ESTE.** *600 Montgomery St (22314). Phone 703/549-9477; fax 703/549-8809. www.villadesterestaurant.com.* Italian menu. Closed major holidays. Lunch, dinner. Bar. Reservations required. **$$$**

D

★ ★ **WHARF.** *119 King St (22314). Phone 703/836-2834; fax 703/836-3028. www.wharfrestaurant.com.* Seafood menu. Closed Jan 1, Thanksgiving, Dec 25. Lunch, dinner. Bar. Children's menu. Late 18th-century building. **$$**

D

Annapolis, MD
40 minutes; 32 miles from Washington, DC

Founded 1649 **Pop** 35,838 **Elev** 57 ft **Area code** 410 and 443

Information Annapolis and Anne Arundel County Conference and Visitors Bureau, 26 West St, 21401; 410/268-TOUR. Information is also available at the Visitor Information Booth located at the city dock.

Web www.visit-annapolis.org

The capital of Maryland, gracious and dignified in the colonial tradition, Annapolis has had a rich history for more than 300 years. Planned and laid out as the provincial capital in 1695, it was the first peacetime capital of the United States (Congress met here November 26, 1783 to August 13, 1784). In 1845, the US Naval Academy was established here at the Army's Fort Severn. Town life centers on sport and commercial water-oriented activities, state government, and the academy. Every May, at commencement time, thousands of visitors throng the narrow brick streets.

What to See and Do

Boat Trips. *980 Awald Rd # 202 (21403). From city dock at foot of Main St. Phone 410/268-7600, 410/269-6776 (Baltimore) or 301/261-2719 (DC).* Forty-minute narrated tours of city harbor, USNA, and Severn River aboard *Harbor Queen* (Memorial Day-Labor Day, daily); 90-minute cruises to locations aboard *Annapolitan II* and *Rebecca,* cruises to St. Michael's aboard the *Annapolitan II* (Memorial Day-Labor Day); 40-minute cruises up Spa Creek, residential areas, city harbor, and USNA aboard the *Miss Anne* and *Miss Anne II* (Memorial Day-Labor Day). Some cruises early spring and late fall, weather permitting. Fees vary.

Chesapeake Bay Bridge. *357 Pier 1 Rd (21666).* The 7 1/4-mile link of US 50 across the Bay. Toll (charged eastbound only) **$$**

Chesapeake Sailing School. *7074 Bembe Beach Rd (21403). Phone 410/ 269-1594; 301/261-2810; toll-free 800/966-0032. www.sailingclasses.com.* There's nothing like sun, water, and a stiff breeze for shaking off doldrums. This school offers everything from weekend sailing classes for beginners (no experience necessary) to live-aboard five-day cruises on gorgeous Chesapeake Bay, with basic and advanced instruction for individuals, families, and corporate groups. Depending on the class, you might cast off in a zippy 22-foot Tanzer or a state-of-the-art catamaran. You can also rent sailboats and go out on your own. (Apr-Oct) **$$$$**

Government House. *101 School St (21401). Between State and Church cirs. Phone 410/974-3531.* (1868) This Victorian structure was remodeled in 1935 into a Georgian country house; furnishings reflect Maryland's history and culture. Tours by appointment (Jan-mid-Apr, Tues and Thurs; rest of year, Tues-Thurs). **FREE**

History and Government in Annapolis

In the years just prior to the American Revolution, the colonial elite flocked to the bustling seaport of Annapolis, Maryland's capital on the Chesapeake Bay. This was the city's "golden age," and many, George Washington among them, were drawn by its spirited social life and elegant mansions built by wealthy tobacco planters. You can see some of the same sights Washington might have enjoyed on a one-hour, one-mile stroll through the city's well-preserved Historic District. Begin at the Visitor Center, 26 West Street, where tourist parking is available. From the center head east (left) on West Street; detour around St. Anne's Church (1859), noting its Tiffany windows; pause on School Street to view Government House, the Georgian-style Maryland Governor's residence (remodeled 1936); and then climb the stairs, as Washington surely did, to the Maryland State House on State Circle (1772), the oldest state capitol in continuous legislative use. Perched atop the city's highest hill, the State House provides a panoramic view of the bay. Inside, the Old Senate Chamber appears as it did on December 23, 1783, when Washington resigned his commission as the victorious commander of the Continental Army. At 21 State Circle, the John Shaw House (1720s) was the home of the city's premier cabinet maker, whose furniture is displayed in the State House. Continue east from State Circle on Maryland Avenue, lined with antique shops, to the Hammond-Harwood Home (1774) at No. 19. A house museum, this Georgian structure features what is considered by many to be the most beautiful doorway in America. Double back one block on Maryland Avenue, pausing briefly at the Chase-Lloyd House (1769), another elegant Georgian mansion where Francis Scott Key, author of "The Star-Spangled Banner," was married in 1802. Turn toward the harbor (left) onto Prince George Street. The William Paca House (1765) at No. 186 and its 2-acre colonial garden, carefully restored for authenticity, are national treasures. Now a house museum, the Paca house was the home of Maryland's Revolutionary War governor and a signer of the Declaration of Independence. Built in the symmetrical five-part structure of the city's finest colonial homes, it is considered one of the best examples of a Georgian home in America. Neighboring Brice House (1767) at 42 East Street is another magnificent Georgian mansion built by a wealthy merchant. To conclude this tour, continue downhill on Prince George Street, and turn west (right) one block onto Randall Street to City Dark for refreshments at Middleton Tavern. Once an "Inn for Seafaring Men," it has been serving Annapolis visitors since 1754.

Hammond-Harwood House. *19 Maryland Ave (21401), at King George St, one block W of US Naval Academy. Phone 410/269-1714.* (1774) Georgian house designed by William Buckland; antique furnishings; garden. Matthias Hammond, a Revolutionary patriot, was its first owner. Guided tours. (Daily; closed Jan 1, Thanksgiving, Dec 25) **$$**

Historic Annapolis Foundation. *Tours leave from museum store, 77 Main St (21401). Phone 410/267-7619 or 410/269-0432.* Self-guided audiocassette walking tours. Includes Historic District, State House, Old Treasury, US Naval Academy, and William Paca House. (Mar-Nov, daily) **$$**

Historic Annapolis Foundation Welcome Center and Museum Store. *77 Main St (21401). Phone 410/268-5576.* This 1815 building stands on the site of a storehouse for Revolutionary War troops that burned in 1790. Audiocassette walking tours. Products reflecting Annapolis history. (Mon-Sat, also Sun afternoons; closed Thanksgiving, Dec 25)

London Town. *839 Londontown Rd, Edgewater (21037). 8 miles SE via MD 2 S, (Mayo Rd). Phone 410/222-1919.* (Circa 1760) Once considered a site for Maryland's capital; the only surviving structure of the Lost Town is the William Brown House, a Georgian mansion on the banks of South River. Has 8 acres of woodland gardens. Museum and garden shop; boat docking. Special events. Guided tours. (Mon-Sat, also Sun afternoon; closed holidays). **$$**

Sailing Tours. *80 Compromise St (21401). Phone 410/263-8619.* Two-hour narrated trips through Chesapeake Bay aboard 74-foot sailing yacht *Woodwind.* (May-Sept, Tues-Sun four trips daily, Mon Sunset Sail only; Apr, Oct, Nov, schedule varies) Departs from Pusser's Landing next to City Dock. **$$$$**

St. John's College. *College Ave (21401). Phone 410/626-2539.* (1784) 475 students. Nonsectarian liberal arts college. This 36-acre campus, one of the oldest in the country, is a National Historic Landmark. The college succeeded King William's School, founded in 1696. George Washington's two nephews and step-grandson studied here; Francis Scott Key was an alumnus. On campus are

> **Charles Carroll, Barrister House.** *107 Duke of Gloucester St (21401). Phone 410/269-1737.* (1722) Birthplace of the author of the Maryland Bill of Rights; moved in 1955 to the campus and restored; now an administration building. Not open to the public.

> **Elizabeth Myers Mitchell Art Gallery.** *60 College Ave (21401). Phone 410/626-2556.* Displays museum-quality traveling exhibitions. (Academic year, Tues-Sun) **FREE**

> **McDowell Hall.** *60 College Ave (21401).* (begun 1742, finished 1789) Named for St. John's first president; originally built as the Governor's Mansion. Lafayette was feted here in 1824. Not open to the public.

Sandy Point State Park. *1100 E College Pkwy (21401). 7 miles E on US 50, at W end of Chesapeake Bay Bridge. Phone 410/974-2149.* On 786 acres. The park's location on the Atlantic Flyway makes it a fine area for bird-watching; view of Bay Bridge and oceangoing vessels. Swimming in the bay at two guarded beaches, two bathhouses, surf fishing, crabbing, boating (rentals, launches); concession. Standard fees. (See SPECIAL EVENTS)

State House. *91 State Cir (21401). Center of town. Phone 410/974-3400.* (1772-1779) Oldest state house in continuous legislative use in US, this was the first peacetime capitol of the US. Here in 1784, a few weeks after receiving George Washington's resignation as commander-in-chief, Congress ratified the Treaty of Paris, which officially ended the Revolutionary War. Visitors Information Center. Guide service (closed Jan 1, Thanksgiving). (Daily; closed Dec 25) **FREE**

Three Centuries Tours of Annapolis. *Morning tour leaves from Visitor Center at 26 West St; afternoon tour leaves from Visitor Information Booth on City Dock. Phone 410/263-5401, to confirm departure points and schedule.* Walking tours of US Naval Academy and Historic District conducted by guides in colonial attire. Tour includes historic Maryland State House, St. John's College, Naval Academy Chapel, crypt of John Paul Jones, Bancroft Hall dormitory, and Armel-Leftwich Visitor Center. (Apr-Oct, daily) **$$$**

United States Naval Academy. *121 Blake Rd (21402). From Baltimore, take I-97 S or Maryland Rte 2 S for 26 miles and get off on Rowe Blvd (exit 24). Take Rowe Blvd 1.6 miles to where it dead-ends at College Ave and turn left. At the first stoplight, which is King George St, turn right. Follow King George St for two blocks. Enter Gate 1; visitor parking is on your right. Phone 410/263-6933. www.usna.edu.* Opened in 1845, the Naval Academy is located in Maryland's picturesque capital, Annapolis, a 30-minute drive from Baltimore. The beautiful campus sits at the edge of the Chesapeake Bay and Severn River, occupying 338 acres. Tours of the campus are available through the academy's Armel-Leftwich Visitor Center, where you can immerse yourself in naval history and life. You will see the tomb of John Paul Jones, the chapel, the midshipmen's living quarters, and the naval museum. The center also shows the orientation film *To Lead and to Serve,* exhibits the original wooden figurehead of the *Tecumseh,* and displays the *Freedom 7* space capsule. If you time your visit right, you can witness the Noon Formation. During this impressive daily event, all present midshipmen gather, line up, and march in for the noon meal with military precision. **Note:** Access to the Academy grounds is limited. Please check the current security restrictions before planning a visit. All visitors over the age of 16 must have a valid picture ID. (Daily; closed major holidays) **$$**

William Paca Garden. *186 Prince George St (21401). Phone 410/263-5553.* Restored 2-acre pleasure garden originally developed in 1765 by William Paca, a signer of the Declaration of Independence and governor of Maryland during the Revolutionary War. Includes waterways, formal parterres, and a garden wilderness. (Mon-Sat, also Sun afternoons; closed Thanksgiving, Dec 25) **$$** Also here is

William Paca House. Paca built this five-part Georgian mansion in 1765. (Mon-Sat, also Sun afternoons; closed Thanksgiving, Dec 25) **$$**

Special Events

Annapolis by Candlelight. *18 Pinkney St (21401). Phone 410/267-7619.* For information and reservations contact Historic Annapolis Foundation. Usually early Nov.

Chesapeake Appreciation Days. *Sandy Point State Park. 1100 E College Pkwy (21401). Phone 410/974-2149.* Skipjack sailing festival honors state's oystermen. Usually last weekend in Oct.

Christmas in Annapolis. Features decorated 18th-century mansions, parade of yachts, private home tours, pub crawls, concerts, holiday meals, First Night celebration, caroling by candlelight at the State House and other events. For free events calendar, phone 410/268-8687. Thanksgiving-Jan 1.

Maryland Renaissance Festival. *1821 Crownsville Rd (21401). Phone 410/266-7303.* Food, crafters, minstrels, dramatic productions. Usually last week in Aug-third weekend in Oct.

Maryland Seafood Festival. *Sandy Point State Park. 1100 E College Pkwy (21401). Phone 410/974-2149. www.mdseafoodfestival.com.* This family-friendly event offers up hearty portions of Maryland's favorite seafood dishes, including crab cakes, flounder, oysters, clams, trout, and shrimp salad. Held at Sandy Point State Park near historic Annapolis, visitors will enjoy the beauty of the Chesapeake Bay, more than 50 quality arts and crafts exhibitors, and live musical entertainment. The nearby National Aquarium and US Naval Academy make nice side trips. Weekend after Labor Day.

US Powerboat Show. *City dock and harbor. 100 Severn Ave (21401). Phone 410/268-8828.* Extensive in-water display of powerboats; exhibits of related marine products. Mid-Oct.

US Sailboat Show. *City dock and harbor. 100 Severn Ave (21401). Phone 410/268-8828.* Features world's largest in-water display of sailboats; exhibits of related marine products. Early-mid-Oct.

Motels/Motor Lodges

★ **BEST WESTERN ANNAPOLIS.** *2520 Riva Rd (21401). Phone 410/224-2800; toll-free 800/780-7234; fax 410/266-5539. www.bestwestern.com.* 152 rooms, 2 story. Complimentary continental breakfast. Check-out 11 am. TV; cable (premium). Laundry services. Game room. Pool. **$**

D ⇌ ⊠

★ **COMFORT INN.** *76 Old Mill Bottom Rd (21401). Phone 410/757-8500; toll-free 877/424-6423; fax 410/757-4409. www.comfortinn.com.* 60 rooms, 2 story. Complimentary continental breakfast. Check-out 11 am. TV; cable (premium). Coin laundry. Pool; lifeguard. **$**

D ⇌ ⊠ SC

★ ★ **COURTYARD BY MARRIOTT.** *2559 Riva Rd (21401). Phone 410/266-1555; toll-free 800/321-2211; fax 410/266-6376. www.courtyard.com.* 149 rooms, 3 story. Check-out noon. TV; cable (premium). In-room modem link. Laundry services. Restaurant, bar. In-house fitness room. Indoor pool, whirlpool. **$**

D ⇌ 🏋 ⊠ SC

Hotels

★ ★ ★ **LOEWS ANNAPOLIS HOTEL.** *126 West St (21401). Phone 410/263-7777; toll-free 800/526-2593; fax 410/263-0084. www.loewsannapolis.com.* Located in the heart of downtown Annapolis, this hotel is within walking distance to many of the city's historical sites. It also has 17,000 square feet of flexible meeting space that business travelers will find convenient and comfortable. 217 rooms, 6 story. Pets accepted, some restrictions. Check-out noon. TV; cable (premium). In-room modem link. Restaurant (see also BREEZE), bar. In-house fitness room. Health club privileges. Valet parking. Business center. Concierge. Luxury level. **$**

D ◄ 🏋 🖾 SC 🏃

★ ★ ★ **MARRIOTT ANNAPOLIS WATERFRONT.** *80 Compromise St (21401). Phone 410/268-7555; toll-free 800/228-9290; fax 410/269-5864. www.marriott.com.* With guest rooms overlooking Chesapeake Bay, this hotel is conveniently located to nearby shops and restaurants in colonial Annapolis. 150 rooms, 6 story. Check-out 11 am. TV; cable (premium), VCR available. In-room modem link. Restaurant, bar. In-house fitness room. On the waterfront; 300 foot dockage. **$$$**

D 🏋 🖾

★ ★ **RADISSON HOTEL ANNAPOLIS.** *210 Holiday Ct (21401). Phone 410/224-3150; toll-free 800/333-3333; fax 410/224-3413. www.radisson.com.* 220 rooms, 6 story. Pets accepted, some restrictions; fee. Check-out noon. TV; cable (premium). In-room modem link. Restaurant, bar. Room service. Pool. **$**

D ◄ 🏊 🖾 SC

★ ★ ★ **SHERATON BARCELO ANNAPOLIS.** *173 Jennifer Rd (21401). Phone 410/266-3131; toll-free 800/625-5144; fax 410/266-6247. www.sheraton.com.* 197 rooms, 6 story. Check-out noon. TV; cable. In-room modem link. Restaurant, bar. Room service. In-house fitness room, sauna. Health club privileges. Indoor pool, whirlpool. **$**

D 🏊 🏋 🖾 SC

B&B/Small Inns

★ ★ **CHESAPEAKE BAY LIGHTHOUSE BED AND BREAKFAST.** *1423 Sharps Point Rd (21401). Phone 410/757-0248; fax 410/757-0248.* 5 rooms, 2 story. No room phones. Children over 12 only. Complimentary continental breakfast. Check-out 11 am, check-in 3-7 pm. TV in sitting room. Working lighthouse on Chesapeake Bay. Totally nonsmoking. **$**

🛴 🖾

★ ★ **GIBSON'S LODGINGS.** *110 Prince George St (21401). Phone 410/268-5555; fax 410/268-2775. www.avmcyber.com/gibson.* 20 rooms, 13 share bath in 3 buildings, 3 story. Complimentary continental breakfast. Check-out 11 am, check-in 2 pm. TV in some rooms; cable, VCR available. Some room phones. Totally nonsmoking. **$**

D 🖾

★ ★ ★ **GOVERNOR CALVERT HOUSE.** *58 State Cir (21401). Phone 410/263-2641; toll-free 800/847-8882; fax 410/268-3813. www.annapolis inns.com/calverthouse.html.* Formerly inhabited by two Maryland governors named Calvert, this tastefully restored colonial and Victorian residence also has a contemporary conference center. One side of the property faces the Colonial Gardens, the other faces the State House. The atrium lobby is a terrific place to gather. 51 rooms, 4 story. Check-out noon, check-in 3 pm. TV; cable (premium). In-room modem link. Valet parking. 18th-century statehouse with modern addition; colonial gardens, atrium. **$$**

[D] [🖼] [SC]

★ ★ **MARYLAND INN.** *58 State Cir (21401). Phone 410/263-2641; toll-free 800/847-8882; fax 410/268-3813. www.annapolisinns.com/marylandinn.html.* 44 rooms, 4 story. Check-out noon, check-in 3 pm. TV; cable (premium). In-room modem link. Restaurant (see also TREATY OF PARIS). Bar; entertainment. Valet parking. Historic inn built in 1772. View of bay. **$$**

[🖼] [SC]

★ ★ ★ **PRINCE GEORGE INN.** *232 Prince George St (21401). Phone 410/263-6418; fax 410/626-0009. www.princegeorgeinn.com.* Step back in time at this quiet, charming bed-and-breakfast originally built in the late 1800s. With a full gourmet breakfast and intimate, antique-filled guest rooms, visitors will feel like they've been to grandma's house. 4 rooms, 2 share bath, 3 story. No room phones. Complimentary full breakfast. Check-out noon, check-in 4-6 pm. TV; VCR. Victorian townhouse built in 1884. Totally nonsmoking. **$**

[🖼]

★ ★ **ROBERT JOHNSON HOUSE.** *23 State Cir (21401). Phone 410/263-2641; toll-free 800/847-8882; fax 410/268-3613.* 29 rooms, 4 story. Check-out noon, check-in 3 pm. TV; cable (premium). In-room modem link. Valet parking. Consists of 18th-century mansion plus two connecting town houses of the same period. **$**

[D] [🖼] [SC]

★ ★ **WILLIAM PAGE INN.** *8 Martin St (21401). Phone 410/626-1506; toll-free 800/364-4160; fax 410/263-4841. www.williampageinn.com.* 5 rooms, 2 share bath, 3 story. Complimentary full breakfast. Check-out noon, check-in 4-6 pm. Former clubhouse (1908). Totally nonsmoking. **$$**

[🖼]

Restaurants

★ ★ ★ **BREEZE.** *126 West St (21401). Phone 410/263-1299; fax 410/263-0084. www.loewsannapolis.com.* Located in the Loews Annapolis Hotel (see), this restaurant has a creative menu with tempting flavors. Seafood, steak menu. Breakfast, lunch, dinner, Sun brunch. Bar. Children's menu. Valet parking. **$$$**

[D] [SC]

★ ★ **CAFE NORMANDIE.** *185 Main St (21401). Phone 410/263-3382; fax 410/263-3566.* French, seafood menu. Breakfast, lunch, dinner. **$$**

D

★ ★ **CARROL'S CREEK.** *410 Severn Ave, Eastport (21403). Phone 410/263-8102; fax 410/269-7536. www.carrollscreek.com.* Seafood menu. Lunch, dinner, Sun brunch. Bar. Outdoor seating. On the water. **$$**

D

★ ★ **FRED'S.** *2348 Solomon's Island Rd (21401). Phone 410/224-2386; fax 410/224-2539.* Continental menu. Closed Thanksgiving, Dec 25. Lunch, dinner. Bar. Children's menu. Victorian décor; antiques. **$$$**

D

★ ★ **GRIFFIN'S.** *22 Market Space (21401). Phone 410/268-2576; fax 410/280-0195. www.griffins-citydock.com.* Seafood, steak menu. Closed Dec 25. Lunch, dinner, Sun brunch. Bar. Children's menu. **$$**

D

★ ★ ★ **HARRY BROWNE'S.** *66 State Cir (21401). Phone 410/263-4332; fax 410/263-8049. www.harrybrownes.com.* Known as one of the best upscale restaurants in town, Harry Browne's overlooks the Maryland State House in downtown Annapolis. The fare is consistently good, the ambience inviting, and the service pleasurable. Continental menu. Closed Jan 1, Dec 25. Lunch, dinner. Bar. Entertainment Mon, Fri, Sat. Valet parking Fri, Sat. **$$**

D

★ ★ **LEWNES' STEAKHOUSE.** *401 4th St (21403). Phone 410/263-1617. www.lewnessteakhouse.com.* Seafood, steak menu. Closed Thanksgiving, Dec 25. Dinner. Bar. Reservations required. **$$$**

D

★ **MARIA'S SICILIAN RESTAURANT & CAFE.** *12 Market Pl (21401). Phone 410/268-2112. www.landmarks.com/marias/.* Italian menu. Lunch, dinner. Bar. Casual attire. Outdoor seating. **$$**

★ ★ **MIDDLETON TAVERN.** *2 Market Space (21401). Phone 410/263-3323; fax 410/263-3807. www.middletontavern.com.* Seafood menu. Lunch, dinner. Bar. Entertainment. Restored building (1750), traditional tavern décor. Outdoor seating. **$$$**

★ ★ ★ **NORTHWOODS.** *609 Melvin Ave (21401). Phone 410/268-2609; fax 410/268-0930.* This rustic, upscale seafood restaurant has a warm and romantic feel with great views of Annapolis Harbor. With a good wine selection and a variety of fresh local seafood, it is a favorite for both business and intimate dinners. Continental menu. Closed most major holidays. Dinner. Outdoor seating. **$$**

D

★ ★ **O'LEARY'S SEAFOOD.** *310 3rd St (21403). Phone 410/263-0884; fax 410/263-5869.* Seafood menu. Closed Thanksgiving, Dec 24-25. Dinner. Bar. Children's menu. **$$$**

★ ★ ★ **TREATY OF PARIS.** *58 State Cir (21401). Phone 410/263-2641; fax 410/268-3813. www.annapolisinns.com/marylandinn.html.* This landmark is praised for its game and seafood selections. With menu items such as warm duck breast salad, beef Wellington, or rack of lamb, guests will bask in both the presentation and flavors of the masterful fares. Continental menu. Closed Jan 1. Lunch, dinner, Sun brunch. Bar. Reservations required. Valet parking (dinner). **$$**

SC

Arlington County (Ronald Reagan Washington-National Airport Area), VA

10 minutes; 5 miles from Washington, DC
See also Alexandria, Fairfax; also see Washington, DC

Originally a part of the District of Columbia laid out for the capital in 1791, Arlington County, across the Potomac River from Washington, was returned to Virginia in 1846. The community is the urban center of northern Virginia.

Web www.co.arlington.va.us

Services and Information

Airlines. Air Canada, Alaska Airlines, America West, American, American Eagle, ATA, Continental, Continental Express, Delta, Delta Connnection, Frontier Airlines, Midwest Express, Northwest, United, US Airways, US Airways Express.

Transportation

AIRPORTS
Ronald Reagan Washington-National Airport. Information 703/417-8000; lost and found 703/417-8560; weather 202/936-1212; cash machines at Main Terminal, main level near Travelers Aid.

CAR RENTAL AGENCIES
See IMPORTANT TOLL-FREE NUMBERS.

PUBLIC TRANSPORTATION

Subway trains and buses (Metro Transit System), phone 202/962-1234. Information 202/637-7000.

RAIL PASSENGER SERVICE

Amtrak 800/872-7245.

What to See and Do

Arlington Farmers' Market. *N Courthouse Rd and N 14th St. Adjacent to Arlington County Courthouse. Phone 703/228-6423. www.arlingtonfarmers market.com.* Irresistibly fresh berries, peaches, and heirloom tomatoes are just some of the pleasures available at this lively market, which has been featuring the produce of farmers within 125 miles of Arlington since 1979. Don't miss the grass-fed meats, specialty goat cheeses, and unusual varieties of familiar fruits and vegetables (one longtime vendor grows 35 different types of apples). Expect a great selection in any season at this year-round market: more than 30 producers are on hand on a typical Saturday. (Sat)

⭐ **Arlington National Cemetery.** *W end of Memorial Bridge. Phone 703/979-0690 or 703/607-8000. www.arlingtoncemetery.org.* The solemn grounds of Arlington National Cemetery are a profoundly stirring sight. Gentle hills are studded as far as the eye can see with white stones marking the graves of more than 260,000 Americans who served in the nation's military, from the American Revolution to more recent conflicts. Many visitors stop at the Tomb of the Unknowns, which contains the unidentified remains of servicemen killed in the world wars and the Korean conflict and provides quiet tribute to anonymous sacrifice. Most also pay their respects at the eternal flame marking the granite-paved gravesite of President John F. Kennedy and his wife, Jacqueline, and that of Robert F. Kennedy nearby. These graves are situated on a grassy slope below Arlington House, the elegantly columned mansion that was Civil War general Robert E. Lee's home for 30 years and is now maintained as a public memorial to him. **FREE** Also located here are

Arlington House, the Robert E. Lee Memorial. *Phone 703/557-0613 or 703/235-1530. www.nps.gov/arho/.* National memorial to Robert E. Lee. Built between 1802 and 1818 by George Washington Parke Custis, Martha Washington's grandson and foster son of George Washington. In 1831 his daughter, Mary Anna Randolph Custis, married Lieutenant Robert E. Lee; six of the seven Lee children were born here. As executor of the Custis estate, Lee took extended leave from the US Army and devoted his time to managing and improving the estate. It was the Lee homestead for 30 years before the Civil War. On April 20, 1861, following the secession of Virginia, Lee made his decision to stay with Virginia. Within a month, the house was vacated. Some of the family possessions were moved for safekeeping, but most were stolen or destroyed when Union troops occupied the house during the Civil War. In 1864, when Mrs. Lee could not appear personally to pay property tax, the estate was confiscated by the federal government; a 200-acre section was set aside for a national cemetery. (There is some evidence that indicates this was done to ensure the Lee family could never again live on the estate.) G. W. Custis Lee, the general's son, later regained title to the property through a Supreme Court decision and sold it to the US government in 1883 for $150,000. Restoration of the house to its 1861 appearance was begun in 1925. The Classic Revival house is furnished with authentic pieces of the period, including some Lee family originals. From the grand portico with its six massive, faux-marble Doric columns there is a panoramic view of Washington, DC. (Daily; closed Jan 1, Dec 25)

Memorial Amphitheatre. This impressive white marble edifice is used for ceremonies such as Memorial Day, Easter sunrise, and Veterans Day services.

Tomb of the Unknowns. On November 11, 1921, the remains of an unknown American soldier of World War I were entombed here. A memorial was erected in 1932 with the inscription "Here rests in honored glory an American soldier known but to God." On Memorial Day 1958, an unknown warrior who died in World War II and another who died in the Korean War were laid beside him. On Memorial Day 1984, an unknown soldier from the Vietnam War was interred here. Sentries stand guard 24 hours a day; changing of the guard is every hour on the hour Oct-Mar, every 30 minutes Apr-Sept.

Crystal City Shops. *Crystal Dr between 15th and 23rd sts (22202). Phone 703/922-4636 or 703/413-INFO. www.thecrystalcityshops.com.* Crystal City, a mixed-use residential and commercial development, has an underground shopping complex and a lot of street-level activity. It's currently being upgraded to provide more of a "Main Street" feel, with outdoor cafés and other seating as well as improved landscaping and opportunities for window-shopping. You'll find jewelry and gift shops, men's and women's apparel, books, and home furnishings, as well as a Japanese steakhouse, two American steakhouses, and a Legal Sea Foods. (Daily)

Fashion Centre at Pentagon City. *1100 S Hayes St (22202). Off I-395 at jct S Hayes St and Army-Navy Dr, S of the Pentagon. Phone 703/415-2400.* The presence of the Ritz-Carlton Hotel dictates a glamorous tone at this huge, glittering mall, anchored by Macy's and Nordstrom and home to more than 150 other tantalizing shops and restaurants. Of-the-moment women's fashions and accessories are everywhere—don't miss bebe, Betsey Johnson, and MAC Cosmetics. For home furnishings, check out Crate & Barrel and Williams-Sonoma; Bang & Olufsen is here, too, if your needs are aural. Recover from strenuous browsing at the skylit food court. (Daily; closed Thanksgiving, Dec 25)

Iwo Jima Statue. *On Arlington Blvd, near Arlington National Cemetery.* Marine Corps War Memorial depicts raising of the flag on Mount Suribachi, Iwo Jima, February 23, 1945; this is the largest sculpture ever cast in bronze. Sunset Parade concert with performances by US Marine Drum and Bugle Corps, US Marine Corps Color Guard, and the Silent Drill Team (late May-late Aug, Tues evenings).

⭐ **The Newseum.** *1101 Wilson Blvd (22209). Phone 888/NEWSEUM or 703/284-3700.* This 72,000-square-foot interactive museum of news takes visitors behind the scenes to see and experience how and why news is made. Be a reporter or newscaster; relive great news stories through multimedia exhibits; see today's news as it happens on a block-long video wall. (Wed-Sun; closed holidays) **FREE** Located on the grounds is

Freedom Park. Nearly 1,000 feet in length, the park occupies a never-used bridge. The park also features a memorial to the journalists killed in the line of duty and various icons of freedom.

The Pentagon. *Bounded by Jefferson Davis Hwy, Washington Blvd, and I-395. Phone 703/695-1776. www.defenselink.mil/pubs/pentagon/.* With some 6 million square feet of floor area, this is one of the largest office buildings in the world; houses offices of the Department of Defense. Tours of the Pentagon are available to schools, educational organizations, and other select groups by reservation only. Groups interested in touring the Pentagon should contact the Pentagon Tour Office at the number listed above. **FREE**

Sur La Table. *1101 S Joyce St, Suite B-20 (22202). Phone 703/414-3580. www. surlatable.com.* In the 1970s, Seattle spawned this clearinghouse for hard-to-find kitchen gear, and it soon became known as a source for cookware, small appliances, cutlery, kitchen tools, linens, tableware, gadgets, and specialty foods. Sur La Table has since expanded to include cooking classes (**$$$$**), chef demonstrations, and cookbook author signings, as well as a catalog and online presence. Cooking connoisseurs discover such finds as cool oven mitts, zest graters, copper whisks, onion soup bowls, and inspired TV dinner trays. (Daily)

Special Events

Arlington County Fair. *3308 S Stafford St (22206). Phone 703/920-4556; 703/228-6400.* Countywide fair; arts, crafts, international foods, children's activities. Aug.

Army 10-miler. *Phone 202/685-3361.* America's largest 10-mile road race, attracting thousands of military and civilian runners. Early Oct.

Marine Corps Marathon. *Starts and ends near the intersection of Rte 110 and Marshall Dr (22201). Phone toll-free 800/786-8762.* Cheer on your favorite runner at the Marine Corps Marathon—with 16,000 contestants participating, there will be awesome physiques to admire everywhere you look. The 26-mile, 385-yard route starts and ends near the Iwo Jima Memorial and winds through Arlington, Georgetown, and DC, passing the Capitol, the Pentagon, and other inspiring sights along the way. The Marine Corps Marathon 5K race, organized in conjunction with the Special Olympics competition, starts at the Memorial at 9:10 am. Late Oct. **FREE**

Memorial Day Service Ceremony. *Arlington National Cemetery. Memorial Dr (22111). Phone 703/685-2851.* Wreaths placed at the Tomb of the Unknown Soldier. The National Symphony Orchestra gives a free concert later in the evening on the lawn of the Capitol.

Motels/Motor Lodges

★ **BEST WESTERN KEY BRIDGE.** *1850 Fort Myer Dr (23692). Phone 703/522-0400; toll-free 800/780-7234; fax 703/524-5275. www.bestwestern.com.* 178 rooms, 11 story. Pets accepted; fee. Check-out noon. TV; cable (premium). In-house fitness room. Health club privileges. Pool. **$**

D ⌚ 🛏 🏋 ⤵ SC

★ ★ **COMFORT INN.** *1211 N Glebe Rd (22201). Phone 703/247-3399; toll-free 800/228-5150; fax 703/524-8739. www.comfortinn.com.* 126 rooms, 3 story. Complimentary continental breakfast. Check-out 11 am. TV; cable (premium). In-room modem link. Laundry services. Restaurant, bar. Room service. **$**

D ⤵ SC

★ ★ **COURTYARD BY MARRIOTT.** *2899 Jefferson Davis Hwy (22202). Phone 703/549-3434; toll-free 800/321-2211; fax 703/549-7440. www.courtyard.com.* 272 rooms, 14 story. Check-out 1 pm. TV; cable (premium), VCR available. In-room modem link. Laundry services. Restaurant, bar. Room service. In-house fitness room. Health club privileges. Indoor pool, whirlpool. Garage parking. Free airport transportation. **$$**

D 🛏 🏋 ✈ ⤵ SC

★ ★ **COURTYARD BY MARRIOTT.** *1533 Clarendon Blvd (22209). Phone 703/528-2222; toll-free 800/321-2211; fax 703/528-1027. www.courtyard.com.* 162 rooms, 10 story. Check-out noon. TV; cable (premium). Laundry services. Restaurant, bar. Room service. In-house fitness room. Health club privileges. Indoor pool, whirlpool. Garage parking. **$$**

D 🛏 🏋 ⤵ SC

★ **HAMPTON INN & SUITES.** *2000 Jefferson Davis Hwy (22202). Phone 703/418-8181; toll-free 800/329-7466; fax 703/920-2840. www.hampton inn.com.* 247 rooms, 8 story. Check-out 11 am. TV; cable (premium). In-room modem link. Laundry services. In-house fitness room. Pool. Garage parking. Free airport transportation. **$**

D 🛏 🏋 ✈ ⤵ SC

★ ★ **HOLIDAY INN.** *2650 Jefferson Davis Hwy (22202). Phone 703/684-7200; toll-free 800/465-4329; fax 703/684-3217. www.holiday-inn.com.* 279 rooms, 11 story. Check-out noon. TV; cable. In-room modem link. Laundry services. Restaurant, bar. In-house fitness room. Health club privileges. Pool. Garage parking. Free airport, train station transportation. Business center. **$**

D 🛏 🏋 ⚡ ⤵ 🏃

★ ★ **QUALITY INN.** *1501 Arlington Blvd (22209). Phone 703/524-5000; toll-free 800/228-5151; fax 703/522-5484. www.qualityinn.com.* 141 rooms, 1-3 story. Check-out noon. TV; cable (premium), VCR available. In-room modem link. Laundry services. Restaurant (in season), bar. Room service.

In-house fitness room. Health club privileges. Indoor pool, poolside service. **$**

D 🏊 🚶 ⛷ SC

★ ★ **QUALITY INN.** *1200 N Courthouse Rd (22201). Phone 703/524-4000; toll-free 800/221-2222; fax 703/522-6814. www.qualityhotelarlington.com.* 392 rooms, 1-10 story. Pets accepted, some restrictions; fee. Check-out noon. TV; cable (premium). In-room modem link. Laundry services. Restaurant, bar. In-house fitness room, sauna. Pool. Concierge. Luxury level. **$**

D 🐾 🏊 🚶 ⛷ SC

Hotels

★ ★ **CROWNE PLAZA.** *1489 Jefferson Davis Hwy (22202). Phone 703/416-1600; toll-free 800/2-CROWNE; fax 703/416-1615. www.crowneplaza.com.* 308 rooms, 11 story. Check-out noon. TV; cable (premium). In-room modem link. Restaurant, bar. In-house fitness room. Pool. Free airport transportation. Business center. **$$**

D 🏊 🚶 ✈ ⛷ SC 🏃

★ ★ **DOUBLETREE HOTEL.** *300 Army Navy Dr (22202). Phone 703/416-4100; toll-free 800/222-8733; fax 703/416-4126. www.doubletree.com.* Ideally located in the Crystal City area, this hotel is close to the airport and within walking distance of a major shopping mall. The Metro system is also close at hand and will take guests quickly to all the sights of Washington, DC. 632 rooms, 15 story. Check-out noon. TV; cable (premium). In-room modem link. Restaurant, bar; entertainment. In-house fitness room, sauna. Health club privileges. Indoor pool. Free airport transportation. Business center. Concierge. Luxury level. **$$**

D 🏊 🚶 ✈ ⛷ SC 🏃

★ ★ ★ **HILTON ARLINGTON AND TOWERS.** *950 N Stafford St (22203). Phone 703/528-6000; toll-free 800/468-3571; fax 703/812-5127. www.hilton.com.* This hotel is part of the Balliston Metro Center and is close to shopping and the National Science Foundation. 209 rooms, 7 story. Check-out 1 pm. TV; cable (premium). In-room modem link. Restaurant, bar. Indoor pool, whirlpool. Concierge. Luxury level. Metro stop in building. **$$**

D 🏊 ⛷ SC

★ ★ ★ **HYATT ARLINGTON.** *1325 Wilson Blvd (22209). Phone 703/525-1234; toll-free 800/233-1234; fax 703/875-3393. www.hyatt.com.* This hotel is located across the bridge from Washington and close to Arlington National Cemetery. 304 rooms, 16 story. Check-out noon, check-in 3 pm. TV; cable (premium), VCR available. In-room modem link. Laundry services. Restaurant, bar. Babysitting services available. In-house fitness room. Health club privileges. Business center. **$$**

D 🚶 ⛷ SC 🏃

★ ★ ★ **HYATT REGENCY CRYSTAL CITY.** *2799 Jefferson Davis Hwy (22202). Phone 703/418-1234; toll-free 800/233-1234; fax 703/418-1289. www.hyatt.com.* This hotel is located across the Potomac River from Washington, DC, and is within walking distance to Georgetown University. 685 rooms, 20 story. Check-out noon. TV; cable (premium), VCR available. In-room modem link. Restaurant, bar. Babysitting services available. In-house fitness room, sauna. Health club privileges. Pool, whirlpool, poolside service. Airport transportation. Business center. Concierge. **$$**

[D] [≈] [⊀] [✈] [⊴] [SC] [⊀]

★ ★ ★ **MARRIOTT CRYSTAL CITY AT REAGAN NATIONAL AIRPORT.** *1999 Jefferson Davis Hwy (22202). Phone 703/413-5500; toll-free 800/228-9290; fax 703/413-0192. www.marriott.com.* This hotel is convenient to the airport and the Metrorail for easy travel to all of DC. 343 rooms, 12 story. Check-out 1 pm, check-in 4 pm. TV; cable (premium), VCR available. In-room modem link. Laundry services. Restaurant, bar. Babysitting services available. In-house fitness room, sauna. Health club privileges. Indoor pool, whirlpool. Valet parking. Free airport transportation. Business center. Concierge. Luxury level. **$$**

[D] [≈] [⊀] [✈] [⊴] [⊀]

★ ★ ★ **MARRIOTT CRYSTAL GATEWAY.** *1700 Jefferson Davis Hwy (22202). Phone 703/920-3230; toll-free 800/228-9290; fax 703/271-5212. www.marriott.com.* This hotel is just minutes from Washington National Airport. With easy access to the mass transit system, guests are close to the many attractions of Washington, DC, and several activities are nearby. 697 rooms, 16 story. Check-out 1 pm, check-in 4 pm. TV; cable (premium). In-room modem link. Restaurant, bar. Babysitting services available. In-house fitness room, sauna. Health club privileges. Indoor, outdoor pools; whirlpool. Free airport transportation. Business center. Concierge. Luxury level. Original artwork. **$$**

[D] [≈] [⊀] [✈] [⊴] [SC] [⊀]

★ ★ ★ **MARRIOTT KEY BRIDGE.** *1401 Lee Hwy (22209). Phone 703/524-6400; toll-free 800/228-9290; fax 703/524-8964. www.marriott.com.* Just minutes from Washington, DC, and the airport, this hotel has many amenities for guests. 584 rooms, 2-14 story. Check-out 1 pm. TV; cable (premium), VCR available. In-room modem link. Restaurant (see also J. W.'S STEAKHOUSE). Bar; entertainment Thurs-Sat. In-house fitness room, sauna. Health club privileges. Indoor, outdoor pools; whirlpool; poolside service. Business center. Concierge. Luxury level. Overlooks Washington across Potomac River. **$$**

[D] [≈] [⊀] [⊴] [⊀]

★ ★ ★ ★ **THE RITZ-CARLTON, PENTAGON CITY.** *1250 S Hayes St (22202). Phone 703/415-5000; res 800/241-3333; fax 703/415-5061. www.ritzcarlton.com.* Five minutes from Washington National Airport, The Ritz-Carlton, Pentagon City provides its guests with an effortless way to visit the capital region. Although businesses, monuments, and other attractions are only minutes away, visitors leave the hectic pace behind when staying here. Tailored elegance is the hallmark of this hotel, and the guest rooms are no exception. Feather beds and Egyptian cotton linens make demanding travelers loyal fans; updated technology is a boon for business travelers; and club-level accommodations take pampering to another plane. Massages and personal fitness assessments are available at the fitness center, and the indoor access to the area's popular Fashion Centre puts smiles on the faces of devoted shoppers. Afternoon tea takes on a whimsical edge with the Winnie the Pooh children's tea service in the Lobby Lounge, and The Grill never ceases to delight diners with its all-day dining. 366 rooms, 18 story. Check-out noon, check-in 3 pm. TV; cable (premium), VCR available (movies). In-room modem link. Restaurant, bar; entertainment. Children's activity center. Babysitting services available. In-house fitness room, massage, sauna, steam room. Indoor pool, whirlpool. Valet parking. Business center. Concierge. Luxury level. **$$$**

[D] [≈] [⬆] [↘] [☂]

★ ★ ★ **SHERATON CRYSTAL CITY HOTEL.** *1800 Jefferson Davis Hwy (22202). Phone 703/486-1111; toll-free 800/325-3535; fax 703/769-3970. www.sheraton.com.* This hotel is just 1 mile from Washington National Airport. Shopping, as well as many sites and activities of Washington are close by. 210 rooms, 15 story. Check-out 1 pm, check-in 3 pm. TV; cable (premium). In-room modem link. Restaurant, bar; entertainment. In-house fitness room, sauna. Outdoor pool. Free airport transportation. Business center. Luxury level. **$$**

[D] [≈] [⬆] [✈] [↘] [SC] [☂]

All Suite

★ ★ **EMBASSY SUITES.** *1300 Jefferson Davis Hwy (22202). Phone 703/979-9799; toll-free 800/EMBASSSY; fax 703/920-5947. www.embassy suites.com.* Convenient to downtown Washington and close to the airport, this property is in the center of Crystal City. 267 rooms, 11 story. Complimentary full breakfast. Check-out noon. TV; cable (premium). In-room modem link. Restaurant, bar. Room service. In-house fitness room. Health club privileges. Pool. Free airport transportation. **$$**

[D] [⚓] [≈] [⬆] [☂] [✈] [↘]

Extended Stay

★ ★ **RESIDENCE INN BY MARRIOTT.** *550 Army Navy Dr (22202). Phone 703/413-6630; toll-free 800/331-3131; fax 703/418-1751. www.residenceinn.com.* 299 rooms, 17 story. Complimentary continental breakfast. Check-out noon. TV; cable (premium). Laundry services. In-house fitness room. Health club privileges. Indoor pool, whirlpool. Garage parking. Free airport transportation. Concierge. **$$**

[D] [≈] [⬆] [↘]

Restaurants

★ ★ **ALPINE.** *4770 Lee Hwy (22207). Phone 703/528-7600; fax 703/528-7625.* Italian menu. Closed Mon; most major holidays. Lunch, dinner. Bar. **$$**

D

★ ★ **BISTRO BISTRO.** *4021 S 28th St (22206). Phone 703/379-0300; fax 703/931-1036. www.bistro-bistro.com.* Closed Thanksgiving, Dec 24-25. Lunch, dinner, Sun brunch. Bar. Outdoor seating. **$$**

D

★ **CAFE DALAT.** *3143 Wilson Blvd (22201). Phone 703/276-0935.* Vietnamese menu. Closed July 4, Thanksgiving, Dec 25; also Chinese New Year. Lunch, dinner. Totally nonsmoking. **$$**

★ ★ **CARLYLE GRAND CAFE.** *4000 S 28th St (22206). Phone 703/931-0777; fax 703/931-9420. www.greatamericanrestaurants.com/carlyle/em.htm.* Closed Thanksgiving, Dec 25. Lunch, dinner, Sun brunch. Bar. Outdoor seating. Totally nonsmoking. **$$**

★ **COWBOY CAFE.** *4792 Lee Hwy (22207). Phone 703/243-8010. www.washingtonpost.com/cowboycafe.* Breakfast, lunch, dinner. Bar. Musicians Thurs-Sat. **$**

D

★ **FACCIA LUNA.** *2909 Wilson Blvd (22201). Phone 703/276-3099. www.faccialuna.com.* Italian menu. Closed Thanksgiving, Dec 24-25. Lunch, dinner. Bar. Children's menu. Outdoor seating. Upscale trattoria. **$$**

D

★ ★ ★ **THE GRILL.** *1250 S Hayes St (22202). Phone 703/412-2760; fax 703/415-5061. www.ritzcarlton.com.* The Grill at the Ritz-Carlton offers upscale American classics in a warm, clubby dining room decked out in mahogany wood. It features a crackling fireplace and fresh flowers. The Grill's formal yet inviting atmosphere makes it ideal for all sorts of gatherings, whether business, pleasure, or both. The seasonal menu features lots of pin-up worthy dishes. Lobster, filet mignon, foie gras, caviar, and oysters are in attendance in abundance, giving those in need of culinary luxury an easy and delicious fix. Weekends are busy for The Grill, as it houses one of the best brunches in the area. American, continental menu. Breakfast, lunch, dinner, brunch. Pianist Fri, Sat evenings. Children's menu. Casual attire. Valet parking available. Afternoon tea. **$$$**

D

★ ★ **J. W:S STEAKHOUSE.** *1401 Lee Hwy (22209). Phone 703/524-6400; fax 703/524-8964. www.marriot.com.* Seafood, steak menu. Closed Jan 1. Dinner, Sun brunch. Bar. **$$$**

D

★ ★ **LA COTE D'OR CAFE.** *6876 Lee Hwy (22213). Phone 703/538-3033; fax 703/573-0409. www.lacotedor.com.* French menu. Closed Jan 1, Dec 25. Lunch, dinner, Sun brunch. Bar. Outdoor seating. **$$**

[D]

★ ★ **LITTLE VIET GARDEN.** *3012 Wilson Blvd (22201). Phone 703/522-9686.* Vietnamese menu. Closed Thanksgiving, Dec 25. Lunch, dinner. Bar. Outdoor seating. **$**

[D]

★ **MATUBA.** *2915 Columbia Pike (22204). Phone 703/521-2811.* Japanese menu. Lunch, dinner. **$$**

★ ★ **QUEEN BEE.** *3181 Wilson Blvd (22201). Phone 703/527-3444; fax 703/525-2750.* Vietnamese menu. Lunch, dinner. Totally nonsmoking. **$**

[D]

★ ★ **R. T.'S SEAFOOD KITCHEN.** *2300 Clarendon Blvd (22201). Phone 703/841-0100; fax 703/841-0597. www.seafoodkitchen.com.* Cajun menu. Closed holidays. Lunch, dinner. Bar. Children's menu. Outdoor seating. **$$**

[D]

★ **RED HOT AND BLUE.** *1600 Wilson Blvd (22209). Phone 703/276-8833. www.redhotandblue.com.* Barbecue menu. Closed Thanksgiving, Dec 25. Lunch, dinner. Bar. Memphis blues memorabilia. **$$**

[D]

★ **SILVER DINER.** *3200 Wilson Blvd (22201). Phone 703/812-8667; fax 703/812-8669.* Closed Dec 25. Breakfast, lunch, dinner, Sat-Sun brunch. Children's menu. **$$**

[D] [SC]

★ ★ **TIVOLI.** *1700 N Moore St (22209). Phone 703/524-8900; fax 703/524-4971. www.tivolirestaurant.net.* Italian menu. Closed Sun; major holidays. Lunch, dinner. Bar. Reservations required. **$$**

[D]

★ **VILLAGE BISTRO.** *1723 Wilson Blvd (22209). Phone 703/522-0284; fax 703/522-7797.* Continental menu. Closed Thanksgiving, Dec 25. Lunch, dinner. Bar. Outdoor seating. Monet prints on walls. **$$**

[D]

★ ★ **WOO LAE OAK.** *1500 S Joyce St (22202). Phone 703/521-3706; fax 703/521-0014. www.woolaeoak.com.* Korean menu. Closed Jan 1. Lunch, dinner. **$$**

[D]

Bethesda, MD

19 minutes; 8 miles from Washington, DC
Also see Washington, DC

Pop 55,277 **Elev** 305 ft **Area code** 301

Information The Greater Bethesda-Chevy Chase Chamber of Commerce, Landow Building, 7910 Woodmont Ave, Suite 1204, 20814; 301/652-4900

Web www.bccchamber.org

A suburb of Washington, DC, Bethesda is the home of both the National Institutes of Health, research arm of the Public Health Service, and Bethesda Naval Hospital.

What to See and Do

Cabin John Regional Park. *7700 Tuckerman Ln, Rockville (20854). Approximately 3 miles N on MD 355 then W on Tuckerman Ln. Phone 301/299-0024.* This 551-acre park has playgrounds, miniature train ride; nature center; concerts (summer evenings; free); tennis courts, game fields, ice rink, nature trails, and picnicking. Fee for some activities. (Daily)

Clara Barton National Historic Site. *5801 Oxford Rd (20812). 8 miles NW in Glen Echo, MD. Phone 301/492-6245. www.nps.gov/clba.* Thirty-six-room house (1891) of unusual architecture was both the national headquarters of the Red Cross and the home of Clara Barton for the last 15 years of her life. Contents include many items belonging to the founder of the American Red Cross. Period costumes worn during some special programs. Guided tours only. (Daily; closed Jan 1, Thanksgiving, Dec 25) **FREE**

National Library of Medicine. *8600 Rockville Pike (20894). Phone 301/496-6308.* World's largest biomedical library; rare books, manuscripts, prints; medical art displays. (Mon-Sat; closed holidays and Sat before Mon holidays) Visitors center and guided tour (Mon-Fri, one departure each day). **FREE**

Motel/Motor Lodge

★ ★ **HOLIDAY INN.** *5520 Wisconsin Ave, Chevy Chase (20815). Phone 301/656-1500; toll-free 800/465-4329; fax 301/656-5045. www.holiday-inn.com.* 215 rooms, 12 story. Pets accepted, some restrictions; fee. Check-out noon. TV; cable (premium), VCR available. In-room modem link. Laundry services. Restaurant, bar. Health club privileges. In-house fitness room. Pool. Business center. **$$**

🄳 🐾 ⬛ 🏃 ⬛ 🏃

Hotel

★ ★ ★ **HYATT REGENCY BETHESDA.** *1 Bethesda Metro Ctr (20814). Phone 301/657-1234; toll-free 800/633-7313; fax 301/657-6453. www.bethesda.hyatt.com.* Guests will delight in all the amenities this hotel has to offer. Located at Metro Center and within steps to restaurants, theaters, and some of the best shopping, this hotel is perfect for both the business and leisure traveler. 390 rooms, 12 story. Check-out noon, check-in 3 pm. TV; cable (premium), VCR available. In-room modem link. Restaurant, bar. Children's activity center. In-house fitness room, sauna. Indoor pool. Covered parking, valet parking. Business center. Luxury level. **$$**

D ⚊ 🏃 🖎 🏃

All Suite

★ ★ ★ **MARRIOTT SUITES BETHESDA.** *6711 Democracy Blvd (20817). Phone 301/897-5600; toll-free 800/228-9290; fax 301/530-1427. www.marriotthotels.com.* Whether for business or pleasure, this hotel welcomes guests with spacious and well-appointed guest rooms with some including an extravagant marbled bath. Nearby attractions include the Kennedy Center, Mormon Temple, and National Zoo. 274 rooms, 11 story. Check-out noon, check-in 4 pm. TV; cable (premium), VCR available. In-room modem link. Restaurant. In-house fitness room. Indoor, outdoor pools; whirlpool. Business center. **$$**

D ⚊ 🏃 🖎 🏃

Restaurants

★ **AUSTIN GRILL.** *7278 Woodmont Ave (20814). Phone 301/656-1366; fax 301/656-1398. www.austingrill.com.* Tex-Mex menu. Closed Thanksgiving, Dec 24-25. Lunch, dinner, Sat-Sun brunch. Bar. Children's menu. Outdoor seating. **$$**

D

★ ★ **BACCHUS BETHESDA.** *7945 Norfolk Ave (20814). Phone 301/657-1722; fax 301/657-4406. www.bacchusrestaurant.com.* Middle Eastern menu. Closed Jan 1, Thanksgiving, Dec 25. Lunch, dinner. Casual attire. Valet parking (dinner). Outdoor seating. **$$**

D

★ **BETHESDA CRAB HOUSE.** *4958 Bethesda Ave (20814). Phone 301/652-3382; fax 301/652-4669. www.bethesdacrabhouse.com.* Closed Dec 25. Lunch, dinner. Rustic décor; established 1961. Outdoor seating. **$$$**

★ ★ **BOMBAY DINING.** *4931 Cordell Ave (20814). Phone 301/656-3373; fax 301/656-2535.* Indian menu. Lunch, dinner, Sat-Sun brunch. Bar. Valet parking (weekends). **$$**

★ ★ **BUON GIORNO.** *8003 Norfolk Ave (20814). Phone 301/652-1400; fax 301/654-5508.* Italian menu. Closed Mon; holidays; also mid-Aug-mid-Sept. Dinner. Bar. Valet parking (dinner). **$$**

D

★ **CADDIE'S ON CORDELL.** *4922 Cordell Ave (20814). Phone 301/215-7730; fax 301/215-7716. www.caddiesoncordell.com.* American menu. Closed Thanksgiving, Dec 25. Lunch, dinner. Bar. Children's menu. Casual attire. Outdoor seating. **$$**

D

★ ★ **CAFE BETHESDA.** *5027 Wilson Ln (20814). Phone 301/657-3383.* Guests will appreciate the professional service in this intimate and relaxed setting. French Bistro menu. Closed Mon; major holidays; also Super Bowl Sun. Lunch, dinner. Casual attire. Valet parking. Outdoor seating. Totally nonsmoking. **$$$**

★ ★ ★ **CESCO TRATTORIA.** *4871 Cordell Ave (20814). Phone 301/654-8333; fax 301/654-8874.* Reminiscent of a Tuscan villa, breads are baked fresh daily in a wood-burning oven which is visible to diners. Entrées are light, yet hearty, and desserts are simply delicious. Italian menu. Closed major holidays. Lunch, dinner. Bar. Casual attire. Valet parking (dinner). Outdoor seating. **$$$**

D

★ ★ **DELRAY VIETNAMESE GARDEN.** *4918 Delray Ave (20814). Phone 301/986-0606.* Vietnamese menu. Closed major holidays. Lunch, dinner. Bar. Reservations required. Valet parking weekends. Outdoor seating. **$$**

D SC

★ ★ **FOONG LIN.** *7710 Norfolk Ave (20814). Phone 301/656-3427; fax 301/215-7985. www.foonglin.com.* Chinese menu. Closed Thanksgiving. Lunch, dinner. Bar. **$$**

D

★ ★ **FRASCATI.** *4806 Rugby Ave (20814). Phone 301/652-9514; fax 301/656-5538. www.ilfrascati.com.* Italian menu. Closed Mon; Jan 1, Easter, Dec 25. Lunch, dinner. Reservations required. Outdoor seating. Totally nonsmoking. **$$**

D

★ ★ **HAANDI.** *4904 Fairmont Ave (20814). Phone 301/718-0121; fax 301/718-0123. www.haandi.com.* Indian menu. Lunch, dinner. Bar. Totally nonsmoking. **$$**

D

★ ★ **JEAN-MICHEL.** *10223 Old Georgetown Rd (20814). Phone 301/564-4910; fax 301/569-4912.* French menu. Closed most major holidays; also Sun July-Aug. Lunch, dinner. **$$**

D

★ ★ ★ **LE VIEUX LOGIS.** *7925 Old Georgetown Rd (20814). Phone 301/652-6816; fax 301/652-8221.* This French restaurant with excellent food and extravagantly colorful décor on the outside with scenes of provincial France is endearingly cluttered on the inside with baskets and kitchen implements. American and Scandinavian cooking adds to the dining experience. French menu. Closed Sun; Jan 1, Dec 25. Dinner. Casual attire. Free valet parking. Outdoor seating. **$$$**

D

★ **MATUBA.** *4918 Cordell Ave (20814). Phone 301/652-7449; fax 301/365-5991.* Japanese menu. Lunch, dinner. Totally nonsmoking. **$$**

D

★ ★ **MONTGOMERY'S GRILLE.** *7200 Wisconsin Ave (20814). Phone 301/654-3595; fax 301/654-3596.* Closed Thanksgiving, Dec 25. Lunch, dinner, Sun brunch. Bar. Children's menu. Outdoor seating. Totally nonsmoking. **$$**

★ ★ **NAM'S.** *4928 Cordell Ave (20814). Phone 301/652-2635; fax 301/652-7937.* Vietnamese menu. Closed Thanksgiving, Dec 25. Lunch, dinner. Bar. **$$**

★ **NAPA THAI.** *4924 St. Elmo (20814). Phone 301/986-8590; fax 301/986-8490.* Thai menu. Closed July 4, Thanksgiving. Lunch, dinner. Casual attire. Outdoor seating. **$$**

★ ★ **PARKERS AN AMERICAN BISTRO.** *4824 Bethesda Ave (20814). Phone 301/654-6366. www.parkersbistro.com.* American menu. Closed major holidays. Lunch, dinner. Bar. Children's menu. Casual attire. Outdoor seating. **$$$**

D

★ **PHILADELPHIA MIKE'S.** *7732 Wisconsin Ave (20814). Phone 301/656-0104; fax 301/656-0105. www.philadelphiamikes.com.* American menu. Closed holidays. Breakfast, lunch, dinner. Children's menu. Casual attire. **$$**

D

★ **RAKU.** *7240 Woodmont Ave (20814). Phone 301/718-8680; fax 301/718-8683.* Pan-Asian menu. Closed Thanksgiving, Dec 25. Lunch, dinner. Children's menu. Outdoor seating. Totally nonsmoking. **$$**

★ ★ **RED TOMATO CAFE.** *4910 St. Elmo Ave (20814). Phone 301/652-4499; fax 301/652-9643. www.redtomato.com.* Italian, American menu. Closed Jan 1, Thanksgiving, Dec 25. Lunch, dinner. Valet parking Thurs-Sat. Totally nonsmoking. **$$**

D

★ ★ ★ **RUTH'S CHRIS STEAKHOUSE.** *7315 Wisconsin Ave (20814). Phone 301/652-7877; fax 301/718-8463. www.ruthschris.com.* This restaurant has interesting décor with a large lobster tank and a cigar lounge with tables and sofa chairs. Closed Thanksgiving, Dec 25. Dinner. Bar. Pianist Thurs-Sat. Reservations required. Valet parking available. Totally nonsmoking. **$$$**

D

★ ★ **TEL-AVIV CAFE.** *4869 Cordell Ave (20814). Phone 301/718-9068; fax 301/718-9069.* Mediterranean menu. Closed Yom Kippur, Passover. Lunch, dinner. Bar. Entertainment Tues, Sat. Outdoor seating. **$$**

D

★ ★ **THYME SQUARE.** *4735 Bethesda Ave (20814). Phone 301/657-9077; fax 301/657-4505.* Seasonal American menu. Closed Dec 24-25. Lunch, dinner. Bar. Reservations required. Totally nonsmoking. **$$**

D

★ ★ ★ **TRAGARA.** *4935 Cordell Ave (20814). Phone 301/951-4935; fax 301/951-0401. www.tragara.com.* Tragara is one of Bethesda's most elegant and romantic restaurants, offering satisfying Italian cuisine and impeccable service. Bathed in soft light, with fresh roses on every linen-topped table, Tragara is serene and relaxing—a lovely place to dine and then linger. Tables fill up quickly at lunch and dinner with smartly dressed business executives and stylish quartets of 30-something couples who have no doubt hired baby-sitters for their escape to the civilized land of adults. The impressive Italian kitchen draws them all in with a tempting menu of pastas, fish, meat, and antipasti, but be sure to save room to indulge in the house-made gelato before saying, "Ciao." Italian menu. Closed holidays. Lunch, dinner. Casual attire. Valet parking available. **$$$**

D

Dover, DE

2 hours; 96 miles from Washington, DC

Founded 1717 **Pop** 32,135 **Elev** 36 ft **Area code** 302 **Zip** 19901

Information Central Delaware Chamber of Commerce, 9 E Loockerman St, Suite 2-A, PO Box 576, 19903; 302/734-7513

Web www.cdcc.net

The capital of Delaware since 1777, Dover was laid out by William Penn around the city's lovely green. For almost 200 years there were coach houses and inns on King's Road between Philadelphia and Lewes. Circling the green north and south on State Street are fine 18th- and 19th-century houses.

Today, because of Delaware's favorable corporation laws, more than 60,000 US firms pay taxes in Dover. At Dover Air Force Base, south off US 113, the Military Airlift Command operates one of the biggest air cargo terminals in the world, utilizing the giant C5-A Galaxy aircraft. Dover is also the home of Delaware State College, Wesley College, and the Terry campus of Delaware Technical and Community College.

What to See and Do

Delaware Agricultural Museum and Village. *866 N DuPont Hwy (US 13) (19901). Phone 302/734-1618. www.agriculturalmuseum.org.* Museum of farm life from early settlement to 1960. Main exhibition hall and historic structures representing a late-19th-century farming community; includes gristmill, blacksmith-wheelwright shop, farmhouse, outbuildings, one-room schoolhouse, store, and train station. Gift shop. (Apr-Dec, Tues-Sun; rest of year, Mon-Fri) **$**

Delaware Public Archives. *121 Duke of York St (19901). Phone 302/739-5318.* Delaware's historical public records.(Mon-Sat; closed holidays) **FREE**

Delaware State Museums. *316 S Governors Ave (19901). www.destate museums.org.* Complex of three buildings:

Delaware Archeology Museum. *316 S Governors Ave (19901). Phone 302/739-3260.* (1790) Housed in an old church, exhibits devoted to archaeology. (Tues-Sat 10 am-3:30 pm; closed holidays) **FREE**

Johnson Victrola Museum. *Bank Ln and New St (19901). Phone 302/739-4266.* Tribute to Eldridge Reeves Johnson, founder of the Victor Talking Machine Company. Collection of talking machines, Victrolas, early recordings, and equipment. (Tues-Sat 10 am-3:30 pm; closed holidays) **FREE**

Museum of Small Town Life. *316 S Governors Ave (19901). Phone 302/739-3261.* Turn-of-the-century drugstore, printing press, pharmacy, carpenter shop, general store, post office, shoemaker's shop, printer's shop; Johnson building. (Tues-Sat 10 am-3:30 pm; closed holidays) **FREE**

Delaware State Visitor Center. *The Green. 406 Federal St (19901). Phone 302/739-4266.* Administered by Delaware State Museums, center offers information on attractions throughout the state. Exhibit galleries. (Mon-Sat, Sun afternoons; closed holidays) **FREE**

Dover Heritage Trail. *1071 S Governors Ave (19901). Departs from State Visitor Center. Phone 302/739-4266.* Guided walking tour of historic areas, buildings, and other attractions. (By appointment only) **$$**

John Dickinson Plantation. *340 Kitts Hummrock Rd (19901). 6 miles SE, near junction US 113 and DE 9. Phone 302/739-3277.* (1740) Restored boyhood residence of Dickinson, the "penman of the Revolution." Reconstructed farm complex. (Tues-Sat; also Sun afternoons Mar-Dec) **FREE**

Killens Pond State Park. *5025 Killens Pond Rd (19901). 13 miles S via US 13. Phone 302/284-4526.* A 1,083-acre park with a 66-acre pond. Swimming pool, fishing, boating (rentals); hiking, fitness trails, game fields, picnicking, camping (hookups, dump station). Standard hours, fees.

The Old State House. *The Green. 406 Federal St (19901). Phone 302/739-4266.* (1792) Delaware's seat of government since 1777, the State House, restored in 1976, contains a courtroom, ceremonial governor's office, legislative chambers, and county offices, including Levy Courtroom. A portrait of George Washington in the Senate Chamber was commissioned in 1802 by the legislature as a memorial to the nation's first president. Although Delaware's General Assembly moved to nearby Legislative Hall in 1934, the State House remains the state's symbolic capitol. (Tues-Sun; closed holidays) **FREE**

Trap Pond State Park. *Rte 24 and Trap Pond Rd (19956).* *Contact RD2 Box 331, Laurel 19956. Phone 302/875-5153.* Boating, canoeing, fishing; hiking, biking, camping. Standard fees.

Special Events

Delaware State Fair. *17 miles S on US 13, Harrington (19952). Phone 302/398-3269.* Arts and crafts, home and trade show, carnival rides, shows; homemaking, agricultural, and livestock exhibits. Mid-July.

Dover Downs. *1131 N DuPont Hwy (19901). Phone 302/674-4600. www.dover downs.com.* Racing events include NASCAR Winston Cup auto racing (June, Sept); harness racing (mid-Nov-Apr). Call for fees and schedule.

Harrington Raceway. *Fairgrounds. 17 miles S on US 13, Harrington (19952). Phone 302/398-7223.* Harness racing. Betting most nights. Sept-Apr.

Old Dover Days. Tours of historic houses and gardens not usually open to the public. Crafts exhibits, many other activities. Contact Kent County Tourism, 800/233-KENT. First weekend in May.

Motels/Motor Lodges

★ **BUDGET INN.** *1426 N DuPont Hwy (19901). Phone 302/734-4433; fax 302/734-4433.* 68 rooms, 2 story. Check-out 11 am. TV. Pool. **$**

★ **COMFORT INN.** *222 S DuPont Hwy (19901). Phone 302/674-3300; toll-free 800/228-5150. www.comfortinn.com.* 84 rooms, 2 story. Complimentary continental breakfast. Check-out noon. TV; cable. Pool; lifeguard. **$**

Hotel

★ ★ ★ **SHERATON DOVER HOTEL.** *1570 N DuPont Hwy (19901). Phone 302/678-8500; toll-free 800/544-5064; fax 302/678-9073. www.sheraton dover.com.* This hotel is conveniently located just minutes from shopping and local attractions in historic Dover. 152 rooms, 7 story. Check-out noon. TV. In-room modem link. Restaurant, bar; entertainment except Sun. Room service. In-house fitness room. Indoor pool, whirlpool. **$**

Restaurant

★ ★ ★ **BLUE COAT INN.** *800 N State St (19901). Phone 302/674-1776; fax 302/674-1807.* Enjoy casual dining at this quaint restaurant serving a variety of menu delights. A great place for a quiet, but cozy, meal. Seafood, steak menu. Closed Dec 25. Lunch, dinner. Bar. Children's menu. Lake setting. **$$$**

Fairfax, VA

24 minutes; 19 miles from Washington, DC
See also Alexandria, Arlington County (Ronald Reagan Washington-National Airport Area); also see Washington, DC

Pop 21,498 **Elev** 447 ft **Area code** 703

Information Fairfax County Convention & Visitors Bureau, 8300 Boone Blvd, Suite 450, Tyson's Corner-Vienna 22182; 703/790-3329, 703/550-2450 (visitor center), or 800/7-FAIRFAX

Web www.visitfairfax.org

What to See and Do

County parks. *12055 Government Center Pkwy (22035). Phone 703/324-8700.* For additional information contact Fairfax County Park Authority, 12055 Government Center Pkwy, Suite 927, 22035.

Burke Lake. *7315 Ox Rd, Fairfax Station (22039). 6 miles S on VA 123. Phone 703/323-6601.* Consists of 888 acres. Fishing, boating (ramp, rentals); picnicking, playground, concession, miniature train, carousel (summer, daily; early May and late Sept, weekends), 18-hole and par-three golf, camping (May-Sept; 7-day limit). Beaver Cove Nature Trail; fitness trail. Fee for activities. (Daily) **$$**

Lake Fairfax. *1400 Lake Fairfax Dr, Reston (20190). On VA 606 near Leesburg Pike. Phone 703/471-5415.* Pool, boat rentals, fishing, excursion boat; picnicking, carousel, miniature train (late May-Labor Day, daily), camping (Mar-Dec; 7-day limit; electric additional fee). Fee for activities. (Daily)

George Mason University. *4400 University Dr (22030). Phone 703/993-1000. www.gmu.edu.* (1957) 24,000 students. This state-supported university, started as a branch of the University of Virginia. Performing Arts Center features concerts, theater, dance; Fenwick Library maintains largest collection anywhere of material pertaining to Federal Theatre Project of the 1930s. Research Center for Federal Theatre Project contains 7,000 scripts, including unpublished works by Arthur Miller, sets and costume designs, and oral history collection of interviews with former Federal Theatre personnel. (Mon-Fri; closed holidays)

Regional parks. *5400 Ox Rd, Fairfax Station (22039). Phone 703/352-5900 or 703/352-3165 (TTY).* Contact Northern Virginia Regional Park Authority at above address.

Algonkian. *47001 Fairway Dr (20165). 6 miles NE on VA 123 to VA 7, then 9 miles NW to Cascades Pkwy N, then 3 miles N near Sterling. Phone 703/450-4655.* An 800-acre park on the Potomac River; swimming (Memorial

Day-Labor Day, fee), fishing, boating (ramp); golf, miniature golf, picnicking, vacation cottages, meeting and reception areas. **FREE**

Bull Run. *7700 Bull Run Dr (20121). From Beltway I-66 W, exit at Centreville, W on US 29 3 miles to park sign. Phone 703/631-0550.* Consists of 1,500 acres. Themed swimming pool (Memorial Day-Labor Day, daily; fee); camping (one to four persons, fee; electricity available; reservations accepted, phone 703/631-0550), concession, picnicking, playground, miniature golf, Frisbee golf, public shooting center, nature trail. (Mid-Mar-Dec) **$$$**

Meadowlark Botanical Gardens. *9750 Meadowlark Gardens Ct, Vienna (22181). On Beulah Rd between Rte 7 and Rte 123. Phone 703/255-3631. www.washacadsci.org/meadowlark-gardens/.* Lilac, wildflower, herb, hosta, native plants, and landscaped gardens on 95 acres. Includes three ponds; water garden; gazebos; trails. Visitor center. (Daily) Children under 7 free. **$$**

Sully. *3601 Sully Rd (20151). 10 miles W on US 50, then N on VA 28 (Sully Rd), near Chantilly. Phone 703/437-1794.* (1794) Restored house of Richard Bland Lee, brother of General "Light Horse Harry" Lee; some original furnishings; kitchen-washhouse, log house store, smokehouse on grounds. Guided tours. (Mon, Wed-Sun; closed Jan 1, Thanksgiving, Dec 25) **$$**

Special Events

Antique Car Show. *3601 Sully Rd (20151).* Four hundred antique cars, flea market, and music. June.

Barns of Wolf Trap. *1624 Trap Rd, Vienna (22182). Phone 703/938-2404. 3/4 miles S of Wolf Trap Farm Park.* A 350-seat theater with chamber music, recitals, mime, jazz, folk, theater, and children's programs. For schedule contact the Barns, 1635 Trap Rd, Vienna 22182. Late Sept-early May.

Quilt Show. *3601 Sully Rd (22181).* Quilts for sale, quilting demonstrations, and antique quilts on display. Sept.

Wolf Trap Farm Park for the Performing Arts. *1624 Trap Rd, Vienna (22182). Phone 703/255-1900. 8 miles NE on VA 123, then W on US 7 to Towlston Rd (Trap Rd), then follow signs.* Varied programs include ballet, musicals, opera, classical, jazz, and folk music. Filene Center open theater seats 3,800 under cover and 3,000 on lawn. Picnicking on grounds, all year. Also free interpretive children's programs, July-Aug. For schedules and prices contact Wolf Trap Foundation at above address. Late May-Sept.

Motels/Motor Lodges

★ ★ **COMFORT INN.** *11180 Main St (22030). Phone 703/591-5900; toll-free 800/228-5150; fax 703/273-7915. www.comfortinn.com.* 205 rooms, 6 story. Complimentary continental breakfast. Check-out 11 am. TV; cable (premium), VCR available (movies). Laundry services. Restaurant, bar. Room service. In-house fitness room. Game room. Indoor, outdoor pools. Free airport, train station transportation. **$**

D ⇔ 🏋 ⇘ SC

★ ★ **COURTYARD BY MARRIOTT.** *11220 Lee-Jackson Hwy (22030). Phone 703/273-6161; toll-free 800/321-2211; fax 703/273-3505. www. courtyard.com.* 144 rooms, 3 story. Check-out noon. TV; cable (premium), VCR available. In-room modem link. Laundry services. Restaurant, bar. In-house fitness room. Health club privileges. Indoor pool, whirlpool. **$**

D ⇔ 🕇 ≋ SC

★ **HAMPTON INN.** *10860 Lee Hwy (22030). Phone 703/385-2600; toll-free 800/426-7866; fax 703/385-2742. www.hamptoninn.com.* 86 rooms, 5 story. Complimentary continental breakfast. Check-out noon. TV; cable (premium). In-room modem link. In-house fitness room. Health club privileges. **$**

D 🕇 ≋ SC

★ ★ **HOLIDAY INN.** *11787 Lee-Jackson Memorial Hwy (22033). Phone 703/352-2525; toll-free 800/465-4329; fax 703/352-4471. www.holiday-inn .com.* 312 rooms, 6 story. Pets accepted; fee. Check-out noon. TV; cable (premium), VCR available. In-room modem link. Laundry services. Restaurant, bar; entertainment. In-house fitness room, sauna. Health club privileges. Game room. Indoor pool. Business center. Concierge. **$**

D 🐾 ⇔ 🕇 🏋 ≋ 🏃

Hotel

★ ★ ★ **HYATT FAIR LAKES.** *12777 Fair Lakes Cir (22033). Phone 703/818-1234; toll-free 800/233-1234; fax 703/818-3140. www.hyatt.com.* Minutes from the Washington Dulles Airport, this striking high-rise hotel in the wooded Fair Lakes Office Park offers large guest rooms. This property features a column-free ballroom and a towering atrium lobby. 316 rooms, 14 story. Check-out noon. TV; cable (premium), VCR available. In-room modem link. Restaurant, bar; entertainment. In-house fitness room, sauna. Health club privileges. Indoor pool, whirlpool. Free airport, train station transportation. Business center. **$$**

D ⇔ 🕇 ≋ SC 🏃

B&B/Small Inn

★ ★ ★ **THE BAILIWICK INN.** *4023 Chain Bridge Rd (22030). Phone 703/ 691-2266; toll-free 800/366-7666; fax 703/934-2112. www.bailiwickinn.com.* A restored Federal-style inn (1800), this majestic bed-and-breakfast offers individually decorated guest rooms, all graciously appointed with antiques. Each room is named after a famous Virginian and includes a small library of books dedicated to the namesake. 14 rooms, some with shower only, 4 story. No elevator. Complimentary full breakfast. Check-out 11 am, check-in 2 pm. TV; VCR available. Restaurant (see also BAILWICK INN). The first Civil War skirmish occured here in June of 1861. Totally nonsmoking. **$$**

D ≋ SC

Restaurants

★ ★ **ARTIE'S.** *3260 Old Lee Hwy (22030). Phone 703/273-7600; fax 703/273-9433. www.greatamericanrestaurant.com.* Closed Thanksgiving, Dec 25. Lunch, dinner, Sun brunch. Bar. **$$$**

D

★ ★ ★ **BAILIWICK INN.** *4023 Chain Bridge Rd (22030). Phone 703/691-2266; fax 703/934-2112. www.bailiwickinn.com.* This Federal-style inn and restaurant, on the National Register of Historic Places, offers French-American cuisine in a quaint, romantic space. Visit for one of the seasonal wine dinners or for traditional-English high tea in one of the intimate parlors. American, Mediterranean, seafood menu. Closed Mon, Tues. Lunch, dinner. In restored inn (1800). Reservations required. Outdoor seating. Totally nonsmoking. **$$$**

SC

★ **BLUE OCEAN.** *9440 Main St (22031). Phone 703/425-7555; fax 703/425-8274. www.blueocean-sushi.com.* Japanese menu. Closed most major holidays. Lunch, dinner. **$$**

D

★ ★ **BOMBAY BISTRO.** *3570 Chain Bridge Rd (22030). Phone 703/359-5810; fax 703/359-5811. www.bombaybistro.com.* Indian menu. Closed Thanksgiving. Lunch, dinner, Sat-Sun brunch. Bar. Outdoor seating. **$$**

D

★ **CASA GRANDE CAFE.** *9534 Arlington Blvd (22031). Phone 703/359-5865; fax 703/359-5866.* Mexican menu. Lunch, dinner. Bar. Children's menu. Casual attire. **$**

★ ★ **CONNAUGHT PLACE.** *10425 North St (22030). Phone 703/352-5959; fax 703/591-2568. www.connaughtplacerestaurant.com.* Indian menu. Closed Thanksgiving, Dec 25. Buffet, lunch, dinner, Sat-Sun brunch. Bar. Sitar Fri, Sat. **$$$**

D

★ **IL LUPO.** *4009 Chain Bridge Rd (22030). Phone 703/934-1655; fax 703/934-7046.* Italian menu. Lunch, dinner. Bar. Casual attire. Outdoor seating. **$$**

D

★ **JAIPUR ROYAL INDIAN CUISINE.** *9401 Lee Hwy (22031). Phone 703/766-1111; fax 703/766-1113.* Indian menu. Lunch, dinner. Bar. Children's menu. Casual attire. Outdoor seating. **$**

★ **P. J. SKIDOO'S.** *9908 Lee Hwy (22030). Phone 703/591-4515; fax 703/591-5407. www.pjskidoos.com.* Closed Thanksgiving, Dec 25. Lunch, dinner, Sun brunch. Bar. Entertainment Tues, Thurs-Sat. Children's menu. **$$**

Gettysburg, PA

1 hour 40 minutes; 86 miles from Washington, DC

Founded 1798 **Pop** 7,490 **Elev** 560 ft **Area code** 717 **Zip** 17325

Information Convention & Visitors Bureau, 35 Carlisle St; 717/334-6274

Web www.gettysburg.com

Because of the historical nature of this area and the many attractions in this town, visitors may want to stop in at the Gettysburg Convention & Visitors Bureau for complete information about bus tours, guide service (including a tape-recorded and self-guided tour) and help in planning their visit here.

Gettysburg: A Town Gripped by War

A three-day Civil War battle in July 1863 unfolded about a mile outside Gettysburg, which was a small rural community at the time. The town also suffered from the battle, and the impact can be seen in a one-hour, 1-mile walking tour that visits several of the well-reserved buildings that witnessed the conflict. Begin at Lincoln Square, the commercial heart of Gettysburg. Abraham Lincoln stayed at the David Wills House, now a small museum at No.12, the night before he gave the "Gettysburg Address" dedicating the nearby National Cemetery. Just outside the door is a life-size statue of Lincoln in somber attire appearing to help a visiting tourist casually dressed in a colorful sweater and cords. Among the townsfolk, it is called the "Perry Como statue," because that's who the tourist looks like. Head south on Baltimore Street to Nos. 242-246, the Jennie Wade Birthplace. Wade, the only civilian to be killed in the battle, is believed to have been shot by a Confederate sharpshooter while baking bread and biscuits for Union troops in her sister's nearby house. That house, on Baltimore Street, is a museum, the Jennie Wade House. Between the two homes, stop at the Schriver house at 309 Baltimore. Built for George Schriver and his family, its garret was occupied by Confederate sharpshooters who poked still-visible holes in the wall for their rifles. Now a museum, the Schriver House details life in the town during and immediately after the battle. Across the street at No. 304, formerly the Methodist parsonage, note the shell near the second-story window in front. The parson's daughter, Laura, was said to have narrowly escaped injury when a shell crashed through the brick wall into her room. Later, the shell was placed in the hole to mark the spot. Return to Lincoln Square via Washington Street. At the corner of West Middle Street, pause in front of the Michael Jacobs House at No. 101. A meteorologist, Jacobs recorded the weather throughout his life, leaving important details to posterity of weather and cloud conditions during the battle.

What to See and Do

A. Lincoln's Place. *571 Steinwehr Ave (17325). Phone 717/334-6049 or 717/334-8003.* Live portrayal of the 16th president; 45 minutes. (Mid-June-Labor Day, Mon-Fri) **$$$**

General Lee's Headquarters. *401 Buford Ave (17325). Phone 717/334-3141.* Robert E. Lee planned Confederate strategy for the Gettysburg battle in this house; contains collection of historical items from the battle. (Mid-Mar-mid-Nov, daily) **$$**

Gettysburg Battle Theatre. *571 Steinwehr Ave (17325). Phone 717/334-6100.* Battlefield diorama with 25,000 figures; 30-minute film and electronic maps program showing battle strategy. (Mar-Nov, daily) **$$$**

Gettysburg College. *300 N Washington St (17325). 3 blocks NW of Lincoln Sq off US 15 Business. Phone 717/337-6000. www.gettysburg.edu.* (1832) 2,000 students. Liberal arts; oldest Lutheran-affiliated college in the US. Pennsylvania Hall was used as Civil War hospital; Eisenhower House and statue on grounds. Tour of campus.

Gettysburg National Military Park. *Visitor center is located tetween Taneytown Rd (State Rte 123) and Steinwehr Ave (Business Rte 15). Phone 717/334-1124. www.nps.gov/gett/.* The hallowed battlefield of Gettysburg, scene of one of the most decisive battles of the Civil War and immortalized by Lincoln's Gettysburg Address, is preserved by the National Park Service. The town itself is still a college community, as it was more than a hundred years ago on July 1-3, 1863, when General Robert E. Lee led his Confederate Army in its greatest invasion of the North. The defending Northerners under Union General George Meade repulsed the Southern assault after three days of fierce fighting, which left 51,000 men dead, wounded, or missing.

The Gettysburg National Military Park has more than 35 miles of roads through 5,900 acres of the battlefield area. There are more than 1,300 monuments, markers, and tablets of granite and bronze; 400 cannons are also located on the field.

Visitors may wish to tour the battlefield with a Battlefield Guide, licensed by the National Park Service (two-hour tour; fee). The guides escort visitors to all points of interest and sketch the movement of troops and details of the battle. Or visitors may wish to first orient themselves at the Electric Map at the Visitor Center; then using the park folder, the battlefield can be toured without a guide. Audio cassettes are also available for self-guided tours.

The late President Dwight D. Eisenhower's retirement farm, a National Historic Site, adjoins the battlefield. It is open to the public on a limited-tour basis. All visitors must obtain tour tickets at the tour information center, located at the lobby of the Visitor Center-Electric Map building. Transportation to the farm is by shuttle (fee). For further information contact Gettysburg National Military Park, 97 Taneytown Rd, Gettysburg 17325; 717/334-1124.

Gettysburg Scenic Rail Tours. *Washington St (17325). Phone 717/334-6932.* A 22-mile round trip to Aspers on a steam train. Also charter trips and special runs. (June, Thurs-Sun; July-Aug, Tues-Sun; Sept Sat-Sun afternoons) **$$$**

Ghosts of Gettysburg Candlelight Walking Tours. *271 Baltimore St (17325). Phone 717/337-0445.* Armed with tales from Mark Nesbitt's *Ghosts of Gettysburg* books, knowledgeable guides lead 1 1/4-hour tours through sections of town that were bloody battlefields 130 years ago. (June-Oct, daily evenings; Apr, May, Nov, weekend evenings) **$$$**

Hall of Presidents and First Ladies. *789 Baltimore St (17325), adjacent to National Cemetery. Phone 717/334-5717.* Costumed life-size wax figures of all the presidents; reproductions of their wives' inaugural gowns; "The Eisenhowers at Gettysburg" exhibit. (Mid-Mar-Nov, daily) **$$$**

Land of Little Horses. *125 Glenwood Dr (17325). 5 miles W off US 30, on Knoxlyn Rd to Glenwood Dr; follow signs. Phone 717/334-7259.* A variety of performing horses—all in miniature. Continuous entertainment; indoor arena; exotic animal races. Saddle and wagon rides. Picnic area, snack bar, gift shop. (May-late Aug, daily; Apr, Sept, Oct, weekends) **$$$**

Lincoln Room Museum. *12 Lincoln Sq (17325). Phone 717/334-8188.* Preserved bedroom in Wills House; collection of Lincoln items; huge plaque inscribed with Gettysburg Address, audiovisual display. (Apr-Nov, daily) **$$**

The Lincoln Train Museum. *425 Steinwehr Ave (17325). 1/2 mile S via US 15 on Steinwehr Ave. Phone 717/334-5678.* Museum features more than 1,000 model trains and railroad memorabilia; Lincoln Train Ride—simulated trip of 15 minutes. (Mar-Nov, daily) **$$$**

Lutheran Theological Seminary. *61 Seminary Ridge (17325). Confederate Ave, 1 mile W of Lincoln Sq on US 30. Phone 717/334-6286. www.itsg.edu.* (1826) 250 students. Oldest Lutheran seminary in US; cupola on campus used as Confederate lookout during battle. Old Dorm, now home of Adams County Historical Society, served as hospital for both Union and Confederate soldiers.

National Civil War Wax Museum. *297 Steinwehr Ave (17325). Phone 717/334-6245.* Highlights Civil War era and Battle of Gettysburg. (Mar-Dec, daily; rest of year, Sat and Sun; closed Jan 1, Thanksgiving, Dec 25) **$$**

Schriver House. *309 Baltimore St (17325). Phone 717/337-2800.* Built prior to the Civil War, this two-story brick house was used by Confederate sharpshooters, who knocked still-visible holes in the garret walls through which to aim their weapons. Private owners have restored and furnished the house as a period museum; the 30-minute guided tour details the Schriver family's experience during the battle, as well as the experience of other townspeople. (Apr-Nov, daily; Dec-Mar, weekends) **$$$**

Ski Liberty. *78 Country Club Trail, Fairfield (17320). 9 miles W on PA 116. Phone 717/642-8282. www.skiliberty.com.* Two quad, three double chairlifts; J-bar, handle tow; patrol, school, rentals; snowmaking; cafeteria, restaurant, bar; nursery, lodge. Longest run approximately 1 mile; vertical drop 600 feet. (Dec-Mar, daily) **$$$$**

Soldiers' National Museum. *777 Baltimore St (17325). Phone 717/334-4890.* Dioramas of major battles, with sound; Civil War collection. (Mar-Nov, daily; schedule may vary) **$$$**

Special Events

Apple Blossom Festival. *South Mountain Fairgrounds. 10 miles NW of Gettysburg on Rte 234.* Early May.

Apple Harvest Festival. *South Mountain Fairgrounds. 10 miles NW of Gettysburg on Rte 234.* Demonstrations; arts and crafts; guided tours of orchard, mountain areas. First and second weekends in Oct.

Civil War Heritage Days. Lectures by historians; Civil War collectors' show; entertainment; Civil War book show; firefighters' festival; fireworks. Late June-early July.

Motels/Motor Lodges

★ **BEST INN.** *301 Steinwehr Ave (17325). Phone 717/334-1188; toll-free 800/237-8466; fax 717/334-1188. www.bestinn.com.* 77 rooms, 2 story. Pets accepted. Check-out noon. TV; cable (premium), VCR available. Bar. Pool. Downhill ski 9 miles, cross-country ski adjacent. **$**

D 🐾 ⛽ ⛱ 🏊 SC

★★ **BEST WESTERN.** *1 Lincoln Sq (17325). Phone 717/337-2000; toll-free 800/780-7234; fax 717/337-2075. www.bestwestern.com.* 83 rooms, 6 story. Check-out 11 am. TV; VCR available (movies). In-room modem link. Restaurant, bar. Pool, whirlpool, poolside service. Downhill ski 8 miles. Free garage parking. Business center. **$**

D ⛽ ⛱ 🏊 SC 🕴

★ **COMFORT INN.** *871 York Rd (17325). Phone 717/337-2400; toll-free 800/221-2222; fax 717/337-0831. www.comfortinn.com.* 81 rooms, 2 story. Complimentary continental breakfast. Check-out 11 am. TV; cable (premium). In-room modem link. Indoor pool, whirlpool. **$**

D ⛱ 🏊 SC

★★ **CROSS KEYS MOTOR INN.** *6110 York Rd (17350). Phone 717/624-7778; fax 717/624-7941.* 64 rooms, 4 story. Crib free. TV; cable, VCR available (movies). Restaurants. Room service. Bar. Check-out 11 am. Meeting rooms. Business services available. Downhill ski 15 miles. Some in-room whirlpools. **$**

⛽ 🏊 SC

★ **DAYS INN.** *865 York Rd (17325). Phone 717/334-0030; toll-free 800/329-7466; fax 717/337-1002. www.daysinngettysburg.com.* 112 rooms, 5 story. Check-out noon. TV; cable (premium), VCR available. In-room modem link. Laundry services. In-house fitness room. Game room. Pool. Downhill ski 10 miles. **$**

D ⚐ ⚏ ⚐ ⚏ SC

★ **HOLIDAY INN EXPRESS.** *869 York Rd (17325). Phone 717/337-1400; toll-free 800/465-4329; fax 717/337-0159. www.holiday-inn.com.* 51 rooms, 2 story. Complimentary continental breakfast. Check-out 11 am. TV; cable (premium). In-room modem link. Indoor pool, whirlpool. Downhill ski 8 miles. **$**

D ⚐ ⚏ ⚏ SC

★ **HOMESTEAD MOTOR LODGE.** *1650 York Rd (17325). Phone 717/334-3866.* 10 rooms. Check-out 10 am. TV. Downhill ski 8 miles. Totally nonsmoking. **$**

⚐ ⚏

★ **QUALITY INN.** *380 Steinwehr Ave (17325). Phone 717/334-1103; toll-free 800/228-5151. www.gettysburgqualityinn.com.* 109 rooms, 2 story. Check-out noon. TV; cable (premium), VCR available. Laundry services. Bar. In-house fitness room, sauna. Indoor, outdoor pools. Downhill, cross-country ski 8 miles. **$**

D ⚐ ⚏ ⚐ ⚏ SC

★ **QUALITY INN.** *401 Buford Ave (17325). Phone 717/334-3141; toll-free 800/228-5050; fax 717/334-1813. www.qualityinn.com.* 41 rooms. Check-out noon. TV; VCR available. Pool. Downhill ski 6 miles. **$**

D ⚐ ⚏ ⚏ SC

★ **RED CARPET INN.** *2450 Emmitsburg Rd (17325). Phone 717/334-1345; toll-free 800/336-1345; fax 717/334-5026.* 25 rooms. Check-out 11 am. TV; cable (premium). Pool. **$**

⚏ ⚏

B&B/Small Inns

★ ★ ★ **BALADERRY INN.** *40 Hospital Rd (17325). Phone 717/337-1342; toll-free 800/220-0025; fax 717/337-1342. www.baladerryinn.com.* 8 rooms, 7 with shower only, 2 story. Children over 14 years only. Complimentary full breakfast. Check-out 11 am, check-in 2 pm. TV in common area; VCR. Outdoor tennis. Downhill ski 10 miles, cross-country ski adjacent. Built in 1812; used as a field hospital during the Civil War battle of Gettysburg. Restored; furnished with antiques and reproductions. **$**

⚐ ⚐ ⚐ ⚏ SC

★ ★ ★ **BATTLEFIELD BED AND BREAKFAST INN.** *2264 Emmitsburg Rd (17325). Phone 717/334-8804; toll-free 888/766-3897. www.gettysburgbattlefield.com.* Built in 1809, this Civil War inn is found on the Gettysburg battlefield. Guests can enjoy a carriage ride and a historic demonstration with real muskets, cannons, and cavalry. 9 rooms, 2 story. No room phones. Complimentary full breakfast. Check-out 11:30 am, check-in 2:30 pm. TV in sitting room; VCR. Fireplaces. Downhill ski 10 miles. Lawn games. Concierge. Restored 1809 farmhouse famous for living history activities. Totally nonsmoking. **$$**

★ ★ **BRAFFERTON INN.** *44 York St (17325). Phone 717/337-3423.* 10 rooms, 2 story. No room phones. Complimentary full breakfast. Check-out 11 am, check-in 2 pm. TV in suites. First house built in town (1786); antiques. **$**

★ ★ ★ **FARNSWORTH HOUSE INN.** *401 Baltimore St (17325). Phone 717/334-8838; fax 717/334-5862. www.gettysburgaddress.com.* 9 rooms, 2 story. No room phones. Complimentary full breakfast. Check-out 11 am, check-in 3 pm. TV in some rooms, sitting room; cable. Restaurant (see also FARNSWORTH HOUSE). Downhill ski 7 miles, cross-country ski 1/4 mile. Concierge. The uppermost level of the inn was once used by Confederate sharpshooters; more than 100 bullet holes still remain in the south wall of the inn. Daily tours. **$**

★ ★ ★ **GASLIGHT INN.** *33 E Middle St (17325). Phone 717/337-9100; toll-free 800/914-5698; fax 717/337-1100.* This bed-and-breakfast is located in the center of historic Gettysburg, near shopping, restaurants, and local attractions. 9 rooms, 3 story. Children over 10 years only. Complimentary full breakfast. Check-out 11 am, check-in 3 pm. TV; VCR (free movies). In-room modem link. Dining room. Concierge. Italianate house (1872) with original exterior trim. Rooms decorated and named in theme of flowers. **$**

★ ★ **GETTYSTOWN INN BED & BREAKFAST.** *89 Steinwehr Ave (17325). Phone 717/334-2100; fax 717/334-6905. www.dobbinhouse.com.* 5 rooms, 2 story. No room phones. Complimentary full breakfast. Check-out 10 am, check-in 2 pm. TV in some rooms; cable. Restaurant (see also DOBBIN HOUSE). Downhill ski 7 miles, cross-country ski 1 mile. Renovated 1860s home; antiques. Overlooks site of Abraham Lincoln's Gettysburg Address. Totally nonsmoking. **$**

★ ★ **THE HERR TAVERN AND PUBLICK HOUSE.** *900 Chambersburg Rd (17325). Phone 717/334-4332; toll-free 800/362-9849; fax 717/334-3332. www.herrtavern.com.* 16 rooms, 3 story. Children over 12 years only. Complimentary full breakfast. Check-out 11 am, check-in 4 pm. TV; VCR (movies). Restaurant. Room service. Downhill ski 5 miles. Built in 1815, served as Confederate hospital. Totally nonsmoking. **$**

★ ★ **JAMES GETTYS HOTEL.** *27 Chambersburg St (17325). Phone 717/337-1334; toll-free 800/900-5275; fax 717/334-2103. www.jamesgettyshotel .com.* 11 rooms, 4 story. Complimentary continental breakfast. Check-out 11 am, check-in 3 pm. TV; VCR available. Laundry services. Downhill ski 10 miles, cross-country ski 1 mile. Concierge. Built in 1804. Totally non-smoking. **$**

D ⊠ ⊠

★ ★ **OLD APPLEFORD INN.** *218 Carlisle St (17325). Phone 717/337-1711; toll-free 800/275-3373; fax 717/334-6228.* 10 rooms, 6 with shower only, 3 story. No room phones. Children over 8 years only. Complimentary full breakfast. Check-out 11 am, check-in 2 pm. Downhill ski 7 miles, cross-country ski 15 miles. Concierge. Victorian mansion (1867); many antiques. Totally nonsmoking. **$**

⊠ ⊠

Restaurants

★ ★ ★ **DOBBIN HOUSE.** *89 Steinwehr Ave (17325). Phone 717/334-2100; fax 717/334-6905. www.dobbinhouse.com.* Built for Reverend Alexander Dobbin in 1776, this colonial restaurant is listed on the National Register of Historic Places. Meals are served against a backdrop of traditional 18th-century décor, including stone walls, fireplaces, and carved woodwork. American, seafood menu. Closed Jan 1, Thanksgiving, Dec 25. Lunch, dinner. Bar. Children's menu. Oldest building in Gettysburg. Totally nonsmoking. **$$**

D SC

★ ★ ★ **FARNSWORTH HOUSE.** *401 Baltimore St (17325). Phone 717/334-8838; fax 717/334-5862. www.farnsworthhousedining.com.* Closed Jan 1, Thanksgiving, Dec 25. Dinner. Bar. Children's menu. Built in 1810; tour available. Outdoor seating. **$$**

D

★ **GINGERBREAD MAN.** *217 Steinwehr Ave (17325). Phone 717/334-1100. www.thegingerbreadman.net.* Closed major holidays. Lunch, dinner. Bar. Children's menu. Varied menu. **$$**

D

★ ★ **THE HERR TAVERN & PUBLICK HOUSE.** *900 Chambersburg Rd (17325). Phone 717/334-4332; fax 717/334-3332. www.herrtavern.com.* Continental menu. Closed Jan 1, Dec 24-25. Lunch, dinner. Bar. Children's menu. Restored antebellum tavern with period art and antiques. **$$**

D

Harpers Ferry, wv

1 hour 15 minutes; 67 miles from Washington, DC

Settled 1732 **Pop** 307 **Elev** 247 ft **Area code** 304 **Zip** 25425

Information Jefferson County Chamber of Commerce, 201 Frontage Rd, PO Box 426, Charles Town 25414; 304/725-2055

Web www.jeffersoncounty.com/chamber

Scene of abolitionist John Brown's raid in 1859, Harpers Ferry is at the junction of the Shenandoah and Potomac rivers, where West Virginia, Virginia, and Maryland meet. A US armory and rifle factory made this an important town in early Virginia; John Brown had this in mind when he began his insurrection. He and 16 other men seized the armory and arsenal the night of October 16 and took refuge in the engine house of the armory when attacked by local militia. On the morning of the 18th, the engine house was stormed, and Brown was captured by 90 marines from Washington under Brevet Colonel Robert E. Lee and Lt. J. E. B. Stuart. Ten of Brown's men were killed, including two of his sons. He was hanged in nearby Charles Town for treason, murder, and inciting slaves to rebellion.

When war broke out, Harpers Ferry was a strategic objective for the Confederacy, which considered it the key to Washington. "Stonewall" Jackson captured 12,693 Union prisoners here before the Battle of Antietam in 1862. The town changed hands many times in the war, during which many buildings were damaged. In 1944, Congress authorized a national monument here, setting aside 1,500 acres for that purpose. In 1963, the same area was designated a National Historical Park, now occupying more than 2,200 acres.

What to See and Do

⭐ **Harpers Ferry National Historical Park.** *Shenandoah and High sts (25425). Phone 304/535-6298. ww.nps.gov/hafe/.* Here the old town has been restored to its 19th-century appearance; exhibits and interpretive presentations explore the park's relation to the water-power industry, the Civil War, John Brown, and Storer College, a school established for freed slaves after the war. A Visitor Center is located just off US 340. Visitors should park there; a bus will take them to Lower Town. Contact the Visitor Center, PO Box 65. **$$** Located in the park are

Camp Hill. *Shenandoah and High sts (25425).* Four restored, private houses built 1832-1850.

Harper House. *Shenandoah and High sts (25425).* Three-story stone house built between 1775-1782 by the founder of the town; both George Washington and Thomas Jefferson were entertained as overnight guests. Restored and furnished with period pieces.

Information Center. *S side of Shenandoah St near High St (25425). Phone 304/535-6029.* Restored Federalist house built in 1859 by US government as residence for the master armorer of the US Armory. During the Civil War, it was used as headquarters by various commanding officers. Also on this street is the site of the US Armory that John Brown attempted to seize; it was destroyed during the Civil War.

Jefferson's Rock. From here Thomas Jefferson, in 1783, pronounced the view "one of the most stupendous scenes in nature."

John Brown's Fort. *Shenandoah and High sts (25425). On Arsenal Sq.* Where John Brown made his last stand; rebuilt and moved near original site.

John Brown Museum. *Arsenal Sq and High St (25425).* Contains an exhibit and film on John Brown and a ten-minute slide presentation on the history of the park. Exiting the museum to the right is High St, which has two Civil War museums and two black history museums.

Lockwood House. (1848) Greek Revival house used as headquarters, barracks, and stable during Civil War; later used as a classroom building by Storer College (1867), which was founded to educate freed men after the war.

Other buildings. Open to the public during the summer are the dry goods store, provost, office, and blacksmith shop.

The Point. *Shenandoah and High sts (25425).* Three states, West Virginia, Virginia, and Maryland, and two rivers, the Shenandoah and Potomac, meet at the Blue Ridge Mountains.

Ruins of St. John's Episcopal Church. Used as a guardhouse and hospital during the Civil War.

John Brown Wax Museum. *168 High St (25425). Phone 304/535-6342 or 304/535-2792.* Sound and animation depict Brown's exploits, including the raid on Harpers Ferry. **$$**

Whitewater rafting. *Phone toll-free 800/225-5982.* Many outfitters offer guided trips on the Shenandoah and Potomac rivers. For a list of outfitters, contact the West Virginia Division of Tourism, Research, and Development, 90 Mac Corkle Ave SW, South Charleston 25303.

Special Events

Election Day 1860. *Along Shenandoah and High sts. Phone 304/535-6298 or 304/535-6881.* More than 100 people in 19th-century attire reenact the 1860 presidential election. Second Sat in Oct.

Mountain Heritage Arts and Crafts Festival. *102 Frontage Rd (25414). Phone 304/725-2055.* More than 190 craftspeople and artisans demonstrate quilting, wool spinning, pottery throwing, vegetable dyeing, and other crafts; concerts. Second full weekend in June and last full weekend in Sept.

Old Tyme Christmas. *Phone 304/725-8019 or 304/535-2511.* Caroling, musical programs, children's programs, taffy pull, candlelight walk. First two weekends of Dec.

Motel/Motor Lodge

★ **COMFORT INN.** *Rte 340 and Union St (25425). Phone 304/535-6391; toll-free 800/535-9909; fax 304/535-6395. www.comfortinn.com.* 50 rooms, 2 story. Complimentary continental breakfast. Check-out 11 am, check-in 3 pm. TV; cable (premium), VCR available (movies). In-room modem link. **$**

D ⊠ SC

Manassas (Bull Run) National Battlefield Park, VA

40 minutes; 32 miles from Washington, DC

(SW of Washington, DC, at junction US 29, VA 234)

This 5,000-acre park was the scene of two major Civil War battles. More than 26,000 men were killed or wounded here in struggles for control of a strategically important railroad junction.

The first major land battle of the war (July 21, 1861) was fought here between poorly trained volunteer troops from both North and South. The battle finally resolved itself into a struggle for Henry Hill, where "Stonewall" Jackson earned his nickname. With the outcome in doubt, Confederate reinforcements arrived by railroad from the Shenandoah Valley and turned the battle into a rout.

Thirteen months later (August 28-30, 1862), in the second battle of Manassas, Robert E. Lee outmaneuvered and defeated Union General John Pope and cleared the way for a Confederate invasion of Maryland.

Contact Park Superintendent, 6511 Sudley Rd, Manassas 22110; phone 703/361-1339. www.nps.gov/mana/. Park (daily; closed Dec 25). **$**

What to See and Do

Chinn House Ruins. *6511 Sudley Rd (20109).* The house served as a field hospital in both engagements and marked the left of the Confederate line at First Manassas; also the scene of Longstreet's counterattack at Second Manassas.

Dogan House. *6511 Sudley Rd (20109).* An original structure at Groveton, a village around which the battle of Second Manassas was fought.

Stone Bridge. *6511 Sudley Rd (20109).* Where Union artillery opened the Battle of First Manassas; it afforded an avenue of escape for the Union troops after both First and Second Manassas.

Stone House. *6511 Sudley Rd (20109). Phone 703/361-1339.* Originally a tavern (circa 1848), used as field hospital in both battles. (Summer, daily)

Unfinished Railroad. *6511 Sudley Rd (20109).* Fully graded railroad bed, never completed, behind which Stonewall Jackson's men were positioned during the second battle.

Visitor Center. *6511 Sudley Rd (20109). On Henry Hill, just N of I-66 off VA 234. Phone 703/361-1339. www.nps.gov/mana/.* Hill affords view of much of the first battlefield. Information; self-guided tours start here (walking tour of First Manassas, directions for driving tour of Second Manassas). Markers throughout park explain various aspects of battles. Ranger-conducted tours (summer). In the same building is

   Battlefield Museum. Exhibits reflect incidents of battles; audiovisual presentations offer orientation. (Daily; closed Dec 25)

Mount Vernon, VA

24 minutes; 15 miles from Washington, DC
See also Alexandria, Fairfax; also see Washington, DC

What to See and Do

Grist Mill. *3 miles W on VA 235 (22121). Phone 703/780-3383.* This mill was reconstructed in 1930 on the original foundation of a mill George Washington operated on Dogue Run. Visitor center, programs. (Memorial Day-Labor Day, daily) **$**

★ **Mount Vernon.** *George Washington Pkwy (22121). 18 miles S of Washington, DC via George Washington Memorial Pkwy. Phone 703/780-2000. www.mountvernon.org.* Touring Mount Vernon, George Washington's home for more than 45 years, gives visitors a fascinating glimpse of the world of landed gentry in 18th-century America, as well as the personal vision of the first US president. Washington designed sections of the beautifully landscaped "pleasure grounds" himself, incorporating woods, meadows, and serpentine walkways into the plan. He also added the red-roofed mansion's cupola, weather vane, and two-story piazza, from which guests may enjoy an awe-inspiring view of the Potomac River. Exploring the working areas of the estate, including the wash house, stable, and kitchen, gives visitors an idea of how Mount Vernon operated: an audio tour describes the lives of some of the more than 300 slaves who lived and worked there. The house has been restored to its 1799 appearance, the year Washington died. He is buried on the estate with his wife, Martha. (Daily; hours vary by season) **$$$**

Potomac Spirit. *Pier 4, 6th and Water sts, Washington, DC (20024). Phone 202/923-4354; res 866/211-3811. www.spiritcitycruises.com.* Offers round-trip, Potomac River cruises from Washington, DC to Mount Vernon. The five-hour excursion is sufficient for a complete tour of the house, gardens, and tomb (late Mar-early June, one trip daily; early June-late Aug, two trips daily). **$$$$**

Woodlawn Plantation. *9000 Richmond Hwy (22309). 3 miles W of George Washington Pkwy on US 1. Phone 703/780-4000. www.woodlawn/805.org.*

(1800-1805) In 1799, George Washington gave 2,000 acres of land as a wedding present to Eleanor Parke Custis, his foster daughter, who married his nephew, Major Lawrence Lewis. Dr. William Thornton, first architect of the US Capitol, then designed this mansion. The Lewises entertained such notables as Andrew Jackson, Henry Clay, and the Marquis de Lafayette. The house was restored in the early 1900s and later became the residence of a US senator; 19th-century period rooms; many original furnishings. Formal gardens. (Mar-Dec, daily; closed Jan-Feb, Thanksgiving, Dec 25) A National Trust for Historic Preservation property. **$$** Also here is

Frank Lloyd Wright's Pope-Leighey House. (1940) Erected in Falls Church in 1940, the house was disassembled (due to the construction of a new highway) and rebuilt at the present site in 1964. Built of cypress, brick, and glass, the house is an example of Wright's "Usonian" structures, which he proposed as a prototype of affordable housing for Depression-era middle-income families; original Wright-designed furniture. (Mar-Dec, daily; closed Jan-Feb, Thanksgiving, Dec 25) A National Trust for Historic Preservation property. Combination ticket (**$$$**) for both houses available. **$$**

Restaurant

★ ★ **MOUNT VERNON INN.** *On the grounds of Mount Vernon (22121). Phone 703/780-0011; fax 703/780-1704. www.mountvernon.org.* Lunch, dinner. Bar. Children's menu. Waiters in colonial costume. Hand-painted murals of colonial scenes. **$$**

[D]

Philadelphia, PA

2 hours 20 minutes; 137 miles from Washington, DC

Founded 1682 **Pop** 1,517,550 **Elev** 45 ft **Area code** 215 & 267

Information Convention & Visitors Bureau, 1515 Market St, 19102; 215/636-3300

Web www.pcvb.org

Suburbs Bristol, Chester, Fort Washington, Jenkintown, Kennett Square, King of Prussia, Media, Norristown, West Chester, Willow Grove; also Wilmington, DE and Camden, NJ.

The nation's first capital has experienced a rebirth in the past few decades. Philadelphia has successfully blended its historic past with an electricity of modern times, all the while keeping an eye on the future. In the mid-18th century it was the second-largest city in the English-speaking world. Now, at the dawn of the 21st century, Philadelphia is the second-largest city on the East Coast and the fifth largest in the country. Here, in William Penn's City of Brotherly Love, the Declaration of Independence was written and adopted, the Constitution was molded and signed, the Liberty Bell was rung,

Betsy Ross was said to have sewn her flag, and Washington served most of his years as president.

This is the city of "firsts," including the first American hospital, medical college, women's medical college, bank, paper mill, steamboat, zoo, sugar refinery, daily newspaper, US mint, and public school for black children (1750).

The first Quakers, who came here in 1681, lived in caves dug into the banks of the Delaware River. During the first year, 80 houses were raised; by the following year, William Penn's "greene countrie towne" was a city of 600 buildings. The Quakers prospered in trade and commerce and Philadelphia became the leading port in the colonies. Its leading citizen for many years was Benjamin Franklin—statesman, scientist, diplomat, writer, inventor, and publisher.

The fires of colonial indignation burned hot and early in Philadelphia. Soon after the Boston Tea Party, a protest rally of 8,000 Philadelphians frightened off a British tea ship. In May 1774, when Paul Revere rode from Boston to Philadelphia to report Boston's harbor had been closed, all of Philadelphia went into mourning. The first and second Continental Congresses convened here, and Philadelphia became the headquarters of the Revolution. After the Declaration of Independence was composed and accepted by Congress the city gave its men, factories, and shipyards to the cause. But British General Howe and 18,000 soldiers poured in on September 26, 1777, to spend a comfortable and social winter here while Washington's troops endured the bitter winter at Valley Forge. When the British evacuated the city, Congress returned. Philadelphia continued as the seat of government until 1800, except for a short period when New York City held the honor. The Constitution of the United States was written here, and President George Washington graced the city's halls and streets.

Since those historic days, Philadelphia has figured importantly in the politics, economy, and culture of the country. Here, national conventions have nominated presidents. During four wars the city has served as an arsenal and a shipyard. More than 1,400 churches and synagogues grace the city. There are over 25 colleges, universities, and professional schools in Philadelphia as well. Fine restaurants are in abundance, along with exciting nightlife to top off an evening. Entertainment is offered by the world-renowned Philadelphia Orchestra, theaters, college and professional sports, outstanding parks, recreation centers, and playgrounds. Shoppers may browse major department stores, hundreds of specialty shops, and antique shopping areas.

For ten blocks between the Delaware River and 9th Street lies a history-rich part of Philadelphia. Here are the shrines of American liberty: Independence Hall, the Liberty Bell Pavilion, and many other historical sites in and around Independence National Historical Park.

Additional Visitor Information

There is also a visitor center at 3rd & Chestnut sts, operated by the National Park Service. (Daily) Phone 215/597-8975 or 215/597-8974 for information on park attractions.

The Visitors Center of the Philadelphia Convention and Visitors Bureau, 16th St and John F. Kennedy Blvd, 19102, has tourist information and maps (daily; closed Thanksgiving, Dec 25). Phone 215/636-1666 or 800/537-7676.

Transportation

AIRPORTS
Philadelphia International Airport. Information 215/937-6800 or 800/PHL-GATE; lost and found 215/937-6888; weather 215/936-1212.

CAR RENTAL AGENCIES
See IMPORTANT TOLL-FREE NUMBERS.

PUBLIC TRANSPORTATION
Subway and elevated trains, commuter trains, buses, trolleys (SEPTA), phone 215/580-7800.

RAIL PASSENGER SERVICE
Amtrak 800/872-7245.

What to See and Do

9th Street Italian Market. *9th St between Wharton and Fitzwater (19147). Phone 215/923-5637. www.phillyitalianmarket.com.* Stroll through this outdoor market and you'll get more than a just a whiff of Italy. Sip on Italian gourmet coffee, inhale imported cheeses, or treat yourself to a cannoli. With more than 100 merchants selling their wares, this is the largest working outdoor market in the US, calling this neighborhood home for more than a century. But there's local flavor here as well. Pinch a Jersey tomato, stop for a famous soft pretzel, or take home fresh-baked Amish bread. And if you want to sit for a while, there are plenty of choices for every budget, from fine Italian dining to lunch counters to an outdoor snack tent. **FREE**

Academy of Music. *Broad and Locust sts (19102). Phone 215/893-1999. www.academyofmusic.org.* (1857). City's opera house, concert hall; home of Philadelphia Orchestra, Philly Pops, Opera Company of Philadelphia and Pennsylvania Ballet.

Academy of Natural Sciences Museum. *1900 Ben Franklin Pkwy (19103). Phone 215/299-1000. www.acnatsci.org.* (1812). Dinosaurs, Egyptian mummies, animal displays in natural habitats, live animal programs, hands-on children's museum. (Daily; closed Jan 1, Thanksgiving, Dec 25) **$$**

African-American Museum Philadelphia. *701 Arch St (19106). Phone 215/574-0380. www.aampmuseum.org.* Built to house and interpret African-American culture. Changing exhibits; public events include lectures, workshops, films, and concerts. (Tues-Sun; closed Jan 1, Thanksgiving, Dec 25) **$$$**

American Swedish Historical Museum. *1900 Pattison Ave (19145). Phone 215/389-1776. www.americanswedish.org.* From tapestries to technology, the museum celebrates Swedish influence on American life. Special exhibits on the New Sweden Colony. Research library, collections. (Tues-Sun; closed holidays) **$$**

Antique Row. *From 9th to 17th Sts along Pine St (19103).* Dozens of antique, craft and curio shops.

Arch Street Meetinghouse. *320 Arch St (19106). Phone 215/627-2667. www.archstreetfriends.org.* (1804) Perhaps the largest Friends meetinghouse in the world. Exhibits, slide show, tours. (Daily except Sun; closed Jan 1, Thanksgiving, Dec 25) **DONATION**

Balch Institute for Ethnic Studies. *18 S 7th St (19106). Phone 215/925-8090. www.balchinstitute.org.* A multicultural library, archive, museum, and education center that promotes intergroup understanding using education; 300 years of US immigration are documented here. Features "Peopling of Pennsylvania," as well as changing exhibits. (Mon-Sat; closed holidays) **$$**

Betsy Ross House. *239 Arch St (19106). Phone 215/686-1252. www.betsy rosshouse.org.* Where the famous seamstress is said to have made the first American flag. Upholsterer's shop, memorabilia. Flag Day ceremonies, June 14. (Apr-Oct, daily; Tues-Sun rest of year; closed Jan 1, Thanksgiving, Dec 25) **DONATION**

Bishop White House. *309 Walnut St (19106).* (1786-1787) House of Bishop William White, first Episcopal Bishop of Pennsylvania. Restored and furnished. Tours. Free tickets at park's Visitor Center. **$**

Blue Cross River Rink. *Columbus Blvd at Spring Garden St (19123). Phone 215/925-RINK. www.riverrink.com.* Few outdoor ice skating rinks are as well located as this one along the Delaware River. Visitors have a great vantage point from which to view the Benjamin Franklin Bridge and the Philadelphia skyline. This Olympic-size rink, at 200 feet x 85 feet, can accommodate 500 skaters. After a hearty skate, warm yourself in the heated pavilion, which features a video game area and concessions. (Daily, Nov-mid Mar) **$$**

The Bourse. *5th St, across from Liberty Bell Pavilion (19106).* (1893-1895) Restored Victorian building houses shops and restaurants.

Burial Ground of Congregation Mikveh Israel. *Spruce and 8th sts (19106).* (1738). Graves of Haym Salomon, Revolutionary War financier, and Rebecca Gratz, probable model for "Rebecca" of Sir Walter Scott's *Ivanhoe.*

Carpenters' Hall. *320 Chestnut St (19106).* (1770) Constructed as guild hall; meeting site of First Continental Congress (1774). Historical museum since 1857; still operated by Carpenters Co. Contains original chairs; exhibits of early tools.

Centipede Tours. *1315 Walnut St (19107). Phone 215/735-3123.* Candlelight strolls (1 1/2 hours) through historic Philadelphia and Society Hill areas led by guides in 18th-century dress; begins and ends at City Tavern. (Mid-May-mid-Oct, Fri-Sat) Reservations preferred. **$$**

Christ Church. *2nd St between Market and Arch Sts (19106). Phone 215/922-1695.* (Episcopal). Patriots, Loyalists, and heroes have worshiped here since 1695. Sit in pews once occupied by Washington, Franklin, and Betsy Ross. (Mar-Dec, daily; rest of year, Wed-Sun; closed Jan 1, Thanksgiving, Dec 25) **FREE**

Christ Church Burial Ground. *5th and Arch sts (19106). Phone 215/922-1695.* Resting place of Benjamin Franklin, his wife, Deborah, and six other signers of the Declaration of Independence. (Call for hours)

City Hall. *Broad and Market sts (19107). Phone 215/686-2840.* A granite statue of William Penn stands 510 feet high above the heart of the city, on top of this municipal building which is larger than the Capitol. It is known as Penn Square and was designated by Penn as the location for a building of "publick concerns." It also functions as Philadelphia's City Hall. It is one of the finest examples of French Second-Empire architectural style and a sculptural achievement. Constructing this building with the tallest statue (37,000 feet) in the world on its top took 30 years. Penn's famous hat is more than 7 feet in diameter, and the brim creates a 2-foot-wide track. There are more than 250 sculptures around this marble, granite, and limestone structure, 20 elevators, and a four-faced, 50-ton clock. Tower tours take place every 15 minutes between 9:30 am-4:30 pm. (Mon-Fri; closed holidays)

Civil War Library and Museum. *1805 Pine St (19103). Phone 215/735-8196.* Four-story brick 19th-century town house filled with 18,000 books and periodicals dealing with events leading up to the American Civil War, the war itself, and early Reconstruction. Unique collection of arms, uniforms, flags of the period, memorabilia, and artifacts begun in 1888 by former officers of the Union Army. Exhibits on Lincoln, Grant, and Meade; also the Navy Room and the Armory. (Thurs-Fri; closed holidays) **$$**

Cliveden. *6401 Germantown Ave (19144), between Johnson and Cliveden sts. Phone 215/848-1777. www.cliveden.org.* (1767) A 2 1/2-story stone Georgian house of individual design built as a summer home by Benjamin Chew, Chief Justice of colonial Pennsylvania. On Oct 4, 1777, British soldiers used the house as a fortress to repulse Washington's attempt to recapture Philadelphia. Used as the Chew family residence for 200 years; many original furnishings. A National Trust for Historic Preservation property. (Apr-Dec, Thurs-Sun afternoons; closed Easter, Thanksgiving, Dec 25) **$$$**

Congress Hall. *6th and Chestnut sts (19106). Phone 215/597-8974.* Congress met here during the last decade of the 18th century. House of Representatives and Senate chambers are restored. **FREE**

Declaration House. *701 Market St (19106). Phone 215/597-8974.* Reconstructed house on the site of the writing of the Declaration of Independence by Thomas Jefferson; two rooms Jefferson rented have been reproduced. Short orientation and movie about Jefferson, his philosophy on the common man, and the history of the house. **FREE**

Deshler-Morris House. *5442 Germantown Ave (19144). Phone 215/596-1748. www.nps.gov/demo/.* (1772-1773) Residence of President Washington in the summers of 1793, 1794; period furnishings, garden. (Wed-Sun afternoons, or by appointment; closed holidays) **$**

Edgar Allan Poe National Historic Site. *532 N 7th St (19123). Phone 215/597-8780. www.nps.gov/edal/.* Where Poe lived before his move to New York in 1844. The site is the nation's memorial to the literary genius of Edgar Allan

Poe. Exhibits, slide show, tours, and special programs. (June-Oct, daily; rest of year, Wed-Sun; closed Jan 1, Dec 25) **FREE**

Electric Factory. *421 N 7th St (19123). Phone 215/569-9400.* This all-ages live music venue offers accessibility to lesser-known bands, although Tori Amos, Garbage, Brian Setzer, and other well-known artists have played here. Because it can accommodate 3,000 people, it can feel crowded; there is no seating on the main level. But early arrivers can position themselves at bar tables in the upstairs balcony overlooking the stage. (Daily)

Elfreth's Alley. *126 Elfreth's Alley (19106). Located on 2nd Street, between Race and Arch. Phone 215/574-0560. www.elfrethsalley.org.* Philadelphians still live in these Georgian- and Federal-style homes along cobblestoned Elfreth's Alley, the nation's oldest continued-use residential street. A few homes have been converted into museums, offering guided tours, a quaint gift shop, and handcrafted memorabilia. Culture and architecture appreciators will pick up all sorts of historical facts through photos and the collections. (Mar-Oct, Mon-Sat, Sun afternoons; Nov-Feb, Thurs-Sat, Sun afternoons) **$**

⭐ **Fairmount Park.** *4231 N Concourse Dr (19131). Begins at Philadelphia Museum of Art, extends NW on both sides of Wissahickon Creek and Schuylkill River. Phone 215/685-0000. www.phila.gov/fairpark.* At 8,900 acres, Fairmount Park is the largest city park in America. The park can please the very active and the moderately active, as well as the artistically and historically inclined. It is home to 100 miles of beautifully landscaped paths for walking and horseback riding. Cyclists love to bike along the Pennypack and Wissahickon trails. Walkers stroll or power-hike in Valley Green alongside the ducks. In-line skaters and rowing and sculling enthusiasts at Boathouse Row enjoy the sights along the Schuykill River on Kelly Drive. Within the park are the Philadelphia Zoo (see), the Shofuso Japanese House, the Philadelphia Museum of Art (see), the outdoor festival center Robin Hood Dell, and the Philadelphia Orchestra's summer amphitheater (Mann Music Center—see also PHILADELPHIA ORCHESTRA), as well as 127 tennis courts and numerous picnic spots. The park contains America's largest collection of authentic colonial homes, features majestic outdoor sculptures, and includes Memorial Hall, the only building remaining from the 1876 Centennial Exhibition. (Daily) In park are

Boathouse Row Rowing Regattas. *On E bank of river. Phone 215/978-6919 for rowing, regatta schedules. www.boathouserow.org.* The Schuylkill River along Kelly Drive beckons competitive rowers. Powerboats are not allowed on this scenic 28-mile river. With Fairmount Park surrounding the 14 historic boathouses where the boats are kept and the Art Museum as a backdrop, it is among the most picturesque rowing courses in the world. Several well-attended events take place here from spring into fall, including the Stotesbury Cup Regatta, the Dad Vail Regatta, the Head of the Schuylkill Regatta, Independence Day Regatta, and the Schuylkill Navy Regatta. **FREE**

Colonial Mansions. *Phone 215/684-7922.* Handsome 18th-century dwellings in varying architectural styles, authentically preserved and furnished, include Mount Pleasant (1761) (Tues-Sun); Cedar Grove (1756) (Tues-Sun); Strawberry Mansion (1797) (Tues-Sun); Sweetbriar (1797) (Mon, Wed-Sun); Lemon Hill (1799) (Wed-Sun); Woodford (1756) (Tues-Sun); Laurel Hill (1760) (Wed-Sun). Further details and guided tours from Park Houses office at Philadelphia Museum of Art. **$**

Japanese Exhibition House. *Fairmount Park Horticulture Center, Horticultural Dr (19131). Phone 215/878-5097.* Re-creates a bit of Japan, complete with a garden, pond, and bridge. (May-Labor Day, Tues-Sun; Labor Day-Oct, Sat and Sun) **$**

Philadelphia Museum of Art. *26th St and Ben Franklin Pkwy (19130). Take I-676 W to the Ben Franklin Pkwy exit (22nd St, museum area), on the right side. At the end of the exit ramp, turn right onto 22nd St and move into the far left lane. Turn left onto the outside lanes of the parkway toward the museum, follow the Art Museum signs, and turn left at the stoplight. Follow this to the west entrance of the museum, where limited parking is available. Phone 215/763-8100. www.philamuseum.org.* Modeled after a Greco-Roman temple, this massive museum amplifies the beauty of more than 300,000 works of art and offers spectacular natural views. From the top of the steps outside (made famous by Sylvester Stallone in the movie *Rocky*), visitors discover a breathtaking view of the Ben Franklin Parkway toward City Hall. Inside, the collections span 2,000 years and many more miles. There's a lavish collection of period rooms, a Japanese teahouse, a Chinese palace hall, and a celebrated selection of Oriental carpets. Art lovers will also find East Asian art costumes, Indian and Himalayan pieces, European decorative arts, Medieval sculptures, Renaissance paintings, Impressionist and Post-Impressionist paintings, and modern and contemporary works in many media. (Tues-Sun; closed holidays) **$$**

Philadelphia Orchestra. *260 S Broad St # 1600 (19102). Phone 215/893-1999. www.philorch.org.* The internationally renowned Philadelphia Orchestra has distinguished itself as a leading American orchestra through a century of acclaimed performances, historic international tours, and best-selling recordings. Performances are held at The Kimmel Center for the Performing Arts at Broad and Spruce Streets; the Mann Center for the Performing Arts, 52nd Street and Parkside Avenue; Saratoga Performing Arts Center in upstate New York; and annually at New York's Carnegie Hall.

Philadelphia Zoo. *3400 W Girard Ave (19104). Located at the corner of 34th St and Girard Ave in Fairmount Park. Phone 215/243-1100. www.philly zoo.org.* The Philadelphia Zoo may have been America's first zoo—it was home to the nation's first white lions and witnessed its first successful chimpanzee birth—but you'll see no signs of old age here. Over the last century, the zoo has transformed itself into much more. The zoo is a preservation spot for rare and endangered animals, as well as a garden and wildlife destination point. Lovers of living things will appreciate the opportunity to see 1,600 live animals, from red pandas to Rodrigues fruit bats, in realistic re-creations of their natural habitats. Inclined to reach out and touch? Take a pony, camel, or elephant ride; feed nectar to a parrot in a walk-through aviary; or engage with a playful wallaby.

Prefer less hands-on contact? Pedal a boat around Bird Lake. If you are happier at arm's length, pretend that you're a giraffe and explore a four-story tropical tree or take a soaring balloon 400 feet up on the country's first passenger-carrying Zooballoon. (Daily; closed Jan 1, Jun 12, Thanksgiving, Dec 24-25, Dec 31) **$$-$$$**

Robin Hood Dell East. *Ridge Ave near 33rd St (19132). Phone 215/685-9560. www.delleast.org.* (See SPECIAL EVENTS)

Fireman's Hall Museum. *147 N 2nd St (19106). Phone 215/923-1438.* Collection of antique firefighting equipment; displays and exhibits of fire department history since its beginning in 1736; library. (Tues-Sat 9 am-4:30 pm; closed holidays) **DONATION**

The First Bank of the United States. *3rd and Walnut sts (19106).* (1797-1811). Organized by Alexander Hamilton; country's oldest bank building; exterior restored. Closed to the public.

First Presbyterian Church. *201 S 21st St (19103). Phone 215/567-0532. www.fpcphila.org.* This more than 300-year-old church was designed in the Victorian Gothic style, combining French and English medieval Gothic cathedral motifs with massive details, flamboyant decoration, and mixed materials, including granite, sand-toned brick, six types of marble, terra cotta, and stone. No plaster was used anywhere within the original building, a matter of some architectural significance toward the end of the 19th century. **FREE**

The Five Spot. *5 S Bank St (19106). Phone 215/574-0070. www.thefivespot.com.* Originally opened as a swing club during the late-1990s "swing trend," The Five Spot is now a live music and dance club that features everything from rock music and live DJs to salsa and swing. The club hosts a live cabaret act called the Peek-a-boo Revue the first Saturday of every month, as well as Latin salsa on Thursdays, open-mike nights on Tuesdays (where many musicians claim to have gotten their start), and weekly swing lessons. (Daily) **$**

Fort Mifflin. *Fort Mifflin Rd and Enterprise Ave (19153). From I-95 S take exit 13 to Island Ave, left at stop sign, follow signs. From I-95 N take exit 10, pass the airport, turn right at Island Ave and follow the road around; turn right onto Fort Mifflin Rd. Phone 215/685-4192. www.libertynet.org/ftmifflin.* Fort Mifflin is a complex of 11 restored buildings that bring the area's only existing fort to life. It was a Revolutionary War fort strategically located in the Delaware River at the mouth of the Schuylkill. Here, you can climb into a bombproof enclosure used to shelter troops; witness the uniform and weapons demonstrations that take place throughout the year; explore the four-foot-thick walls of the Arsenal, soldiers' barracks, officers' quarters, and blacksmith's shop; or simply enjoy the spectacular view of Philadelphia and the Delaware from the Northeast Bastion. Self-guided and one-hour guided tours are available. (Apr-Nov, Wed-Sun) **$$**

Franklin Court. *316-322 Market St (19106). Phone 215/597-8974.* The site of Benjamin Franklin's house has been developed as a tribute to him; area includes working printing office and bindery, underground museum with multimedia exhibits, an archaeological exhibit, and the B. Franklin Free Post Office. **FREE**

Franklin Institute Science Museum. *222 N 20th St (19103). Phone 215/448-1200. sln.fi.edu.* This 300,000-square-foot science museum complex and memorial hall brings biology, earth science, physics, mechanics, aviation, astronomy, communications, and technology to life with a variety of highly interactive exhibits honoring Philadelphia's mechanical inventor Ben Franklin. (A 30-foot marble statue of Franklin sits in a Roman Pantheon-inspired chamber known as the Benjamin Franklin National Memorial.) The kids can play tic-tac-toe with a strategically adept computer, climb into the cockpit of an Air Force jet trainer, experiment with the laws governing flight, or test water quality in the Mandell Center located in a 38,000-square-foot garden. Stargazers can witness the birth of the universe, see galaxies form, or discover wondrous nebulae under the Fels Planetarium dome. Budding physicists and bike fanatics will appreciate the 28-foot-high bicycle perched on a 1-inch cable demonstrating gyroscopic stability in the Sky Bike exhibit. And every member of the family can lose themselves in the 56-speaker sounds and larger-than-life-size images at the Tuttleman IMAX Theater. (Daily; closed major holidays) **$$-$$$$**

Franklin Mills Mall. *1455 Frankling Mills Cir (19154). I-95 and Woodhaven Rd, 15 minutes north of Center City Philadelphia; daily shuttle bus available. Phone 215/632-1500. www.franklin-mills-mall.com.* Bargain hunters will feel like they've hit the jackpot in the more than 200 discount stores in this mega-shopping complex just 15 miles outside Center City Philadelphia, which touts itself as "Pennsylvania's most visited attraction." Shoppers will find outlets of such well-known retailers as Kenneth Cole, Tommy Hilfiger, Casual Corner, The Gap, Old Navy, Nine West, Neiman Marcus, Saks Fifth Avenue, and Marshalls. There is no sales tax on apparel in Pennsylvania, which makes slashed prices even more appealing. Two food courts, seven restaurants, and a 14-screen movie theater will engage any non-shoppers in the group. If you don't want to fight for a parking spot, take advantage of the daily shuttle services from area hotels, airport, and train stations. (Daily)

Free Library. *Logan Sq, 1901 Vine St (19103). Phone 215/686-5322. www.library.phila.gov.* Large central library with over 9 million indexed items in all fields. Rare books, maps, theater scripts, and orchestral scores; automobile reference collections; changing exhibits. (Memorial Day-Labor Day, Tues-Sun; rest of year, daily; closed holidays) **FREE**

The Gallery. *9th and Market sts (19107). Phone 215/925-7162.* Concentration of 250 shops and restaurants in a four-level mall with glass elevators, trees, fountains, and benches.

Gloria Dei Church National Historic Site ("Old Swedes"). *Columbus Blvd and Christian St (19147). 8 blocks S of Chestnut. Phone 215/389-1513. www.nps.gov/glde/.* (1700) State's oldest church. Memorial to John Hansen, president of the Continental Congress under Articles of Confederation. (Daily)

Gray Line bus tours. *3101 Orthodox St (19137). Phone 215/744-1100 or 800/220-3133.*

Haverford College. *370 Lancaster Ave, Haverford (19041). 10 miles W on US 30. Phone 610/896-1000. www.haverford.edu.* (1833) 1,138 students. Founded by members of the Society of Friends. The 204-acre campus includes Founders Hall; James P. Magill Library; Arboretum; Morris Cricket Library and Collection (by appointment only; phone 610/896-1162). Tours of arboretum and campus.

Historical Society of Pennsylvania. *1300 Locust St (19107). Phone 215/732-6200. www.hsp.org.* Museum exhibit features first draft of Constitution, 500 artifacts and manuscripts, plus video tours of turn-of-the-century urban and suburban neighborhoods. Research library and archives house historical and genealogical collections. (Tues-Sat; closed holidays) **$$**

Historic Bartram's Garden. *54th St and Lindbergh Blvd (19143). Phone 215/729-5281. www.bartramsgarden.org.* Pre-Revolutionary home of John Bartram, the royal botanist to the colonies under George III, naturalist, and plant explorer. The 18th-century stone farmhouse (fee), barn, stable, and cider mill overlook the Schuylkill River. Museum shop. (Daily; 10 am-5 pm; closed holidays) Gardens **FREE** House tours **$**

Independence Hall. *5th and Chestnut sts (19106). Phone 215/597-8974. www.nps.gov/inde/.* Built in the mid-1700s, Independence Hall is the site of the first public reading of the Declaration of Independence. It also played host to large political rallies during the country's founding years. It is considered a fine example of Georgian architecture. Visitors often find the Hall a good first stop for their tour of Independence National Historic Park, which includes the Liberty Bell (see), Congress Hall (see), Old City Hall (see), and Carpenter's Hall (see). The building is open for tours only. Admission by tour only. (Daily) **FREE**

★ Independence National Historical Park. *3rd and Chestnuts sts (19106). Phone 215/597-8974. www.nps.gov/inde/.* The park has been called "America's most historic square mile." The Independence Visitor Center at 6th & Marker streets has a tour map, information on all park activities and attractions, and a 30-minute film entitled *Independence.*

Independence Seaport Museum. *211 S Columbus Blvd (19106). Take I-95 to exit 20. At the traffic light turn left onto Columbus Blvd (aka Delaware Ave.). Pass the Hyatt Regency Philadelphia at Penn's Landing on the right; the next building is the Museum. Turn right into the museum just before the bridge. The circular driveway leads to the entrance to the Penn's Landing parking lot. Phone 215/925-5439. www.phillyseaport.org.* Maritime enthusiasts of all ages will appreciate the creative interactive exhibits about the science, history, and art of boat building along the region's waterways at the Independence Seaport Museum. Oral histories of the men and women who have lived and worked here take visitors through immigration, commerce, defense, industry, and the recreational aspects of boats. You can watch how builders assemble a boat, walk (or crawl) through a full-size replica of a Delaware River Shad Skiff, or pull shapes through a 10-foot tank of water to examine drag-affecting speed. Or you can chart a course for Penn's Landing or learn about navigation as you travel beneath a three-story replica of the Ben

Franklin Bridge and make your way along a model of the Delaware River. (Daily 10 am-5 pm; closed Jan 1, Thanksgiving, Dec 25) **$$**

Independence Square. *(Known as State House Yard in colonial times) Bounded by Chestnut, Walnut, 5th and 6th sts (19106).* Contains Independence Hall, Congress Hall, Old City Hall, and Philosophical Hall.

Jeweler's Row. *7th and Sansom sts (19106).* Largest jewelry district in the country other than New York City. More than 300 shops, including wholesalers and diamond cutters.

John Heinz National Wildlife Refuge at Tinicum. *86th and Lindbergh Blvd (19153). S via I-95, W PA 291 exit, right on Bartram Ave, left on 84th St, left on Lindbergh Blvd. Phone 215/365-3118 or 610/521-0662.* Largest remaining freshwater tidal wetland in the state, protecting more than 1,000 acres of wildlife habitat. Area was first diked by Swedish farmers in 1643; Dutch farmers and the colonial government added dikes during the Revolutionary War. More than 280 species of birds and 13 resident mammal species. Hiking, bicycling, nature observation, canoeing on Darby Creek, fishing. (Daily) **FREE**

Laff House Comedy Club. *221 South St (19147). Phone 215/440-4242. www.laffhouse.com.* This humor hub located on the city's artsy and alternative South Street hosts comedy events all week. There are Open Mic nights (**$**), Comedy Spotlights (**$$**), and comedy competitions. Laff Club attracts up-and-comers as well as established comics such as Dave Attell of Comedy Central's "Insomniac."

⭐ **The Liberty Bell.** *Liberty Bell Center, 6th St between Market and Chestnut sts (19106). Phone 215/597-8974. www.nps.gov/inde/liberty-bell.* "Proclaim liberty throughout all the land unto all the inhabitants thereof," reads the inscription on this irreparably damaged, 2,000-pound historic bell housed in the Liberty Bell Center. An international icon and one of the most venerated stops in Independence Park, the bell is a representation of the fragile but enduring nature of the republic it reflects. This mostly copper symbol of religious freedom, justice, and independence is believed to hang from its original yoke. (Daily) **FREE**

Library Hall. *105 S 5th St (19106). Phone 215/440-3400.* Reconstruction of Library Company of Philadelphia (1789-1790) building is occupied by library of American Philosophical Society. Open to scholars. (Mon-Fri)

Manayunk. *Take 76 from the Center City to Manayunk exit 338. At the bottom of the ramp, turn left and cross the Green Ln bridge to the traffic light, which is Main St, and turn right into Manayunk. Phone 215/482-9565. www.manayunk.com* This historic district, just 7 miles from Center City, makes a great destination point or place to hang out. Appreciators of old things will marvel over the rail lines, canal locks, and old textile mills dotting this quaint town. Joggers, walkers, hikers, and off-road cyclists will enjoy traveling the towpath that edges the town while their shop-a-holic counterparts check out the more than 70 boutiques and galleries. The word *Manayunk* is derived from the Lenape Indian word *manaiung*, which means "where we go to drink," after the canal that flows into town, and this town offers a selection of charming watering holes. Serious shoppers will find collectibles, furnishings, crafts, clothing, and accessories that you can't find just anywhere.

Masonic Temple. *1 N Broad St (19107). Phone 215/988-1900. www.pagrandlodge.org/home.html.* Philadelphia's Masonic Temple was designed for the Fraternal Order of Freemasons, of which Benjamin Franklin and George Washington were members. The interior houses seven different halls, including the Gothic Hall, Oriental Hall, and the better-known Egyptian Hall. It showcases treasures of freemasonry, including a book written by Franklin and a Masonic apron of Washington's. A tour helps illuminate the mysteries of this unusual religious order. (Mon-Sat) **FREE**

The Merchant's Exchange. *3rd and Walnut sts (19106).* Designed by William Strickland, this building is one of the East's finest examples of Greek Revival architecture. Exterior restored; now houses regional offices of the National Park Service. Closed to the public.

Morris Arboretum of the University of Pennsylvania. *100 Northwestern Ave (19128). Approximately 12 miles NW in Chestnut Hill; entrance on Northwestern Ave, between Stenton and Germantown Ave. Phone 215/247-5777. www.upenn.edu/arboretum.* (1887). Public garden with more than 14,000 accessioned plants on 166 acres; special garden areas such as Swan Pond, Rose Garden, and Japanese gardens. Tours (Sat and Sun afternoon; one each day) (Daily; closed major holidays) **$$**

Mummer's Museum. *1100 S 2nd St (19147). Phone 215/336-3050. riverfrontmummers.com/museum.* Participatory exhibits and displays highlighting the history and tradition of the Mummer's Parade (see SPECIAL EVENTS). Costumes and videotapes of past parades. Free outdoor string band concerts (May-Sept, Tues evenings, weather permitting); 20 string bands, different every week. (Tues-Sun; closed Mon, major holidays, and Sun in July-Aug) **$**

Museum Shop (Pemberton House). *Chestnust between 3rd and 4th sts (19106).* Reconstruction of Quaker merchant's house; now shop with items relating to historic sites.

Mütter Museum. *19 S 22nd St (19103). Phone 215/563-3737. www.collphyphil .org/muttpg1.shtml.* This collection of one-of-a-kind, hair-raising medical curiosities includes President Cleveland's jawbone; the thorax of John Wilkes Booth; a plaster cast of Siamese twins; human bones shattered by bullets; a liver in a jar; and a drawer full of buttons, coins, and teeth removed from human stomachs *without* surgery. Located at the esteemed College of Physicians of Philadelphia, the gallery holds an internationally revered collection of creepy anatomical and pathological specimens, medical instruments, and illustrations. (Mon-Sun 10 am-5pm; closed Jan 1, Thanksgiving, Dec 25) **$$**

National Museum of American Jewish History. *Independence Mall East, 55 N 5th St (19106). Phone 215/923-3811. www.nmajh.org.* The museum presents experiences and educational programs that preserve, explore, and celebrate the history of Jews in America. (Daily except Sat; limited hours Fri and Sun; closed Jan 1, Thanksgiving, also Jewish holidays) **FREE**

New Hall Military Museum. *4th and Chestnut sts (19106). Phone 215/597-8974.* This reconstruction houses the US Marine Corps Memorial Museum, featuring exhibits on the early history of the Marines, and the Army-Navy Museum. (Daily 2-5 pm)

Old City Hall. *5th and Chestnut sts (19106).* (1789) Built as City Hall, but was also home of first US Supreme Court, 1791-1800. Exterior restored. Interior depicts the judicial phase of the building.

Old Pine Street Presbyterian Church. *412 Pine St (19106). Phone 215/925-8051.* (1768) Colonial church and graveyard, renovated in 1850s in Greek Revival style. (Daily)

Old St. George's United Methodist Church. *235 N 4th St (19106). Phone 215/925-7788.* (1769) Oldest Methodist Church in continuous service in the US. Colonial architecture; collection of Methodist memorabilia; has only Bishop Asbury bible and John Wesley chalice cup in America. (Daily)

Old St. Mary's Church. *252 S 4th St (19106), between Locust and Spruce sts. Phone 215/923-7930.* (1763). Commodore John Barry, "father of the US Navy," is interred in graveyard behind the city's first Catholic cathedral. (Daily)

Penn's Landing. *Columbus Blvd and Spruce St (19106).*

Gazela of Philadelphia. *Columbus Blvd (19106). Phone 215/218-0110.* (1883) Portuguese square-rigger, tall ship. (call for hours)

USS *Olympia*. *Columbus Blvd and Walnut St (19106). Phone 215/925-5439.* Commodore Dewey's flagship during Spanish-American War; restored. Naval museum has weapons, uniforms, ship models, and naval relics of all periods. Also here is World War II submarine, USS *Becuna*. (Daily; closed holidays) **$$$**

Pennsylvania Academy of Fine Arts. *118 N Broad St (19106). Phone 215/972-7600. www.pafa.org.* This is the nation's oldest art museum and school of fine arts. Within the Gothic Victorian structure are paintings, works on paper, and sculptures by American artists ranging from colonial masters to contemporary artists. Many of the nation's finest artists, including Charles Willson Peale, Mary Cassatt, William Merritt Chase, and Maxfield Parrish, were founders, teachers, or students here. (Tues-Sat) **$$$**

Pennsylvania Ballet. *1101 S Broad St (19147). Phone 215/336-2000. www.paballet.org.* This company with a George Balanchine influence includes a varied repertoire of ballets ranging from classics like *The Nutcracker* to original works. Performances are held at the Academy of Music and the Merriam Theatre.

Pennsylvania Hospital. *8th and Spruce sts (19107).* (1751) First in country, founded by Benjamin Franklin.

Pentimenti Gallery. *133 N 3rd St (19106). Phone 215/625-9990. www.pentimenti.com.* Exhibiting works of art in all modes ranging from figurative to abstract by local, regional, and international artists. (Wed-Sat) **FREE**

Philadelphia 76ers (NBA). *First Union Center, 3601 S Broad St (19148). Phone 215/339-7676. www.nba.com/sixers/.* Team plays at First Union Center.

Philadelphia Carriage Company. *500 N 13th St (19123). Phone 215/922-6840.* Guided tours via horse-drawn carriage covering Society Hill and other historic areas; begin and end on 5th St at Chestnut. (Daily, weather permitting; closed Dec 25) **$$$$**

Philadelphia Eagles (NFL). *Lincoln Financial Field, 11th St and Pattison Ave (19148). Phone 215/463-2500. www.philadelphiaeagles.com.* Team plays at Lincoln Financial Field.

Philadelphia Flyers (NHL). *First Union Center, 3601 S Broad St (19148). Phone 215/336-2000.* Team plays at First Union Center.

Philadelphia History Museum—The Atwater Kent. *15 S 7th St (19106). Phone 215/685-4830. www.philadelphiahistory.org.* Hundreds of fascinating artifacts, toys and miniatures, maps, prints, paintings, and photographs reflecting the city's social and cultural history. (Wed-Mon; closed holidays) **$$**

Philadelphia Phillies (MLB). *Citizens Bank Park, on Pattison Ave between 11th and Darien sts (19148). Phone 215/463-5000. www.philadelphiaphillies.mlb .com.* Team will begin the 2004 season in this brand new, state-of-the-art stadium.

Philadelphia Soft Pretzel. The famous Philadelphia soft pretzel is not your average hard, crunchy, plastic-wrapped snack. You know you're getting the real deal when you are handed this hand-rolled, freshly baked, coarsely salted, buttery, golden-brown comfort food in a paper bag. A Philadelphia pretzel's texture is as vital as its taste: that means not too dry (read: stale) and certainly not too moist. Aficionados claim that Amish girls in hairnets sell the best ones at Fishers in Reading Terminal Market. But serious pretzel hunters can also find these chewy twists of dough, considered to be the country's oldest snack food, in food carts at city intersections, family-owned restaurants, and the airport. Try one with a dollop or two of yellow—not Dijon—mustard.

Philosophical Hall. *104 S 5th St (19106). www.amphilsoc.org.* (1785-1789) Home of the American Philosophical Society, oldest learned society in America (1743), founded by Benjamin Franklin. Not open to the public.

Please Touch Museum for Children. *210 N 21st St (19103). Phone 215/963-0667. www.pleasetouchmuseum.org.* A group of artists, educators, and parents conceived of this award-winning, interactive exploratory learning center for children ages 1 to 7 in 1976. The safe, hands-on learning laboratory has since become a model for children's museums nationwide. Story lovers will enjoy having tea with the Mad Hatter or hanging out with Max in the forest "where the wild things are." Children who don't want to sit still can board the life-size bus or shop at the miniature supermarket. The ones who like to get their hands dirty can engage in science experiments. Creature lovers can interact with fuzzy human-made barnyard animals. And the entertainment-minded can see themselves on television or audition for a news anchor position. (Daily) **$$$**

Reading Terminal Market. *12th and Arch sts (19107). Phone 215/922-2317. www.readingterminalmarket.org.* The nation's oldest continuously operating farmers market is alive and well—and thriving—in downtown Philadelphia. An indoor banquet for the senses, the market offers an exhilarating array of baked goods, meats, poultry, seafood, produce, flowers, and Asian, Middle Eastern, and Pennsylvania Dutch foods. Locals recommend the family-run stands, three of which are descendants of the original market. (Mon-Sat 8 am-6 pm)

Rita's Water Ice. *235 South St (19147). Phone 215/629-3910. www. ritasice.com/contact.html.* The best water ice is not a solid and not quite a liquid, and visitors to Philadelphia will find it at Rita's. With locations throughout the city and surrounding area, Rita's is the city's favorite for frozen water ice, offering a changing selection of smooth, savory water ice, as well as ice cream and gelati. (Daily)

Rittenhouse Square. *Bordered by 18th, 19th, and Walnut sts (19103). www.rittenhouserow.org.* In the blocks that surround this genteel urban square in Philadelphia's most fashionable section of town are exclusive shops, restaurants, and cafés. Discover what's new at chic boutiques—Francis Jerome, Sophy Curson, Nicole Miller, or Ralph Lauren—or experience department store shopping of old at the historic Wanamaker's building, which is now a Lord & Taylor.

Rodin Museum. *22nd St and Franklin Pkwy (19101). Phone 215/763-8100. www.rodinmuseum.org.* This museum, built in the Beaux Arts style, houses more than 200 sculptures created by Auguste Rodin (1840-1917) and is considered the largest collection of his works outside his native France. *The Thinker,* Rodin's most famous piece, greets visitors outside at the gateway to the museum. Tours available. (Tues-Sun 10 am-5 pm; closed holidays) **$$**

Schuylkill Center for Environmental Education. *8480 Hagy's Mill Rd (19128). Phone 215/482-7300.* A 500-acre natural area with more than 7 miles of trails; discovery room; gift shop/bookstore. (Daily; closed holidays) **$$**

Sesame Place. *100 Sesame Rd (19047). 20 miles NE via I-95 to Levittown exit (25 E). Follow signs for the Oxford Valley Mall on the US 1 Bypass.*

Shops at the Bellevue. *200 S Broad St (19102). Phone 215/875-8350.* Beaux Arts architecture of the former Bellevue Stratford Hotel has been preserved and transformed; it now contains offices, a hotel, and a four-level shopping area centered around an atrium court. (Mon-Sat)

Society Hill Area. *7th and Lombard sts (19106). Area between the Delaware River and Washington Sq (5th St), bounded by Walnut St to the north and Lombard St to the south. www.ushistory.org/tour/tour_sochill.htm.* Secret parks, cobblestone walkways, and diminutive alleys among beautifully restored brick colonial town homes make this historic area a treasure for visitors. A popular daily 30-minute walking tour will inspire history fans as well architecture lovers. Highlights along the way include a courtyard designed by famed architect I. M. Pei; gardens planted by the Daughters of the American Revolution; a sculpture of Robert Morris, one of the signers of the Declaration of Independence; Greek Revival-style architecture now home to the National Portrait Gallery; and the burial ground of Revolutionary War soldiers. Admire the gardens, immerse yourself in the history of Independence National Historical Park, or stroll through the exquisitely landscaped Washington Square Park. In the summer months, the area hosts outdoor arts festivals in Headhouse Square. It's also home to some of Philadelphia's finest restaurants.

Athenaeum of Philadelphia. *219 S 6th St (19106). Phone 215/925-2688. www.philaathenaeum.org.* Landmark example of Italian Renaissance architecture (1845-1847); restored building has American neoclassical-style decorative arts, paintings, sculpture; research library; furniture and art from the collection of Joseph Bonaparte, King of Spain and older brother of Napoleon; changing exhibits of architectural drawings, photos, and rare books. Tours by appointment. (Mon-Fri; closed holidays) **FREE**

Physick House. *321 S 4th St (19106). Phone 215/925-7866.* (1786) House of Dr. Philip Sung Physick, "father of American surgery," from 1815-1837. Restored Federal-style house with period furnishings; garden. (Thurs-Sun afternoons) **$$**

Powel House. *244 S 3rd St (19106). Phone 215/627-0364.* (1765) Georgian town house of Samuel Powel, last colonial mayor of Philadelphia and first mayor under the new republic. Period furnishings, silver and porcelain; garden. Tours (Thurs-Sun afternoons; closed holidays). **$$**

South Street District. *From the Schuylkill Expy, take the South St exit east. From the Center City area, it's 5 blocks south of Market St. Phone 215/413-3713. www.south-street.com.* On South Street, the young and hip will enjoy the search for thrift store finds, the aroma of incense, the light refracting from crystals, and a fashion show of the pierced and tattooed sort. The rest can rifle through dusty rare books, cruise the art galleries, or try on every manner of hat. These blocks at the southern boundary of the city—as well as the numbered streets just off of it—are chock full of offbeat shops, cafés, street musicians, and water ice stands, all within walking distance of Penn's Landing and Society Hill. For a Philadelphia signature treat, visitors of all tastes should not miss the legendary Jim's Steaks for cheesesteaks.

St. Peter's Church. *3rd and Pine sts (19106). Phone 215/925-5968. www.stpetersphila.org.* (1761 Episcopal) (1761) Georgian colonial architecture; numerous famous people buried in churchyard.

Stenton House. *4601 N 18th St (19140). Phone 215/329-7312. www.stenton .org.* (1723-1730) Mansion built by James Logan, secretary to William Penn. Excellent example of Pennsylvania colonial architecture, furnished with 18th- and 19th-century antiques. General Washington spent Aug 23, 1777, here and General Sir William Howe headquartered here for the Battle of Germantown. Colonial barn, gardens, kitchen. (Apr-Dec, Tues-Sat afternoons; rest of year, by appointment; closed holidays) **$$**

Temple University. *Cecil B Moore Ave and Broad St (19122). Phone 215/204-7000. www.temple.edu.* (1884) 33,000 students. Undergraduate, professional, and research school. Walking tours of campus.

Thaddeus Kosciuszko National Memorial. *3rd and Pine sts (19106). Phone 215/597-1785 (TDD); 215/597-8974 (voice). www.nps.gov/thko/.* House of Polish patriot during his second visit to US (1797-1798). He was one of the 18th century's greatest champions of American and Polish freedom and one of the first volunteers to come to the aid of the American Revolutionary Army. Exterior and second-floor bedroom have been restored. (Daily) **FREE**

Todd House. *4th and Walnut sts (19106).* (1775) House of Dolley Payne Todd, who later married James Madison and became First Lady; 18th-century furnishings depict middle-class Quaker family life. Tours. Free tickets at park's Visitor Center.

The Trocadero Theatre. *1003 Arch St (19107). Phone 215/922-LIVE. www.thetroc.com.* This former 1870s opera house hosted vaudeville, burlesque, and Chinese movies before it became the beautiful, contemporary live music venue that it is today. The theater, which includes upstairs and downstairs seating, now hosts many well-known rock and pop artists, as well as the annual eight-hour Philadelphia Pop Festival held in June, which highlights local bands. Recently, it has gone back to one of its previous incarnations—a movie house. On "Movie Mondays," the theater holds free screenings (on its original screen) of such classic movies as *Apocalypse Now* and *Escape from New York.*

University of Pennsylvania. *Chestnut to Pine Sts and 32nd to 40th sts (19104). Phone 215/898-5000. www.upenn.edu.* (1740) 23,000 students. On campus are the restored Fisher Fine Arts Library (phone 215/898-8325), Annenberg Center for performing arts (phone 215/898-6791); University Museum of Archaeology and Anthropology and the Institute of Contemporary Art, located at 36th and Sansom sts (Wed-Sun; phone 215/898-7108; fee).

University of Pennsylvania Museum of Archaeology and Anthropology. *33rd and Spruce sts (19104). Phone 215/898-4000. www.upenn.edu/ museum/.* World-famous archaeological and ethnographic collections developed from the museum's own expeditions, gifts, and purchases; features Chinese, Near Eastern, Greek, ancient Egyptian, African, Pacific, and North, Middle, and South American materials; library. Restaurant, shops. (Tues-Sun; closed holidays, also Sun in summer) **$$**

US Mint. *5th and Arch sts (19106). On Independence Mall. Phone 215/408-0114. www.usmint.gov.* Produces coins of all denominations. Gallery affords visitors an elevated view of the coinage operations. Medal making may also be observed. Audiovisual, self-guided tours. Rittenhouse Room on the mezzanine contains historic coins, medals, and other exhibits. (July-Aug, daily; rest of year, Mon-Fri; closed Jan 1, Thanksgiving, Dec 25) **FREE**

Wagner Free Institute of Science. *1700 W Montgomery Ave (19121). Phone 215/763-6529.* Victorian science museum with more than 50,000 specimens illustrating the various branches of the natural sciences. Dinosaur bones, fossils, reptiles, and rare species are all mounted in the Victorian style. Reference library and research archives. (Tues-Fri) **FREE**

Walnut Street Theatre. *825 Walnut St (at 9th) (19107). Phone 215/574-3550. www.wstonline.org.* (1809) America's oldest theater. The Walnut Mainstage offers musicals, classical, and contemporary plays. Two studio theaters provide a forum for new and avant-garde works.

Washington Square. *Walnut St from 6th St (19107).* Site where hundreds of Revolutionary War soldiers and victims of the yellow fever epidemic are buried. Life-size statue of Washington has tomb of Revolutionary War's Unknown Soldier at its feet. Across the street is

Philadelphia Savings Fund Society Building. *Walnut and 8th sts (19107).* (1816) Site of oldest savings bank in the US. Not open to the public.

Wok N' Walk Tours of Philadelphia Chinatown. *Located at the corner of 10th and Arch sts in Center City. Phone 215/928-9333. www.josephkpoon.com/ home.* Considered one of the best culinary tours in the country, Joseph Poon's Wok N' Walk Tour is rich with Chinese history and culture as well as calories. This two-and-a-half-hour tour begins at Poon's Asian restaurant. (Be sure to try Chef Poon's trademark potato carvings.) Walkers are treated to a tai chi demonstration, Poon's start-of-the-art kitchen, and a vegetable carving lesson. Along the tour, you visit a Chinese herbal medicine expert, a fortune cookie factory, and a Chinese noodle shop; see exotic fish and places of worship; and, best of all, snack on free samples from a Chinese bakery in one of the city's more vibrant ethnic communities. (Daily) **$$$$**

Special Events

American Music Theater Festival. *123 S Broad St (19109). Phone 215/893-1570.* Repertory includes new opera, musical comedy, cabaret-style shows, revues, and experimental works. Mainstage productions Mar-June.

Army-Navy Football Game. *John F. Kennedy Memorial Stadium or Veterans Stadium.* First Sat in Dec.

The Book and the Cook. *1528 Walnut St (19102). Phone 215/686-3662.* Sample fine cuisine as world-famous cookbook authors team up with the city's most respected chefs to create culinary delights. Wine tastings, market tours, film festival. Mar.

CoreStates US Pro Cycling Championship. *Broad and Walnut sts (19102).* At 156 miles, it's the longest (and richest) single-day cycling event in the country. Mid-June.

Delaware Valley First Fridays. *www.dvfirstfridays.com.* First Fridays is a citywide cultural event that takes place at rotating venues with alternating formats on the first Friday of every month, with socializing and networking as goals. Galleries, shops, theaters, restaurants, and sidewalks in the Old City area along Second and Third streets from Market to Race have hosted record label release parties, live concerts, comedy shows, children's festivals, fashion shows, and vendor expositions. Proceeds go to African-American charitable organizations. First Fri of every month.

Devon Horse Show. *Approximately 20 miles NW via US 30, at Horse Show Grounds, in Devon. Phone 610/964-0550. www.thedevonhorseshow.org.* One of America's leading equestrian events. More than 1,200 horses compete; country fair; antique carriage drive. Nine days beginning Memorial Day weekend.

Elfreth's Alley Fete Days. *126 Elfreth's Alley (19106). Phone 215/574-0560. www.elfrethsalley.org.* Homes open to the public, costumed guides, demonstrations of colonial crafts; food, entertainment. Second weekend in June.

Fairmount Park Historical Christmas Tours. *2600 Ben Franklin Pkwy (19130). Phone 215/684-7922.* Period decorations in 18th-century mansions. Early Dec.

Head House Open Air Craft Market. *Pine and 2nd sts, in Society Hill area in Head House Sq (19147).* Crafts demonstrations, children's workshops. Sat and Sun, June-Aug.

Horse racing. *Philadlphia Park, 3001 Street Rd, Bensalem (19020). Phone 215/639-9000. www.philadelphiapark.com.* Flat racing at Philadelphia Park.

Mann Center for the Performing Arts. *Fairmont Park. 52nd St and Parkside Ave (19131). Phone 215/546-7900 or 215/893-1999 (tickets). www.manncenter.org.* Orchestra performs late June-July, Mon, Wed, and Thurs. Also popular music attractions. June-Sept.

Mummer's Parade. *Phone 215/336-3050. www.mummers.com.* The Mummer's Parade is Philadelphia's version of New Orleans' Mardi Gras or Spain's Carnival. It is an annual tradition to dress in outlandish costumes and noisily parade down the streets of Philadelphia on New Year's Day (the word *mummer* comes from an old French word that means to wear a mask). Jan 1.

The Opera Company of Philadelphia. *Academy of Music. 510 Walnut St (19106). Phone 215/928-2100. www.operaphilly.com.* Oct-Apr.

PECO Energy Jazz Festival. *2301 Market St (19101). Phone 800/537-7676.* Jazz concerts around the city. Four days mid-Feb.

Penn Relays. *Franklin Field, 33rd and South sts (19104). Phone 215/898-6151. www.thepennrelays.com.* These races originally served as a way to dedicate Franklin Field to the University of Pennsylvania. That was in 1895. Today, the Penn Relays hold the record for being the longest uninterrupted amateur track meet in the country. Thousands of men and women, ranging in age from 8 to 80, have competed. More than 400 races take place, one every five minutes, to keep spectators glued. Last weekend in April. **$$$**

The Philadelphia Flower Show. *Pennsylvania Convention Center, 12th and Arch sts (19107). Phone 215/988-8899. www.theflowershow.com/showinfo.* The country's first formal flower show took place here in 1829 in the city's Masonic Hall on Chestnut Street. More than 150 years later, exotic and rare flowers are still on display in this town but in a new location: the Pennsylvania Convention Center. Flower lovers will be dazzled by more than 275,000 flowers from Africa, Germany, Japan, England, France, Holland, Italy, and Belgium. Early Mar. **$$**

Philadelphia Open House. *325 Walnut St (19106). Phone 215/928-1188.* House and garden tours in different neighborhoods; distinguished selection of over 150 private homes, gardens, historic sites. Many tours include lunches, candlelight dinners, or high teas. Late Apr-mid-May.

Philadelphia Theatre Company. *Plays and Players Theatre, 1714 Delancey St (19103). Phone 215/568-1920.* Four contemporary American plays per season. Oct-June.

Robin Hood Dell East. *Fairmount Park. 33rd and Ridge sts (19131). Phone 215/685-9560. www.delleast.org.* Top stars in popular music stage outdoor concerts. July-Aug.

Thanksgiving Day Parade. *Franklin Parkway (19103). Phone 215/878-9700.* Giant floats; celebrities.

Motels/Motor Lodges

★★ **BEST WESTERN CENTER CITY HOTEL.** *501 N 22nd St (19130). Phone 215/568-8300; toll-free 800/780-7234; fax 215/557-0259. www.bestwestern.com.* 183 rooms, 3 story. Pets accepted, some restrictions; fee. Check-out noon. TV; cable (premium). In-room modem link. Restaurant, bar. In-house fitness room. Pool. **$**

D ⬚ ⬚ ⬚ ⬚

★ **BEST WESTERN HOTEL PHILADELPHIA NORTHEAST.** *11580 Roosevelt Blvd (19116). Phone 215/464-9500; toll-free 800/780-7234; fax 215/464-8511. www.bestwestern.com.* 100 rooms, 2 story. Complimentary continental breakfast. Check-out 11 am. TV; cable (premium). Laundry services. Bar. In-house fitness room. Pool. Lawn games. **$**

D ⬚ ⬚ ⬚

★ **COMFORT INN DOWNTOWN HISTORIC AREA.** *100 N Christopher Columbus Blvd (19106). Phone 215/627-7900; toll-free 800/228-5150; fax 215/238-0809. www.comfortinn.com.* 185 rooms, 10 story. Complimentary continental breakfast. Check-out 11 am. TV. In-room modem link. Bar. Airport transportation. View of the Delaware River. **$**

D ⬚ SC

★★ **COURTYARD BY MARRIOTT.** *21 N Juniper St (19107). Phone 215/496-3200; toll-free 800/321-2211; fax 215/496-3696. www.courtyard.com.* Across from City Hall and surrounded by business and government offices, this hotel is also close to restaurants and unique shops. 498 rooms, 15 story. Check-out noon, check-in 3 pm. TV. In-room modem link. Laundry services. Restaurant, bar. Room service. In-house fitness room. Indoor pool, whirlpool. Business center. Concierge. **$**

⬚ ⬚ ⬚ ⬚

★★ **DAYS INN.** *2015 Penrose Ave (19145). Phone 215/336-4600; toll-free 800/537-8483; fax 215/336-6308. www.daysinn.com.* 224 rooms, 17 story. Check-out noon. TV; cable (premium). In-room modem link. Laundry services. Restaurant, bar. In-house fitness room. Pool, children's pool, poolside service. Free airport transportation. **$**

D ⬚ ⬚ ⬚ ⬚ SC

★ ★ **HOLIDAY INN HISTORIC DISTRICT PHILADELPHIA.** *400 Arch St (19106). Phone 215/923-8660; toll-free 800/843-2355; fax 215/923-4633. www.holiday-inn.com.* 364 rooms, 8 story. Check-out 11 am. TV; cable (premium). Laundry services. Restaurant, bar. Rooftop pool. Business center. **$**

⊡ ⇌ ⊠ SC ⚞

★ **HOLIDAY INN EXPRESS.** *1305 Walnut St (19107). Phone 215/735-9300; toll-free 800/465-4329; fax 215/732-2682. www.holiday-inn.com.* 166 rooms, 20 story. Complimentary continental breakfast. Check-out 1 pm. TV; cable (premium). In-room modem link. Pool. **$**

⊡ ⇌ ⊠ SC

Hotels

★ ★ **ADAM'S MARK HOTEL.** *4000 City Line Monument Rd (19131). Phone 215/581-5000; toll-free 800/444-2326; fax 215/581-5069. www.adamsmark.com.* 515 rooms, 23 story. Check-out noon. TV. In-room modem link. Restaurant, bar; entertainment. In-house fitness room, sauna, steam room. Indoor, outdoor pools; whirlpool; poolside service. Airport transportation. Business center. **$**

⊡ ⇌ 木 ✈ ⊠ SC ⚞

★ ★ ★ **BUTTONWOOD SQUARE.** *2001 Hamilton St (19130). Phone 215/569-7000; toll-free 888/456-7626; fax 215/569-7040. www.korman communities.com.* Located just blocks from the business and financial district, this hotel offers its guests a luxurious experience, including enclosed parking, fitness center, outdoor pool, and hot tub. Guest rooms range from studios to suites and feature washer/dryers, kitchenettes, and a wide range of other amenities. 150 rooms, 23 story. Check-out 11 am, check-in 3 pm. TV; cable (premium). In-room modem link. Restaurant, bar. In-house fitness room. Pool, whirlpool, poolside service. Free garage parking. **$**

⊡ ⇌ 木 ⊠ SC

★ ★ **CROWNE PLAZA.** *1800 Market St (19103). Phone 215/561-7500; toll-free 800/2-CROWNE; fax 215/561-4484. www.crowneplaza.com.* 445 rooms, 25 story. Check-out noon. TV; cable (premium). In-room modem link. Laundry services. Restaurant, bar. In-house fitness room. Health club privileges. Pool. Airport transportation. Concierge. **$$**

⊡ ⇌ 木 ⊠ SC

★ ★ **DOUBLETREE HOTEL.** *9461 Roosevelt Blvd (19114). Phone 215/671-9600; toll-free 800/354-4332; fax 215/464-7759. www.doubletree.com.* This hotel has a desirable location for vacation and business travelers alike. Meeting rooms will accommodate up to 200 people. 188 rooms, 6 story.

Check-out 11 am. TV. In-room modem link. Laundry services. Restaurant, bar. In-house fitness room. Indoor pool. Business center. **$**

D ⚊ 🏃 ⬆ SC 🚶

★ ★ **DOUBLETREE HOTEL.** *Broad and Locust sts (19107). Phone 215/893-1600; toll-free 800/222-8733; fax 215/893-1663. www.doubletree.com.* This hotel is conveniently located near many museums and historical sites and offers racquetball and a walking track. 434 rooms, 26 story. Check-out noon. TV; cable (premium), VCR available. In-room modem link. Restaurant, bar. In-house fitness room, sauna, steam room. Health club privileges. Indoor pool, whirlpool. Airport transportation. Concierge. Luxury level. **$**

D ⚊ 🏃 ⬆ SC

★ ★ ★ ★ **FOUR SEASONS HOTEL PHILADELPHIA.** *1 Logan Sq (19103). Phone 215/963-1500; toll-free 800/332-3442; fax 215/963-9506. www.fourseasons.com/philadelphia.* Philadelphia's rich heritage comes alive at the Four Seasons Hotel. Located on historic Logan Square, the hotel puts the city's museums, shops, and businesses within easy reach. The eight-story Four Seasons is a Philadelphia institution in itself, from its dramatic Swann Fountain to its highly rated Fountain Restaurant (see), considered one of the better dining establishments in town. The rooms and suites are a celebration of federalist décor, and some accommodations incorporate little luxuries like deep soaking tubs and high-speed Internet access. City views of the Academy of Natural Science, Logan Square, and the tree-lined Ben Franklin Parkway provide a sense of place for some guests, while other rooms offer tranquil views over the inner courtyard and gardens. The Four Seasons spa focuses on nourishing treatments, while the indoor pool resembles a tropical oasis with breezy palm trees and large skylights. 364 rooms, 8 story. Pets accepted, some restrictions. Check-out noon, check-in 3 pm. TV; cable (premium), VCR available. In-room modem link. Laundry services. Restaurant, bar. Room service 24 hours. Babysitting services available. In-house fitness room, spa, massage, sauna. Indoor pool, whirlpool, poolside service. Business center. Concierge. **$$$**

D 🐾 ⚊ 🏃 ⬆ 🚶

★ ★ ★ **HILTON PHILADELPHIA AIRPORT.** *4509 Island Ave (19153). Phone 215/365-4150; toll-free 800/774-1500; fax 215/937-6382. www.hilton.com.* 334 rooms, 9 story. Check-out noon. TV; cable (premium). In-room modem link. Restaurant, bar. Room service 24 hours. In-house fitness room. Indoor pool, whirlpool. Free airport transportation. Business center. Luxury level. **$**

D ⚊ 🏃 ✈ ⬆ 🚶

★ ★ ★ **HYATT REGENCY PHILADELPHIA AT PENN'S LANDING.** *201 S Columbus Blvd (19106). Phone 215/928-1234; toll-free 800/233-1234; fax 215/521-6600. www.hyatt.com.* 363 rooms, 22 story.

Check-out noon, check-in 3 pm. TV; cable (premium). In-room modem link. Restaurant, bar. In-house fitness room. Indoor pool, whirlpool. Business center. Concierge. **$**

★ ★ ★ **LATHAM HOTEL.** *135 S 17th St (19103). Phone 215/563-7474; toll-free 877/528-4261; fax 215/568-0110. www.lathamhotel.com.* This charming hotel is a favorite of guests looking for an intimate setting in downtown Philly. Conveniently located, it is just blocks away from Independence Hall and the Pennsylvania Convention Center. 139 rooms, 14 story. Check-out noon. TV; cable (premium), VCR available (movies). In-room modem link. Restaurant, bar. In-house fitness room. Health club privileges. Valet parking. Business center. Concierge. **$**

★ ★ ★ **LOEWS PHILADELPHIA HOTEL.** *1200 Market St (19107). Phone 215/627-1200; fax 215/231-7312. www.loewshotels.com.* 583 rooms, 32 story. Check-out noon, check-in 3 pm. TV; cable (premium). In-room modem link. Restaurant, bar. In-house fitness room, sauna. Indoor pool, whirlpool. Business center. Concierge. **$$**

★ ★ ★ **MARRIOTT PHILADELPHIA AIRPORT.** *One Arrivals Rd (19153). Phone 215/492-9000; toll-free 800/228-9290; fax 215/492-6799. www.marriott.com.* 424 rooms, 15 story. Check-out noon, check-in 3 pm. TV; cable (premium). In-room modem link. Restaurant, bar. In-house fitness room. Indoor pool, whirlpool. Business center. Concierge. **$$**

★ ★ ★ **MARRIOTT PHILADELPHIA DOWNTOWN.** *1201 Market St (19107). Phone 215/625-2900; toll-free 800/228-9290; fax 215/625-6000. www.marriott.com.* Located downtown in the heart of the business district and conveniently connected to the Convention Center, this hotel is a business traveler's oasis. 1,408 rooms, 20 story. Check-out noon. TV; cable (premium), VCR available. In-room modem link. Laundry services. Restaurant, bar. In-house fitness room, sauna. Indoor pool, children's pool, whirlpool. Valet parking. Business center. Concierge. Luxury level. **$$$**

★ ★ ★ **MARRIOTT PHILADELPHIA WEST.** *111 Crawford Ave (19428). Phone 610/941-5600; toll-free 800/237-3639; fax 610/941-4425. www.marriott.com.* This hotel is located just miles from the Valley Forge National Park, Philadelphia Zoo, Musuem of Art, and the Franklin Institute, as well as many other local points of interest. 286 rooms, 17 story. Check-out noon. TV; cable (premium), VCR available. In-room modem link. Restaurant, bar. In-house fitness room, sauna. Indoor pool, whirlpool, poolside service. Airport transportation. Concierge. Luxury level. One block from the Schuylkill River. **$$**

★ ★ ★ **OMNI HOTEL AT INDEPENDENCE PARK.** *401 Chestnut St (19106). Phone 215/925-0000; toll-free 800/THE-OMNI; fax 215/925-1263. www.omnihotelindependencepark.com.* The Omni is a very functional hotel located just steps away from historic Independence Hall. There is a restaurant, Azalea (see), and the lobby lounge is quite pleasant. The rooms are quite spacious, and many have excellent panoramic views of historic Philadelphia. 150 rooms, 14 story. Check-out 11 am. TV; cable (premium), VCR available. In-room modem link. Restaurant, bar; entertainment Tues-Sat. Room service 24 hours. In-house fitness room, sauna. Indoor pool, whirlpool. Valet parking. Business center. Concierge. **$$**

D ⊷ ⟨X⟩ ⟨N⟩ SC ⟨X⟩

★ ★ ★ **PARK HYATT PHILADELPHIA.** *Broad and Walnut sts (19102). Phone 215/893-1234; toll-free 800/228-9000; fax 215/732-8518. www.hyatt.com.* Located in the heart of Philadelphia, this restored national historic landmark provides guests with old-world charm along with first-class amenities. Relax in spacious and elegantly appointed guest rooms. Enjoy the restaurant's fabulous cuisine while overlooking the lights of downtown. Work off the calories in the state-of-the-art fitness center adjacent to the hotel, which offers guests four levels and 93,000 square feet of ways to sweat the week's stress away, or free the mind and enjoy getting pampered at the full-service European Day Spa and Salon. 172 rooms, 5 story. Check-out 11 am. TV; cable (premium), VCR. In-room modem link. Restaurant, bar. Room service 24 hours. Massage, sauna. Whirlpool. Business center. Concierge. **$$$**

D ⟨N⟩ SC ⟨X⟩

★ ★ ★ **PENN'S VIEW HOTEL.** *Front and Market sts (19106). Phone 215/922-7600; toll-free 800/331-7634; fax 215/922-7642. www.penns viewhotel.com.* The inn, which was built in 1828, is located in Old City Philadelphia overlooking the Delaware River. Some guest rooms have river views, working fireplaces, and large marble baths with Jacuzzi tubs. 54 rooms, 5 story. Complimentary continental breakfast. Check-out noon, check-in 3 pm. TV. In-room modem link. Fireplaces. Dining room. Airport transportation. Concierge. **$$**

D ⟨N⟩ SC

★ ★ **RADISSON HOTEL PHILADELPHIA NORTHEAST.** *US 1 at Old Lincoln Hwy (19053). Phone 215/638-8300; toll-free 800/333-3333; fax 215/638-4377. www.radisson.com.* Conveniently located just 3 miles from the Northeast Philadelphia Airport and 10 miles from the Williowgrove Airport, this hotel is perfect for business travelers. 282 rooms, 6 story. Check-out noon. TV. In-room modem link. Laundry services. Restaurant, bar. In-house fitness room. Indoor, outdoor pool; poolside service. Concierge. **$**

D ⊷ ⟨X⟩ ⟨N⟩

★ ★ ★ **THE RADISSON PLAZA WARWICK HOTEL.** *1701 Locust St (19103). Phone 215/735-6000; toll-free 800/333-3333; fax 215/790-7766.*

www.radisson.com. For over 75 years, this landmark hotel has welcomed guests to enjoy the atmosphere and elegance of a century gone by. Guests will delight in such amenities as fitness facilities, a beauty salon/barber shop, and dry cleaning service. 545 rooms, 21 story. Check-out noon. TV; cable (premium), VCR available. In-room modem link. Restaurant, bar. In-house fitness room. Concierge. **$$**

D 🏃 ➳ SC

★ ★ ★ **RADNOR HOTEL.** *591 E Lancaster Ave (19087). Phone 610/688-5800; toll-free 800/537-3000; fax 610/341-3299. www.radnorhotel.com.* Located in the western suburbs of Philadelphia, this multi-service property caters to both business and leisure travelers. The meeting spaces are perfect to hold an important board meeting or a lavish wedding. Guests will enjoy the state-of-the-art fitness facility that is open 24 hours a day. 171 rooms, 4 story. Check-out noon. TV; cable (premium), VCR available. In-room modem link. Microwaves available. Restaurant, bar; entertainment weekends. Room service 24 hours. Health club privileges. In-house fitness room. Game room. Pool, wading pool, lifeguard. Airport transportation. Meeting rooms. Business center. Luxury level. **$$**

D ➳ 🏃 ➳ SC 🏃

★ ★ ★ **RENAISSANCE PHILADELPHIA AIRPORT HOTEL.** *500 Stevens Dr (19113). Phone 610/521-5900; toll-free 888/887-7951; fax 610/521-4362. www.renaissancehotels.com.* Conveniently located just 1 mile from the airport and surrounded by a small pond, this hotel offers guests a relaxing place to stay and unwind. Guests will find the rooms to be spacious and the service to be warm and friendly. 351 rooms, 12 story. Check-out noon. TV. In-room modem link. Restaurant, bar. In-house fitness room. Game room. Indoor pool, whirlpool, poolside service. Free airport transportation. Business center. **$**

D ➳ 🏃 ✈ ➳ 🏃

★ ★ ★ ★ **THE RITTENHOUSE HOTEL.** *210 W Rittenhouse Sq (19103). Phone 215/546-9000; toll-free 800/635-1042; fax 215/732-3364. www.rittenhousehotel.com.* The Rittenhouse Hotel is a jewel in the heart of Philadelphia. This intimate hotel occupies a particularly enviable address across from the leafy Rittenhouse Square and among the prestigious town houses of this exclusive area. The accommodations are among the most spacious in the city and are decorated with a sophisticated flair. Guests at The Rittenhouse are treated to the highest levels of personalized service. Fitness and business centers cater to travelers visiting for work or pleasure, while the Adolf Biecker Spa and Salon pampers and primps its clients in a peaceful setting. From the mood-lifting décor of the gracious Cassatt Lounge and the striking contemporary style of Lacroix (see) to the rowing memorabilia of Boathouse Row Bar and the traditional steakhouse feel of Smith & Wollensky, the Rittenhouse Hotel also provides memorable dining experiences to match every taste. 98 rooms, 9 story. Pets accepted, some restrictions. Check-out 1 pm, check-in 3 pm. TV; cable (premium), VCR available. In-room modem link. Restaurant, bar; entertainment. Room service. Babysitting services available. In-house fitness room, sauna, steam room, spa, massage. Indoor pool. Business center. Garage, valet parking. Concierge. **$$$**

[icons: D 🛏 🏊 ✕ 🚶]

★ ★ ★ ★ **THE RITZ-CARLTON, PHILADELPHIA.** *Ten Avenue of the Arts (19102). Phone 215/523-8000; toll-free 888/505-3914; fax 215/568-0942. www.ritzcarlton.com.* The Ritz-Carlton breathes new life into a magnificent historic building in the center of Philadelphia's downtown business district. This one-time home to Girard and Mellon Banks was designed in the 1900s by the architectural firm of McKim, Mead, and White, and was inspired by Rome's Pantheon. Marrying historic significance with trademark Ritz-Carlton style, this Philadelphia showpiece boasts handsome and striking décor. Impressive marble columns dominate the lobby, where guests can pause for reflection over light meals in the Rotunda. The rooms and suites are the last word in luxury, while Club Level accommodations transport guests to heaven with a private lounge filled with five food and beverage selections daily. Dedicated to exceeding visitors' expectations, The Ritz-Carlton even offers a pillow menu, a bath butler, and other unique services. Dining options are plentiful, and the Sunday jazz brunch is a local favorite. 330 rooms, 31 story. Pets accepted, some restrictions; fee. Check-out noon, check-in 3 pm. TV; cable (premium). In-room modem link. Restaurant, bar. In-house fitness room. Business center. Concierge. **$$$**

[icons: 🍴 ✕ 🚶]

★ ★ ★ **SHERATON PHILADELPHIA AIRPORT HOTEL.** *4101 Island Ave (19079). Phone 215/365-6600; toll-free 800/362-3535; fax 215/ 365-6035. www.sheraton.com.* Conveniently located near the Philadelphia Airport. Amenities include a fitness center and a swimming pool. For guests who enjoy golfing, a golf course is nearby. 178 rooms, 5 story. Check-out noon. TV; cable (premium), VCR available. Laundry services. Restaurant, bar. Pool. Free airport transportation. **$**

[icons: D 🏊 ✈ 🚶 SC]

★ ★ ★ **SHERATON RITTENHOUSE SQUARE HOTEL.** *227 S 18th St (19103). Phone 215/546-9400; toll-free 800/325-3535; fax 215/875-9457. www.sheratonrittenhouse.com.* This state-of-the-art hotel is a gratifying, eco-smart hotel. It is able to offer high-tech features while maintaining an environmentally friendly atmosphere. From the nontoxic materials, such as the organically grown cotton for the organic sleep systems, to the filtered rooms offering fresh air, this hotel offers a refreshing stay. 193 rooms, 16 story. Complimentary continental breakfast. Check-out noon, check-in 3 pm. TV; cable (premium), VCR available. Restaurant, bar. Room service 24 hours. Supervised children's activities. In-house fitness room. Valet parking available. Free airport transportation. Business center. **$$$**

[icons: D ✕ ✈ 🚶 SC 🚶]

★ ★ ★ **SHERATON SOCIETY HILL.** *One Dock St (19106). Phone 215/238-6000; toll-free 800/325-3535; fax 215/238-6736. www.sheraton.com.* Situated in downtown Philadelphia, this hotel is conveniently located near Independence Hall, Society Hill, the Liberty Bell, the Philadelphia Zoo, and the Pennsylvania Convention Center. 378 rooms, 4 story. Check-out noon. TV; cable (premium), VCR available. In-room modem link. Restaurant, bar. Room service 24 hours. In-house fitness room, massage, sauna. Indoor pool, children's pool, whirlpool, poolside service. Concierge. **$**

D ⇌ 🏃 ⇝ SC

★ ★ ★ **SHERATON UNIVERSITY CITY.** *36th and Chestnut sts (19104). Phone 215/387-8000; toll-free 888/625-5144; fax 215/387-7920. www.sheraton.com.* 374 rooms, 15 story. Check-out noon, check-in 3 pm. TV; cable (premium). In-room modem link. Restaurant, bar. In-house fitness room. Pool, whirlpool. Business center. Concierge. **$**

⇌ 🏃 🏃

★ ★ ★ **SOFITEL.** *120 S 17th St (19103). Phone 215/569-8300; toll-free 800/SOFITEL; fax 215/569-1492. www.sofitel.com.* 306 rooms, 14 story. Pets accepted, some restrictions; fee. Check-out noon, check-in 3 pm. TV; cable (premium). In-room modem link. Restaurant, bar. In-house fitness room. Pool, whirlpool. Business center. Concierge. **$$**

🐾 ⇌ 🏃 🏃

★ ★ ★ **THE WESTIN PHILADELPHIA.** *99 S 17th St (19103). Phone 215/563-1600; toll-free 800/937-8461; fax 215/567-2822. www.westin.com.* Located near Restaurant Row and the Pennsylvania Convention Center, this stately hotel exudes old-fashioned elegance despite its fairly recent opening. Guest rooms are modestly sized but extremely comfortable with plush-down bedding and an attractive, European-style décor. Afternoon tea in the relaxing lobby lounge and fine, French cuisine at The Grill Room are both wonderful culinary experiences. 290 rooms, 15 story. Check-out noon, check-in 3 pm. TV; cable (premium). Restaurant, bar. Room service 24 hours. Valet parking available. Business center. Concierge service. **$$**

D ⇝ 🏃

★ ★ **WYNDHAM PHILADELPHIA AT FRANKLIN PLAZA.** *2 Franklin Plz (19103). Phone 215/448-2000; toll-free 877/999-3223; fax 215/448-2864. www.wyndham.com.* 758 rooms, 26 story. Check-out noon. TV; cable (premium). In-room modem link. Restaurant, bar. In-house fitness room, massage, sauna, steam room. Indoor pool, whirlpool, poolside service. Outdoor tennis. Business center. **$$**

D 🤸 ⇌ 🏃 ⇝ 🏃

All Suites

★ ★ **DOUBLETREE GUEST SUITES.** *640 W Germantown Pike, Plymouth Meeting (19462). Phone 610/834-8300; toll-free 800/222-8733; fax 610/879-4242. www.doubletree.com.* This hotel is located in Philadelphia's fastest growing business corridor. Their newly renovated suites will make you feel at home with a separate living room and bedroom. 252 rooms, 7 story. Check-out noon. TV; VCR available. In-room modem link. Laundry services. Restaurant, bar. In-house fitness room, sauna. Indoor pool, children's pool, whirlpool, poolside service. Airport transportation. **$$**

[D] [⇔] [⼤] [⤢]

★ ★ ★ **SHERATON SUITES PHILADELPHIA AIRPORT.** *4101 Island Ave (19153). Phone 215/365-6600; toll-free 800/222-8733; fax 215/492-9858. www.sheraton.com.* This hotel is located in the heart of Philadelphia's business district near Restaurant Row and the Pennsylvania Convention Center. 251 rooms, 8 story. Check-out noon. TV; cable (premium), VCR available. In-room modem link. Restaurant, bar. In-house fitness room, sauna, steam room. Indoor pool, whirlpool. Airport transportation. Business center. **$$**

[D] [⇔] [⼤] [⼦] [✈] [⤢] [SC] [⼤]

B&B/Small Inns

★ ★ **1011 CLINTON.** *1011 Clinton St (19107). Phone 215/923-8144; fax 215/923-5757.* 8 rooms, 3 story. Pets accepted, some restrictions. Complimentary continental breakfast. Check-out noon, check-in 3 pm. TV; VCR (movies). In-room modem link. Laundry services. Street parking. Concierge service. Built in 1836; enclosed courtyard. No elevators. Totally nonsmoking. **$$**

[⤹] [⤢] [SC]

★ **THOMAS BOND HOUSE.** *129 S 2nd St (19106). Phone 215/923-8523; toll-free 800/845-2663; fax 215/923-8504. www.bnbinns.com.* 12 rooms, 2 story. No elevator. Complimentary continental breakfast. Check-out noon, check-in 3-9 pm. TV. Airport transportation. Restored guest house (1769) built by Dr. Thomas Bond, founder of the country's first public hospital. Individually decorated rooms. **$$**

[SC]

Restaurants

★ **ANJOU.** *206 Market St (19106). Phone 215/923-1600; fax 215/923-4981. www.anjouphilly.com.* French, Asian, sushi menu. Lunch, dinner. Bar. Casual attire. Outdoor seating. **$$$**

[D]

★ ★ ★ **AZALEA.** *401 Chestnut St (19106). Phone 215/925-0000; fax 215/925-1263. www.omnihotelindependencepark.com.* Just a block from historic Independence Hall and the Liberty Bell, this restaurant at the Omni Hotel at Independence Park (see) is a restful spot to enjoy a meal. The décor is stylishly eclectic, and executive chef Peter Paul Meyer's menus are rooted in classic French technique, and feature contemporary touches and international accents. Dishes range from comfortingly rich (house-made herb spaetzle baked with Gruyere and Emmantal cheeses and assorted summer vegetables) to heart-healthy (mustard-glazed salmon over golden whipped potatoes with a sauce ver jus and baby bok choy). American menu. Dinner. Bar. Casual attire. Valet parking. **$$$**

D

★ **BILLY WONG.** *50 S 2nd St (19106). Phone 215/829-1128.* Chinese menu. Dinner. Bar. **$$$**

★ ★ **BOOKBINDER'S.** *215 S 15th St (19102). Phone 215/545-1137; fax 215/732-2560.* Seafood menu. Closed Thanksgiving, Dec 25. Lunch, dinner. Bar. Children's menu. Casual attire. **$$$**

D

★ ★ ★ **BRASSERIE PERRIER.** *1619 Walnut St (19103). Phone 215/568-3000; fax 215/568-7855. www.brasserieperrier.com.* Brasserie Perrier, the less formal, younger sibling of Le Bec-Fin, is a terrific spot for first-rate modern French fare with Italian and Asian influences. While the menu is more reasonably priced than the one at its more refined relative, the quality here remains just as high. In traditional French brasserie style, you'll find plats du jour, steak frites, and frisee aux lardons among other perfectly prepared standards. The kitchen also departs from the traditional brasserie-style menu, offering a fantastic selection of sweet and savory fondues (a ton of fun to share as an appetizer or for dessert), as well as creative takes on pasta and entrées painted with eclectic flavors from around the globe. The impressive wine list is mostly French, although some American bottles are also featured. The modern Art Deco dining room is warmed by plush banquettes, vintage silver leaf ceilings, light cherry wood, and golden lighting, making it a wonderful choice for many occasions, from an after-work drink to a lunch meeting. French menu. Closed holidays. Lunch, dinner. Bar. Reservations required. Valet parking. Outdoor seating. Totally nonsmoking. **$$$**

D

★ ★ **BRIDGET FOY'S SOUTH STREET GRILL.** *2nd and South sts (19147). Phone 215/922-1813; fax 215/922-6551. www.bridgetfoys.com.* Closed Thanksgiving, Dec 25. Lunch, dinner. Bar. Outdoor seating. **$$**

★ ★ ★ **BUDDAKAN.** *325 Chestnut St (19106). Phone 215/574-9440; fax 215/574-8994. www.buddakan.com.* Slick, sexy, and spectacular, Buddakan is one of Philadelphia's hottest spots for dining, drinking, and lounging. Whether you're seated in the shadow of the restaurant's 10-foot gilded Buddha at the elevated communal table or at one of the other more intimate tables for two in chairs backed with black-and-white photo portraits, you will never guess that this den of fabulousness was once a post office. If your mail carrier were feasting on Buddakan's brand of splashy Asian fusion re, like lobster fried rice with Thai basil and saffron and crisp thin pizza topped with seared tuna and wasabi, you can be sure that the mail would never arrive on time. Entrées are meant for sharing and arrive steamy and fragrant, arranged with a minimalist, Zenlike artistry. The wine and sake list is impressive, as is the lengthy selection of house cocktails. A nice way to kick off the evening is with the signature Buddalini, a sexy sipper made from Champagne, Cointreau, and fresh mango juice. Modern Asian menu. Closed most major holidays. Dinner. Casual attire. **$$$**

D

★ ★ **CAFE SPICE.** *35 S 2nd St (19106). Phone 215/627-6273; fax 215/ 627-6280. www.cafespice.com.* Indian menu. Lunch, dinner, late night. Bar. Outdoor seating. **$$**

D

★ ★ ★ **CIRCA.** *1518 Walnut St (19102). Phone 215/545-6800; fax 215/ 545-7683. www.circarestaurant.com.* Still echoing its past function as a bank, the building that houses Circa offers guests the chance to dine in a vault, or under the soaring cathedral ceiling of the original bank proper. Austere setting aside, executive chef Tom Harkin's Mediterranean menu is all warmth and sunshine. Wood-grilled prawns come with sweet corn mashed potatoes and sun-dried tomato reduction. There's a superb Moroccan lamb sirloin with grilled fennel, tomato, and chicken puree, and the pan-roasted organic chicken is stuffed with sweet sausage and served with a confit of leg meat and mustard spaetzle. Desserts also glow. Menu changes seasonally. Closed Jan 1, Dec 25. Lunch, dinner. Bar. Valet parking. **$$$**

D

★ ★ **CITY TAVERN.** *138 S 2nd St (19106). Phone 215/413-1443; fax 215/ 413-3043. www.citytavern.com.* 18th-century American menu. Closed Mon in Jan. Lunch, dinner. Bar. Entertainment Sat. Children's menu. Historical colonial tavern (1773). Outdoor seating. **$$$**

D

★ ★ **CUVEE NOTRE DAME.** *1701 Green St (19130). Phone 215/765- 2777.* Belgian menu. Closed Thanksgiving, Dec 25. Lunch, dinner, Sun brunch. Bar. Children's menu. Outdoor seating. **$$**

D

★ **DARBAR GRILL.** *319 Market St (19106). Phone 215/923-2410; fax 215/923-2409. www.darbargrill.com.* Indian menu. Lunch, dinner. Children's menu. Casual attire. **$$**

D

★ ★ **DARK HORSE.** *Head House Sq (19147). Phone 215/928-9307; fax 215/928-0232. www.dickensinn.com.* Continental menu. Closed Mon; Jan 1, Dec 25. Lunch, dinner, Sun brunch. Bar. Children's menu. In historic Harper House (1788); Victorian décor; artwork imported from England. **$$**

D

★ ★ ★ **DEUX CHEMINEES.** *1221 Locust St (19107). Phone 215/79*‹ *0200; fax 215/790-0202. www.deuxchem.com.* Featuring classic and regional French cuisine in five beautifully appointed dining rooms, Deux Cheminees ("two fireplaces") is a testament to the fact that some traditions endure for good reason. Located in two 19th-century town houses, the formal restaurant offers fixed-price five-course menus and special value three-course dinners for early diners. This is the place for foie gras, pates and terrines, sweetbreads and escargot. And the house specialty—rack of lamb for two—is roasted to order and served with truffle-filled sauce Perigord. French menu. Menu changes daily. Closed Sun, Mon; major holidays. Dinner. Totally nonsmoking. **$$$$**

★ **DIMITRI'S.** *795 S 3rd St (19147). Phone 215/625-0556.* Mediterranean menu. Dinner. Closed Easter, Thanksgiving, Dec 24, 25. **$$**

★ ★ **DINARDO'S.** *312 Race St (19106). Phone 215/925-5115; fax 215/ 592-1112. www.dinardos.com.* Seafood menu. Closed Easter, Thanksgiving, Dec 25. Lunch, dinner. Bar. Children's menu. Historic building (1740). **$$** D

★ **FAMOUS 4TH STREET DELI.** *700 S 4th St (19147). Phone 215/922- 3274; fax 215/922-7097. www.famouscookies.com.* Family owned since 1923, this Jewish delicatessen is worth a stop for a corned beef, roast beef, roast turkey brisket, or smoked fish sandwich. But it's the freshly baked award-winning cookies that put the Famous in "Famous 4th Street Deli." These large, chunky cookies come in chocolate chip, chocolate walnut, peanut butter, and oatmeal raisin. Closed Rosh Hashanah, Yom Kippur. Breakfast, lunch. **$**

★ ★ **FELICIA'S.** *1148 S 11th St (19147). Phone 215/755-9656; fax 215/ 755-6056.* Italian menu. Closed Mon; most major holidays. Lunch, dinner. Bar. Reservations required. Valet parking. **$$$** D

★ ★ **FORK.** *306 Market St (19106). Phone 215/625-9425; fax 215/625- 9435. www.forkrestaurant.com.* American menu. Closed some major holidays. Dinner. Bar. Children's menu. Outdoor seating. **$$** D

★ ★ ★ **THE FOUNDERS.** *Broad and Walnut sts (19102). Phone 215/ 790-2814; fax 215/731-0342. www.hyatt.com.* Located on the 19th floor, atop the historic Park Hyatt Philadelphia at the Bellevue (see), The Founders features floor-to-ceiling 45-foot-high palladium windows, offering soaring views of the city. Bronze sculptures of the city founders it's named for—David Rittenhouse, William Peale, Benjamin Franklin, and William Penn—populate the dining room where the menu is overseen by executive chef C. David Wolf. Changing seasonally, menus feature American cuisine with French influence. French menu. Breakfast, lunch, dinner, Sat-Sun brunch. Bar. Entertainment. Elegant turn-of-the-century décor. Jacket required (dinner). Valet parking. **$$$** D

★ ★ ★ **FOUNTAIN RESTAURANT.** *1 Logan Sq (19103). Phone 215/963-1500; fax 215/963-9506. www.fourseasons.com/philadelphia.* The wine list at The Fountain, the stunning flagship restaurant of the Four Seasons Hotel Philadelphia (see), weighs as much as a light barbell. If you need to work your biceps, it makes for a good substitute. The extensive list—covering all of France as well as Germany, Italy, the United States, Australia, New Zealand, and South America—is just one of the highlights of dining here. Other highlights include refined service and an exquisitely prepared menu of seasonal, contemporary American fare. The kitchen often serves ingredients from local producers and includes the farms' names on the menu, so you'll know which farmer planted your baby greens and where your beets were picked. This thoughtfulness adds to the experience by giving you a real sense of connection to the food and the care that is taken to find the best ingredients. As you'll see here, the best ingredients really do make a difference. Plates return to the kitchen spotless, and portions are easily manageable. The staff is also concerned that their diners' specific dietary restrictions are accommodated. Vegetarian items are available on request, and the kitchen offers several selections that are marked "nutritionally balanced, healthier fare." If you choose one of these "lighter" options, you can definitely opt for the heavenly chocolate soufflé for dessert. Since it is a house specialty, you really should make a point of having it regardless of what you decide to eat for dinner. *Secret Inspector's Notes:* The dining room at The Fountain is just lovely, ideal for a special occasion or business dinner. Consult the fantastic sommelier for wine assistance, but in case it's an off-evening, be prepared for absent-minded staff and food that on occasion lacks interesting flavor and textural excitement. Continental menu with French Provençal influence. Breakfast, lunch, dinner, Sun brunch. Bar. Entertainment. Children's menu. Jacket required. Valet parking. **$$$$**

D

★ **GENO'S.** *1219 S 9th St (19147). Phone 215/389-0659; fax 215/389-4166. www.genosteaks.com.* Closed Dec 24, Dec 25. Lunch, dinner. Entertainment. Outdoor seating. No credit cards accepted. **$**

D

★ ★ **ITALIAN BISTRO.** *211 S Broad St (19107). Phone 215/731-0700; fax 215/731-0702. www.italianbistro.com.* Italian menu. Closed Thanksgiving, Dec 25. Lunch, dinner. Bar. Children's menu. **$$**

D

★ **JACK'S FIREHOUSE.** *2130 Fairmount Ave (19130). Phone 215/232-9000; fax 215/765-7920. jacksfirehouse.com.* American menu. Closed Dec 25. Lunch, dinner. Bar. Children's menu. Casual attire. Outdoor seating. **$$**

D

★ ★ ★ ★ **JAKE'S RESTAURANT.** *4365 Main St, Manayunk (19127). Phone 215/483-0444; fax 215/487-7122. www.jakesrestaurant.com.* Located in Manayunk, Philadelphia's funky, high-energy, artsy neighborhood, Jake's Restaurant is a lively, sexy spot to meet friends for drinks and stay for dinner. Be warned, though; this is a place you may not want to leave. Chef-owner Bruce Cooper's chic regulars make a habit of staying all night, savoring his unique brand of stylish, regional American food. While at the bar, go for one of Jake's wild house cocktails or take a chance on a unique microbrew. After drinks, settle into the lively, butter-yellow dining room and get ready for a fabulous meal. While fine dining can be pretentious or stuffy, at Jake's it is neither. The kitchen is in sync with its customers' desire for both fun and flavor in their food. For instance, on a recent visit, the prix fixe menu was titled "Jake's Clam Bake." Currently, it is offered Sunday through Thursday nights and features a popular four-course clam bake-style shellfish menu paired with wine. Unfortunately, sunshine and the seashore are not included, but with the steady buzz from the bright energy in the room, you won't need them. New American menu. Lunch, dinner, Sun brunch. Bar. Reservations required. Outdoor seating. Totally nonsmoking. **$$$**

D

★ ★ **JOSEPH POON.** *1002 Arch St (19107). Phone 215/928-9333; fax 215/928-9368. www.josephpoon.com.* Chinese menu. Closed Mon; Thanksgiving, Dec 25; also Chinese New Year. Lunch, dinner. Bar. **$$**

D

★ ★ ★ **KANSAS CITY PRIME.** *4417 Main St, Manayunk (19127). Phone 215/482-3700; fax 215/483-1515. www.kansascityprime.com.* If butter-tender beef is your thing, independently owned Kansas City Prime is the place. Exclusive rights (in Philadelphia) to Japanese Kobe beef guarantee exceptional quality in the red meat department, and the chef's seafood and game selections are equally pleasing. For true indulgence, try the Kobe burger, 10 ounces of Kobe beef with seared foie gras and black truffle mayo on a Parmesan roll. Steak menu. Closed Thanksgiving. Dinner. Bar; entertainment Tues-Sat. Casual attire. **$$$**

D

★ ★ **KNAVE OF HEARTS.** *230 South St (19147). Phone 215/922-3956.* Closed Dec 25. Lunch, dinner, Sun brunch. Bar. **$$**

★ ★ ★ ★ **LACROIX AT THE RITTENHOUSE.** *210 W Rittenhouse Sq (19103). Phone 215/790-2533; fax 215/732-3364. www.rittenhousehotel.com.* Set in the stately Rittenhouse Hotel, Lacroix is a restaurant of understated elegance featuring the haute culinary creations of chef Jean-Marie Lacroix. The kitchen plays up fresh local ingredients with a delicate French hand, while guests dine in posh, sophisticated luxury and enjoy transporting views of the charming Rittenhouse Square. For an intimate dinner party, consider the private dining room that can seat up to 18 guests. French menu. Breakfast, lunch, dinner. Bar. Children's menu. Jacket required. **$$$**

★ ★ ★ **LA FAMIGLIA.** *8 S Front St (19106). Phone 215/922-2803; fax 215/922-7495. www.la-famiglia.com.* Occupying the shell of a colonial tea warehouse since 1976, this Society Hill Italian restaurant is just one of the Sena-family operations. The classic menu includes items such as Vitello Papa Sena's, a combination of veal picante, involtino, and Capri. The dining room is elegant, filled with paintings and family collectibles, and the wine cellar is one of the finest in the country. Italian menu. Closed Mon; holidays; also the last week in Aug. Lunch, dinner. Bar. Built in 1878 in one of the city's first blocks of buildings. Jacket required. Reservations required. Valet parking. **$$$**

★ ★ ★ **LE BAR LYONNAIS.** *1523 Walnut St (19102). Phone 215/567-1000; fax 215/557-7494. www.lebecfin.com.* Since Georges Perrier added Le Bar Lyonnais to his internationally renowned Le Bec-Fin restaurant in 1990, the bar has achieved status as one of Philadelphia's best French bistros, winning kudos for its comfortable setting and accessible menu. Open from lunch to late-night, the bistro features dishes such as a cassolette of snails in champagne and hazelnut butter sauce, grilled Dover sole with herb gnocchi in beurre blanc, and veal tenderloin with calves liver and onions. Best bar munchies? The crisp frites with dipping sauces. French menu. Closed Sun; major holidays. Lunch, dinner. Bar. Valet parking available. **$$$$**

★ ★ ★ ★ ★ **LE BEC-FIN.** *1523 Walnut St (19102). Phone 215/567-1000; fax 215/568-1151. www.lebecfin.com.* Still sparkling from its recent renovation, George Perrier's Le Bec-Fin, which opened in 1970, remains a shining star for elegant haute cuisine of the French variety. Perrier unveiled his better-than-ever culinary temple after closing the restaurant for one month. During that time, he had architects, draftsmen, designers, and painters working around the clock to transform the Louis XVI-style room into a "turn-of-the-century Parisian dining salon." Indeed, the room is a bastion of civility with fresh flowers, tawny-toned carpeting, amber lighting, and finely dressed tabletops. In addition to the stunning physical changes to the space, the menu has been treated to a warm wave of fresh air. Perrier's talented team brings out the brilliance in classic dishes while offering several new creations that are destined to be classics. Perrier's signature crab cake with haricot verts has remained on the menu through the renovation. It joins an exciting menu divided between Les Entrees (appetizers); an impressive and unusual selection of Les Poissons (fish), depending on availability; and an equally terrific assortment of Les Viandes (meats), also listed according to season and availability. Le Cave, as the restaurant's wine cellar is known, has also seen improvement. The list has been expanded from 200 to 700 bottles and includes many sought-after vintages and rare selections from private collections. Reborn, Le Bec-Fin is better than ever. *Secret Inspector's Notes:* The service here is as warm and attentive as you could imagine. Each guest's wants and needs are consistently attended to, and the staff manages to keep the interaction fun and light while achieving the utmost professionalism. French menu. Closed Sun; holidays. Lunch, dinner. Bar. Jacket required. Valet parking (dinner). **$$$$**

D

★ **MANAYUNK BREWING AND RESTAURANT.** *4120 Main St (19127). Phone 215/482-8220; fax 215/482-3555. www.manayunkbrewery.com.* Lunch, dinner. Entertainment. Children's menu. On the river. **$**

D

★ **MANAYUNK DINER.** *3720-3740 Main St (19127). Phone 215/483-4200; fax 215/483-0840.* American menu with Greek influences. Breakfast, lunch, dinner, late night. Bar. Children's menu. Casual attire. Outdoor seating. **$$**

D

★ ★ **MICHAEL'S.** *824 S 8th St (19147). Phone 215/922-3986; fax 215/922-3294. www.michaelsristorante.com.* Italian menu. Closed Mon. Dinner. Bar. Valet parking. Exposed brick, stucco walls; statuary in alcoves. Bronze, glass chandeliers. **$$**

★ ★ ★ **MONTE CARLO LIVING ROOM.** *150 South St (19147). Phone 215/925-2220; fax 215/925-9956.* Rounding the corner on this, their showcase restaurant's 20th year, Giorgio Giuliani and Umberto Degli Estosti recently completed an extensive remodel. The resulting ambience in the 45-seat dining room and club upstairs is elegant, warm, and welcoming. The chef's weekly-changing menus represent fine contemporary Mediterranean cuisine at its best. A starter duet of foie gras and sweetbreads is coupled with Firelli pears and aged balsamic vinegar, and in the entrée section, the roasted lamb is fragrant with sage and paired with cranberry beans and Barolo sauce. Cheese course selections are well thought out, and the desserts are creative. Northern Italian menu. Closed major holidays. Dinner. Bar. Jacket required. **$$$$**

★ ★ ★ **MOONSTRUCK.** *7955 Oxford Ave (19111). Phone 215/725-6000; fax 215/722-7177. www.moonstruckrestaurant.com.* Formerly known as Ristorante DiLullo, this elegantly casual northern Italian gem has been doing business for more than 20 years. Menus let customers choose among a wide range of antipasti, primi piatti (pasta appetizers), secondi piatti (second courses), and piatti tradizionale (traditional classics). The latter menu section features one special dish per night, ranging from Friday's caciucco—a bouillabaisse of seafood and fish—to Tuesday's osso buco, braised veal shank with pesto risotto. Italian menu. Closed Jan 1, July 4, Dec 25. Dinner. **$$**

★ ★ ★ **MORIMOTO.** *723 Chestnut St (19106). Phone 215/413-9070; fax 215/413-9075. www.morimotorestaurant.com.* Japanese fusion cuisine from "Iron Chef" Masaharu Morimoto of New York's Nobu fame (he was executive chef at Nobu Matsuhisa's restaurant for six years) pulsates with life and creativity. His Philadelphia outpost—stunningly shaped by local restaurant impresario Stephen Starr—is Morimoto's first restaurant in the US. Ceilings undulate, booths change color, and the sushi bar at the back never stops bustling. The best way to challenge your taste buds is to select one of Morimoto's omakase (multicourse tasting) menus. Japanese menu. Closed Jan 1, Thanksgiving, Dec 25. Lunch, dinner. Bar. Reservations required. **$$$**

D

★ **NAIS CUISINE.** *13-17 W Benedict Ave (19083). Phone 610/789-5983.* French, Thai menu. Dinner. Reservations required. **$$**

D

★ ★ ★ **OPUS 251.** *251 S 18th St (19103). Phone 215/735-6787; fax 215/735-6170. www.opus251.com.* Charmingly situated in the Philadelphia Arts Alliance's former parlor and dining room, Opus 251 is a lovely "two-fer," steeping guests in both visual and culinary art at the same time. The assertive American menu is featured at brunch (try the strawberry mascarpone-stuffed French toast with crisp Philadelphia scrapple), lunch, and dinner. The chef surprises with interesting accents. A lunch entrée of seared Lancaster County ostrich comes with braised Belgian endive and a golden gooseberry salad. At dinner, braised West Coast halibut comes in a Savoy cabbage wrapper with grilled ratatouille and yellow pepper carrot fume. Lunch and dinner menus change daily, featuring a $21 three-course fixed price menu at lunch, plus dinner's pre-theater three-course fixed-price menu for $41 and a four-course fixed price for $61. American menu. Closed Mon; Memorial Day, Thanksgiving, Dec 25. Lunch, dinner, Sun brunch. Bar. Outdoor seating. **$$$**

★ ★ ★ **OVERTURES.** *609 E Passyunk Ave (19147). Phone 215/627-3455.* Chef/proprietor Peter LamLein has been creating his finely tuned menus of French/Mediterranean fare for Philadelphians for more than a decade. The setting is elegantly Empire, with murals on the garden room walls and additional paintings by pastry chef Ron Weisberg throughout. There's a nice selection of à la carte dishes, including an appetizer of fresh anchovies in lemon oil with garlic and roasted peppers, and an entrée of veal sweetbreads in hazelnut crumbs with orange Cognac sauce. But the best values are LamLein's fixed-price menus—$50 for four courses and $20.04 (the price matches the year) for three courses—three nights a week. Bring your own alcoholic beverages, as there is no bar. Fresh juices and mixers are stocked, however, and the waitstaff will uncork and pour your wines. Mediterranean menu. Closed Mon; holidays. Dinner. Reservations required. **$$$**

D

★ ★ ★ **THE PALM.** *200 S Broad St (19102). Phone 215/546-7256; fax 215/546-3088. www.thepalm.com.* Closed most major holidays. Lunch, dinner. Bar. Valet parking available. Counterpart of a famous New York restaurant. Caricatures of celebrities adorn the walls. **$$$**

D

★ ★ **PALOMA.** *6516 Castor Ave (19149). Phone 215/533-0356. www. palomarestaurant.com.* French, Mexican menu. Closed Mon; Dec 25. Dinner. Bar. Children's menu. **$$$**

D

★ ★ ★ **PASION!** *211 S 15th St (19102). Phone 215/875-9895; fax 215/875-9935. www.pasionrestaurant.com.* Award-winning chef Guillermo Pernot's passion is Nuevo Latino cuisine—a melding of ancient cooking influences plumbed from Mexico, Central America, and South America with fun, contemporary stylings. Known for his meal-starting seviches (five different versions are featured daily), Pernot is equally creative with main courses, such as a plantain and wasabi pea-crusted salmon with creamy fufu and recao beurre blanc sauce. The upscale Latin-themed dining room, run by Pernot's business partner Michael Dombkoski, was recently doubled in size and features newly updated fabrics and furniture. Latin menu. Closed major holidays. Dinner. Casual attire. **$$$**

D

★ ★ **PHILADELPHIA FISH.** *207 Chestnut St (19106). Phone 215/625-8605; fax 215/625-9529. www.philadelphiafish.com.* Seafood menu. Closed Thanksgiving, Dec 25. Dinner. Bar. Children's menu. Casual attire. Outdoor seating. **$$**

D

★ ★ **PLOUGH & THE STARS.** *123 Chestnut St (19106). Phone 215/733-0300; fax 215/829-1097. www.ploughstars.com.* This upscale Irish pub is situated in a spectacular location in a beautiful historically preserved building with 245-foot ceilings, molded Corinthian columns, and dramatic 16-foot windows. Plan to stop here for Irish tea and scones after a day of touring Philadelphia's historic places, as it's just a few blocks from art galleries and several movie theaters as well as the Liberty Bell, Independence Hall, and Penn's Landing. Pints of Guinness and shepherd's pie are the specialties of the house, made more festive around the roaring fireplace or, in good weather, outdoors. Contemporary Irish menu. Dinner. Bar. Children's menu. Outdoor seating. **$$**

D

★ ★ **POD.** *3636 Sansom St (19104). Phone 215/387-1803. www.podphilidelphia.com.* Pan-Asian menu. Lunch, dinner. Bar. **$$$**

D

★ ★ **RANGOON BURMESE RESTAURANT.** *112 N 9th St (19107). Phone 215/829-8939; fax 215/629-2370. www.chinatown.com.* Burmese menu. Closed Thanksgiving. Lunch, dinner. Bar. Totally nonsmoking. **$$**

D

★ **THE RESTAURANT SCHOOL.** *4207 Walnut St (19104). Phone 215/222-4200. www.phillyrestaurants.com.* Continental, seasonal menu. Closed Sun, Mon; also during student breaks. Dinner. Bar. Unique dining experience in a "restaurant school." Consists of two buildings: a restored 1856 mansion is linked by a large atrium dining area to a new building housing the kitchen and classrooms. **$**

D

★ ★ ★ **RISTORANTE PANORAMA.** *Front and Market sts (19106). Phone 215/922-7800; fax 215/922-7642. www.pennsviewhotel.com.* Located right at the bridge to Penn's Landing in a building that's on the National Register of Historic Places, Panorama is part of the Penn's View Hotel (see). The cuisine is gutsy old-world Italian, featuring dishes such as paillard of beef rolled in garlic, cheese, egg, and herbs, slow-cooked in tomato sauce, and served with house-made gnocchi. But it's wine that this place is known for. Daily wine lists offer from 22 to 26 different flights (five wines per flight), plus dozens more by-the-glass options. The quality—made possible by the restaurant's cruvinet preservation and dispensing system—is exceptional, earning Panorama numerous "Best Wines by the Glass" awards from national food magazines. Northern Italian menu. Closed most major holidays. Dinner. Bar. Casual attire. **$$$**

D

★ ★ ★ **THE SALOON.** *750 S 7th St (19147). Phone 215/627-1811; fax 215/627-6765.* Richard Santore has been operating this venerable establishment in Philadelphia's Bellavista neighborhood, bordering Center City and South Philly, for more than 30 years. The food is classic Italian fare, served for lunch and dinner, in a dining room featuring lots of framed mirrors and old glass. Appetizers include poached pear and gorgonzola salad with roasted walnuts, baby greens, and red onion with pear vinaigrette. Fettuccini Lobster Amatriciana is a toss of house-made fettuccini with lobster, bacon, onion, fresh tomato, and pecorino cheese in tomato sauce. Daily dinner specials range from beef carpaccio drizzled with truffle essence and served with fava beans to a double veal chop marinated in white wine, pan seared and served with Yukon gold potatoes. Italian menu. Closed Sun; holidays. Lunch, dinner. Bar. **$$**

D

★ ★ **SERRANO.** *20 S 2nd St (19106). Phone 215/928-0770; fax 215/928-0805. www.tinangel.com.* International menu. Closed major holidays. Dinner. Bar. Entertainment Wed-Sat. **$$**

D

★ ★ **SONOMA.** *4411 Main St (19127). Phone 215/483-9400; fax 215/487-7894. www.sonomarestaurant.com.* California menu. Closed Thanksgiving. Lunch, dinner. Bar. Children's menu. Casual attire. Valet parking. Outdoor seating. **$$$**

D

★ **SOUTH STREET DINER.** *140 South St (19147). Phone 215/627-5258; fax 215/629-3954.* Greek menu. Closed Dec 25. Open 24 hours. Bar. Children's menu. Outdoor seating. **$$**

D

★ **SPASSO ITALIAN GRILL.** *34 S Front St (19106). Phone 215/592-7661. www.spassoitaliangrill.com.* Italian menu. Closed Dec 25. Lunch, dinner. Bar. Children's menu. Casual attire. Outdoor seating. **$$**

D

★ ★ **STEPHEN'S.** *1415 City Line Ave (19096). Phone 610/896-0275.* Northern Italian menu. Closed Jan 1, Dec 25. Lunch, dinner. Bar. Reservations required. Valet parking. **$$**

D

★ ★ ★ **STRIPED BASS.** *1500 Walnut St (19102). Phone 215/732-4444; fax 215/732-4433. www.mealticket.org.* Striped Bass makes quite a visual impression. Set in a former brokerage house, the room boasts towering 30-foot ceilings, red marble columns, potted palms, terra cotta-colored walls, and a high-energy open kitchen. It is a breathtaking room. Luckily, the treat for the eyes extends to the stomach. The menu, a loving showcase of virtually every fish in the sea, changes daily. If it once swam, you'll find it on the menu. (But if you're hungry for meat, head elsewhere. This is not the place for steak.) A magnificent raw bar tempts you with briny oysters, sweet clams, and plump, juicy shrimp. Don't hesitate to indulge here, but save room for the Raw Fish selection: a shimmering array of tartars, ceviches, and carpaccios deliciously tinged with Asian (wasabi, ginger, miso), Latin American (cilantro, chilies, lime), and Italian (olive oil, herbs, pine nuts) flavors. If you're feeling flush, a caviar sampler includes 30 grams each of sevruga, osetra, and beluga. Caviar or not, you'll find no losers on this menu. With global flair drawing inspiration from Cuba to Provence, the kitchen deftly demonstrates fish that can be as exciting and have as much personality as meat, if not more. *Secret Inspector's Notes:* The room and atmosphere at Striped Bass are still as impressive and awe-inspiring as ever, but the food and service may have gone downhill in the last few years of its long reign as one of Philadelphia's top tables. The incredibly renovated bank building is still worthy of a visit, with the proper expectations. Seafood menu. Menu changes daily. Closed holidays. Lunch, dinner. Bar. Reservations required. Valet parking. **$$$**

D

★ ★ ★ **SUSANNA FOO.** *1512 Walnut St (19102). Phone 215/545-2666; fax 215/546-9106. www.susannafoo.com.* Thanks to the plethora of greasy Chinese takeout joints, Chinese food has been much maligned over the years. But at Susanna Foo, a Zenlike dining oasis, the delicious, traditional cuisine of China sheds its unfortunate reputation and gains the respect it deserves. For the past 20 years, chef/owner Susanna Foo has been dressing up the dishes of her native land with sophisticated French flair and modern, global accents. Foo's dim sum can be a meal on their own, and that's a wonderful way to approach dinner here, as long as you order the stellar signature Hundred Corner crabcakes. The entrées are equally mouthwatering, especially the famous tea-smoked Peking duck breast. You may never be able to order takeout again. Chinese, French menu. Closed holidays. Lunch, dinner. Bar. Jacket required. Reservations required. Valet parking. **$$**

D

★ ★ ★ **SWANN CAFE.** *1 Logan Sq (19103). Phone 215/963-1500; toll-free 866/516-1100; fax 215/963-9562. www.fourseasons.com/philadelphia.* Named for the spectacular Logan Square fountain situated right in front of the Four Seasons Hotel (see) that houses this café, Swann is the more accessible of the hotel's exceptional restaurants. (The other, Fountain Restuarant (see), is one of Philadelphia's premier special-occasion restaurants.) Menus are overseen by executive chef Martin Hamann and range from light and lovely dishes such as an appetizer ragout of forest mushrooms and asparagus tips to a zesty sandwich of pulled osso bucco with aged provolone and spicy pepper and onion relish on a Stirato roll. American menu. Lunch, dinner. Bar. Entertainment. Children's menu. Casual attire. Valet parking. **$$**

D

★ ★ **THOMAS' RESTAURANT AND BAR.** *4201 Main St (19127). Phone 215/483-9075; fax 215/483-2109. www.bar-hop.com/thomas.htm.* American, Asian, French menu. Closed Jan 1, Thanksgiving, Dec 25. Dinner, Sat-Sun brunch. Bar. Outdoor seating. **$$**

D

★ ★ **UMBRIA.** 7131 Germantown Ave (19119). Phone 215/242-6470. Eclectic menu. Blackboard menu changes daily. Closed Sun-Tues; major holidays. Dinner. Totally nonsmoking. **$$**

★ ★ ★ **VETRI.** 1312 Spruce St (19107). Phone 215/732-3478; fax 215/ 732-3487. www.vetriristorante.com. Chef Marc Vetri learned to prepare rustic Italian cuisine (rabbit loin and sweetbreads wrapped in pancetta with morels; baby goat poached in milk and then oven roast to crispness) from Italy's best chefs and then brought his skills home to Philly. Ensconced in the tiny, 35-seat space once occupied by other pinnacle establishments (Le Bec-Fin, Chanterelle), Vetri is intent on creating likewise legendary meals. Sweet quirkiness is his trademark (Vetri shaves prosciutto on a 1936 Berkel meat slicer right in the dining room). The wine list has been nationally lauded, and the service is seamless. On Saturdays, indulge in Vetri's five- or seven-course fixed-price menus (not available during the summer). Italian menu. Closed Sun; holidays. Dinner. Casual attire. **$$$**

★ ★ **WHITE DOG CAFE.** 3420 Sansom St (19104). Phone 215/386-9224; fax 215/386-1185. www.whitedog.com. Closed Thanksgiving, Dec 25. Lunch; dinner; Sat-Sun brunch. Bar. Children's menu. Former house (circa 1870) of author Madame Blavatsky, founder of the Theosophical Society. Outdoor seating. **$$**

★ ★ ★ **ZANZIBAR BLUE.** 200 S Broad St (19102). Phone 215/732-4500; fax 215/732-4550. www.zanzibarblue.com. This noisy beneath-the-street venue is considered a major stop on the jazz circuit. It blends Southern-style (as well as some Latin and French) fine dining with a plush, low-lit downstairs jazz club and bar. With live jazz seven nights a week, it draws locally, nationally, and internationally known artists. Eclectic/International menu. Dinner. Bar. Entertainment. **$$$**

D

★ ★ **ZOCALO.** 3600 Lancaster Ave (19104). Phone 215/895-0139. Contemporary Mexican menu. Closed holidays. Lunch, dinner. Bar. Outdoor seating. **$$**

Richmond, VA

1 hour 45 minutes; 106 miles from Washington, DC

Settled 1607 **Pop** 197,790 **Elev** 150 ft **Area code** 804

Information Convention and Visitors Bureau, 550 E Marshall St, 23219; 804/782-2777 or 800/370-9004

Web www.richmondva.org

There have been few dull moments in Richmond's history. Native Americans and settlers fought over the ground on which it now stands. In 1775, Patrick Henry made his "liberty or death" speech in St. John's Church, and in 1780, the city was named capital of the state. At that time, Virginia extended all the way to the Mississippi. British soldiers plundered it brutally in the Revolutionary War. As the capital of the Confederacy from 1861 to 1865, it was constantly in danger. Finally, in 1865, the city was evacuated and retreating Confederate soldiers burned the government warehouse; a portion of the rest of the city also went up in flames.

However, Richmond did survive. As Virginia's capital, it proudly exemplifies the modern South. It is a city industrially aggressive yet culturally aware, respectful of its own historical background yet receptive to new trends in

Richmond's Historical Legacy

Richmond was the Civil War "Capital of the Confederacy," and this aspect of its past can easily be recalled on a two-hour, 2-mile walking tour of the city center. The city also enjoys other, less-troubling claims to historical fame, which will be pointed out along the way. Begin this walk at the Virginia State Capitol, designed in 1785 by Thomas Jefferson, himself a state governor, in the style of a classical temple. Surrounded by Capitol Square's expanse of well-tended lawn, it displays such majesty that it still commands the eye despite the modern-day structures that surround it. Step inside the Rotunda to see the famous life-size statue of George Washington, the only one executed of him from life. From Capitol Square, walk north (right) on 9th Street across Broad Street to the neighborhood once known as Court End, which now bustles with students and faculty of the Medical College of Virginia. At 818 East Marshall Street (intersecting 9th) stands the most important residence of Court End, the home of John Marshall, the distinguished chief justice of the US Supreme Court from 1801 to 1835. Built in 1790, the two-story brick house where he lived for 45 years is a museum dedicated to his memory. Though it's a seven-block detour, head west on Marshall Street to 2nd Street and turn north (right) two blocks to 110 East Leigh Street, the Maggie Walker National Historic Site. A museum, the modest two-story brick home on a quiet residential street honors a black woman of impressive ability. Despite physical handicaps, Walker became America's first female bank president, establishing the Penny Savings Bank in 1903 as a way of helping local blacks during the Jim Crow period. Double back via Marshall Street past the John Marshall House to the Valentine Museum at 1015 East Clay Street. A small, innovative museum with a contemporary outlook, it focuses on the people and history of Richmond. Conclude the tour a block down the street at 12th and East Clay at the adjacent Museum of the Confederacy and the White House of the Confederacy. Not surprisingly, the museum emphasizes Southern leaders, featuring mementos of General Robert E. Lee. The White House, a neoclassical mansion built in 1818, recounts the home life during the Civil War of Confederate President Jefferson Davis and his wife, Varina.

architecture and modes of living. Richmond esteems both the oldest monuments and the newest skyscrapers.

Tobacco and tobacco products, paper and paper products, aluminum, chemicals, textiles, printing and publishing, and machinery contribute to the city's economy. Richmond is also an educational center; Virginia Commonwealth University, Virginia Union University, and the University of Richmond are based here.

What to See and Do

17th Street Farmers' Market. *17th St and Main St (23219). Phone 804/646-0477. www.17thstreetfarmersmarket.com.* Farmers market built on the site of a Native American trading village. Seasonal produce, flowers, and holiday greens. (Daily)

6th Street Marketplace. *6th St between Coliseum and Grace St (23219), downtown.* Restored area of shops, restaurants, and entertainment.

Agecroft Hall. *4305 Sulgrave Rd (23221). Phone 804/353-4241. www.agecrofthall.com.* Half-timbered Tudor manor built in the late 15th century near Manchester, England. Disassembled, brought here, and rebuilt during the late 1920s in a spacious setting of formal gardens and grassy terraces overlooking the James River. English furnishings from 16th and 17th centuries. Audiovisual presentation explains the history of the house. (Tues-Sun; closed holidays) **$$**

★ **Capitol Square.** *9th and Grace sts (23219). Bounded by Broad, Governor, Bank, and 9th sts, downtown. Phone 804/784-5736.*

Equestrian Statue of Washington. By Thomas Crawford; cast in Munich over an 18-year period. Base features allegorical representations of six famous Revolutionary War figures from Virginia.

Governor's Mansion. *E of State Capitol. Phone 804/371-2642.* (1813) This two-story Federal-style house was built after the capital was moved from Williamsburg. Oldest governor's mansion in the US still in use as a governor's residence. Tours (by appointment). **FREE**

State Capitol. *Phone 804/698-1788.* (1785-1788) Modeled after La Maison Carrée, an ancient Roman temple at Nîmes, France, the Capitol was designed by Thomas Jefferson. In this building, where America's oldest continuous English-speaking legislative bodies still meet, is the famous Houdon statue of Washington. The rotunda features the first interior dome in the US; here Aaron Burr was tried for treason, Virginia ratified the Articles of Secession, and Robert E. Lee accepted command of the forces of Virginia; the Confederate Congress also met in the building. (Mon-Sat, also Sun afternoons; closed Jan 1, Thanksgiving, Dec 25)

Virginia State Library and Archives. *800 E Broad St (23219). Phone 804/692-3500. www.lva.lib.va.us.* Outstanding collection of books, maps, and manuscripts. (Mon-Sat; closed holidays) **FREE**

Carytown. *W Cary St, between Boulevard St and I-95 (23220).* Eight blocks of shops, restaurants, and theaters adjacent to the historic Fan neighborhood.

Church Hill Historic Area. *Bounded by Broad, 29th, Main, and 21st sts, E of Capitol Sq (23223).* Neighborhood of 19th-century houses, more than 70 of which predate Civil War. Some Church Hill houses are open during Historic Garden Week (see SPECIAL EVENTS). In the center of Church Hill is

> **Edgar Allan Poe Museum.** *1914-1916 E Main St (23223). Phone 804/648-5523. www.poemuseum.org.* Old Stone House portion is thought to be oldest structure in Richmond (1737). Three additional buildings house Poe mementos; James Carling illustrations of "The Raven"; scale model of the Richmond of Poe's time. Guided tours. (Tues-Sun; closed some major holidays). **$$**

> **St. John's Episcopal Church.** *25th and Broad sts (23223). Phone 804/648-5015.* (1741) Where Patrick Henry delivered his stirring "liberty or death" speech. Reenactment of the Second Virginia Convention (late May-early Sept, Sun). Guided tours. (Daily; closed holidays)

City Hall Observation Deck. *900 E Broad St (23219). Phone 804/646-7000.* Eighteenth-floor observation deck offers a panoramic view of the city, including the capitol grounds, James River, and Revolutionary and Civil War-era buildings contrasted with modern skyscrapers. (Mon-Fri) **FREE** Across the street is the old **City Hall** (1886-1894), a restored Gothic Revival building featuring an elaborate central court with arcaded galleries.

★ **The Fan and Monument Avenue.** *Bounded by Franklin St and Monument Ave, Boulevard, Main, and Belvidere sts (23220). Phone 804/643-3589.* Named for the layout of streets that fan out from Monroe Park toward the western part of town. Historical neighborhood has restored antebellum and turn-of-the-century houses, museums, shops, restaurants, and famed Monument Avenue. The fashionable boulevard, between Lombard and Belmont streets, is dotted with imposing statues of Generals Lee, Stuart, and Jackson; of Jefferson Davis; and of Commodore Matthew Fontaine Maury, inventor of the electric torpedo. Within this area are

> **Children's Museum of Richmond.** *2626 W Broad St (23220). Phone 804/474-2667; toll-free 877/295-2667. www.c-mor.org.* Exhibits on arts, nature, and the world around us designed for children 2-12 years old; many hands-on exhibits. (July-Aug, daily; rest of year, Tues-Sun; closed holidays) **$$**

> **Science Museum of Virginia.** *2500 W Broad St (23220), N of Monument Ave. Phone 804/864-1400. www.smv.org.* Hands-on museum. Major exhibits include aerospace, computers, electricity, visual perception, physical phenomena and astronomy, and Foucault pendulum. The Ethyl Universe Planetarium Space Theater features Omnimax films and planetarium shows (inquire for schedule). (Tues-Sun; closed Thanksgiving, Dec 25) **$$-$$$**

> **Virginia Historical Society.** *428 N Boulevard St (23220). Phone 804/358-4901. www.vahistorical.org.* Comprehensive collection of Virginia history housed in the Museum of Virginia History with permanent and changing exhibits, and the Library of Virginia History with historical and genealogical research facilities. (Mon-Sat, museum also Sun afternoons; closed holidays) **$$**

Virginia Museum of Fine Arts. *2800 Grove Ave (23221). Phone 804/340-1400. www.vmfa.state.va.us.* America's first state-supported museum of art. Collections of paintings, prints, and sculpture from major world cultures; Russian Imperial Easter eggs and jewels by Faberge; decorative arts of the Art Nouveau and Art Deco movements; sculpture garden; changing exhibits. Cafeteria. (Tues-Sun; closed holidays) **FREE**

Federal Reserve Money Museum. *701 E Byrd St (23219), downtown, on first floor of bank. Phone 804/697-8000. www.rich.frb.org/econed/museum/.* Exhibits of currency, include rare bills; gold and silver bars; money-related artifacts. (Mon-Fri 9:30 am-3:30 pm; closed holidays) **FREE**

Historic Richmond Tours. *707 E Franklin St (23219). Phone 804/649-0711.* Offers guided van tours with pickup at Visitor Center and major hotels (daily); reservations required. Also guided walking tours (Apr-Oct, daily; fee). **$$$$**

Hollywood Cemetery. *412 S Cherry St (23220). At Albemarle St. Phone 804/648-8501. www.hollywoodcemetery.org.* (1847) James Monroe, John Tyler, Jefferson Davis, other notables, and 18,000 Confederate soldiers are buried here; audiovisual program (Mon-Fri). (Daily 8 am-5 pm; walking tours Apr-Oct, Mon-Sat at 10 am) **FREE**

Jackson Ward. *Broad and Belvidere sts (23218). Bounded by I-95, 7th, Broad, and Belvidere sts.* Historic downtown neighborhood that was home to many famous black Richmonders, including Bill "Bojangles" Robinson. The area has numerous 19th-century, Greek Revival, and Victorian buildings with ornamental ironwork that rivals the wrought iron of New Orleans. Within the ward are

    Bill "Bojangles" Robinson Statue. *Corner of Leigh and Adams sts (23218).* Memorial to the famous dancer who was born at 915 N 3rd St.

    Black History Museum and Cultural Center. *00 Clay St (23219). Phone 804/780-9093. www.blackhistorymuseum.org.* Limited editions, prints, art, photographs; African memorabilia; Sam Gilliam collection. (Tues-Sun 10 am-5 pm) **$$**

    Maggie Walker National Historic Site. *110 1/2 E Leigh St (23223). Phone 804/771-2017. www.nps.gov/malw/.* Commemorates the life and career of Maggie L. Walker, daughter of former slaves, who overcame great hardships to become successful in banking and insurance; early advocate for women's rights and racial equality. Two-story, red brick house was home to her family from 1904 to 1934. (Mon-Sat; closed Jan 1, Thanksgiving, Dec 25) **FREE**

John Marshall House. *818 E Marshall St (23219). Phone 804/648-7998.* (1790) Restored house of famous Supreme Court justice features original woodwork and paneling, family furnishings, and mementos. (Tues-Sun; closed holidays) Combination ticket available for Marshall House, Valentine Museum, Museum of the Confederacy, and White House of the Confederacy. **$**

Kanawha Canal Locks. *12th and Byrd sts (23219), downtown. Phone 804/780-0107 (walking tour) or 804/649-2800 (cruise tour).* Impressive stone locks were part of the nation's first canal system, planned by George Washington. Narrated audiovisual presentation explains the workings of the locks and canal. Picnic grounds. (Mon-Sat) **FREE**

Meadow Farm Museum. *General Sheppard Crump Memorial Park. 8600 Dixon Powers Dr (23273). Phone 804/501-5520. www.co.henrico.va.us/rec/ mfarm.htm.* Living history farm museum depicting rural life in the 1860s. Orientation center, farmhouse, barn, outbuildings, crop demonstration fields, and 1860s doctor's office. Also a 150-acre park with picnic shelters, playground. (Mar-Dec, Tues-Sun) **$**

Monumental Church. *1224 E Broad St (23219), N of Capitol Sq.* (1812) Located on the Medical College of Virginia campus of Virginia Commonwealth University. Octagonal domed building designed by Robert Mills, architect of the Washington Monument. Commemorative structure was built on the site where many prominent persons, including the governor, perished in a theater fire in 1811. Interior closed. Behind the church is the distinctive **Egyptian Building** (1845).

Museum of the Confederacy. *1201 E Clay St (23219), N of Capitol Sq. Phone 804/649-1861. www.moc.org.* Contains the nation's largest collection of Confederate military and civilian artifacts, including uniforms; equipment; flags; personal belongings of Jefferson Davis, Robert E. Lee, and J. E. B. Stuart; documents; manuscripts; and artwork. (Mon-Sat 10 am-5 pm, Sun noon-5 pm; closed Jan 1, Thanksgiving, Dec 25) **$$**

Paddlewheeler *Annabel Lee.* *Departs from Intermediate Terminal. Broad St E to 21st St, turn right on 21st St to Dock St, turn left on Dock, follow until you reach the terminal. Phone 804/377-2020; toll-free 800/752-7093. www.spiritcitycruises.com/richmond/onboard/.* Triple-decked, 350-passenger, 19th-century-style riverboat cruises the James River. Narrated tour; entertainment. Lunch, brunch, dinner, and plantation cruises. (Apr-Dec, at least one cruise Tues-Sun)

Parks. *Phone 804/780-5733.* For general information, contact the Department of Parks and Recreation.

Bryan. *Bellevue Ave and Hermitage Rd (23227).* A 279-acre park, 20 acres of which are an azalea garden with more than 55,000 plants (best viewed late Apr-mid-May). Picnic facilities, tennis courts. **FREE**

James River. *W 22nd St and Riverside Dr (23225).* Hiking. **FREE**

Lewis Ginter Botanical Garden. *1800 Lakeside Ave (23228). Phone 804/ 262-9887. www.lewisginter.org.* Victorian-era estate features the Grace Arents Garden and the Henry M. Flagler Perennial Garden; seasonal floral displays; emphasis on daffodils, daylilies, azaleas, and rhododendrons. (Daily) **$$**

Maymont. *1700 Hampton St at Pennsylvania Ave (23220). Phone 804/ 358-7166.* Dooley mansion, late Victorian in style, houses an art collection and decorative arts exhibits (Tues-Sun; fee). Also here are formal Japanese and Italian gardens, an arboretum, a nature center with wildlife habitat for native species, an aviary, a children's farm, and a working carriage collection. (Daily) **FREE**

Pocahontas State Park. *10301 State Park Rd (23838). S on US 10, then W on VA 655. Phone 804/796-4255. www.dcr.state.va.us/parks/pocahont.htm.* More than 7,000 acres; Swift Creek Lake. Swimming, pool, bathhouse, fishing, boating (launch, rentals, electric motors only); hiking trails, bicycle path (rentals), picnicking, concession, tent and trailer sites (seasonal), group cabins. Nature center; evening interpretive programs (summer). Standard fees. (Daily)

William Byrd. *Boulevard St and Idlewood Ave (23220).* Includes 287 acres of groves, artificial lakes, picnic areas. Tennis courts, softball fields, and a fitness course. Amphitheater (June-Aug). Virginia's World War I memorial, a 240-foot, pink brick carillon tower.

Plantation tours. *401 E Marshall St (23220). Phone 804/783-7450.* The Richmond-Petersburg-Williamsburg area has many fine old mansions and estates. Some are open most of the year; others only during Historic Garden Week (see SPECIAL EVENTS). The Metro Richmond Visitors Center has maps, information folders, and suggestions.

Shockoe Slip. *E Cary St between 12th and 14th sts (23219), downtown.* Restored area of historic buildings and gaslit cobblestone streets; shopping, restaurants, and galleries.

St. Paul's Church. *815 E Grace St (23219), W of Capitol Sq. Phone 804/643-3589. www.stpauls-episcopal.org. (*Episcopal) Established in 1843, the church survived the Civil War intact. It was here that Jefferson Davis received news of Robert E. Lee's retreat from Petersburg to Appomattox. Beginning in 1890, the church added many fine stained-glass windows, including eight from the Tiffany studios. Sanctuary ceiling features decorative plasterwork interweaving Greek, Hebrew, and Christian motifs around a central panel. A Tiffany mosaic of da Vinci's *Last Supper* surmounts the altar. (Daily; closed holidays)

Valentine Museum. *1015 E Clay St (23219), N of Capitol Sq. Phone 804/649-0711. www.valentinemuseum.com.* Traces the history of Richmond. Exhibits focus on city life, decorative arts, costumes and textiles, and industrial and social history; tour of restored 1812 Wickham House. Lunch is served in a walled garden (Apr-Oct). (Daily; closed holidays). **$$**

Virginia Aviation Museum. *5701 Huntsman Rd (23250). At Richmond International Airport. Phone 804/236-3622. www.vam.smv.org.* Exhibits and artifacts on the history of aviation, with an emphasis on Virginia pioneers. (Daily; closed Thanksgiving, Dec 25) **$$**

Virginia House. *4301 Sulgrave Rd (23221), 1/2 mile off VA 147 (Cary St). Phone 804/353-4251. www.vahistorical.org.* A Tudor building constructed of materials from Warwick Priory (built in England in 1125 and rebuilt in 1565 as a residence); moved here in 1925. The west wing is modeled after Sulgrave Manor, at one time the home of Lawrence Washington. Furniture, tapestries, and paintings from the 15th to 20th centuries. Formal gardens. Tours by appointment only except during Historic Garden Week (see SPECIAL EVENTS). (Fri-Sat 10 am-4 pm, Sun 12:30-5 pm, otherwise by appointment; closed holidays) **$$**

Virginia War Memorial. *621 S Belvidere St (23220), downtown at N end of Robert E. Lee Bridge. Phone 804/786-2060. www.vawarmemorial.org.* Honors Virginians who died in World War II and the Korean and Vietnam wars. Mementos of battles; eternal flame; more than 12,000 names engraved on glass and marble walls. (Daily) **FREE**

White House of the Confederacy. *12th and E Clay sts (23219), N of Capitol Sq. Phone 804/649-1861. www.moc.org/exwhite.htm.* Classical Revival house (1818) used by Jefferson Davis as his official residence during the period when Richmond was the capital of the Confederacy. Abraham Lincoln met with troops here during the Union occupation of the city. Restored to pre-wartime appearance; original furnishings. (Daily; closed Jan 1, Thanksgiving, Dec 25) **$$**

Wilton House Museum. *215 S Wilton Rd (23226) off Cary St, 8 miles W. Phone 804/282-5936. www.wiltonhousemuseum.org.* (1753) Georgian mansion built by William Randolph III. Fully paneled, authentic 18th-century furnishings. Headquarters of the National Society of Colonial Dames in Virginia. (Tues-Sun; closed holidays) Open during Historic Garden Week (see SPECIAL EVENTS). **$**

Special Events

Historic Garden Week in Virginia. *12 E Franklin St (23219). Phone 804/644-7776. www.vagardenweek.org.* Many private houses and gardens of historic or artistic interest are opened for this event, which includes more than 200 houses and gardens throughout the state. Tours. Mid-late Apr.

June Jubilee. *Downtown.* Performing and visual arts festival with ethnic foods, folk dances, music, and crafts. First weekend in June.

Richmond Newpapers Marathon. Last Sun in Oct.

Virginia State Fair. *600 E Laburnum Ave (23222). Phone 804/228-3200. www.statefair.com.* Animal and 4-H contests, music, horse show, and carnival. Late Sept-early Oct.

Motels/Motor Lodges

★ ★ **COURTYARD BY MARRIOTT.** *6400 W Broad St (23230). Phone 804/282-1881; toll-free 800/321-2211; fax 804/288-2934. www.courtyard.com.* 145 rooms, 3 story. Check-out noon. TV; cable (premium). In-room modem link. Laundry services. Restaurant, bar. In-house fitness room. Pool, whirlpool. **$**

[D] [≈] [⊼] [⊠]

★ **FAIRFIELD INN.** *7300 W Broad St (23294). Phone 804/672-8621; toll-free 800/228-2800; fax 804/755-7155. www.fairfieldinn.com.* 124 rooms, 2 story. Complimentary continental breakfast. Check-out noon. TV; cable (premium). In-room modem link. Laundry services. Pool. **$**

[D] [≈] [⊠] [SC]

★ **HAMPTON INN.** *10800 W Broad St, Glen Allen (23060). Phone 804/747-7777; fax 804/747-7069. www.hamptoninn.com.* 136 rooms, 5 story. Complimentary continental breakfast. Check-out noon, check-in 3 pm. TV; cable (premium). In-room modem link. In-house fitness room. Pool. **$**

[D] [≈] [⊼] [⊠]

★ **LA QUINTA INN.** *6910 Midlothian Tpke (23225). Phone 804/745-7100; toll-free 800/531-5900; fax 804/276-6660. www.laquinta.com.* 130 rooms, 3 story. Pets accepted. Complimentary continental breakfast. Check-out noon. TV; cable (premium). In-room modem link. Pool. **$**

[D] [⌫] [≈] [⊠] [SC]

★ **QUALITY INN.** *8008 W Broad St (23294). Phone 804/346-0000; toll-free 800/228-5151; fax 804/527-0284. www.qualityinn.com.* 191 rooms, 6 story. Pets accepted; fee. Complimentary continental breakfast. Check-out 11 am. TV; cable (premium). In-room modem link. In-house fitness room. Pool. **$**

[D] [⌫] [≈] [⊼] [⊠] [SC]

★ **RED ROOF INN.** *4350 Commerce Rd (23234). Phone 804/271-7240; toll-free 800/733-7663; fax 804/271-7245. www.redroof.com.* 108 rooms, 2 story. Pets accepted, some restrictions. Check-out noon. TV; cable (premium). **$**

[D] [⌫] [⊠]

Hotels

★ ★ ★ **THE BERKELEY HOTEL.** *1200 E Cary St (23219). Phone 804/780-1300; toll-free 888/780-4422. www.berkeleyhotel.com.* This hotel opened in 1988 but appears to be a property of days gone by. It is located at the crossroads of the business district and Historic Shockoe Slip. Dark wood paneling adorns the lobby and dining room. Dramatic windows to the ceiling give it a European appearance, and diners at the hotel's restaurant get a view of the Slip's cobblestone and lamplights. 56 rooms, 6 story. Check-out noon. TV; cable (premium), VCR available. In-room modem link. Restaurant, bar. Valet parking. Concierge. **$**

[D] [⊠] [SC]

★ ★ ★ **CROWNE PLAZA.** *555 E Canal St (23219). Phone 804/788-0900; toll-free 800/2-CROWNE; fax 804/788-0791. www.richmondcrowneplaza.com.* Just 9 miles from Richmond International Airport, this hotel is situated in the heart of the historic district and minutes from area attractions such as Shockoe Slip, Sixth Street Market Place, museums, theaters, and fine dining. 299 rooms, 16 story. Check-out noon. TV; cable (premium). In-room modem link. Laundry services. Restaurant, bar. Room service. In-house fitness room, sauna. Health club privileges. Indoor pool, whirlpool. Garage, valet parking. Business center. Concierge. Luxury level. **$**

[D] [≈] [⊼] [⛵] [⊠] [⊼]

★ ★ ★ **DOUBLETREE HOTEL RICHMOND AIRPORT.** *5501 Eubank Rd, Sandston (23150). Phone 804/226-6400; toll-free 800/445-8667; fax 804/226-1269. www.doubletree.com.* This hotel is just 40 minutes from Colonial Williamsburg and directly across from the Richmond International Airport. Area attractions include Kings Dominion, Busch Gardens, Richmond Coliseum, Aviation Museum, and the Museum of the Confederacy. 160 rooms, 5 story. Check-out noon. TV; cable (premium). In-room modem link. Laundry services. Restaurant, bar. Room service 24 hours. In-house fitness room. Pool, whirlpool. Free airport transportation. Luxury level. **$**

🄳 ⌁ 🕴 ✈ ⋈ SC

★ ★ ★ ★ ★ **THE JEFFERSON HOTEL.** *101 W Franklin St (23220). Phone 804/788-8000; toll-free 800/424-8014; fax 804/225-0334. www.jefferson-hotel.com.* The Jefferson Hotel is an institution in the heart of Richmond. Imaginations run wild at this historic landmark, dating to 1895. It's easy to conjure a beautifully dressed debutante gliding down the hotel's sweeping staircase, or influential politicians having a heated debate under the impressive marble-style columns. The guest rooms are furnished in a traditional style defined by antique reproductions and fine art, while modern amenities and inimitable Southern hospitality ensure the comfort of all guests. Pedigreed residents take afternoon tea here. TJ's provides a casual setting for fine dining with local dishes like oyster chowder and peanut soup. The hotel's star restaurant is Lemaire (see), with its sparkling ambience and refined menu. 264 rooms, 9 story. Pets accepted; fee. Check-out noon, check-in 3 pm. TV; cable (premium), VCR available. In-room modem link. Restaurant, bar. Room service 24 hours. Children's activity center; babysitting services available. In-house fitness room. Indoor pool. Valet parking. Business center. Concierge. **$$$**

🄳 🔧 ⌁ 🕴 ⋈ SC 🕴

★ ★ ★ **MARRIOTT RICHMOND.** *500 E Broad St (23219). Phone 804/643-3400; toll-free 800/228-9290; fax 804/788-1230. www.marriott.com.* This hotel has a direct connection to the convention center. 410 rooms, 17 story. Check-out noon, check-in 3 pm. TV; cable (premium). In-room modem link. Laundry services. Restaurant, bar. In-house fitness room, sauna. Game room. Indoor pool, whirlpool, poolside service. Business center. Concierge. Luxury level. **$$**

🄳 ⌁ 🕴 ⋈ 🕴

★ ★ ★ **OMNI RICHMOND HOTEL.** *100 S 12th St (23219). Phone 804/344-7000; toll-free 800/THE-OMNI; fax 804/648-1029. www.omnihotels.com.* This contemporary hotel is located in the center of the financial and historic districts and features views of the scenic James River. 369 rooms, 19 story. Check-out noon. TV; cable (premium). In-room modem link. Restaurant, bar. Indoor pool, poolside service. Business center. Concierge. Luxury level. **$$**

🄳 ⌁ ⋈ 🕴

★★ **SHERATON RICHMOND WEST HOTEL.** *6624 W Broad St (23230). Phone 804/285-2000; toll-free 800/228-9000; fax 804/288-3961. www.starwood/sheraton/richmondwest.com.* 372 rooms, 3-8 story. Check-out noon, check-in 3 pm. TV; cable (premium), VCR available. In-room modem link. Restaurant, bar; entertainment. Room service. Babysitting services available. In-house fitness room. Indoor, outdoor pools. Outdoor tennis. Airport transportation. Business center. Luxury level. **$$**

[D] [icons] [SC]

All Suites

★ **AMERISUITES.** *4100 Cox Rd, Glen Allen (23060). Phone 804/747-9644; toll-free 800/833-1516; fax 804/346-9320. www.amerisuites.com.* 126 suites, 6 story. Complimentary continental breakfast. Check-out noon, check-in 3 pm. TV; cable (premium). Laundry services. In-house fitness room. Pool. Business center. **$**

[D] [icons] [SC] [icon]

★★ **EMBASSY SUITES.** *2925 Emerywood Pkwy (23294). Phone 804/672-8585; toll-free 800/362-2779; fax 804/672-3749. www.embassy-suites.com.* 224 rooms, 8 story. Complimentary full breakfast. Check-out noon. TV; cable (premium). In-room modem link. Laundry services. Restaurant, bar. In-house fitness room, sauna. Indoor pool, whirlpool. Business center. **$**

[D] [icons] [SC] [icon]

B&B/Small Inns

★★ **EMMANUEL HUTZLER HOUSE.** *2036 Monument Ave (23220). Phone 804/353-6900. www.bensonhouse.com.* 4 rooms, 3 story. Children over 12 years only. Complimentary full breakfast. Check-out noon, check-in 4 pm. TV. Built in 1914; antiques. Totally nonsmoking. **$**

[icon]

★★ **LINDEN ROW INN.** *100 E Franklin St (23219). Phone 804/783-7000; toll-free 800/348-7424; fax 804/648-7504. www.lindenrowinn.com.* 68 rooms, 4 story. Complimentary continental breakfast. Check-out 11 am, check-in 3 pm. TV; cable (premium). In-room modem link. Laundry services. Dining room (public by reservation). Room service. Concierge. In a block of Greek Revival row houses (1847), around a courtyard thought to be the playground of Edgar Allan Poe; antique and period furnishings and décor. **$**

[icon]

★ **THE PATRICK HENRY INN.** *2300 E Broad St (23223). Phone 804/225-0477.* 3 rooms. Complimentary continental breakfast. Check-out noon, check-in 3 pm. TV. Street parking. **$**

[SC]

Extended Stay

★ ★ **RESIDENCE INN BY MARRIOTT.** *2121 Dickens Rd (23230). Phone 804/285-8200; toll-free 800/331-3131; fax 804/285-2530. www.residenceinn.com.* 80 rooms, 2 story. Pets accepted; fee. Complimentary continental breakfast. Check-out noon. TV; cable (premium), VCR available (movies). In-room modem link. Laundry services. Pool, whirlpool. Outdoor tennis. **$**

D 🐾 🏃 🛏 🏊

Restaurants

★ ★ **1421 RISTORANTE ITALIANO.** *1421 E Cary St (23219). Phone 804/648-0808; fax 804/648-2900. www.1421restaurant.com.* Italian menu. Closed Sun. Lunch, dinner. Bar. Casual attire. **$$**

★ ★ **ACACIA.** *3325 W Cary St (23221). Phone 804/354-6060; fax 804/354-6062. www.acaciarestaurant.com.* Closed Sun. Lunch, dinner. Entertainment. In an old renovated church. **$$**

D

★ ★ **AMICI.** *3343 W Cary St (23221). Phone 804/353-4700; fax 804/278-6291. www.amiciristorante.net.* Northern Italian menu. Closed major holidays. Lunch, dinner. Bar. Outdoor seating. **$$**

★ **AVALON.** *2619 W Main St (23220). Phone 804/353-9709.* Global menu. Closed Thanksgiving, Dec 25. Dinner. Bar. Casual attire. **$**

★ **BYRAM'S LOBSTER HOUSE.** *3215 W Broad St (23230). Phone 804/355-9193. www.byrams.com.* Continental, seafood menu. Closed Jan 1, Dec 25. Lunch, dinner. Bar. **$$**

SC

★ ★ **CABO'S CORNER BISTRO.** *2053 W Broad St (23220). Phone 804/355-1144.* Seafood menu. Closed Sun, Mon. Dinner. Bar. Casual attire. **$$**

D

★ ★ **CAFE MANDOLIN.** *1309 W Main St (23220). Phone 804/355-8558.* International menu. Closed Sun, Mon. Lunch, dinner. Bar. Casual attire. Outdoor seating. **$$**

D

★ **CAFFE DI PAGLIACCI.** *214 N Lombardy St (23220). Phone 804/353-3040; fax 804/358-2509. www.caffedipagliacci.com.* Italian menu. Closed Mon; major holidays. Dinner, Sun brunch. Bar. Casual attire. **$$**

★ ★ ★ **THE DINING ROOM AT THE BERKELEY HOTEL.** *1200 E Cary St (23219). Phone 804/225-5105; fax 804/343-1885. www.berkleyhotel.com.* Located in a European-style hotel, this handsomely decorated dining room serves elegant, impeccably prepared meals in an atmosphere that is sophisticated and tranquil. Many fine Virginia products are served, and classical preparation prevails. Breakfast, lunch, dinner. Entertainment. Children's menu. **$$$**

D

★ **FAROUK'S HOUSE OF INDIA.** *3033 W Cary St (23221). Phone 804/ 355-0378. www.faroukshouseofindia.com.* Indian menu. Lunch, dinner. **$**

D SC

★ ★ **HALF WAY HOUSE.** *10301 Jefferson Davis Hwy (23237). Phone 804/275-1760.* Lunch, dinner. Bar. Antique-furnished manor house (1760) was a stop on the Petersburg stagecoach line until the late 19th century; hosted Washington, Lafayette, Patrick Henry, and Jefferson, among others. Used as a Union headquarters during the 1864 siege of Richmond. **$$$**

★ ★ **HELEN'S.** *2527 W Main St (23220). Phone 804/358-4370; fax 804/ 358-4553.* Menu changes weekly. Closed Mon, major holidays. Dinner. Entertainment. **$$**

★ ★ ★ **KABUTO JAPANESE HOUSE OF STEAK.** *8052 W Broad St (23294). Phone 804/747-9573.* Japanese menu. Closed Thanksgiving, Dec 25. Lunch, dinner. Bar. Children's menu. **$$**

D

★ ★ **LA PETIT FRANCE.** *2108 Maywill St (23230). Phone 804/353-8729; fax 804/353-4692. www.lapetitefrance.net.* French menu. Closed Sun, Mon; major holidays; also last two weeks in Aug. Lunch, dinner. Children's menu. Jacket required (dinner). **$$$**

D

★ ★ ★ **LEMAIRE.** *101 W Franklin (23220). Phone 804/788-8000; fax 804/344-5162. www.jefferson-hotel.com.* Old-world fine dining comes to life at Lemaire, located in the historic Jefferson Hotel (see). The restaurant is named for Etienne Lemaire, who served as maitre d' to President Jefferson and was widely credited for introducing the fine art of cooking with wines to America. His love of food and wine is continued at Lemaire, where contemporary Southern cooking goes upscale with French accents, homegrown herbs, featherweight sauces, and seasonal ingredients. Professional and friendly service and quiet, intimate surroundings make dining at Lemaire a delight. American menu. Closed Memorial Day. Breakfast, lunch, dinner. Bar. Pianist. Children's menu. Jacket required. Valet parking available. Seven small dining rooms. **$$$**

D

★ **MILLIE'S.** *2603 E Main St (23223). Phone 804/643-5512; fax 804/648- 4321. www.milliesdiner.com.* Thai menu. Closed Mon. Lunch, dinner, Sun brunch. Entertainment. In front of old tobacco warehouses; huge collection of old 45 singles with mini-jukeboxes in booths. **$$**

D

★ **NUCCIO'S TRATTORIA & PIZZA.** *1108 Courthouse Rd, Suite A (23236). Phone 804/594-0040; fax 804/594-0994.* Italian menu. Lunch, dinner. Bar. Casual attire. **$**

D

★ **O'TOOLES.** *4800 Forest Hill Ave (23225). Phone 804/233-1781; fax 804/232-1737.* Seafood, steak menu. Closed Dec 24-25. Lunch, dinner. Bar. Pianist. Children's menu. **$$**

D

★ ★ ★ **THE OLD ORIGINAL BOOKBINDER'S.** *2306 E Cary St (23223). Phone 804/643-6900; fax 804/643-6690. www.oldoriginalbookbinders .com.* Seafood, steak menu. Closed major holidays. Dinner. Bar. Children's menu. Valet parking. **$$$**

★ ★ **PEKING PAVILION.** *1302 E Cary St (23219). Phone 804/649-8888; fax 804/649-8147.* Chinese menu. Closed Thanksgiving. Lunch, dinner, Sun brunch. Bar. **$$**

★ ★ **RIVAH BISTRO.** *1417 E Cary St (23219). Phone 804/344-8222. www.rivahbistro.com.* French bistro menu. Lunch, dinner. Bar. Children's menu. Casual attire. Outdoor seating. **$$**

D

★ ★ ★ **RUTH'S CHRIS STEAK HOUSE.** *11500 Huguenot Rd (23113). Phone 804/378-0600; fax 804/378-0776. www.sizzlingsteak.com.* Located in the historic Bellgrade Plantation House, this restaurant offers fine dining with elegant Southern hospitality. Dine on the patio or in a private room with period furnishings. For those seeking a ribeye or a New York strip, Ruth's Chris definitely lives up to its name as the home of serious steaks. Closed some major holidays. Dinner. Bar. Outdoor seating. Organist Tues-Sun. **$$**

D

★ ★ **SAM MILLER'S WAREHOUSE.** *1210 E Cary St (23219). Phone 804/644-5465; fax 804/644-5470. www.sammillers.com.* Seafood menu. Closed Labor Day, Dec 25. Lunch, dinner. Children's menu. In a historic district; display of antique mirrors. Casual attire. Lobster tank. **$$$**

★ ★ **SKILLIGALEE.** *5416 Glenside Dr (23228). Phone 804/672-6200; fax 804/755-1312. www.skilligalee.com.* Seafood menu. Closed Thanksgiving, Dec 25. Lunch, dinner. Bar. Children's menu. **$$$**

D

★ **STRAWBERRY STREET CAFE.** *421 Strawberry St (23220). Phone 804/353-6860; fax 804/358-3569. www.strawberrystreetcafe.com.* Lunch, dinner. Entertainment. Children's menu. Stained glass throughout the restaurant. **$$**

★ **TANGLEWOOD ORDINARY.** *2210 River Rd W, Maidens (23102). Phone 804/556-3284. www.ordinary.com.* Traditional Southern menu. Closed Mon-Tues; some major holidays. Dinner. Totally nonsmoking. Collection of *The Saturday Evening Post* dating from 1913. No credit cards accepted. **$**

★ ★ **TOBACCO COMPANY.** *1201 E Cary St (23219). Phone 804/ 782-9555; fax 804/788-8913. www.thetobaccocompany.com.* Closed Jan 1,

Dec 25. Lunch, dinner, Sun brunch. Bar. Band Mon-Sat. In a former tobacco warehouse (circa 1880); built around a skylit atrium with an antique cage elevator; many unusual antiques. **$$$**

D

★ **TRAK'S.** *9115 Quioccasin Rd (23229). Phone 804/740-1700; fax 804/740-1700.* Mediterranean menu. Closed Sun; also some major holidays. Lunch, dinner. Children's menu. **$$**

D

★ ★ **YEN CHING.** *6601 Midlothian Tpke (23225). Phone 804/276-7430. www.yenchingdining.com.* Chinese menu. Closed Thanksgiving. Lunch, dinner. Bar. **$$**

D

Shenandoah National Park, VA

1 hour 20 minutes; 70 miles from Washington, DC

About 450 million years ago, the Blue Ridge was at the bottom of a sea. Today, it averages 2,000 feet above sea level; some 300 square miles of the loveliest Blue Ridge area are included in Shenandoah National Park.

The park is 80 miles long and 2-13 miles wide. Running its full length is the 105-mile Skyline Drive. Main entrances are the North Entrance (Front Royal), from I-66, US 340, US 522, and VA 55; Thornton Gap Entrance (31.5 miles south), from US 211; Swift Run Gap Entrance (65.7 miles south), from US 33; and the South Entrance (Rockfish Gap), from I-64, US 250, and the Blue Ridge Parkway (see). The drive, twisting and turning along the crest of the Blue Ridge, is one of the finest scenic trips in the East. Approximately 70 overlooks give views of the Blue Ridge, the Piedmont, and, to the west, the Shenandoah Valley and the Alleghenies.

The drive offers much, but the park offers more. Exploration on foot or horseback attracts thousands of visitors who return again and again. Most of the area is wooded, predominantly in white, red, and chestnut oak, with hickory, birch, maple, hemlock, tulip poplar, and nearly 100 other species scattered here and there. At the head of Whiteoak Canyon are hemlocks that are more than 300 years old. The park bursts with color and contrast in the fall, which makes this season particularly popular with visitors. The park is a sanctuary for deer, bears, foxes, and bobcats, along with more than 200 varieties of birds.

Accommodations are available in the park, with lodges, motel-type units, and cabins at Big Meadows and Skyland and housekeeping cabins at Lewis Mountain. For reservations and rates (which vary), contact ARA-MARK

Virginia Sky-Line Company, Inc, PO Box 727, Luray 22835-9051; phone toll-free 800/999-4714. Nearby communities provide a variety of accommodations. In the park, there are restaurants at Panorama, Skyland, and Big Meadows; light lunches and groceries are available at Elkwallow, Big Meadows, Lewis Mountain, and Loft Mountain waysides.

The park is open all year; lodge and cabin accommodations, usually Mar-Dec; phone ahead for the schedule. Skyline Drive is occasionally closed for short periods during Nov-Mar. As in all national parks, pets must be on a leash. The speed limit is 35 miles per hour. $10 per car per week, annual permit $20; Golden Age, Golden Access, and Golden Eagle Passports are accepted (see MAKING THE MOST OF YOUR TRIP).

Park Headquarters is 5 miles east of Luray on US 211. Detailed information and pamphlets may be obtained by contacting the Superintendent, Shenandoah National Park, 3655 US 211 E, Luray 22835; phone 540/999-3500.

What to See and Do

Camping. *Phone 800/365-CAMP.* First-come, first-served tent and trailer sites (no hookups) at Mathews Arm, Lewis Mountain, and Loft Mountain. Big Meadows requires reservations (phone 800/365-CAMP). Fourteen-day limit. Campers must register and check out (spring-fall). Write to the Park Superintendent, 3655 US 211 E, Luray 22835, for information. **$$$$**

Fishing. Trout. Regulations and directions at entrance stations, Dickey Ridge, Panorama, Big Meadows, and Loft Mountain. State or five-day non-resident license necessary.

Hiking. The 500 miles of trails include 101 miles of the Appalachian Trail. Along the trail, which winds 2,100 miles from Maine to Georgia, are numerous side trails to mountaintops, waterfalls, and secluded valleys. The trail crosses Skyline Drive at several points and can be entered at many overlooks. Overnight backcountry use requires a permit. No open fires are allowed. Regulations and permits may be obtained at any park entrance station, visitor center, or at Park Headquarters. The backcountry may be closed during periods of high fire danger. Visitor centers and lodges post schedules of evening programs and ranger-led hikes. Self-guided walks ranging from 1/2 to two hours are at Dickey Ridge (mile 4.6), Skyland (mile 1.7), Big Meadows (mile 51.1), Lewis Mountain (mile 57.5), and Loft Mountain (mile 79.5).

Interpretive program. Guided walks, illustrated campfire talks. (Usually mid-June-mid-Oct; rest of year, on a limited basis) Obtain a schedule at Park Headquarters, entrance stations, visitor centers, or concessions.

Picnicking. Near Dickey Ridge Visitor Center, Elkwallow, Pinnacles, Big Meadows, Lewis Mountain, South River, and Loft Mountain.

★ **Points of special interest on Skyline Drive.** Mileposts are numbered north to south, starting at Front Royal. Periods of operation are estimated—phone ahead.

Big Meadows. *Mile 51.1.* (3,500 feet) Accommodations, restaurant; store, gas; tent and trailer sites; picnic grounds; nature trail. (Usually Apr-Nov)

Byrd Visitor Center. *Mile 51.* Exhibits, information, book sales, orientation programs, maps. (Usually Apr-Nov, daily)

Dickey Ridge Visitor Center. *Mile 4.6.* Exhibits, programs, information, book sales; picnic grounds. (Usually Apr-Nov, daily)

Elkwallow. *Mile 24.1.* (2,445 feet) Picnic grounds; food, store. (May-Oct, daily)

Lewis Mountain. *Mile 57.5.* (3,390 feet) One- and two-bedroom cabins with heat; tent and trailer sites; picnic grounds, store. (Usually May-Oct)

Loft Mountain. *Mile 79.5.* (3,380 feet) Picnicking, camping (May-Oct); wayside facility; gas, store (May-Oct).

Loft Mountain Information Center. *Mile 79.5.* Exhibits, information; programs, nature trail. (Usually May-Nov)

Mary's Rock Tunnel. *Mile 32.4.* (2,545 feet) Drive goes through 600 feet of rock (clearance 13 feet).

Panorama. *Mile 31.5, at junction US 211.* (2,300 feet) Dining room, gift shop. Trail to Mary's Rock. Closed in winter.

Pinnacles. *Mile 36.7.* (3,500 feet) Picnic grounds.

Skyland. *Mile 41.7.* (3,680 feet) Accommodations, restaurant, gift shop; guided trail rides; Stony Man Nature Trail.

South River. *Mile 62.8.* (2,940 feet) Picnic grounds, 2 1/2-mile round-trip trail to falls.

Riding. Many miles of horseback trails. Trail rides (ponies for children) for rent at Skyland.

Washington, VA

1 hour 30 minutes; 67 miles from Washington, DC

Founded 1796 **Pop** 183 **Elev** 690 ft **Area code** 540 **Zip** 22747

The oldest of more than 25 American towns to be named after the first president, this town was surveyed in 1749 by none other than George Washington himself. The streets remain laid out exactly as surveyed and still bear the names of families who owned the land on which the town was founded. It is romantically rumored that Gay Street was named by the 17-year-old Washington after the lovely Gay Fairfax.

The town, seat of Rappahannock County, is situated in the foothills of the Blue Ridge Mountains, which dominate the western horizon.

What to See and Do

Mount Vernon. (see).

B&B/Small Inns

★ ★ **BLEU ROCK INN.** *12567 Lee Hwy (22747). Phone 540/987-3190; fax 540/987-3193. www.bleurockinn.com.* 5 rooms, 2 story. No room phones. Closed Mon, Tues; Jan 1, Dec 24-25. Complimentary full breakfast. Check-out 11 am, check-in 3 pm. Restaurant (see BLEU ROCK INN). Restored farmhouse (1899) on lake; rustic setting; vineyard. **$**

D ⬡ ⬡

★ ★ ★ ★ ★ **THE INN AT LITTLE WASHINGTON.** *309 Main St (22747). Phone 540/675-3800; fax 540/675-3100.* Savvy epicureans book a room—and a table—at The Inn at Little Washington. Just far enough away from the nation's capital and tucked away in a sweet village in the foothills of the Blue Ridge Mountains, The Inn offers visitors a taste of the good life. Urban warriors are swayed by the Victorian charms of the public and private rooms, and the pastoral setting in Virginia's hunt country soothes even the most frayed nerves. Sophisticated without being pretentious, this romantic country house's amiable staff welcomes visitors with the comforts of home, including a delightful afternoon tea with scones and tartlets. Tempting as it may be to indulge, guests save their appetites for the evening's superlative cuisine. Many make special trips just for the talented chef's award-winning and artfully prepared meals, although lucky guests recount their memorable feasts while ensconcing themselves in one of the inn's lovely rooms. 14 rooms, 2 story. Inn closed Tues (except May and Oct); also Dec 24-25. Complimentary continental breakfast. Check-out noon, check-in 3 pm. Restaurant (see THE INN AT LITTLE WASHINGTON). Bar. Bicycles. Airport transportation. **$$$$**

D ⬡

★ ★ ★ **MIDDLETON INN.** *176 Main St (22747). Phone 540/675-2020; toll-free 800/816-8157; fax 540/675-1050. www.middleton-inn.com.* This historic country estate was built in 1850 by Middleton Miller, who designed and manufactured the Confederate uniform of the Civil War. The inn faces the Blue Ridge Mountains, and the original slaves' quarters have been converted into a two-story guest cottage. 4 rooms, 2 with shower only, 2 story. 1 cabin. Children over 12 years only. Complimentary full breakfast. Check-out 11 am, check-in 3 pm. TV; cable (premium), VCR available (movies). Lawn games. Totally nonsmoking. **$$**

⬡ ⬡ ⬡ ⬡

★ ★ **SYCAMORE HILL HOUSE AND GARDENS.** *110 Menefee Mountain Ln (22747). Phone 540/675-3046. www.sycamorehillhouseand gardens.com.* 3 rooms, 1 with shower only, 2 story. No room phones. Children over 12 years only. Complimentary full breakfast. Check-out 11 am, check-in 2 pm. Lawn games. On top of a hill, with a view of the mountains. Totally nonsmoking. **$**

D ⬡

Restaurants

★ ★ ★ **BLEU ROCK INN.** *12567 Lee Hwy (22747). Phone 540/987-3190. www.bleurockinn.com.* This country-inn farmhouse is located on 80 acres of rolling hillside overlooking the Blue Ridge Mountains and adjoining vineyards. It is a great place to stop between Harrisonburg and Washington, DC. American, French menu. Closed Mon, Tues; Dec 25. Dinner, brunch. Outdoor seating. **$$$**

★ ★ **FOUR AND TWENTY BLACKBIRDS.** *650 Zachary Taylor Hwy (22627). Phone 540/675-1111.* Closed Mon, Tues; July 4, Dec 25; also the first two weeks of Jan and Aug. Dinner, Sun brunch. Entertainment. Originally built in 1910 as carpenter's shop. Totally nonsmoking. **$$**

★ ★ ★ ★ ★ **THE INN AT LITTLE WASHINGTON.** *309 Main St (22747). Phone 540/675-3800; fax 540/675-3100.* Opulent, luxurious, romantic, mind-altering, and magnificent: these are just a handful of adjectives that come to mind after experiencing dinner at The Inn at Little Washington. Set in the foothills of the Blue Ridge Mountains, the Inn's dining room is heavy with charm, appointed with rich draperies, tasseled lampshades, and vases overflowing with elaborate flower arrangements. As for the food, it's spectacular. Chef Patrick O'Connell has amassed almost every culinary award in existence. (He must have a separate house for all his plaques and trophies.) For the wonderful opportunity to be a guinea pig in his gifted presence, you will fork over a tidy sum, but your financial indulgence will be well rewarded. Plates are breathtaking, assembled from pristine seasonal ingredients that sparkle and balanced flavors that dazzle. Seasonal dishes that should be considered required eating include the crab cake "sandwich" with fried green tomatoes and tomato vinaigrette; the sesame-crusted Chilean seabass with baby shrimp, artichokes, and grape tomatoes; the rabbit braised in apple cider with wild mushrooms and garlic mashed potatoes; and, for dessert, the pistachio and white chocolate ice cream terrine with blackberry sauce. An amazing wine list will give you the right buzz to match your meal. To make matters even better, coddling is a specialty of the house, so be prepared to have your every whim catered to with grace and warmth. Closed Tues (except in May and Oct), Dec 24-25. Dinner. Reservations required. Valet parking available. **$$$$**
D

Wilmington, DE

1 hour 50 minutes; 109 miles from Washington, DC
See also Philadelphia, PA

Settled 1638 **Pop** 72,664 **Elev** 120 ft **Area code** 302

Information Greater Wilmington Convention & Visitors Bureau, 100 W 10th St, 19801; 302/652-4088

Web www.wilmcvb.org

Wilmington, the "chemical capital of the world," international hub of industry and shipping, is the largest city in Delaware. The Swedish, Dutch, and British have all left their marks on the city. The first settlement was made by Swedes seeking their fortunes; they founded the colony of New Sweden. In 1655, the little colony was taken without bloodshed by Dutch soldiers under Peter Stuyvesant, governor of New Amsterdam. Nine years later, the English became entrenched in the town, which grew, under the influence of wealthy Quakers, as a market and shipping center. Abundant water power in creeks of the Brandywine River Valley plus accessibility to other eastern ports stimulated early industrial growth. When Eleuthére du Pont built his powder mill on Brandywine Creek in 1802, the valley had already known a century of industry. From here come vulcanized fiber, glazed leathers, dyed cotton, rubber hose, autos, and many other products.

Wilmington's Public Art

The Brandywine Valley, just outside Wilmington, is noted for its magnificent museums and gardens. What is often overlooked is the wealth of outdoor statuary in public squares and office courtyards in the historic heart of the old city. Much of it is representational, but there are abstract pieces and a whimsical work or two. *Indeed,* a picture book describing the collection, has been published for several years. On a one-hour, 1-mile walk through the city's commercial center, you can almost imagine you are in a sculpture garden. Begin at Rodney Square outside the elegant Hotel du Pont at 11th and Market streets. Dominating the view is the famous 1923 statue of Caesar Rodney, which shows him astride his horse galloping toward Philadelphia, about 30 miles north, to cast the deciding vote for the Declaration of Independence in 1776. A city hallmark, the *Rodney Statue* is one of the world's rare equestrian sculptures of a horse in full gallop, its two front legs in the air and the weight of the statue resting on the two rear hooves. The challenge of balancing the statue was solved in part by weighting the horse's tail. Head north on Market Street to 13th Street and two blocks west (left) to Orange Street to the Brandywine Gateway, where you'll see the intriguing kinetic fountain at the foot of the Hercules Building (facing 13th Street) in Hercules Plaza. Three solid granite balls rest on three marble pillars in the middle of a large pool. The spheres are arranged so that water flowing over them suggests they are rotating. Retrace your path to 8th and Market and then turn east (left) to Spencer and Freedom plazas between French and Market streets. In Spencer Plaza, *Father and Son,* a larger-then-life bronze statue, touchingly depicts a black man with a child in his arms. It is the work of Charles Park, a local artist. A plaque notes that this was the one-time site of the Mother African Union Methodist Protestant Church, the first black church in America wholly controlled by descendants of Africans. Just across French Street in Freedom Plaza, in the shadow of a cluster of modern municipal buildings, is an arresting statue, *The Holocaust*. Both abstract and realistic, it shows the tortured bodies of the victims pressed against three unyielding pillars, a symbol of the force of destruction. End your tour on a more positive note at the plaque honoring abolitionists Harriet Tubman and Thomas Garrett and the Underground Railroad, the road north to freedom for Southern slaves before the Civil War.

What to See and Do

Amtrak Station. *Martin Luther King Blvd and French St (19801).* Restored Victorian railroad station, which continues to function as such, designed by master architect Frank Furness. (Daily)

Banning Park. *22 S Heald St (19801). Phone 302/323-6422.* Fishing; tennis, playing fields, picnicking, and pavilions. (Daily) **FREE**

Bellevue State Park. *800 Carr Rd (19809). 4 miles NE via I-95, Marsh Rd exit. Phone 302/577-3390. www.destateparks.com/bvsp/bvsp.htm.* Fishing; nature, fitness, and horseback riding trails; bicycling, tennis, game courts, picnicking (pavilions). Standard hours, fees.

Brandywine Creek State Park. *Rtes 92 and 100 (19807). 4 miles N on DE 100. Phone 302/577-3534. www.destateparks.com/bcsp/bcsp.asp.* A 1,000-acre day-use park. Fishing; nature and fitness trails; cross-country skiing. Picnicking. Nature center. Standard hours, fees.

Brandywine Springs Park. *3300 Faulkland Rd (19805), 4 miles W on DE 41. Phone 302/395-5652.* Site of a once-famous resort hotel (1827-1845) for Southern planters and politicos. Here, Lafayette met Washington under the Council Oak before the Battle of Brandywine in 1777. Picnicking, fireplaces, pavilions, baseball fields. Pets on leash only. (Daily) **FREE**

Brandywine Zoo and Park. *1001 N Park Dr (19802). On both sides of Brandywine River, from Augustine to Market St bridges. Phone 302/571-7788. www.destateparks.com/wilmsp/zoo.* Designed by Frederick Law Olmsted, the park includes Josephine Garden with a fountain and roses; stands of Japanese cherry trees. The zoo, along North Park Drive, features animals from North and South America (daily). Picnicking, playgrounds (daily 10 am-4 pm). **$**

Delaware Art Museum. *2301 Kentmere Pkwy (19806). Phone 302/571-9590. www.delart.org.* Expanded facility features Howard Pyle Collection of American illustrations with works by Pyle, N. C. Wyeth, and Maxfield Parrish; American painting collection, with works by West, Homer, Church, Glackens, and Hopper; Bancroft Collection of English Pre-Raphaelite art, with works by Rossetti and Burne-Jones; and Phelps Collection of Andrew Wyeth works; also changing exhibits, children's participatory gallery; store. (Tues-Sun; closed holidays) Guided tours by appointment. **$$**

Delaware History Museum. *504 Market St (19801). Phone 302/656-0637. www.hsd.org/dhm.htm.* Changing exhibits on history and decorative arts. (Tues-Sat; closed holidays) **$**

Delaware Museum of Natural History. *4840 Kennett Pike (19807). 5 miles NW on DE 52. Phone 302/658-9111. www.delmnh.org.* Exhibits of shells, birds, mammals; also the largest bird egg and a 500-pound clam. (Daily; closed holidays) **$**

Fort Christina Monument. *Foot of E 7th St (19801). Phone 302/652-5629.* Monument marks the location where Swedes settled in 1638. The monument was presented in 1938 to Wilmington by the people of Sweden. It consists of black granite plinth surmounted by pioneers' flagship, the *Kalmar Nyckel,* sculpted by Carl Milles. Complex includes nearby log cabin, moved to this location as a reminder of Finnish and Swedish contributions to our nation.

Grand Opera House. *818 Market St Mall (19801). Phone 302/658-7898; 302/652-5577 (box office). www.grandopera.org.* (1871) Historic landmark built by Masons, this restored Victorian theater now serves as Delaware's Center for the Performing Arts, home of Opera Delaware (Nov-May) and the Delaware Symphony (Sept-May). The façade is fine example of the style of the Second Empire interpreted in cast iron.

Hagley Museum. *298 Buck Rd (19807). 3 miles NW off DE 141. Phone 302/ 658-2400. www.hagley.lib.de.us/museum.html.* Old riverside stone mill buildings, one-room schoolhouse, and millwright shop highlight 19th-century explosive manufacturing and community life; 240-acre historic site of E. I. du Pont's original black powder mills includes an exhibit building with working models and dioramas, an operating waterwheel, a stationary steam engine, and a fully operable 1875 machine shop. Admission includes a bus ride along the river for a tour of 1803 Eleutherian Mills, a residence with antiques reflecting five generations of du Ponts, a 19th-century garden, and a barn with a collection of antique wagons. Museum store. (Mid-Mar-Dec, daily; rest of year, Sat and Sun, limited hours Mon-Fri; closed holidays) **$$$**

Holy Trinity (Old Swedes) Church and Hendrickson House. *606 Church St (19801). Phone 302/652-5629. www.oldswedes.org.* Founded by Swedish settlers in 1698, the church stands as originally built and still holds regular services. The house, a Swedish farmhouse built in 1690, is now a museum containing 17th- and 18th-century artifacts. (Mon-Sat; closed holidays) **DONATION**

Longwood Gardens. *Rte 1, Kennett Sq, PA (19348). Phone 610/388-1000. www.longwoodgardens.org.* Longwood Gardens is a stately horticultural display garden created by Pierre S. du Pont, offering more than 1,000 acres of indoor and outdoor gardens, woodlands, and meadows. Lovers of living things are treated to greenhouses heated year-round, more than 10,000 different types of plants, spectacular fountains, flower shows, and gardening demonstrations. Children's programs are available as well. The Orangery and Exhibition Hall are centerpieces, with a sunken marble floor flooded with reflective water. (Daily) **$$$**

Nemours Mansion and Gardens. *1600 Rockland Rd (19899). Phone 302/651-6912. www.nemours.org/mansion.* Country estate (300 acres) of Alfred I.

du Pont. Mansion (1910) is modified Louis XVI, by Carrére and Hastings, with 102 rooms of rare antique furniture, Asian rugs, tapestries, and paintings dating from the 12th century. Formal French gardens extend 1/3 of a mile along the main vista from the house with terraces, statuary, and pools. Tours (May-Nov, Tues-Sun; reservations required). Over 16 years only. **$$$**

Rockwood Museum. *610 Shipley Rd (19809). Phone 302/761-4340.* A 19th-century Gothic Revival estate with gardens in English Romantic style. On grounds are manor house, conservatory, porter's lodge, and other outbuildings. Museum furnished with English, European, and American decorative arts of the 17th to 19th centuries. Guided tours (Mar-Dec, Tues-Sun; Jan and Feb, Tues-Sat). (See SPECIAL EVENTS) **$$**

Willingtown Square. *505 N Market St Mall (19801). Phone 302/655-7161.* Historic square surrounded by four 18th-century houses moved to this location between 1973 and 1976. Serves as office and conference space.

Wilmington & Western Railroad. *Greenbank Station, 2201 Newport Gap Pike (19808). 4 miles SW, near junction DE 2 and DE 41. Phone 302/998-1930. www.wwrr.com.* Round-trip steam-train ride (9 miles) to and from Mount Cuba picnic grove. (May-Oct, Sun; rest of year, schedule varies) **$$$**

Winterthur Museum, Garden, and Library. *Rte 52 (Kennett Pike), Winterthur (19735). 6 miles NW on DE 52. Phone 302/888-4907; toll-free 800/448-3883. www.winterthur.org.* Henry Francis du Pont established this world-class antiques museum, naturalistic garden, and Americana library on a 979-acre grand country estate in the early 1950s. Inspiring period rooms showcase thousands of objects made or used in America between 1640 and 1860, ranging from historic clothing and craftsmen's tools to metalworks, ceramics, and paintings. On the grounds are rolling hills, streams, meadows, and forests and a garden that blooms from late January to November. Cooks will enjoy demonstrations of open-hearth cooking and kitchen gardening. Little ones can ride a garden tram or gently finger growing things in a fairy-tale garden or the Enchanted Woods. Walkers can stroll on gentle paths, and history buffs will enjoy African-American history presentations as well as the thousands of exquisite collectibles. (Tues-Sun; closed Jan, Feb, Easter, Jul 4, Thanksgiving, Dec 24-25) **$$$**

Special Events

Harvest Moon Festival. *Ashland Nature Center. 3511 Barley Mill Rd, Hockessin (19707), 3 miles NW via US 41. Phone 302/239-2334. www. delawarenaturesociety.org.* Cider-pressing demonstrations, hay rides, nature walks, farm animals, arts and crafts, musical entertainment, pony rides, and games. First weekend in Oct.

Horse racing. Delaware Park. *777 Delaware Park Blvd (19804). 7 miles S on I-95 exit 4 B. Phone 302/994-2521. www.delpark.com.* Thoroughbred racing. Late-Apr-mid-Nov.

Victorian Ice Cream Festival. *Rockwood Museum. 610 Shipley Rd (19809). Phone 302/761-4340.* Victorian festival featuring high-wheeled bicycles, hot-air balloons, marionettes, old-fashioned medicine show, baby parade, and crafts; homemade ice cream. Mid-July.

Wilmington Garden Day. *Phone 302/428-6172.* Tour of famous gardens and houses. First Sat in May.

Winterthur Point-to-Point Races. *Phone 302/888-4600.* May.

Motels/Motor Lodges

★ **BEST WESTERN BRANDYWINE VALLEY INN.** *1807 Concord Pike (19803). Phone 302/656-9436; toll-free 800/537-7772; fax 302/656-8564. www.bestwestern.com.* 95 rooms, 2 story. Pets accepted. Check-out noon. TV; cable (premium), VCR available. In-room modem link. In-house fitness room. Pool, children's pool, whirlpool. **$**

D ⬛ ⬛ ⬛ ⬛

★ ★ **COURTYARD BY MARRIOTT.** *1102 West St (19801). Phone 302/429-7600; toll-free 800/321-2211; fax 302/429-9167. www.courtyard.com.* 126 rooms, 10 story. Check-out noon. TV; cable (premium). In-room modem link. Guest laundry. In-house fitness room. Health club privileges. Airport transportation. **$**

D ⬛ ⬛

★ ★ **HOLIDAY INN.** *4000 Concord Pike (19803). Phone 302/478-2222; toll-free 800/465-4329; fax 302/479-0850. www.holiday-inn.com.* 138 rooms, 2 story. Check-out noon. TV; cable (premium). In-room modem link. Coin laundry. Restaurant, bar. Room service. Pool; lifeguard. **$**

D ⬛ ⬛ SC

Hotels

★ ★ **DOUBLETREE HOTEL.** *4727 Concord Pike (19803). Phone 302/478-6000; toll-free 800/222-TREE; fax 302/477-1492. www.doubletree.com.* 154 rooms, 7 story. Check-out noon. TV; cable (premium), VCR available (movies). In-room modem link. Restaurant, bar. In-house fitness room. Health club privileges. Pool. **$$**

D ⬛ ⬛ ⬛ SC

★ ★ ★ **HOLIDAY INN SELECT.** *630 Naamans Rd, Claymont (19703). Phone 302/792-2700; toll-free 800/465-4329; fax 302/798-6182. www.holiday-inn.com.* This hotel is conveniently located just minutes from the airport. 193 rooms, 7 story. Pets accepted; fee. Check-out noon. TV; cable (premium). In-room modem link. Restaurant, bar. In-house fitness room. Pool. Free airport transportation. **$**

D ⬛ ⬛ ⬛ ⬛ SC

★ ★ ★ ★ **HOTEL DU PONT.** *11th and Market sts (19801). Phone 302/594-3100; toll-free 800/441-9019; fax 302/594-3108. www.hoteldupont.com.* The Hotel du Pont has been a Delaware institution since its opening in 1913. Constructed to rival the grand hotels of Europe, this palatial hotel carries a distinguished air. Located in downtown Wilmington, the hotel enjoys proximity to the city's attractions while remaining in the heart of the scenic Brandywine Valley, where championship golf and estate tours are de rigueur.

Luxury is in the details here, from the ornate plasterwork to the gleaming brass. The guest rooms are classically decorated with mahogany furnishings, cream tones, and imported linens. Patrons dine on sublime French cuisine while listening to the gentle strains of a harp at the Green Room. From its coffered ceiling to its oak-paneled walls, its turn-of-the-century décor is the height of elegance. The Brandywine Room offers a delightful change of pace with its inviting ambience resembling a private club and its contemporary American fare. 217 rooms, 10 story. Pets accepted, $100. Check-out noon, check-in 3 pm. TV; cable (premium), VCR available. In-room modem link. Restaurant, bar; entertainment. Room service 24 hours. Babysitting services available. In-house fitness room, massage, sauna. Valet parking. Airport transportation. Business center. Concierge. **$$$**

D 🐾 🏋 🖉 SC 🏃

★ ★ ★ **WYNDHAM WILMINGTON HOTEL.** *700 King St (33140). Phone 302/655-0400; toll-free 800/WYNDHAM; fax 302/655-0430. www.wyndham.com.* 219 rooms, 9 story. Check-out noon, check-in 3 pm. TV; cable (premium). In-room modem link. Restaurant, bar. In-house fitness room. Pool, whirlpool. Business center. Concierge. **$$**

D 🏊 🏋 🖉 SC 🏃

All-Suites

★ ★ **BRANDYWINE SUITES HOTEL.** *707 N King St (19801). Phone 302/656-9300; toll-free 800/756-0070; fax 302/656-2459.* Located in the heart of Wilmington, this small, luxurious European-style hotel offers intimate attention to visitors. Guest suites are comfortable and spacious. 49 rooms, 4 story. Complimentary continental breakfast. Check-out noon, check-in 3 pm. TV; cable (premium), VCR available (movies). In-room modem link. Restaurant, bar. Free airport transportation. **$**

D 🖉 SC

★ ★ ★ **SHERATON SUITES WILMINGTON.** *422 Delaware Ave (19801). Phone 302/654-8300; fax 302/654-6036. www.sheraton.com.* 228 rooms, 16 story. Check-out noon, check-in 3 pm. TV; cable (premium), VCR available. In-room modem link. Laundry services. Restaurant, bar. In-house fitness room. Health club privileges. Sauna. Indoor pool. Airport transportation. Business center. **$**

D 🏊 🏋 🖉 🏃

B&B/Small Inns

★ ★ ★ **THE BOULEVARD BED AND BREAKFAST.** *1909 Baynard Blvd (19802). Phone 302/656-9700; fax 302/656-9701.* This red brick inn, built in 1913, provides relaxation and comfort. Wake up to a delicious breakfast that might include lemon pancakes with raspberry syrup, or enjoy mulled apple cider in the afternoon. 6 rooms, 2 share bath, 3 story. Complimentary full breakfast. Check-out 11 am, check-in 2 pm. TV; cable (premium), VCR (free movies). In-room modem link. **$**

🖉

★ ★ ★ **DARLEY MANOR INN.** *3701 Philadelphia Pike, Claymont (19703). Phone 302/792-2127; toll-free 800/824-4703; fax 302/798-6143. www.darinn.com.* Visitors will appreciate this intimate bed-and-breakfast set in the quiet countryside. 6 rooms, 3 story. No elevator. Children over 6 years only. Complimentary full breakfast. Check-out noon, check-in 4 pm. TV; VCR. In-house fitness room. Totally nonsmoking. **$**

★ ★ ★ ★ **INN AT MONTCHANIN VILLAGE.** *Rte 100 and Kirk Rd, Montchanin (19710). Phone 302/888-2133; toll-free 800/269-2473; fax 302/888-0389. www.montchanin.com.* Experience the charm of a 19th-century hamlet while staying at The Inn at Montchanin Village in Delaware's historic Brandywine Valley. Once part of the Winterthur Estate and located on the National Register of Historic Places, the inn endears itself to visitors with its white picket fence, winding walkways, and country sensibilities. This winsome inn is a perfect base for travelers perusing nearby antique stores, enjoying scenic country drives, or admiring the glorious blooms at Longwood Gardens (see). The warm innkeepers pay meticulous attention to detail, incorporating luxurious amenities while maintaining the integrity of this quaint village. Four-poster and canopy beds set a romantic tone, while marble bathrooms add a sophisticated element to the lovely guest rooms. Gourmets cross state lines just for a meal at Krazy Kat's (see), where refined nouvelle cuisine takes on the tranquil countryside. 28 rooms, 1-3 story. Check-out 11 am, check-in 3 pm. TV; VCR available. In-room modem link. Fireplaces. Restaurant. Room service. Babysitting services available. In-house fitness room, health club privileges. Concierge. Totally nonsmoking. **$$**

Restaurants

★ ★ ★ **BACK BURNER.** *425 Hockessin Corner (19707). Phone 302/239-2314; fax 302/234-3212. www.backburner.com.* Enjoy intimate conversation at this darkly lit restaurant converted from an old barn. Closed Sun; Jan 1, Dec 25. Lunch, dinner. Bar. Elegeant dining in a country atmosphere; renovated barn with arched walls and a display kitchen. Reservations required. **$$**

[D]

★ ★ ★ **BISTRO 1717.** *1717 Delaware Ave (19806). Phone 302/777-0464; fax 302/777-3477. www.blacktrumpetbistro.baweb.com.* A sister operation of chef/owner Karen Boyd's Black Trumpet Bistro, this slightly more casual spot offers creative salads, sandwiches, entrées, and house-made desserts. The Trolley Square location has a relaxed, urban atmosphere and offers take-out for diners on the run. French bistro menu. Closed Sun. Lunch, dinner. Guitarist Mon-Thurs. **$$**

[D]

★ ★ **BRANDYWINE ROOM.** *11th and Market sts (19801). Phone 302/594-3156; fax 302/594-3070. www.hoteldupont.com.* American menu. Closed Fri, Sat. Dinner. Bar. Casual attire. **$$$**

[D]

★ ★ ★ **COLUMBUS INN.** *2216 Pennsylvania Ave (19806). Phone 302/571-1492; fax 302/571-1111. www.columbusinn.com.* This charming restaurant attracts an eclectic crowd with cuisine that has a flavorful twist. American menu. Closed Memorial Day, Labor Day, Dec 25. Lunch, dinner. Bar. Entertainment Fri, Sat. Children's menu. Early American décor in a 200-year-old house. Casual attire. Valet parking. Outdoor seating. **$$$**

D

★ ★ ★ **GREEN ROOM.** *11th and Market sts (19801). Phone 302/594-3154; toll-free 800/441-9019; fax 302/594-3070. www.hoteldupont.com.* As this restaurant is upscale and expensive, patrons are expected to play the part with proper attire. The menu offers a variety of selections with a continental flair. French menu. Breakfast, lunch, dinner, Sun brunch. Bar. Live music. Children's menu. Jacket required (dinner). Valet parking available. **$$$**

D

★ ★ ★ **HARRY'S SAVOY GRILL.** *2020 Naaman's Rd (19810). Phone 302/475-3000; fax 302/475-9990. www.harrys-savoy.com.* Seafood menu. Closed Dec 25. Lunch, dinner, Sun brunch. Bar. Musicians Fri, Sat; magicians perform at tables Tues evenings. Children's menu. Outdoor seating. **$$**

D

★ **KID SHELLEENS.** *1801 W 14th St (19806). Phone 302/658-4600; fax 302/658-7910. www.kidshelleens.com.* American menu. Closed Thanksgiving, Dec 25. Lunch, dinner. Bar. Children's menu. Casual attire. Outdoor seating. **$$**

D

★ ★ ★ **KRAZY KAT'S.** *Rte 100 and Kirk Rd, Montchanin (19710). Phone 302/888-2133; toll-free 800/269-2473; fax 302/888-0389. www.montchanin.com.* Serving bold yet refined French-Asian cuisine, Krazy Kat's is set in a romantic 19th-century blacksmith's shop neighboring the charming and historic Inn at Montchanin Village (see). With its wild, whimsical animal-themed décor (the seats are covered in plush zebra and leopard prints), you may not know what to expect. But the food here is phenomenal and far from silly—although it will make you smile because the plates are truly exquisite. The kitchen's inventive menu includes signatures like grilled wild boar tenderloin satay with ginger jus, sesame-roasted fingerling potatoes, and red cabbage daikon slaw—a robust warmer for a cold winter's night. Fresh seafood, seasonal salads, organic chicken, filet mignon, and Muscovy duck are also on the menu, each perfectly prepared in French style and gently accented with Asian flavors. The wine list is extensive and spans the globe, from America's Northwest to Italy, France, Australia, and New Zealand. Eclectic/International menu. Breakfast, lunch, dinner. Jacket required. Outdoor seating. Totally nonsmoking. **$$$**

D

★ ★ ★ **PICCOLO MONDO.** *3604 Silverside Rd (19810). Phone 302/478-9028; fax 302/478-9028.* For good, no-frills Italian cooking, this restaurant is a great choice. Italian menu. Closed Sun; most major holidays. Lunch, dinner. Bar. **$$**

D

★ ★ ★ **RESTAURANT 821.** *821 Market St (19801). Phone 302/652-8821; fax 302/652-4481. www.restaurant821.com.* Located directly across from Wilmington's historic opera house, this is the perfect spot for taking in dinner before or after a show. The atmosphere is sophisticated, and the American menu with international accents includes many excellent choices. Closed Sun. Lunch, dinner. Entertainment. **$$$**

D

★ ★ ★ **TOSCANA KITCHEN AND BAR.** *1412 N DuPont St (19806). Phone 302/654-8001; fax 302/655-8090. www.toscanakitchen.com.* This restaurant is a favorite for private and intimate parties. Italian menu. Closed major holidays. Dinner. Bar. Casual attire. Reservations required. **$$**

D

★ ★ ★ **VINCENTE'S.** *1601 Concord Pike (19803). Phone 302/652-5142; fax 302/652-0514.* With a variety of creative menu items, this upscale but casual restaurant is always superb, and diners will leave with a happy palate. French, Italian menu. Closed Sun; most major holidays. Lunch, dinner. Bar. Children's menu. Casual attire. Reservations required. **$$$**

D

★ ★ ★ **ZANZIBAR BLUE.** *1000 West St (19801). Phone 302/472-7000; fax 302/472-7002. www.zanzibarblue.com.* Eclectic menu. Lunch, dinner, Sun brunch. Bar. **$$$**

D

After taking in all the indoor attractions that Washington, DC has to offer, dial it down a notch, commune with nature, and head out to Chesapeake Bay. Just a 3 1/2-hour drive from DC, Chesapeake Bay offers the perfect respite from the frantic pace of our nation's capital.

Chesapeake Bay Bridge Area, MD

3 hours 30 minutes; 210 miles from Washington, DC

The majestic twin spans of the Chesapeake Bay Bridge carry visitors to the Eastern Shore, a patchwork of small picturesque towns, lighthouses, and fishing villages tucked away from the city. Scenic rivers and bays, wildlife, gardens, and wildflowers fill the countryside. The main attractions of any visit, however, are the many fine inns and the restaurants specializing in local seafood.

What to See and Do

Wye Oak State Park. *MD Rte 662, on the Eastern Shore in Talbot County, approximately 1 mile from the jct of Rtes 50 and 404 (21657). Phone 410/820-1668.* The official state tree of Maryland is in this 29-acre park; it is the largest white oak in the US (108 feet high, 28 feet around) and believed to be over 460 years old; a new tree has been started from an acorn. A restored 18th-century one-room schoolhouse and the Old Wye Mill (late 1600s) are nearby.

Motel/Motor Lodge

★ **COMFORT INN.** *3101 Main St, Grasonville (21638). Phone 410/827-6767; toll-free 800/228-5150; fax 410/827-8626. www.comfortinn.com.* 86 rooms, 4 story. Complimentary continental breakfast. Check-out 11 am. TV; cable (premium). Indoor pool; whirlpool. Coin laundry. Meeting rooms. Business services available. In-house fitness room; sauna. Refrigerators, microwaves. **$**

D ⚊ 🏋 ⊠ SC

All-Suite

★ **COMFORT SUITES.** *160 Scheeler Rd, Chestertown (21666). Phone 410/810-0555; fax 410/810-0286. www.chestertown.com/comfortsuites.* 53 suites, 3 story. Complimentary continental breakfast. Check-out 11 am. TV; cable. Indoor pool. Meeting rooms. Business services available. Coin laundry. Health club privileges. Refrigerators, microwaves. **$**

D 🔌 ⊠ SC

B&B/Small Inns

★ ★ **HUNTINGFIELD MANOR.** *4928 Eastern Neck Rd, Rock Hall (21661). Phone 410/639-7779; toll-free 800/720-8788; fax 410/639-2924. www.huntingfield.com.* 6 rooms, 2 story. No room phones. Pets accepted, some restrictions. Complimentary continental breakfast. Check-out noon, check-in 2 pm. Telescope-type house on a working farm that dates to the middle 1600s. **$**

D 🐾 ⊠

★ ★ ★ **INN AT MITCHELL HOUSE.** *8796 Maryland Pkwy, Chestertown (21620). Phone 410/778-6500; fax 410/778-2861. www.innatmitchellhouse .com.* Built in 1743, this elegant and historic manor house welcomes guests with friendly service and a serene atmosphere, set amidst lush woods and 10 beautiful acres. Guests will delight in views of the Stoneybrook Pond and the tranquility of this charming inn. 5 rooms, 2 story. No room phones. Complimentary breakfast. Check-out noon, check-in 3 pm. TV. Dinner available Fri, Sat at 7 pm; reservations required. Totally nonsmoking. **$**

🐾 ⊠

★ ★ **KENT MANOR INN & RESTAURANT.** *500 Kent Manor Dr, Stevensville (21666). Phone 410/643-5757; toll-free 800/820-4511; fax 410/ 643-8315. www.kentmanor.com.* 24 rooms, 3 story. Complimentary continental breakfast. Check-out 11 am, check-in 3 pm. TV. Restaurant. Pool. Built in 1820. On Thompson Creek. **$$**

D 🐾 ⊠ ⊠

★ ★ **WHITE SWAN TAVERN.** *231 High St, Chestertown (21620). Phone 410/778-2300; fax 410/778-4543. www.chestertown.com/whiteswan/.* 6 rooms, 2 story. No room phones. Complimentary continental breakfast. Check-out noon, check-in 3 pm. TV. Health club privileges. Game room. Former house and tavern built in 1733 and 1793, respectively; restored with antique furnishings; museum. **$$**

D 🐾 ⚡ 🐾 ⊠

Restaurants

★ ★ **FISHERMAN'S INN AND CRAB DECK.** *316 Main St, Kent Narrows (21638). Phone 410/827-8807; fax 410/827-5705. www.fishermans inn.com.* Seafood menu. Closed Dec 24-25. Lunch, dinner. Bar. **$$**

D

★ **HARRIS CRAB HOUSE.** *433 Kent Narrows Way N, Grasonville (21638). Phone 410/827-9500; fax 410/827-9057. www.harriscrabhouse.com.* Seafood menu. Closed Thanksgiving, Dec 25. Lunch, dinner. Bar. Outdoor seating. Gazebo. **$**

D

★ ★ ★ **NARROWS.** *3023 Kent Narrows Way S, Grasonville (21638). Phone 410/827-8113; fax 410/827-8436.* This restaurant offers waterfront dining with a spectacular view of the narrows. Regional Eastern Shore menu. Specializes in seafood, traditional Maryland recipes. Closed Dec 24-25. Lunch, dinner, brunch. Bar. Children's menu. **$$**

D

★ ★ **OLD WHARF INN.** *Cannon St, Chestertown (21620). Phone 410/778-3566; fax 410/778-2989.* Closed Dec 25. Lunch, dinner, Sun brunch. Bar. Children's menu. Specializes in fresh seafood, steak, salad. Outdoor seating. View of river. **$$**

D SC

★ **WATERMAN'S CRAB HOUSE.** *21055 Sharp St, Rock Hall (21661). Phone 410/639-2261; fax 410/639-2819.* Seafood menu. Closed Thanksgiving; also Jan-Feb. Lunch, dinner. Bar. Children's menu. Outdoor seating. On Rock Hall Harbor. **$**

D

Index

Notes

Notes

Notes